Rhonda Suddreth

Making
Your Love
Last Forever

Making Your Love Last Forever

A Book for Couples

COMMUNICATION: KEY TO YOUR MARRIAGE

MORE COMMUNICATION KEYS FOR YOUR MARRIAGE

THE SECRETS OF A LASTING MARRIAGE

Three Bestselling Books Complete in One Volume

H. NORMAN WRIGHT

INSPIRATIONAL PRESS

NEW YORK

First Inspirational Press edition published in 1998.

Inspirational Press
A division of BBS Publishing Corporation
386 Park Avenue South
New York, NY 10016

Inspirational Press is a registered trademark of BBS Publishing Corporation.

Published by arrangement with Regal Books, a division of Gospel Light, 2300 Knoll Drive, Ventura, California 93006.

Library of Congress Catalog Card Number: 98-75432

ISBN: 0-88486-240-2

Printed in the United States of America.

Contents

Communication
Key to Your Marriage

Contents

Foreword

LET US FACE IT. In recent years marriage has been getting "bad press." That once permanent bastion of security and "'til death do us part" commitment has become for too many an impermanent gamble lasting "'til divorce seems convenient."

In the church or out, the problems are there. The ardor, enthusiasm and excitement of courtship fade into a grey routine of work, raising kids, and sitting glassy-eyed in front of the tube until the eleven o'clock news signs off. Life grinds on and inevitably there is a decline in understanding as the communication gap grows wider and wider. Many couples lack the elementary communication skills needed to produce the understanding necessary for a marriage to grow strong, or even exist, in these times of "swapping, swinging and shacking."

What can be done? Is there a way to make marriage work better—or work at all? What about the ideal called "Christian marriage"? Is a Christian marriage possible today?

Books on marriage and marriage problems abound. This book is designed to take you beyond the problems and start working on the solutions. Real communication between husband and wife is possible. Over the last several years Norm Wright has proved it—in classes, seminars, workshops, retreats—wherever he can get a group of married (or planning to be married) people together.

As a practicing marriage counselor, licensed in California, Norm has the experience and background to speak with authority on marital problems and why lack of communication is at the bottom of most of them.

As one of the most popular professors in his seminary and a much-in-demand speaker and teacher across the land, he has the educational know-how to do what this book is all about—communicate.

One of the best things about this book is that it's more than a book. It's an experience in learning, sharing and communicating. You don't simply read this book; you dialogue with it—and, hopefully, with your partner. You don't just talk about communicating. You *do* it—perhaps for the first time.

Don't just "dip into" this book. Jump in with both feet. Interact with the "What Do You Think?" and "What's Your Plan?" sections in each chapter. Above all, interact with your mate and *communicate,* more deeply, personally and honestly than you ever have before. Communication is the key to *your* marriage.

Fritz Ridenour

Introduction
Marriage: The Only Game
Both Players Can Win!

Does the institution called "marriage" have a future? Some experts are saying that marriage as we now know it is on the way out. As divorce rates continue to climb, or at least stay at appallingly high levels, many people, in and out of the church, are growing pessimistic about marriage. Even for seemingly "perfectly matched" couples, marriage grows to be more and more of a gamble.

There are three major changes taking place in the institution of marriage today:

1. A decline in understanding between marriage partners.
2. The loss of determination to stay married.
3. The development of unrealistic marriage expectations.

Decline of understanding and lack of communication go together. Many couples today lack the kind of communication skills that produce the understanding necessary for a marriage to grow strong, or even exist. Understanding in a marriage doesn't mean that there are no differences. It does mean that you and your mate are able to talk about the differences and come to an understanding of each other's views. You are able to accept the fact that your partner was raised in a different fashion and because of that will react differently than you. Just because something was done in a certain manner in your home when you were growing up does not mean that it has to be done that same way in your new home.

Two people who love one another but are unable to understand each other suffer pain—a continual biting pain in their relationship. Understanding may not come easily, but a willingness to share views, to see the "other side of the question," to talk things out can help a husband and wife adjust and adapt to their honest differences of opinion.

Someone has likened this adjustment to two porcupines who lived in Alaska. When the deep and heavy snows came they felt the cold and began to draw close together. However, when they drew close they began to stick one another with their quills. When they drew apart they felt the cold once again. In order to keep warm they had to learn how to adjust to one another.

Lack of determination to stay married is seen today on every hand. To have had more than one husband or wife is not considered at all unusual. As one woman filled out an application for a new job, she came to the question, "Married or Single?" Her answer: "Between marriages."

Many enter marriage today with the attitude that if they do not get along they can break the relationship and try again. Many people are too impatient with their marriages. They do not want to live "happily ever after." They want to live "happily right away" and when this does not happen, they bail out.

Too many young couples enter marriage blinded by unrealistic expectations. They believe the relationship should be characterized by a high level of continuous romantic love. As one young adult said: "I wanted marriage to fulfill all my desires. I needed security, someone to take care of me, intellectual stimulation, economic security immediately—but it just wasn't like that!" People are looking for something "magical" to happen in marriage.

But magic doesn't make a marriage work: hard work does. When there are positive results it is because of two people working together one step at a time.

"WHEN I GOT MARRIED
I WAS LOOKING FOR AN IDEAL —
THEN IT BECAME AN ORDEAL
AND NOW I WANT A NEW DEAL."

One rather cynical description of marriage is that it is "the only game of chance at which both players can lose." I prefer to see it as the only game in which both players can win! I agree wholeheartedly with Richard Lessor, when he writes in his book, *Love, Marriage and Trading Stamps*: "It isn't a case of marriage having been tried and found wanting. In the twentieth century world, true marriage is deeply wanted but largely untried."[1]

And how do you go about trying "true marriage"? It will do little good to look to society for help. Society struggles with the crisis but continues to become hopelessly entangled in its own web of conflicting values and ideas. Society seeks answers but only provides more and more questions.

Is the whole thing hopeless? Not at all. Society has not provided a way to a truly happy marriage, but God has! God has given a definite pattern for marriage and if a man and woman will follow that pattern, they will find the happiness and harmony they seek.

Charles Shedd in his book, *Letters to Phillip*, tells the story of two rivers flowing smoothly and quietly along until they came together and joined. When this happened they clashed and hurled themselves at one another. As the newly formed river flowed downstream, however, it gradually quieted down and flowed smoothly again. But now it was much broader, more majestic and had much more power. Dr. Shedd suggests that "A good marriage is often like that. When two independent streams of existence come together, there will probably be some dashing of life against life at the juncture. Personalities rush against each other. Preferences clash. Ideas contend for power and habits vie for position. Sometimes like the waves, they throw up a spray that leaves you breathless and makes you wonder where has the loveliness gone. But that's all right. Like the two rivers, what comes out of their struggle may be something deeper, more powerful than what they were on their own."[2]

Two Christians have the best possibilities for a happy marriage because they have a third Person—the Lord Jesus Christ—working with them and strengthening them. But there *must* be communication—between them and their Lord and between themselves. That's what the rest of this book is all about. Truly, communication—with Christ and each other—is the key to your marriage.

1
What Is a "Christian" Marriage?

As you read this chapter, you will discover . . .
   . . . the definition of a Christian marriage
   . . . what it means to be "one flesh"
   . . . how to evaluate your own marriage and take
      steps to enrich and improve it.

How would you describe being married? What do you think of when you hear the word "marriage"? Joy, love, happiness, bliss? Misery, hatred, frustration? Or just boredom and the blahs?

Definitions of marriage are a dime a dozen, and a lot of them don't seem to put much more value on marriage than that!

Meander said, "Marriage, if one will face the truth, is an evil, but a necessary evil."

Montaigne said, "Marriage happens as with cages: the birds without despair to get in and those within despair of getting out."

Sidney Smith's statement about marriage is clever, yet contains a great deal of wisdom. He said, "Marriage resembles a pair of shears, so joined that they cannot be separated; often moving in opposite directions, yet always punishing anyone who comes between them."

WHAT DO YOU THINK? #1

The definitions of marriage given above have touches of cynicism or at least satire. What is *your* definition of marriage? Write it below.

Marriage: A Contract with an Escape Clause?

Some psychologists, marriage counselors and ministers have suggested that marriage is a contract and many people are quick to agree. But is this really true? Is marriage really a contract?

In every contract there are certain conditional clauses. A contract between two parties, whether they be companies or individuals, involves the responsibility of both parties to carry out their part of the bargain. These are CONDITIONAL CLAUSES or "IF CLAUSES." If you do this, the other person must do this, and if the other person does this, you must do this. But in the marriage relationship and the marriage ceremony there are no conditional clauses. Nowhere does the marriage ceremony say, "If the husband loves his wife then the wife continues in the contract." Or, "If the wife is submissive to her husband then the husband carries out the contract." Marriage is an unconditional commitment into which two people enter.

In most contracts there are ESCAPE CLAUSES. An escape clause says that if the party of the first part does not carry out his responsibilities, then the party of the second part is absolved. If one person does not live up to his part of the bargain, the second person can get out of the contract. This is an escape clause. In marriage there is no escape clause.

WHAT DO YOU THINK?   #2

Rate yourself on a scale of 1 to 5 (1—very uncomfortable; 2—slightly more comfortable; 3—could be; 4—probably so; 5—sounds good) regarding your response to the following concepts. (Circle the appropriate one.)

1. Marriage is a necessary evil.
   1 2 3 4 5

2. It is normal—even desirable—for marriage partners to be moving in opposite directions in life.
   1 2 3 4 5

3. Most couples have unwritten conditional clauses in their marriage that both know about but never discuss.
   1 2 3 4 5

4. It would be to your advantage to have an escape clause in the marriage contract to protect you because if the marriage goes sour it will probably be the other person's fault.
   1 2 3 4 5

5. Marriage is an unconditional commitment of the total person for total life.
   1 2 3 4 5

Marriage: Blending, Not Rending

In his book, *The Essence of Marriage,* ordained minister and marriage counselor Julius A. Fritze describes marriage as follows:

"Marriage is an emotional fusion of two personalities into a functional operation, yet both retaining their own identities. The Biblical concept is contained in Genesis 2:24—'One flesh'." Fritze goes on to illustrate the marriage relationship by talking about two lumps of clay. He points out that if you were to hold a lump of dark green clay in your left hand and a lump of light green clay in your right hand, you could clearly see the different shades. However, if you were to take both of these pieces of clay and mold and push them together, you would see just one lump of green clay—at first glance. But if you were to inspect the lump closely you would see the distinct and separate lines of dark green and light green clay. This is like the marriage relationship—two people blended together so they appear as one, yet each retaining his own distinct identity or personality.[1] It's one new life existing in two people.

Christian marriage, however, involves more than the blending of two people. It also includes a *third Person*—Jesus Christ—who gives meaning, guidance and direction to the relationship. When Jesus Christ presides in a marriage, then and only then is it a Christian marriage.

Various writers have given definitions of "Christian marriage."

Wayne Oates, professor at Southern Baptist Theological Seminary, says: "Marriage is a covenant of responsible love, a fellowship of repentance and forgiveness."

David Augsburger, Mennonite minister and author of *Cherishable: Love and Marriage*, defines marriage by first asking, "Is marriage a private action of two persons in love, or a public act of two pledging a contract?" Then he goes on to say, "Neither. It is something other. Very much other!

> "Basically the Christian view of marriage is not that it is primarily or even essentially a binding legal and social contract. The Christian understands marriage as a covenant made under God and in the presence of fellow members of the Christian family. Such a pledge endures, not because of the force of law or the fear of its sanctions, but because an unconditional covenant has been made. A covenant more solemn, more binding, more permanent than any legal contract."[2]

Dwight Small, experienced counselor and author of several books on marriage, defines marriage as: "One new life existent in two persons."

Elton Trueblood, author of *Company of the Committed* and other books on Christian discipleship, calls marriage, "A system by means of which persons who are sinful and contentious are so caught up by a dream and a purpose bigger than themselves that they work through the years, in spite of repeated disappointment, to make the dream come true."

Dr. David Hubbard, president of Fuller Theological Seminary, has said: "Marriage does not demand perfection. But it must be given priority. It is an institution for sinners. No one else need apply. But it finds its fullest glory when sinners see it as God's way of leading us through His ultimate curriculum of love and righteousness."

WHAT DO YOU THINK?   #3

From the five definitions of Christian marriage given above, circle the name of the writer whose definition you like the best.

Oates   Augsburger   Small   Trueblood   Hubbard

In the definition that you picked as "best" what ideas appeal to you the most?

Of the five definitions of marriage given above, which one appealed to you the least?

Oates   Augsburger   Small   Trueblood   Hubbard

What bothers you the most about that definition?

Use the five definitions of Christian marriage plus your own ideas to compile your own definition of "Christian marriage."

What Does the Bible Say About Marriage?

What, then, are God's purposes for marriage?

One basic purpose is procreation—to bring children into the world. God created man in His own image and then said: "Be fruitful and multiply, and fill the earth, and subdue it . . ." (Gen. 1:28). Psalm 127:3–5 teaches that *"children are a gift of the Lord. . . . like arrows in the hand of a warrior. . . . How blessed is the man whose quiver is full of them"* (NASB).

Procreation also involves providing adequate care and training for your children. *"Train up a child in the way he should go,"* says the well-known verse from Proverbs, *"even when he is old he will not depart from it"* (Prov. 22:6, NASB).

But there is much more to marriage than the procreation, care and training of children. Genesis 2:18–25 teaches that marriage was God's idea and that He had several divine purposes in mind.

18. *Then the Lord God said, "It is not good that the man should be alone; I will make him a helper fit for him."*

19. *(So) out of the ground the Lord God formed every beast of the field and every bird of the air, and brought them to the man to see what he would call them; and whatever the man called (every) living creation, that was its name.*

20. *The man gave names to all the cattle, and to the birds of the air, and to every beast of the field, but for the man there was not found a helper fit for him.*

21. *So the Lord God caused a deep sleep to fall upon the man, and while he slept took one of his ribs and closed up its place with flesh;*

22. *and the rib which the Lord God had taken from the man he made into a woman and brought her to the man.*

23. *Then the man said, "This at last is bone of my bones and*

flesh of my flesh; she shall be called Woman, because she was taken out of Man."

24. *Therefore a man leaves his father and his mother and cleaves to his wife, and they become one flesh.*

25. *And the man and his wife were both naked, and were not ashamed. (RSV)*

God created marriage for *companionship.* As John Milton observed, ". . . Loneliness was the first thing God's eye named not good." Loneliness and isolation are contradictions to the purpose in God's creative act. God made man to live with others, and the first "other" was woman.

God also created marriage for *completeness.* The woman was to be . . . *a helper fit for him* (Gen. 2:18). The woman was created to be a complement or counterpart, suitable for the man. The woman assists man in making his life (and hers, too) complete. She fills up the empty places. She shares his life with him, draws him out of himself and into a wider area of contact through the involvement they have with one another. She is one who can enter into responsible companionship. The partners in a marriage relationship are actually fulfilling God's purpose of completeness or wholeness to life.

The companionship and completeness that God intended for marriage grow out of *communication* as two people share each day and the meaning of their lives. As Dwight Small says, "The heart of marriage is its communication system. . . . But no couple begins marriage with highly developed communication. It is not something they bring into marriage ready made but something to be continually cultivated through all of the experiences of their shared life."[3] Satisfying companionship and a sense of completeness develop as husband and wife learn to communicate with openness and understanding.

Marriage—A New Relationship

Genesis 2:24 puts an emphasis upon two verbs: *leave* and *cleave.* The word *leave* means to abandon, forsake, to sever one relationship before establishing another. Unfortunately, many individuals do not make this break. They leave home *physically* but remain there *psychologically.* The attachment to home and parents should be replaced by the attachment to one's mate. This does not mean disregarding or dishonoring one's parents, but rather breaking a tie to one's parents and assuming one's own responsibility for a spouse.

The second word, *cleave,* means to weld, grip or adhere together. When a man "cleaves" to his wife, they become *one flesh.* The term "one flesh" is a beautiful capsule description of the oneness, completeness and permanence God intended in the marriage relationship. "One flesh" suggests a unique oneness—a total commitment to intimacy in all of life together, symbolized by sexual union.

The Jewish rabbis taught that man is restless while he misses the rib that was taken out of his side and the woman is restless until she gets under the arm of the man—from where she came. With all of the flap in recent years over women's lib, here is a majestic statement of just how the Bible views woman. She is not man's *property.* She is man's *partner*—a full partner in every sense of the word.

St. Augustine lived in the fifth century, but what he said fits perfectly into today's heated discussions of women's rights. He wrote: "If God meant woman to rule over man, He would have taken her out of Adam's head. Had He designed her to be his slave, He would have taken her out of his feet. But God took woman out of man's side, for He made her to be a helpmate and an equal to him."

In his book, *After You've Said I Do,* Dwight Small emphasizes

HOW CAN YOU BE ONE
WHEN YOU'RE NOT EQUAL?

the Bible's consistent equalitarian and democratic view of marriage. "There can be no true oneness," writes Small, "except as there is equal dignity and status for both partners. The wife who came from man's side is to stand at his side, to share every responsibility and enjoy every privilege. This is the goal."

Small goes on to admit that achieving this goal is not easy. What is needed is *dialogue*. He believes that "dialogue takes place when two people communicate the full meaning of their lives to one another, when they participate in each other's lives in the most meaningful ways in which they are capable."[4]

From Genesis 2:18–24, you can gather three distinctly Christian views of marriage:

1. As mentioned, marriage is to be permanent, for life. When two become one flesh, there is to be no division, no severing, because of the irreparable damage that will occur.

2. Marriage is to be monogamous. There are examples of polygamy in Scripture, but these are descriptions of what men did, not of what Scripture teaches as good and right. Again, one flesh means one flesh. A man cannot become one flesh with more than one woman and have it mean what is meant here.

3. Finally, Christian marriage demands fidelity. Today's new morality claims that a man can become "one flesh" with as many women as he wishes, that fornication and a little adultery are "healthy" pastimes that broaden experience and deepen relationships.

God's description of marriage, however, speaks of deep and lasting intimacy, a companionship between husband and wife that leads to mutual enrichment, happiness and welfare. Adultery is to marriage what a knife is to a back. Today's advocates of "new morality" can think of all kinds of excuses for adultery and fornication. They come up with what might be called a "pretzel" morality, in which facts, sound principles for good human relationships and responsibilities are all twisted and bent into shapes that seemingly, in some cases, justify infidelity as a "good and loving thing in the situation."

As Dwight Small says in his book, *Design for Christian Marriage,* "A Christian marriage can never fail, but the people in that marriage can fail. There is a vast difference between the two possibilities. So if the marriage of two Christians seems to fail, it is either that they were ignorant of God's purposes, or unwilling to commit themselves to it."[5]

Way back in the beginning God spelled it out. As early as the second chapter of Genesis, He made it clear that marriage is a *total*

commitment of the *total* person for *total* life.

Anything less is not Christian marriage. Anything less can easily fail. But when man and wife come together, committed to God and committed to communicating the full meaning of their lives to each other, they cannot help but succeed.

WHAT'S YOUR PLAN?

If you are studying this book with your spouse, best results can be obtained if you complete the following material individually and then discuss your answers together. As you compare ideas, feelings and attitudes you will achieve new levels of communication and understanding in your marriage.

Part 1

Think back to before you were married . . .

1. What did you think marriage would be like? Did it turn out the way you expected?

2. Did you and your spouse have different expectations for marriage? How did you discover the differences? Have you talked directly about these differences?

3. I expected marriage to change my life-style by . . .

4. I believe my mate expected me to be . . .

5. I expected my mate to be more . . .

Part 2

1. If you were going to describe your marriage at this time with one word, what word would you use?

2. What word do you think your spouse would use to describe your marriage?

3. What benefits are you getting from your marriage relationship that you wouldn't have received if you had remained single? Be very specific.

4. What strengths do you see in your spouse? Have you ever told him or her that you are aware of these strengths and appreciate them?

5. What does your spouse do that makes you feel loved or of value?

6. What do you do that expresses your love and appreciation toward your spouse?

7. What are the strengths in your marriage? Who contributes most of these strengths, you or your spouse?

8. What do you feel is the weakest area in your marriage? In what ways might you be responsible for this weak area?

9. What efforts are you now making to make your marriage a happy one?

10. What efforts do you see your spouse making?

11. What are your present goals for your marriage? What are you going to do to reach these goals? What can you do differently that will enable you to reach them?

Here are some suggestions for you to consider:

- I will show more of an interest in my spouse's activities by asking questions.
- I will spend more time thinking about positive factors in my marriage relationship and attempt to discover ways to be what my spouse wants and needs.
- I will take time to pray for and with my family, especially my spouse.
- If I have any resentments against the family members—and particularly my spouse—I will forgive them now.

Other goals I want to set:

2
Who's in Charge Here?

As you read this chapter, you will discover . . .
. . . why there is a "leadership vacuum" in many homes today
. . . the Biblical definition of the role of the wife
. . . what it means to submit to your husband
. . . the Biblical definition of the role of the husband
. . . what it means to "love your wife."

In today's world there is some confusion in the role and responsibility of the wife-mother and that of the husband-father. Who is the head of the home or *is* there to be a head?

Imagine a Martian coming to our world and landing in our front yard. He steps out of his spaceship and rings the doorbell at your home. Suppose one of your children opens the door and the Martian says, "Take me to your leader." To whom would the child go? To the father? To the mother? To both? Or would the child say, "I am the leader." Who is the head or leader in your home today?

Jokes and stories abound about the ineffectiveness of the man as a leader. We have heard the statement that behind every successful man stands an understanding and helpful wife. One writer said, "Baloney! Behind every successful man stands a surprised mother-in-law!" Statements and jokes like these are clever and yet for some family situations they are painfully true.

"He brags that he's the boss in his home, but he lies about other things too."

"When she wants his opinion, she gives it to him."

"The only time he opens his mouth is to ask for the apron, and the vacuum cleaner."

She snaps, "Are you a man or a mouse?—squeak up!"

"The last big decision she let him make was whether to wash or dry."

Today there seems to be a new husband-father image. Basically the man has assumed the role of financial provider in the family (this, too, is changing in many homes!) and leaves all of the other functions to his wife. Many men appear to be assistants to their wives in areas that once were their responsibility. In most marriages the couple begins by sharing interest and responsibilities; then specialization gradually gets in. The man becomes engrossed with his job (the economic side of life) and neglects his other responsibilities. The wife is left in charge or simply "takes charge" because of the leadership vacuum.

Another factor contributing heavily to the "leadership gap" is a belief by many families in what they think is "pure democracy." Everyone in the family, including the children, casts an equal vote. Is this proper? Is this what the Scripture teaches? Many so-called "Christian" homes today are on the verge of disintegration because of the lack of a leader. They are on shaky ground because they purposely choose to ignore the guidelines that have been set down for them in Scripture.

WHAT DO YOU THINK? #4

1. According to the preceding paragraphs, there is a lack of male leadership in many homes because the husband becomes engrossed in his career and making money and neglects his other responsibili-

ties. From what you have experienced and observed, would you agree?

2. List some responsibilities you think husbands tend to neglect because of their involvement in their career.

What is the Biblical Role of the Wife?

Ephesians 5:22–33 contains the clearest Biblical definition of marriage roles. In Ephesians 5:22–24 Paul speaks particularly to the wife about her responsibilities to her husband:

You wives must submit to your husband's leadership in the same way you submit to the Lord. For a husband is in charge of his wife in the same way Christ is in charge of his body the church. (He gave his very life to take care of it and be its Savior!) So you wives must willingly obey your husbands in everything, just as the church obeys Christ (TLB).

Genesis 2:18–20 teaches that the woman was created to be a "helpmeet," one who is to be a complement to the man and assist him. In a real sense the wife is a fulfillment of the husband's life.

Ephesians 5:22–24 teaches that the wife is to be "subject" or "submissive" to her husband. How are these two concepts wed together? How can the wife be a "completer" of her husband and also be submissive to him? What does this mean in a practical sense?

First, a wife's submission to her husband is from complete freedom and love, not from compulsion or fear. The Church submits to the Lordship of Christ on a voluntary basis—in response to His love. The wife's motivation in submitting to her husband should be the same.

But what does it mean to submit? It does not mean to "be a doormat." The Scriptures say submit, but they do not say "sell out." The wife is *not* to become a nothing, a pawn in her husband's hand. She retains her distinctiveness as an individual with the right to her own ideas and feelings. She is not a servant. She remains a person with a distinct personality and personal needs. She needs to accept responsibility and make decisions as much as her husband does.

The marriage relationship functions smoothly when the Biblical guidelines are followed. Traffic laws enable a driver to reach his destination with the least possible chance of accident or injury. Biblical guidelines help a couple reach their destination of a happy, growing relationship. One of these guidelines is for the wife to submit to her husband as the leader in their relationship. She submits to her husband not because he demands it but because Christ directs her to in His Word. Lack of submission to her husband is as much a spiritual problem as it is a marital problem!

The wife encourages and strengthens her husband's masculine leadership role and *never* tries to destroy, usurp, weaken or eliminate it. A wife is to respect her husband and affirm his leadership.

Dwight Small suggests that "each is an active participant in building the relationship. . . . Precluded forever is any assumption of superiority-inferiority." He (Paul) affirms the principle of "personal interdependency in marriage."[1]

"God has charged the husband with headship," writes Gladys Hunt. "In fact, he hangs the responsibility of the Fall on the man *(as by one man sin entered the world; the woman was deceived but not the man).* He now makes the husband the head of his wife. He says to the wife, 'Don't make it rough for him. Help him to be what I want him to be. Support him in his role; don't compete for headship.'

"That does not mean that she never has an original thought, never says she disagrees, etc. It does mean that her spirit is controlled by God's Spirit. She doesn't have to prove her worth by grabbing her husband's job."[2]

WHAT DO YOU THINK?   #5

Do you agree or disagree that . . .

1. It was God's idea that a wife should immediately give up everything to go with her husband.
   a. Agree strongly
   b. Agree with reservations
   c. Disagree strongly
   d. Disagree with reservations

2. It is all right for an obedient wife to instruct and give advice to her husband.
   a. Agree strongly
   b. Agree with reservations
   c. Disagree strongly
   d. Disagree with reservations

3. A wife has the right to disobey her husband when she feels he is dictating to her.
   a. Agree strongly
   b. Agree with reservations
   c. Disagree strongly
   d. Disagree with reservations

4. Since the wife is assigned the subordinate position in marriage, she is not on an equal basis with man.
   a. Agree strongly
   b. Agree with reservations
   c. Disagree strongly
   d. Disagree with reservations

5. The wife is to be regarded as the one who does the cooking, washing, training of the children, and at the same time she is to be a "helpmeet" to her husband.
   a. Agree strongly
   b. Agree with reservations
   c. Disagree strongly
   d. Disagree with reservations

Now, rewrite on another sheet each of the statements to indicate your own belief and convictions.

And What About the Husband's Role?

In Ephesians 5:25–32 Paul deals specifically with the husband's responsibilities:

> And you husbands, show the same kind of love to your wives as Christ showed to the church when he died for her, to make her holy and clean, washed by baptism and God's Word; so that he could give her to himself as a glorious church without a single spot or wrinkle or any other blemish, being holy and without a single fault. That is how husbands should treat their wives, loving them as parts of themselves. For since a man and his wife are now one, a man is really doing himself a favor and loving himself when he loves his wife! No one hates his own body but lovingly cares for it, just as Christ cares for his body the church, of which we are parts.
>
> (That the husband and wife are one body is proved by the Scripture which says, "A man must leave his father and mother when he marries, so that he can be perfectly joined to his wife, and the two shall be one.") I know this is hard to understand, but it is an illustration of the way we are parts of the body of Christ (TLB).

In Ephesians 5:23 Paul declares that the husband is the head of the wife. Unfortunately, too many men only read that much of the Scripture and fail to read the rest of the verse—"as Christ is the Head of the church." Authority is given to the man, but Paul did not mean that husbands should be bosses over their wives. Being the head does not mean being the victor in a struggle. The husband sets the pace by being a leader. The authority is there but he is always answerable to God for his use of it.

As the husband submits to Christ, his authority is transformed by Christ into sacrificial care. The basic truth of this passage is *not* control and domination, but sacrificial love for the wife. The husband is nowhere given the prerogative to rule with a rod of iron. He may *not* impose his own selfish will upon his wife and overshadow her feelings. He is not to demand leadership. The Scripture does not emphasize that Jesus Christ dominates or dictates to the Church. Christ gave Himself for the Church. He takes the initiative to love and serve the Church; *this is the pattern that husbands are to follow in caring for their wives.* When a husband does not do this, he has a spiritual problem (disobedience to the Word) as well as a marital problem.

A loving husband is willing to give all that is required to fulfill the life of his wife. His love is ready to make any sacrifice for her good. The man's first responsibility is to his wife. His love for her enables him to give himself to her.

His love is also a purifying love. The husband never asks his wife to do something which would degrade or harm her. His caring love for his wife is compared to his love for his own body. A man certainly cares for and nourishes his own body. A loving husband does not try to extract service from his wife nor does he make sure that his own physical comfort is assured; he does not love her for the sake of convenience. He does not regard his wife as a kind of permanent servant who simply cooks, washes and trains the children. Rather, the loving husband sees his wife as a person whom he is to cherish and strengthen. A caring love is a serving love. A husband's love is to be patterned after the caring love of Christ.

WHAT DO YOU THINK?   #6

Do you agree or disagree that . . .

1. The Scripture teaches that the husband is the head of the family. Thus, the wife should be submissive and obedient to her husband in everything even if he is an unbeliever.
   a. Agree strongly
   b. Agree with reservations
   c. Disagree strongly
   d. Disagree with reservations

NOT "I WILL IF YOU WILL" BUT "WE WILL REGARDLESS"

2. Since man is the head of the family, and this headship is patterned after that of Christ, therefore, the husband should be the "boss" of his wife.
   a. Agree strongly
   b. Agree with reservations
   c. Disagree strongly
   d. Disagree with reservations

3. It is all right for the husband to demand obedience or order his
   wife to respect his authority.
   a. Agree strongly
   b. Agree with reservations
   c. Disagree strongly
   d. Disagree with reservations

4. Usually the husband should make the final decision when he
   and his wife cannot agree upon a decision that must be made.
   a. Agree strongly
   b. Agree with reservations
   c. Disagree strongly
   d. Disagree with reservations

Now, rewrite on a separate sheet each of the statements to indicate your own belief and conviction.

Where Do We Go from Here?

As you study Ephesians 5:22–33 you should remember to apply
these truths in a *very personal and specific way.* Do not concern
yourself with your partner's role. Concentrate on your *own responsibility* in your marriage, according to what God's Word teaches.
We all like to apply the Scriptures to "someone else." Applying it
personally often gets too close to home. And in Ephesians 5 Paul is
"close to home," indeed.

For example, some wives react to Paul's teaching in Ephesians by
saying, "I will submit to my husband if he does his part and loves
me the way I want to be loved."

But in Ephesians 5:21–24 Paul doesn't say that. Paul says to wives,
in so many words. "Forget what the man is to do and concern yourself with your own responsibility. Don't base your attitudes and actions on the idea that if your husband does one thing you will do
another. Your attitudes and actions are to be the result of your commitment and obedience to Christ, who should be at the center of
your marriage."

The same thing is true for husbands. Some men take Paul's teaching and deduce that, "I'm boss in my house. My wife has to obey
me. Scripture is on my side."

But notice in Ephesians 5:22–33 Paul does not emphasize the husband's *authority* over his wife. Instead Paul focuses on the husband's *responsibility* to have a self-giving love for his wife. A master illustrator, Paul reminds the husband that he loves his own body; does he love his wife as much? Christ loved His "body," the Church. He set the example that the husband is to follow.

As the husband, you do not demand obedience. You do not order your wife to respect your authority. You do not say, "You be submissive and obedient and *then* I will love you as Scripture tells me to." Instead, you focus on your responsibility to give love. You *give your wife the freedom to decide to submit to you.* Submission, according to Paul, is her responsibility, not yours. And, of course, as she submits, she returns your love freely and joyfully, *because she knows she is loved.*

In Ephesians 5:33 Paul puts his teaching into one capsule statement:

So again I say, a man must love his wife as a part of himself; and the wife must see to it that she deeply respects her husband— obeying, praising and honoring him (TLB). Husband or wife, here is the blueprint for a truly happy marriage. Meet your responsibility and give your mate the freedom to meet his or hers. Then you will build a marriage in which both partners are free to communicate openly and honestly. With good communication, there will be no leadership gap. As husband and wife fulfill their respective Biblical roles, love and submission intertwine. The result is an atmosphere of trust and security where both partners grow and mature as God intends.

WHAT'S YOUR PLAN?

If you are studying this book with your spouse, best results can be obtained if you complete the following material individually and then discuss your answers together. As you compare ideas, feelings and attitudes you will achieve new levels of communication and understanding in your marriage.

Set aside time this week to study Ephesians 5:22–33. Read the passage two or three times and then complete the following:

1. List the instructions given to the wife. Describe in detail what these instructions mean as far as you are concerned.

2. List the instructions given to the husband. Describe in detail what the instructions mean to you.

3. What do you feel will be the consequences if one or the other marriage partner fails to follow these instructions? Be specific.

4. How do you feel the guidelines given in Ephesians 5:22–33 match with the attitudes of marriage partners in today's world?

5. What changes or additions to your life-style do you feel you should make to measure up to the instructions given in Ephesians 5:22–33? Describe these changes and additions in some detail.
A husband might say:
I can show more love by asking my wife where she would like to go on our next vacation.
I can consider her feelings and opinions when it comes time to decide on that new car.
I can sit down and talk to my wife about something that interests her.
I can tell her that I love her.
Add your own ideas of things you want to say and changes you want to make. . . .

A wife might say:
I can seek to discover the needs of my husband and see that they are met.
I can watch my tone of voice when he comes home late from work and hasn't called to tell me he will be late.
I can support him more by encouraging and building him up in areas where confidence is lacking.
Add your own ideas of things you want to say and changes you want to make. . . .

3
How Do You Make It Work?

As you read this chapter, you will discover . . .
. . . the "when," "how," and "who" of decision making in a marriage
. . . principles from 1 Peter 3 concerning the role of the husband and the role of the wife
. . . how to make changes in your attitudes or behavior that will build a stronger marriage.

Ephesians 5 makes it clear. The husband is to be the loving leader of the home. His wife is to lovingly submit to his leadership. These are great principles, but how do they work out in the nitty-gritty situations of daily life? For example, what about the dozens of decisions that must be made each day?

According to family specialist Nathan Ackerman, "Delineation of the expected family role functions of male and female is often unclear. Issues of cooperation, division of labor, and sharing of authority are consequently confused. Each parent competes with the other and fears being bested. Neither is sure, yet each pretends to superior competence. Paradoxically each passes the buck to the other for the responsibility of decisions. The strife of competition reduces empathic sympathy, distorts communications, impairs the mutuality of support and sharing and decreases satisfaction of personal need. In effect, intelligent cooperation lessens, and bickering and recrimination mount. The inevitable consequence is progressive emotional alienation in parental relations.

"With the father absent much of the day, the mother assumes the dominant position in the home.

"The father strives mightily to show success as a man. He pursues what has been called 'the suicidal cult of manliness.' To prove his merit, it is not enough to be a man; he must be a superman. In his daily work, he serves some giant industrial organization, or he is a lone wolf in the jungle warfare of modern competitive enterprise. The more he succeeds, the more he dreads failure. He brings his work worries home. Depleted by his exertions, he has little emotional stamina left over to give freely of his love to wife and children.

"He wants to be buttressed for the war of tomorrow, but he finds his wife absorbed in her own busy life. He feels deserted and alone and angry that his wife gives him so little understanding. She reproaches him for not taking a more responsible role in the family. She demands more consideration for herself and the children. For the difficulties with the children she feels guilty. But she denies this guilt and projects it to father. Father takes it. He thinks it must really be his fault. Though confused and angry, he appeases mother because of his need for her. He tries to be useful to win her favor.

"Both parents therefore act unnatural. They are suspicious of any open show of emotion, which they regard as weakness. A free flow of emotion is felt to be dangerous, as if all emotion were equated with something bad and destructive. Therefore it must be curbed. Anxiety over loss of control is constant. Tender sentiment is avoided or, if expressed, is ignored; it spells weakness and the threat of loss of control. Thus the behavior of both parents becomes overcontrolled, unspontaneous, and reduced in vitality. Both parents are burdened with anxiety, guilt and doubt. They are afraid of life and have lost their zest for play and sense of adventure. They settle down to a stereotyped way of living, a safe conforming routine. They strive to live up to the Joneses with all the external accoutrements of conventional success—a home, a new car, the latest gadgets."[1]

WHAT DO YOU THINK? #7

1. How do you feel about who makes the decisions in your family? (Circle the appropriate statements.)
    a. I feel comfortable about who makes the decisions.
    b. I don't like to make decisions.
    c. I feel I make too many decisions.
    d. I feel that I don't make enough decisions.
    e. I am reluctant to give up making any of the decisions I now make.
    f. Decisions? What decisions?

Who Is Responsible?

Unclear roles and confusion over who is responsible for things like making decisions, disciplining the children, or handling the money, do cause many marriage problems. But how can a husband and wife know what to do about decision making and other practical "who is responsible?" problems?

James Jauncey, in his book *Magic in Marriage,* points out that the Christian husband and wife have specific help for everyday problems, not only from the guidelines in Scripture, but also in the daily presence of the Holy Spirit. As Jauncey says, "God through His Holy Spirit seeks our best welfare and happiness. He seldom does this by a supernatural act. Instead, He seeks to permeate our thinking until our judgments are His.

"In marriage He has two people to work through. The husband's authority does not carry infallibility with it. Since the two have become 'one flesh' the guidance has to come through both. This means that except in cases of emergency, decisions affecting the whole family should not be put into effect until they are unanimous."[2]

This view is also held by Lionel Whiston. In his book *Are You Fun to Live With?* he says, "By far the most productive and ideal method of dealing with decisions is to make them together under God. This rules out the possibility of taking over areas of responsibility in open defiance, in secret, by emotional blackmail, or by constantly placating the offended partner.

"The prelude to making joint decisions under God is the commitment of the partners to Him, as individuals and as a team. It relies on wisdom and direction greater than that of either partner, claimed by faith. Practically, it means examining all the factors involved, 'putting the cards on the table,' including pertinent data, inner motives and desires, the recognition of which spouse has greater experience in the particular area, and lessons learned in the past."[3]

This view presupposes that both individuals are honestly and truthfully seeking the will of God for their lives and are completely willing to follow the will of God. Many times a husband and wife decide that it is better for one or the other to make decisions in different areas of responsibility. Many a wise husband, realizing the capabilities and strengths of his wife, has delegated definite responsibilities and authority where the wife can best complement him. Each relies upon the strength and wisdom of the other person. What happens when the husband and wife cannot agree upon a decision that must be made? In cases like this perhaps the husband should decide. This does not mean it will be the best decision but God will hold the man responsible for the decision, not the woman.

For Biblical guidelines in working out decisions together, a passage with many specific practical suggestions is 1 Peter 3:1–9, where the apostle Peter talks about what marriage partners should do and be. Peter completes chapter 2 of his first letter with a stirring description of how Christ submitted Himself to sacrifice and suffering. He set a personal example that all Christians should follow. (See 1 Pet. 2:21.) Then Peter opens chapter 3 with practical applications of how to follow Christ's example by saying:

1. *In the same way, you wives, be submissive to your own husbands so that even if any of them are disobedient to the word, they may be won without a word by the behavior of their wives,*

2. *as they observe your chaste and respectful behavior.*

3. *And let not your adornment be external only—braiding the hair, and wearing gold jewelry, and putting on dresses;*

4. *but let it be the hidden person of the heart, with the imperishable quality of a gentle and quiet spirit, which is precious in the sight of God.*

5. *For in this way in former times the holy women also, who hoped in God, used to adorn themselves, being submissive to their own husbands.*

6. *Thus Sarah obeyed Abraham, calling him lord, and you have become her children if you do what is right without being frightened by any fear.*

7. *You husbands likewise, live with your wives in an understanding way, as with a weaker vessel, since she is a woman; and grant her honor as a fellow-heir of the grace of life, so that your prayers may not be hindered.*

8. *To sum up, let all be harmonious, sympathetic, brotherly, kind-hearted, and humble in spirit;*

9. *not returning evil for evil, or insult for insult, but giving a blessing instead; for you were called for the very purpose that you might inherit a blessing (NASB).*

Why So Much Advice for Wives?

It is interesting that the advice Peter gives to the wives in this passage is six times as long as his advice to the husbands. There is a reason for this. At the time Peter wrote, if the husband became a Christian his wife automatically followed him into the church. But if the wife became a believer, it created tensions and difficulties. In Peter's day, men and women did not hold equal places in the family.

This inequality was even reflected in the Jewish form of morning prayer. One of the sentences that a Jewish man prayed each morning was, "I thank God that He did not make me a Gentile, or slave or a woman." The view of women that permeated all of the Jewish law was that the woman was not a person, but a thing. She had no legal rights; she was absolutely in her husband's possession to do with her as he pleased!

Now, in theory the Jews had a high ideal of marriage. The rabbis said, "Every Jew must surrender his life rather than commit idolatry, murder or adultery." "The very altar sheds tears when a man divorces the wife of his youth." That was theory! The fact was, that in the time of Christ, divorce was tragically easy!

The divorce laws at that time were strange. The wife had no rights of divorce at all, unless her husband became a leper, an apostate or engaged in a "disgusting trade." But under the law a man could divorce his wife for almost any cause. The woman was helpless and defenseless. And the entire process of obtaining a divorce was very easy. The law said that a man who wished a divorce had to hand his wife a bill of divorcement which read, "Let this be from me your letter of divorce and letter of dismissal and deed of liberation, that you may marry whatever man you want." The husband handed the bill of divorcement to his wife in the presence of two witnesses and the marriage was over.

In the Greek world at the time of Christ the situation was worse. Women of the respectable classes in Greece led a completely se- cluded life. They took no part in public life; they never appeared on the streets alone; they never even appeared at meals or at social occasions. Each woman had her own living quarters and no one but her husband might enter. It was the man's job to keep the woman secluded so she might see as little as possible, hear as little as pos- sible and ask as little as possible. Companionship and fellowship in marriage were unheard of in that day. A man found these pleasures outside of marriage.

Peter has all these conditions in mind as he talks to the ladies about how to be good wives, even if they are Christians and their husbands are not. His advice isn't profound; it is surprisingly simple. Be a good wife. That is all. Nothing more. Nothing less. By the silent preaching of her behavior the Christian wife will win her husband.

Many Christian women have fallen into the trap of being a walk- ing tape recorder. They virtually remember every word of the pas- tor's sermon and when they get home they parrot what they have heard. Other women, in their efforts to reach their husbands for Christ, mention God in every statement and the husband feels that a normal conversation is a rarity. He even gets a sermon out of how God created the wonderful cows which makes it possible for him to have steak on his plate!

A wife accomplishes more by her Christian behavior than by what she says. As one woman stated, "I haven't told my husband that I've accepted the Lord. I want to wait until he sees such a change in me that he will ask, 'What's going on with you? Why are you so differ- ent?' Then when I tell him it will make sense."

Peter goes on to explain how a wife is to be a good wife. She is to be submissive. This means she is voluntarily unselfish. A good wife is also pure and respectful. A respectful wife is one who tries never to say or do anything that embarrasses her husband or makes him feel unsure or ashamed. She is concerned about his welfare, building him up instead of tearing him down. A good wife is worthy of being trusted. She is faithful and doesn't engage in what some call "inno- cent flirtations."

A third principle from this passage is that a quality wife knows what to wear. As Peter wrote this he was not telling women how to dress. He was simply giving a principle: a beautiful woman is one who has an inner beauty and radiance.

As William Coleman says, "Naturally, within reason a woman

HUSBANDS DON'T USUALLY appreciate THE AGGRESSIVE APProach

wants to look both contemporary and attractive. But she does not want to appear brash. To many young women the emphasis seems to be sexuality. What a shame if they never understand femininity!

"Do you know how a female rhino selects her male rhino? She is nearsighted, so when she sees her beau she first backs up. Then she charges him at thirty miles an hour, hitting him broadside and knocking him to the ground. Then she proceeds to gouge and step on him. While he is literally bleeding and bruised he gets the message, 'she loves me!'

"The Christian woman is not this way. She is feminine. She is gentle, sweet and kind because she knows what femininity is all about. There are very few men who would want a drill sergeant for a wife."[4]

Peter didn't want the Christian woman to demand attention just because she was a woman. Instead he encouraged her to develop an inner beauty that reflects femininity, gentleness, thoughtfulness and love.

WHAT DO YOU THINK?   #8

(For Wives Only)

1. First Peter 3:1–6 gives several specific suggestions how a wife can live out her role in the marriage relationship. To apply this passage to yourself, complete the following sentences:

I am submissive to my husband when I . . .

I respect my husband when I . . .

I show a gentle and quiet spirit when I . . .

2. Following are four of Peter's words to wives. Which one say something to you about decision making in your marriage? Why?
Submissive

Respectful

Gentle

Quiet

3. Do Peter's words to wives—submissive, respectful, gentle and quiet—indicate that you are to always let your husband make the decisions in your family? Why? Why not?

4. Circle the feelings that are a part of you:

I listen to my husband comfortably.
    Always   Sometimes   Seldom   Never

I wish my husband would listen more to my ideas.
    Always   Sometimes   Seldom   Never

I really have the best understanding of how to handle discipline with the children.
    Always   Sometimes   Seldom   Never

I think it's important to let my husband feel he's the leader even if I do most of the planning.
    Always   Sometimes   Seldom   Never

Wives today should not be expected to actually obey their husbands.
    Always   Sometimes   Seldom   Never

I enjoy knowing that my husband is the leader in our family; it makes me feel safe.
    Always   Sometimes   Seldom   Never

I wish my husband would help me more with handling the money.
    Always   Sometimes   Seldom   Never

Peter Talks to Husbands

The apostle Peter takes only one brief paragraph—1 Peter 3:7—to speak to the husbands, but in that paragraph he gives much valuable advice. In fact, Peter gives the husbands three principles to live by.

First, a husband must be understanding. This means he is willing to listen to his wife's point of view. He's willing to think with her. He is sensitive to her feelings, moods and ideas. He tries to discover his wife's needs in order to meet them and do what is best for her. Here we see the selfless attitude being important in the husband's role as well as in the role of the wife.

Second, the husband is to be a protector. Recognizing that his wife is not as rugged physically as he is, the Christian husband is not to let his wife overwork. He knows when to take her out for dinner, or even away for the weekend without the kids. (This is good for both husband and wife!) Also, the husband doesn't let the children get away with being disrespectful to their mother. He treats his wife with respect, love and consideration, and protects her from hurtful situations.

In the third place, Peter tells husbands to remember that wives have spiritual rights that are equal to theirs. They are joint-heirs of God's grace. God loves wives just as much as He loves husbands.

WIVES APPRECIATE CONSIDERATION and UNDERSTANDING

What happens if husbands do not follow the instructions in 1 Peter 3? Peter explains one significant consequence. He says, "Otherwise, you won't be able to pray." In other words, if your relationship isn't right with others it won't be right with God.

WHAT DO YOU THINK?   #9

(For Husbands Only)

1. First Peter 3:7 gives specific suggestions for how a husband can live out his role in the marriage relationship. To apply this passage to yourself, complete the following:

I show consideration and understanding for my wife by . . .

I honor her and protect her by . . .

I treat my wife as my spiritual equal by . . .

2. Following are the three key statements Peter makes to husbands. What do they say to you about decision making in your marriage?

Be understanding

Be a protector

Know that God loves your wife as much as He loves you.

3. If you are an understanding protector who knows God loves your wife as much as He loves you, does this suggest you are to make all the decisions in your family? Why? Why not?

4. Check the feelings that are a part of you:

I listen to my wife comfortably.
    Always   Sometimes   Seldom   Never

My wife has outlandish ideas.
    Always   Sometimes   Seldom   Never

I wish my wife would listen more to me and my ideas.
    Always   Sometimes   Seldom   Never

I am afraid that my role of disciplinarian makes me the "bad guy" in the eyes of my children.
    Always   Sometimes   Seldom   Never

I'd rather not talk about who's the leader in our home.
    Always   Sometimes   Seldom   Never

Some tasks around the house are definitely feminine, others definitely masculine.

Always   Sometimes   Seldom   Never

Start Making Some Changes—in Yourself

Note that in 1 Peter 3:8,9 Peter points out the characteristics that are part of the marriage relationship when husband and wife are living by God's plan. Peter says, "You should be like one big happy family, full of sympathy toward each other, loving one another with tender hearts and humble minds."

Read these guidelines from 1 Peter with yourself in mind. Compare Peter's instructions for each marriage partner with what is going on in your marriage now. Is the wife respectful and submissive to the husband's views? Is the husband careful, strong, thoughtful and loving, protecting his wife from the pressures and buffeting of life? Just who is making the decisions? Is one spouse making them all, without really trying to communicate or share ideas?

Perhaps you see changes that need to be made. Perhaps it is easier to see changes your mate should be making. But how can you begin?

Don't begin with your mate.

Begin with yourself.

"Before you can have any hope of changing your partner, you will need to make some very crucial changes.

"Since criticizing and suggesting changes only increase the problem by decreasing understanding, love and acceptance between you, discard it. Stop it all. Determine to give the most wholehearted love and acceptance possible—without conditions. But then, if you can't criticize and correct the other, how will you proceed?

"By being a different sort of person. Instead of accepting with spoken or unspoken reservations, genuinely accept him or her as you promised in that long ago ceremony. Vows are nothing if they do not become a way of life—a daily commitment of life. And your vows were not to educate, reform and restructure your mate, but to love. The crucial commitment of marriage is the pledge to be the right mate to the other person. Forget whether you 'found the right mate.' Who could know? Who could say? And so what if you did or didn't discover just-the-very-very-right-and-perfect-person-for-grand-old-you?

"What kind of person are you being? Are you committed to being the right mate here and now? Do that, be that, and you'll make a change for the better in both of you. Almost instantly."[5]

WHAT'S YOUR PLAN?

If you are studying this book with your spouse, best results can be obtained if you complete the following material individually and then discuss your answers together. As you compare ideas, feelings and attitudes you will achieve new levels of communication and understanding in your marriage.

Set aside time this week to study 1 Peter 3:1–9. Read the passage two or three times and note words or phrases that seem especially significant to you. Then complete the following in a personal notebook:

1. Describe the behavior or attitude that you want to change (for example: wanting to have the last word, wanting to make all or most of the major decisions, feeling your way is really best, etc.).

2. List several very personal reasons for giving up this behavior or attitude. What will changing this mean to you personally?

3. Motivation to change is very important. From your reasons for giving up the behavior or attitude select the *most important reason*. Write it down.

4. Begin to think about *how* you should change your behavior if you wish to succeed. Write these ideas down.

5. Adopt a positive attitude. What has been your attitude toward changing this in the past? Describe. How will you maintain your new attitude? Write it down.

6. Many times when you eliminate a behavior or attitude that you dislike a vacuum or void will remain. Frequently a person prefers the bad or poor behavior to this emptiness so he reverts back to the previous pattern. In order for this *not* to happen decide what *positive behavior* you want to substitute in place of the negative one you are giving up. Describe this positive behavior attitude.

7. Search for Scriptures that will help you in this problem area and your determination to change. Read Ephesians 4:31,32. Choose any word, phrase or thought that encourages you or gives you a specific guideline. For encouragement read Philippians 4:13,19.

4
What Was That
I Never Heard You Say?

As you read this chapter, you will discover . . .
. . . why communication can be such a problem
. . . that communication is more than talking
. . . listening is an essential part of building strong lines of communication in a marriage
. . . the valuable Biblical guidelines for communicating
. . . how husbands and wives frustrate each other (and how to avoid it)
. . . specific ways you can improve your communication skills.

"But why can't we communicate?"

That's a familiar question, especially for a lot of husbands and wives. But before asking "Why no communication?" take time to ask yourself, "What does the word communication mean to me?"

WHAT DO YOU THINK?   #10

My definition of communication is . . .

Communication Is a Process

There are many definitions of communication. One very good and simple definition is that communication is a process (either verbal or nonverbal) of sharing information with another person in such a way that he understands what you are saying. *Talking* and *listening* and *understanding* are all involved in the process of communication.

One of the key problems in communicating is making yourself understood. (See cartoon next page.) We often *do* think we understand what our mate is saying, but often what we heard is not what he or she means at all. In fact, our spouses may not be sure they themselves know what they mean in the first place!

When you stop to think about all that's involved in getting your message across it's apparent why misunderstandings often occur. Communication specialists point out that when you talk with another person there are actually six messages that can come through.

1. What you mean to say.
2. What you actually say.
3. What the other person hears.
4. What the other person thinks he hears.
5. What the other person says about what you said.
6. What you think the other person said about what you said.

Discouraging? Rather. But it does illustrate why communication is often hard work. We want the other person not only to listen, but

to understand what we mean. The old proverb, "Say what you mean and mean what you say," is a worthy goal, but not an easy one to achieve.

WHAT DO YOU THINK?   #11

Here are three questions to help you think about yourself as a communicator.

1. Is communicating with your spouse difficult for you?

     Often   Sometimes   Almost never

2. Does your mate seem to have difficulty understanding what you mean?

     Often   Sometimes   Almost never

3. What do you think your mate would say about your ability to communicate?

Great   So-so   Impossible

To Communicate—Listen More, Talk Less

In his book *Herein Is Love*, Reuel Howe says, "If there is any indispensable insight with which a young married couple should begin their life together, it is that they should try to keep open, at all cost, the lines of communication between them."[1]

Unfortunately, it is not uncommon for communication lines to be down. Sometimes these breaks in communication are due to the husband and/or wife not being willing or able to talk about what's happening in his or her life. But just as often it is the result of marriage partners not really listening when the other talks. There cannot be strong lines of communication without real listening.

Someone has suggested that listening intently with one's mouth shut is a basic communication skill needed in marriages. Think about your own communication pattern. Do you listen? How much of what is said do you hear? It has been estimated that usually a person hears only about 20 percent of what is said. What is involved in effective listening?

Listening effectively means that when someone is talking you are not thinking about what you are going to say when the other person stops. Instead, you are totally tuned in to what the other person is saying. As Paul Tournier says, "How beautiful, how grand and liberating this experience is, when people learn to help each other. It is impossible to overemphasize the immense need humans have to be really listened to."

Listening is more than politely waiting for your turn to speak. It is more than hearing words. Real listening is receiving and accepting the message as it is sent—seeking to understand what the other person really means. When this happens you can go further than saying, "I hear you." You can say, "I hear what you mean."

While listening is generally regarded as a passive part of communication, this is not true. Sensitive listening is reaching out to the other person, actively caring about what he says and what he wants to say.

In his book *After You've Said I Do*, Dwight Small points out that listening does not come naturally nor does it come easily to most people. Listening is not our natural preference. Most people prefer to be the one speaking. We like to express our ideas. We feel more comfortable identifying our position, asserting our opinions and feelings. Actually, most people do not want to hear as much as they want to speak and to be heard. Because of this we concentrate more on getting our word into the conversation, rather than giving full attention to what the other person is saying. Also, all too often we filter the other person's remarks through our own opinions and our own needs.

For example, a wife mentions that she's tired of housework. Her husband hears what she says, but the message he receives is that she is unhappy because he isn't providing her with household help like her mother has. That's not what the wife had in mind, but it is what the husband heard. Ever since they were married it has bothered him that he cannot provide help for the home like his wife's father does. It is easy to see how the message came through differently than the wife intended. Filtered messages are seldom accurate and cause much misunderstanding.[2]

When both husband and wife recognize the importance of listening objectively, and giving each other full attention, they are taking big steps toward building strong lines of communication.

WHAT DO YOU THINK?   #12

How would you describe yourself as a listener?

1. As your mate talks to you, do you find it difficult to keep your mind from wandering to other things?
    Yes   No   Sometimes

2. When your mate talks, do you go beyond the facts being discussed and try to sense how he or she is feeling about the matter?
    Yes   No   Sometimes

3. Do certain things or phrases your mate says prejudice you so that you cannot objectively listen to what is being said?
    Yes   No   Sometimes

4. When you are puzzled or annoyed by what your mate says, do you try to get the question straightened out as soon as possible?
    Yes   No   Sometimes

5. If you feel it would take too much time and effort to understand something, do you go out of your way to avoid hearing about it?

Yes   No   Sometimes

6. When your mate talks to you, do you try to make him or her think you are paying attention when you are not?

Yes   No   Sometimes

7. When you are listening to the other person, are you easily distracted by outside sights and sounds (such as the TV set)?

Yes   No   Sometimes

Look back over your answers. Do they give you clues for improving your listening attitudes and skills?

The Bible Speaks of Word Power

Children attending school soon learn to chant the sing-song poem, "Sticks and stones may break my bones, but words will never hurt me." But experience quickly teaches that this is untrue. Words can and do hurt a person. The Bible recognizes this and talks about word power in both the Old and New Testaments.

Proverbs 18:21 states what many have discovered: *Death and life are in the power of the tongue (NASB).* Proverbs 26:22 also speaks of how words really get to a person: *The words of a whisperer . . . go down to the innermost parts of the body (NASB).* This was what Job was experiencing when he cried in frustration, *How long will you torment me, and crush me with words? (NASB).* Or as *The Living Bible* puts it, *How long are you going to trouble me, and try to break me with your words?* (Job 19:2).

James 3:2–10 talks about the power of words and why it is so important to control the tongue. Surely here are key ideas for improving communications in a marriage:

If anyone can control his tongue, it proves that he has perfect control over himself in every other way. We can make a large horse turn around and go wherever we want by means of a small bit in his mouth.

And a tiny rudder makes a huge ship turn wherever the pilot wants it to go, even though the winds are strong.

So also the tongue is a small thing, but what enormous damage

WE FiLTEP WHaT WE HEAP THPOUGH
OUP FEELINGS

it can do. A great forest can be set on fire by one tiny spark. And the tongue is a flame of fire. It is full of wickedness, and poisons every part of the body. And the tongue is set on fire by hell itself, and can turn our whole lives into a blazing flame of destruction and disaster.

Men have trained, or can train, every kind of animal or bird that lives and every kind of reptile and fish, but no human being can tame the tongue. It is always ready to pour out its deadly poison. Sometimes it praises our heavenly Father, and sometimes it breaks out into curses against men who are made like God. And so blessing and cursing come pouring out of the same mouth. Dear brothers, surely this is not right! (TLB).

James compares the power of the tongue to the rudder of a ship, as far as power is concerned. Comparatively speaking, a rudder is a small part of the ship, yet it can turn the ship in any direction and control its destiny. What husbands and wives say to one another can turn their marriage in different directions (and in some cases cause them to wind up going in a vicious circle).

Continuing to emphasize the tongue's potency, James compares it to a flame of fire. Great forests can be leveled by one tiny spark. In the same way, a marriage can be damaged and in some cases even "set on fire" by one remark, or (more typically) by continually chopping and snipping away at each other.

Words do spread like fire. Did you ever try to stop a rumor? Did you ever attempt to squelch an unkind story once it was told? Impossible! Who can unsay words or wipe out what has been heard?

James continues to bear down on the difficulty in controlling the tongue when he writes that man's ingenuity has succeeded in taming almost every kind of living creature; yet he has failed in taming his own tongue! According to the dictionary "to tame" means "to control" and "to render useful and beneficial." Man has not been able to do that with his tongue on any widespread basis.

Each person must be responsible for his own tongue-training program. Controlling the tongue needs to be a continuing aim for each husband and wife because *everything* that is said either helps . . . or hinders; heals . . . or scars; builds up . . . or tears down.

According to Scripture, the husband or wife who just blurts out whatever he or she is thinking or feeling without considering the consequences is in a bad way indeed: *Do you see a man who is hasty in his words? There is more hope for a fool than for him* (Pro. 29:20, *NASB*).

First Peter 3:10 sums it up nicely: *If you want a happy, good life, keep control of your tongue, and guard your lips . . . (TLB)*. To control your tongue is not easy to accomplish in your own strength, but the Christian who depends on the Holy Spirit for teaching and guidance has help and strength far beyond his own. Remember how good it feels when you have a comfortable, "building-up" kind of conversation with your spouse? You concentrate on choosing words that are kind and appropriate for the time and purpose. And your mate does the same. And the result is that you build up each other and create a rewarding situation for yourself. Proverbs 25:11 describes the beauty of such a moment: *A word fitly spoken is like apples of gold in a setting of silver (RSV)*. Or as Proverbs 15:23 says, *How wonderful . . . to say the right thing at the right time (TLB)*.

The Bible also gives tips on how to listen. The ability to use words well isn't all that is required to make a person an effective communicator. An anonymous wit once pointed out that the Lord created man with one mouth and two ears and perhaps this is an indication of how much talking and how much listening we should do!

Proverbs 18:13 gives an important reason for listening carefully: *He who gives an answer before he hears, it is folly and shame to him (NASB)*. According to Scripture, listening means taking time to know what the situation is before jumping to conclusions (and going off with your tongue half-cocked).

In James 1:19 the Christian is told to *be quick to hear* or as it is put in the *Amplified* version: *be a ready listener*. Too many of us are ready talkers, but we have little or no desire to listen. Yet, one of the keys to a successful marriage is *wanting* to hear your mate out. You must make the effort to listen.

To be sure, listening takes effort but at the same time it frees us from ourselves and from our own interests and makes it possible for us to take in what the other person has to say. In so many cases, communication breaks down in a marriage because each partner is so wrapped up and enslaved by his own interests and ideas that he fails to try to understand his mate. And of course the result is that his mate does not understand him. But when husband and wife start to listen to one another an amazing thing happens: they start to feel understood by each other.

One of the difficulties in listening is that one partner tries to second guess the other. It is easy to think that you know what your partner is going to say, so you cut your partner off and finish the sentence or interrupt his idea with something that he or she doesn't mean at all. All too often a husband or wife blurts out an opinion that is miles from the wavelength that the other partner is on. This is what the writer of Proverbs had in mind when he said: *What a shame—yes, how stupid—to decide before knowing the facts!* (Prov. 18:13, *TLB*).

To Understand—Communicate!

In his book, *The Art of Understanding Your Mate,* Cecil Osborne suggests several ways in which men and women frustrate one another in the marriage relationship. For example, women frustrate their husbands by "taking over" and assuming dominance, or by tending to become emotional in a discussion. Men are also frustrated when women refuse to abandon the romantic dreams of girlhood.

On the other hand, men frustrate their wives by failing to understand the somewhat volatile emotions of their wives. Women often have strong mood swings and may be depressed or made happy by events that do not deeply affect a man. Women are also frustrated by men failing to understand that "little things" as he sees them, are often "big things" to her. For instance, outside activities of the husband, like sports, hobbies and even work, are frequently sources of frustration to the wife.

But, as Osborne points out, the major source of frustration for wives by their husbands is *that men do not communicate with or listen to their wives.* And to be fair, this can be the case with wives as well.

An additional source of frustration is that all too often husbands and wives concentrate on the talking aspect of communication because they are overly concerned about getting their ideas across. In doing this they fail to listen to the other party. When this happens husbands and wives have no real idea of what the other is really thinking or feeling. They may talk, but do they really say anything? Or hear anything? Many conversations are dominated with responses like "unhuh," "Yes," and "I see," and then five minutes later both husband and wife wonder what went on.[3]

Such lack of communication can produce real marriage problems. In fact, many marriage counselors say that the number one problem in marriage is poor communication.

Marriage is an intimate relationship built on mutual understanding, but in order to truly understand another person you must be able to communicate with him. A husband and wife can know a great deal *about* each other without really knowing one another. Communication is the process that allows people to know each other, to relate to one another, to understand the true meaning of the other person's life.

WHAT'S YOUR PLAN?

If you are studying this book with your spouse, best results can be obtained if you complete the following material individually and then discuss your answers together. As you compare ideas, feelings and attitudes you will achieve new levels of communication and understanding in your marriage.

1. Circle the phrase that you feel describes the quality of communication in your marriage:
   a. needs no improvement
   b. highly effective
   c. satisfactory
   d. inconsistent

e. superficial
f. frustrating
g. highly inadequate

Now go back and underline the phrase which you think your spouse would choose.

2. List three things *you* can do to improve communication between yourself and your spouse. "I plan to improve our communication by:
   a.

   b.

   c.

I will start doing these three things *(date)* _____ *(time)* _____"

3. Make an "appointment" with your mate when you can sit down (perhaps over a cup of coffee) and plan together how you can improve your communication.

(date) _____ *(time)* _____

As you do your planning together be sure to cover the four following points:

a. Share and discuss your responses to question 1 on the quality of communication in your marriage.

b. Also share your responses to question 2 on how you plan to improve communication. Ask your mate's opinion to see if he or she feels if your suggestion will actually improve communication. If not, work out alternate ideas that both of you approve of.

c. Commit yourself to following your plans for improving communication and stick to it for at least one week.

d. Set a date for one week from now to get together again and evaluate how successful your plan has been. If necessary, revise your plan at that time and repeat the process until you both feel that communication between you is improving.

5
Why Can't We Talk About It?

As you read this chapter, you will discover . . .
. . . four hangups that keep people from communicating
. . . that we communicate at five different levels, from shallow clichés to deep honest openness
. . . that Scripture teaches a definite relationship between self-acceptance (through God's love) and the willingness to accept and communicate with others
. . . that communication with God is vital to communication with each other
. . . how to plan specific ways to improve communication with God and each other.

"But I just don't want to talk about it!" Ever hear that from the other half? Ever use it yourself when you are out of patience (or ideas) about what to say next?

There are basic reasons why a lot of us can't get through or can't be reached. And there are basic Scriptural principles which will help us communicate more effectively.

Reasons for Not Communicating

Why is it that some people do not communicate? They often have basic hangups or weaknesses such as these:

1. A few people do not have the ability to talk with another person. They have never learned how to share openly with someone else and they have difficulty forming the words.

2. Others are fearful of exposing what they feel or think. They do not want to run the risk of being rejected or hurt if someone else disagrees with them. This is a protective device. The ability to communicate is not lost when married couples grow apart. It is the desire to communicate that undergoes change. When one or the other no longer wants to be understood or to be understanding, then distance will develop.

3. Others have the attitude that talking won't do any good, so why bother? They are unable to get through to the other person so they stop trying.

4. Some people do not believe that they as a person have anything to offer. They do not think that their ideas are worthwhile. They have what is called a poor self-image and, as a result, they withhold their comments and personal feelings. They have difficulty accepting themselves.

There are times when it is easy to identify the obstacles to good communication. Other times there is a complex mixture of reasons that is hard to pin down. Think back to a situation when you and your spouse couldn't communicate. What was the *real* reason?

WHAT DO YOU THINK?   #13

1. Which reason for not communicating applies to you?
   - ☐ can't talk to others
   - ☐ afraid to expose thoughts
   - ☐ feel "why bother?"
   - ☐ ideas not worthwhile

2. Which reason for not communicating applies to your mate?
   - ☐ can't talk to others
   - ☐ afraid to expose thoughts
   - ☐ feel "why bother?"
   - ☐ ideas not worthwhile

3. Maybe you have another reason for not wanting to communicate. If so, describe it in ten words or less.

The Five Levels of Communication

In his excellent book, *Why Am I Afraid to Tell You Who I Am?*, John Powell asserts that we communicate on at least five different levels, from shallow clichés to deep personal honesty. Hangups such as fear, apathy or a poor self-image keep us at the shallow level, but if we can be freed from our weaknesses, we can move to the deeper, more meaningful level.

Powell's five levels of communication include:

Level Five: Cliché Conversation. This type of talk is very safe. We use words such as "How are you?" "How is your family?" "Where have you been?" "I like your suit." In this type of conversation there is no personal sharing. Each person remains safely behind his screen.

Level Four: Reporting the Facts About Others. In this kind of conversation we are content to tell others what someone else has said, but we offer no personal commentary on these facts. We just report the facts like the five o'clock news each day. We share gossip and little narrations but we do not commit ourselves as to how we feel about it.

Level Three: My Ideas and Judgments. This is where some real communication begins. The person is willing to step out of his solitary confinement and risk telling some of his ideas and decisions. He is still cautious, however, and if he senses that what he is saying is not being accepted he will retreat.

Level Two: My Feelings or Emotions. Now the person shares how he feels about facts, ideas and judgments. The feelings underneath these areas are revealed. If a person is to really share himself with another individual he must get to the level of sharing his feelings.

Level One: Complete Emotional and Personal Truthful Communication. All deep relationships, especially marriage relationships, *must* be based on absolute openness and honesty. This may be difficult to achieve because it involves a risk—the risk of being rejected because of our honesty, but it is vital for relationships to grow in marriage. There will be times when this type of communication is achieved and other times when the communication is not as complete as it could be.[1]

These are five suggested levels of communication. Only you know at what level communication is occurring in your marriage. But ask yourself, "What *is* our communication like? On which level are we? How can we move toward Level One in our relationship?"

WHAT DO YOU THINK?   #14

1. Write down subjects or topics which you discuss with your spouse at the Level One stage of communication—complete emotional and personal truthful communication:

2. Now write down subjects or topics you do not discuss at Level One:

3. What prevents you from communicating on certain subjects at Level One?

4. What do you think can be done about this? List what you can do to help your partner share more deeply with you.

What About Communication with God?

We have been talking about communication especially as it pertains to husband and wife. But what about our communication with God? Are we open in the presence of God or do we use Level Four or Five communication there? Do we share ourselves with Him? Do we do all the talking or do we sit and listen?

In Christian marriage we realize that there are three people involved—God, husband and wife. As you see on the diagram we have a triangle with God as the top or the center. You also see the word communication between each member here. If there is a breakdown in communication between one member and God this will affect the communication between that person and his mate. If there is a breakdown in communication between this person and his mate this will affect his communication between himself and God! The communication lines between God and your mate must be open and you must work on keeping these open at all times. One author has suggested that "Lines open to God invariably open to one another, for a person cannot be genuinely open to God and closed to his mate. . . . God fulfills His design for Christian marriage when lines of communication are first opened to Him."[2]

What is it that really frees a person to open his life to another, to reach out to share and to love another person? Before we can love someone, we must have had two basic experiences in our life. First of all, we must have experienced love from someone else and then we must also love ourselves. But what if we grew up never having experienced true unconditional love that is necessary for us to begin loving ourselves? How can one begin to love others and himself when he's an adult? Is it really possible or are we just fooling ourselves? We find that it is possible to experience this unconditional love—from Jesus Christ! Often called the apostle of love, John puts it this way:

9. *By this the love of God was manifested in us, that God has sent His only begotten Son into the world so that we might live through Him.*

10. *In this is love, not that we loved God, but that He loved us and sent His Son to be the propitiation for our sins.*

11. *Beloved, if God so loved us, we also ought to love one another.*

18. *There is no fear in love; but perfect love casts out fear. . . .*

19. *We love, because He first loved us (1 John 4:9–11,18,19, NASB).*

KEEP all the LINES OPEN

The ability to love yourself and other people is the result of God reaching out and loving you first. When you accept God's forgiveness and acceptance you experience His love. But for many people, right here is where the "catch" comes in. God doesn't cause the problem, we Christians do. Deep down, we really don't believe God accepts us—and the result is that we really don't accept ourselves.

But if Scripture plainly says that God forgives and accepts you, why go on rejecting yourself? Why reject what God has accepted? And not only has God accepted you, but He *accepts you unconditionally.* God attaches no strings to your relationship with Him, so why should you? Why not drop your guard as far as God is concerned? Relax in His presence and your confidence in yourself—as well as in Him—will grow.

As John points out. *There is no fear in love; but perfect love casts our fear . . .* (1 John 4:18, *NASB*). So, let it happen. Let God love you His way—with no conditions, no improvements on your part to make yourself "worthy" of God's love. If you try to "shape up" for God and be "worth loving," you play the same game with Him that you play with others—especially your mate. You set a standard of what you think is lovable. When you don't reach it, or your mate doesn't reach it, you freeze, clutch, or blow up. Fear casts out, or suppresses, the love you want to have for yourself and others.

WHAT DO YOU THINK?   #15

Analyze just how much you accept what God has done for you and how He feels about you by completing the following multiple choice statements. Don't choose answers because they look "right." Instead choose answers that really match your true feelings.

1. I think of God as
   ☐ a distant power
   ☐ my friend
   ☐ my policeman
   ☐ my _____

2. When I pray I feel
   ☐ relaxed and close to God
   ☐ strained and uncertain
   ☐ afraid God is displeased with me
   ☐ _____

3. As a Christian I
☐ try to do better so I will deserve God's love
☐ feel God can't love me the way I act
☐ feel unhappy because I belong to God's family
☐ _____

4. Describe a lovable person in twenty-five words or less. How would God describe a lovable person? How would He describe an unlovable person?

Doorways to Communication

As you open up to God, you will discover new ability to open up to others. You will be able to communicate at those deeper levels described earlier in this chapter. It works like this:

1. Christ accepts us.
2. We accept Christ's love.
3. We accept ourselves.
4. We accept others.
5. We communicate! (See cartoon.)

Christ's love and acceptance of us gives us the confidence to share ourselves with others. He accepts us with our failures and defects and sees the great potential that lies within us. This potential can now be developed because Christ is in us. Because God accepts us, we can learn to accept ourselves. When we accept ourselves and develop a better self-image, we learn to accept others which leads to a willingness to communicate with those around us. Jesus Christ provides the way for a person to move to the first level of communication!

WHAT'S YOUR PLAN?

If you are studying this book together, best results can be obtained if you complete the following material individually and then discuss your answers with your spouse. As you compare ideas, feelings and attitudes you will achieve new and deeper levels of communication and understanding.

Choose three of the following ideas and try them out during the coming week.

1. Decide if there are areas in your relationship with your spouse that could be improved if you would be willing to share how you feel (Level Two communication). Choose one thing that you will talk about with your mate and share your true feelings. Choose a time that's appropriate and honestly tell him or her that you want to share your feeling about something because you believe it would help you feel better.

2. Decide if there are areas in your relationship with God that would be improved if you were willing to tell Him how you really feel. (He knows anyway!) Take some time alone this week to tell God your true feelings about yourself and how you feel about Him.

3. Discuss with your mate how he or she feels about God. If your feelings do not agree does this mean that God loves either one of you more than the other? Does your faith in God's acceptance of you "just as you are" help you accept your marriage partner just as he or she is? Can you feel comfortable for your mate to have ideas on certain subjects that do not agree with yours?

4. Write a letter to God telling Him how you feel about His acceptance of you. For ideas read Psalm 103.

5. List ways that you protect yourself or cut yourself off from communicating with your mate. Your list may include things like: reading at mealtime; ironing or doing some task that gives me a degree of privacy; turning on TV rather than continue a conversation; taking a bath so your mate will be asleep when you go to bed; etc., etc. At the end of the week decide which barriers you want to "tear down."

6. Plan a time when you can spend some time with your husband or wife in a relaxed situation (when the children are asleep or with a sitter, for example). It should be a time when you are not in a hurry, a time you can enjoy. Perhaps you will want to take a walk, read aloud to each other or share a snack or just talk about hopes and plans for the future.

7. Plan for one way that you really want to begin to communicate on "Level One" with your husband or wife. Think through what it would really mean to talk about a certain area of your relationship with complete emotional and personal truthfulness. Will talk be enough? What else will you have to do to prepare your husband or wife for your openness? Are there things you can do to build a credibility bridge that will make your openness meaningful and acceptable?

6
Is Anger Always a "No-No"?

As you read this chapter, you will discover . . .
. . . how anger blocks communication
. . . what anger is
. . . why people get angry
. . . what Scripture says about being angry
. . . typical reactions to anger
. . . how you respond to anger and how you can make needed
     changes in your attitude toward anger.

Most couples want to communicate with one another. Communication is vitally important when one or both of the partners is angry.

Yet anger is one of the main causes of the breakdown of communication in marriage.

Have you ever tried to define the feeling of anger or hostility? Perhaps the simplest definition is a *strong emotion of displeasure.* Emotions generate energy within us. Anger generates energy which impels us to hurt or destroy that which angers us. Anger is the natural, reflexive result of frustration—our reaction to having a goal blocked.

WHAT DO YOU THINK?   #16

What is your definition of anger? Do you agree with the definition given above? Why? Why not?

Positive and Negative Points on Anger

Too often we think of anger negatively. But anger also has its positive points. For example, one of our built-in goals is survival. When it appears that that goal is threatened (or may not be reached), the frustration resulting from the blocked goal makes us angry. This emotion can spur us on to almost impossible feats in order to survive.

. . . *Let justice roll down like waters and righteousness like an ever-flowing stream,* God said through Amos the prophet (Amos 5:24, *NASB*). Many of us desire to see justice and righteousness prevail. When this goal is not reached we become angry. And that is a good thing. When we see injustices around us—other people being hurt or taken advantage of—or when we see suffering we become angry because these conditions should not be so! The energy produced by this anger can motivate us to correct the injustices.

Of course, we do not always become angry for such noble reasons. Often our anger results from concern for ourselves—we are selfish. We do not get our own way and we are frustrated and become angry. We make plans, our mate does not agree with them and refuses to cooperate and we become angry.

"But I've already made reservations at the mountain resort," he states.

"You know how my allergy reacts to all that pollen," she retorts. "I want to go to the beach."

"Yeah, but I *always* get sunburned at the beach. Why can't you take your allergy pills?" he questions.

"For the same reason you don't use suntan lotion," she jabs.

And so it goes. Anger can result from the frustration of not getting your own way. Our unconscious goal is to have and do what we want when we want it. Usually anger stemming from this blocked goal strains our relationship with our spouse.

The prophet Jeremiah observed that *"the heart is the most deceitful thing there is, and desperately wicked"* (Jer. 17:9, TLB). We often fail to know when we are angry because we hide it behind other reactions. Our anger often conceals itself behind a cloak of resentment, aggression, frustration, hate, fury, indignation, outrage, wrath, antagonism, crossness, hostility, bitterness, destructiveness, spite, rancor, ferocity, scorn, disdain, enmity, malevolence and defiance. Regardless of how we describe it, when we get down to cases we are simply angry.

Our vocabulary is also rich in describing other people who are angry. We call people mad, bitter, frustrated, griped, fed up, sore, excited, seething, annoyed, troubled, antagonistic or antagonized, exasperated, vexed, indignant, furious, provoked, hurt, irked, irritated, sick, cross, hostile, ferocious, savage, deadly, dangerous, and on the offense.

Anger often produces behavior which prevents communication between husband and wife. We describe such communication-shattering behavior as: to hate, wound, damage, annihilate, despise, scorn, disdain, loathe, vilify, curse, despoil, ruin, demolish, abhor, abominate, desolate, ridicule, tease, kid, get even, laugh at, humiliate, goad, shame, criticize, cut, take out spite on, rail at, scold, bawl out, humble, irritate, beat up, take for a ride, ostracize, fight, beat, vanquish, compete with, brutalize, crush, offend and bully. When we find our feelings or actions described by these terms we should stop kidding ourselves. We are angry. Face that fact so that it can be dealt with.

Some Biblical Thoughts on Anger

What does the Bible say about anger in the lives of men? The Bible gives us several directives and thoughts about this emotion called anger.

The Bible says to put some kinds of anger away.

Let all bitterness and indignation and wrath (passion, rage, bad temper) and resentment (anger, animosity) and quarreling (brawling, clamor, contention) and slander (evil-speaking, abusive or blasphemous language) be banished from you, with all malice (spite, ill will or baseness of any kind) (Eph. 4:31, *Amplified*).

In this verse, Paul is referring to anger as a turbulent emotion, the boiling agitation of the feelings. It is passion boiling up within us.

The Christian is also to put away the anger that is abiding and habitual, the kind of anger which seeks revenge:

But now put away and rid yourselves completely of all these things: anger, rage, bad feeling toward others, curses and slander and foulmouthed abuse and shameful utterances from your lips! (Col. 3:8, *Amplified*).

Scripture teaches us not to provoke others to anger:

The terror of a king is as the roaring of a lion; whoever provokes him to anger or angers himself against him sins against his own life (Prov. 20:2, *Amplified*).

Fathers, do not provoke or irritate or fret your children—do not be hard on them or harass them; lest they become discouraged and sullen and morose and feel inferior and frustrated; do not break their spirit (Col. 3:21, *Amplified*). (See also Eph. 6:4.)

The Bible directs us to be "slow to anger" (that is, to control our anger) and to be careful of close association with others who are constantly angry or hostile.

He who is slow to anger is better than the mighty, and he who rules his own spirit than he who takes a city (Prov. 16:32, *Amplified*).

A hot-tempered man stirs up strife, but the slow to anger pacifies contention (Prov. 15:18, *NASB*).

Make no friendships with a man given to anger, and with a wrathful man do not associate, lest you learn his ways and get yourself into a snare (Prov. 22:24,25, *Amplified*).

Scripture also speaks of "justified anger." An example of justified anger is found in the life of the Lord Jesus:

> *And He glanced around at them with vexation and anger, grieved at the hardening of their hearts, and said to the man, Hold out your hand. He held it out, and his hand was (completely) restored* (Mark 3:5, *Amplified*).

In Ephesians 4:26 the apostle Paul speaks of two different kinds of anger and how to deal with both:

> *When angry, do not sin; do not ever let your wrath—your exasperation, your fury or indignation—last until the sun goes down* (Eph. 4:26, *Amplified*).

In the phrase, "When angry, do not sin," Paul is describing the kind of anger that is an abiding, settled attitude against sin and sinful things. You are aware that you are angry and you are in control of your anger. In this verse, God is actually instructing us to be angry—but about the right thing! Anger is an emotion created by God; He created us as emotional beings. The phrase, "do not sin," is a check against going too far. The kind of anger that is justified because it is against sin and sinful things and fully under your control is the kind of anger that has God's approval.

In the phrase, *"Do not ever let your wrath . . . last until the sun goes down,"* Paul has another meaning. Here he links anger to irritation, exasperation and embitterment. As earlier mentioned in Ephesians 4:31 and Colossians 3:8, we are supposed to put this kind of anger away. If we do get angry in this negative sense, we should deal with it quickly, "before sundown." Scripture counsels us to never take irritation or embitterment to bed. If we do we are sure to lose sleep (not to mention peace, friends and even our health).

WHAT DO YOU THINK?   #17

1. Using the previous Biblical descriptions of anger, describe the kind of anger that you usually experience.

How do you express this anger?

2. Describe the kind of anger your spouse seems to usually experience.

How does your spouse usually express this anger?

3. What can a person do to make himself "slow to anger"?

4. Describe how a person can "be angry and sin not."

How We Respond to Anger

How do people react when they are angry—especially in the husband-wife relationship? What choices do they seem to make almost automatically? For most of us there are at least four basic reactions that we have to anger.

1. *We suppress anger.* To suppress anger is like building a fence around it. You recognize you are angry and consciously try to keep your anger under control instead of letting your bad feelings spill out in uncontrolled actions or words.

Suppressing anger is what the writer of Proverbs had in mind when he said: *A [self-confident] fool utters all his anger, but a wise man keeps it back and stills it* (Prov. 29:11, *Amplified*). The same idea is found in Proverbs 14:29: *A wise man controls his temper. He knows that anger causes mistakes (TLB).*

In the New Testament James gives good advice on how to suppress

anger: . . . *let every one be quick to hear, slow to speak and slow to anger* (Jas. 1:19, *NASB*). To "be quick to hear" is another way to say, "listen carefully." If you can listen to what's going on and hold back long enough to think about what you are going to say, you can usually control your anger in a healthy way. As Dr. William Menninger says, "Do not talk when angry but after you have calmed down."[1]

It is important, however, to eventually talk about your anger. Somewhere, somehow the anger has to be recognized and released in a healthy manner. Otherwise your storage apparatus will begin to overflow at the wrong time and the wrong place.

2. *We express anger.* The opposite reaction to suppressing anger is to express it. Anger is a strong emotion and it needs expression in some way. Some people go so far as to advocate cutting loose and expressing exactly how you feel, when you feel it, no matter how much damage you do.

Granted, expressing anger with violent passion, yelling, sharp words and high emotions does get results but the results are usually not too positive. We like to say that we feel better because we "got it off our chest," but chances are, neither you nor the people you blast really profit from uncontrolled expressions of anger. Waiting until you've cooled off is better for all concerned. Reread Proverbs

EXPRESS ANGER—LET IT ALL HANG OUT

29:11 and Proverbs 14:29. In most cases Solomon makes it clear that a fool goes off half-cocked with uncontrolled anger while the wise man holds on to his temper.

This doesn't mean that you don't express anger in some way. Some people learn to express their anger by redirecting it. They get busy doing something that gives them time to cool off as they use up some of the emotional energy they've generated by becoming angry. Some people go out into the yard and cut the grass or dig in the garden. Some walk around the block and others ride a bicycle. Others find it helpful to sit down and write out exactly how they feel. Scrubbing a floor, washing a car or doing anything that takes physical effort can be a good way of working out the strong, pent-up feelings of anger. Whatever helps you calm down and control your feelings is a good course of action for you as long as it does not hurt others or damage their property.

3. *We repress anger.* The person who represses anger refuses to accept the fact that he is angry. Many Christians practice repression.

As a Christian you may honestly think that because you know Christ you are not supposed to become angry—the anger is not a legitimate emotion for you. Therefore, when angry feelings arise you attempt to ignore them and refuse to accept their presence. Because of what you've been taught in sermons and possibly in things that you have read, you feel that anger is always a sin and therefore off limits for anyone practicing Christian behavior.

But this isn't the case and it isn't what Scripture actually teaches. Anger is a God-given emotion. The Bible doesn't teach us to repress anger but to control it. In a way, we need anger as part of our personality and makeup.

As Dr. J. H. Jowett says, "A life incapable of anger is destitute of the needful energy for all reform. There is no blaze in it, there is no ministry of purification. . . . We are taught in the New Testament that this power of indignation is begotten by the Holy Spirit. The Holy Spirit makes us capable of healthy heat, and it inspires the fire within us. The Holy Spirit doesn't create a character that is lukewarm, neutral or indifferent."[2]

Ignoring anger and refusing to recognize its presence is NOT HEALTHY. Repressing anger is like taking a wastepaper basket full of paper and putting it in a closet and setting it on fire. True the fire can burn itself out OR it can set the entire house on fire and burn it down. Actually, ulcers, anxiety, headaches or depression are common results of repressing anger.

Dr. David Augsburger observes, "Repressed anger hurts and keeps on hurting. If you always deal with it simply by holding it firmly in check or sweeping it under the rug, without any form of release or healing it can produce rigidity and coldness in personality . . . Or repressed anger may come out indirectly in critical attitudes, scapegoating or irritableness."[3]

John Powell sums it up nicely when he says, "When I repress my emotions my stomach keeps score."[4]

If you are afraid of recognizing anger in your own life remember that God's Word recognizes the presence of anger, and although it gives advice to avoid anger and to control it, the Bible does not say to ignore your angry feelings.

Anger does serve a purpose. God Himself has anger against what is wrong. *For God's [holy] wrath and indignation are revealed from heaven against all ungodliness and unrighteousness of men* (Rom. 1:18, *Amplified*). Mark 3:5 tells about one of the times that Christ was angry, *And He glanced around at them with vexation and anger, grieved at the hardening of their hearts (Amplified).*

As already mentioned, the apostle Paul recognized that anger is a part of life. That's why he wrote: *When angry, do not sin* . . . (Eph. 4:26, *Amplified*). Notice that he did not write, "do not sin by being angry."

The point is this. Admitting the presence of anger is a healthy way to respond to anger in your life. Ignoring anger and repressing your feelings of anger only make matters worse. Getting angry is not necessarily a sin, but repression of anger is always a sin.

Dr. William Menninger writes, "Sometimes we push each other away and the problem between us festers and festers. Just as in surgery, free and adequate drainage is essential if healing is to take place."[5]

Repression of anger is the worst possible response that we can make to being angry. Unfortunately, it is an all too common response among Christians.

4. *We confess anger.* Some people react to anger by recognizing they are getting angry and they can confess it before their feelings get out of control. This is an excellent response to make to your mate when things are getting a little tense. The secret is to confess your anger in a way that your spouse will be able to accept. You might say, "You know, the way the discussion is going I'm starting to get angry. Now I don't want to get angry and I know you don't want me to get angry so perhaps we could stop the discussion, start over and see if I can get my feelings under control."

CONFESS ANGER — GET IT OUT IN THE OPEN.

Whatever you do don't say, "You're making me angry." This puts your spouse at fault and will put him or her on the defensive. *Always recognize that you are responsible for your own emotional reaction toward another person.* Confessing your anger to the other person simply means that you are willing to admit that you have a problem. You might say: "I'm sorry I'm angry. What can I do now so we can work this thing out?"

The Living Bible paraphrase of Ephesians 4:26,27 gives some good clues on responding to anger by confessing it:

> *If you are angry, don't sin by nursing your grudge. Don't let the sun go down with you still angry—get over it quickly; for when you are angry you give a mighty foothold for the devil (TLB).*

Paul was well aware that when you nurse a grudge you can grow a consuming hatred. Paul advises the Ephesian Christians (and us) to never nurse a grudge and let anger fester and rage within. To confess anger is to get it out in the open where you can discuss the cause of the trouble.

Confessing anger is a response that is usually more difficult for most of us, because by the time we admit we are angry it has already become obvious to our spouse, or whomever we are angry with, that we are definitely irritated and uptight. The key is to learn how to confess anger in a way that does not make the other person feel that you are angry with him already!

WHAT DO YOU THINK? #18

1. What is your usual response when you get angry?
   Suppress   Express   Repress   Confess

2. Do you agree with John Powell when he says, "When I repress my emotions my stomach keeps score"? What are other possible ways that repressed anger seems to affect you? Does it make you irritable? critical? touchy? Would you say that you are aware that you sometimes repress anger and don't want to admit that you are angry?

3. Does confessing anger seem like a real possibility for you? That is, is it something that you do easily or think that you could start doing? What would people say if you were honest and let them know when they were making you angry?
   My spouse would say:

   My friends would say:

   My boss would say:

Make the Most of Your Anger

In his book, *Be All That You Can Be,* David Augsburger suggests the following ways to make the most of anger. First of all a person must understand that "anger is a vital, valid, natural emotion. As an emotion, it is in itself neither right nor wrong. The rightness or wrongness depends on the way it is released and exercised."

"Be angry, but be aware. You are never more vulnerable than when in anger. Self-control is at an all-time low, reason decreases, common sense usually forsakes you."

"Be angry, but be aware that anger quickly turns bitter, it sours into resentment, hatred, malice, and even violence unless it is controlled by love."

"Be angry, but only to be kind. Only when anger is motivated by love of your brother, by love of what is right for people, by what is called from you by love for God, is it constructive, creative anger."

"Make the most of your anger. Turn it from selfish defensiveness to selfless compassion."[6]

WHAT'S YOUR PLAN?

If you are studying this book with your spouse, best results can be obtained if you complete the following material individually and then discuss your answers together. As you compare ideas, feelings and attitudes you will achieve new levels of communication and understanding.

Use the following questionnaire to evaluate your own attitude toward anger—what being angry does to you and what you do to others when you get angry. After each question write in "yes," "no," or a more accurate response (using as few words as possible).

1. Do you have a temper?

2. Do you control it?

3. Do others know when you are angry?

4. Describe how you feel when angry.

5. Does your anger surge up quickly?

6. Do you hold resentments?

7. Does your anger affect you physically?

8. Have you ever hit someone or something?

9. When was the last time?

10. How do you control your anger?

11. Who taught you?

12. Are others afraid of your anger?

13. Are others afraid of your criticism?

14. What causes your anger or criticism?

15. How often do you get angry?

16. What are you dissatisfied with in life?

17. Do you get mad at people or things?

18. What do you do about your anger?

19. How do you handle anger directed toward you?

20. Do you repress your anger?

21. Do you suppress it?

22. Do you express or confess it?

23. Do you know of Scriptures that can help you?

24. Do you regularly memorize Scriptures?

25. Do you openly and honestly pray about your emotions?

26. Do you really expect God to help you change your emotions?

27. Do YOU want to change?

If you are not satisfied with the way you respond to anger, then what are you going to do now to change your attitudes and behavior? Look back over the previous chapter and think of some specific things you can do to change and list them here.

7
How to Handle Anger
(Before It Handles You)

As you read this chapter, you will discover . . .
  . . . how a critical attitude can communicate anger
  . . . the difference between healthy and unhealthy approaches to
      anger
  . . . ten practical principles for dealing constructively with angry
      feelings
  . . . how to use Scriptural guidelines to deal with attitudes of
      anger, criticism or hostility.

Like it or not, anger is a part of life—including married life. In
fact, as the previous chapter points out, anger is an emotion given

to man by God Himself. Our problem is that we don't handle anger very well. We tend to become angry for the wrong reason or we tend to express angry feelings in a hurtful or damaging way rather than trying to help others and ourselves.

How Critical Are You?

For example, one "wrong reason" for anger is a critical attitude. The angry, hostile person is almost always a critical person. He attacks other people verbally or subtly. If you constantly dislike what you see in other people you may be this way. When you look for and are overly aware of the faults and weaknesses in others you are too critical and hostile. A person with a critical or hostile disposition is not going to be happy and will alienate those about him.

Are you really critical? Ask yourself these questions: Do you spend more time criticizing people in your mind than looking at their strong points? Do others do things that bother you so much that you feel you have to tell them? Do you talk about others in a derogatory manner behind their back? Do you have standards for others that you can't live up to yourself? Do you pressure others to conform to your standards so you can accept them easier?

These reactions indicate a critical or hostile attitude.

Why are we critical? It gets attention off of us. It may make us feel better at the expense of others. In his *Psychology and Morals,* Dr. J. A. Hadfield writes: "It is literally true that in judging others we are trumpeting abroad our own secret faults. We personalize our unrecognized failings, and hate in others the sins to which we are secretly addicted." He goes on to say that the real reason for our condemnation of certain sins in others is that these same sins are a temptation to ourselves. It is for this very reason that we denounce so vehemently the miserliness, bigotry or cynicism of others. Whatever fault we are most intolerant of in others is likely to be amongst our own besetting sins. "Most of our emotions are directed against ourselves," writes Dr. Hadfield. "Allow any man to give free vent to his feelings and then you may, with perfect safety, turn and say: Thou are the man.'"[1]

Whenever we find intense prejudice, intolerance, excessive criticism, and cynicism, we are likely to find projection of our feelings into someone else. We are prone to see in others our own undesirable tendencies.

WHAT DO YOU THINK?   #19

1. List the things about which you tend to criticize others:

2. What does this tell you about yourself?

3. How do these attitudes/characteristics compare with the fruit of the Holy Spirit (Gal. 5:22,23)?

4. Stop now and thank God for His forgiveness and ask Him to replace your critical spirit with the fruit of the Holy Spirit. (See Rom. 14:13.)

Healthy and Unhealthy Approaches to Anger

While a critical attitude is a problem for some people, even more of a problem for most of us is expressing angry feelings in a damaging way. Let's suppose you are going through the day and not feeling particularly critical of anyone or anything. But then feelings of anger suddenly (or not so suddenly) well up within. What do you do with them? Are you helpless? Must you blow your top because "that's the way you are"? That's a copout. Anger won't render you "helpless" unless you want it to—unless you secretly enjoy blowing off steam.

The truth is, you *do* have a choice about anger. You can react to anger in one of two ways: healthy or unhealthy.

First take a look at unhealthy reactions that will keep you enslaved, "helplessly" angry:

Unhealthy Reactions

First, be sure to ignore your emotional reactions. Even though you may be angry with your spouse, tell yourself that your angry feelings have nothing to do with the argument anyway. Even better, if you want to compound the problem, convince yourself that you're not getting upset at all. So you're perspiring a little—it's probably just warm in the room.

Be sure to keep your anger down in the pit of your stomach, where it won't bother your head. Keep everything on an intellectual level but don't let your spouse know how you feel.

Next, be sure to keep on denying your emotions. Keep telling yourself, "I'm not mad." So your stomach is in a knot and you're perspiring profusely. Keep insisting to your mate that you aren't angry at all. Your mate will believe you (?).

Also, make sure you keep your mind on the argument and how you can get back at your spouse. It's obvious the one with the right moves and bright lines is going to break this whole discussion wide open and come away the winner. And that's what's important, isn't it? Winning the argument? Especially if you are arguing with your spouse, right?

If you really get mad, blame your spouse. Surely it's his (or her) fault! When arguing with your mate, be sure to raise the volume. Find some defect in your spouse and point it out with great precision and accuracy (and a little exaggeration, too, if you can think of it). Very helpful rational things such as, "It's impossible to discuss anything with you. You're just too arrogant. You never (generalizations like this are good, too) listen. You think you're God, don't you?" Naturally, as a good Christian, you will be saying all this to speak the truth in love.

Finally, don't learn from your emotions. Walk out in a huff, take a couple of aspirins and concentrate on how unreasonable your spouse was, is, and always will be![2]

Obviously, the "unhealthy" reactions listed above are a perfect prescription for disaster in a marriage. Unfortunately, these reactions are all too typical with many husbands and wives. In their book, *Learning for Loving*, Robert McFarland and John Burton point out that "few couples have self-sufficient social skills and emotional maturity to fight constructively for the good of their marriage. We

1. IGNORE YOUR FEELINGS
2. LET YOUR STOMACH HANDLE IT.
3. KEEP SAYING... "I'M NOT ANGRY."

UNHEALTHY REACTIONS TO ANGER

4. CONCENTRATE ON "SCORING POINTS" AGAINST YOUR OPPONENT.
5. BLAME YOUR MATE (AS LOUDLY AS YOU CAN).
6. WALK OUT AND FEEL SORRY FOR YOURSELF.

believe consequently that most couples urgently need to develop skills and increase their emotional strength sufficiently to engage themselves in such encounters. We believe that many couples seek to avoid constructive conflict because one or both of them feel that changes will have to take place if adequate communication occurred between them."³

But in order to do this couples must be willing to trust each other—to trust one another with their feelings and with their admittals that what they are hearing and feeling hurts or is disturbing. All too often husbands and wives are too proud to admit to each other that they are uncomfortable, angry, hurt, etc. And the result is a stalemate in communication. Dwight Small observes, however, "All communication in an intimate relationship is built upon mutual trust. To confide in another is to be relatively sure, first of all, that a ground of confidence is shared. Mutual trust grows as each partner takes the other into account as a person whose happiness is bound up with his own."⁴

And how about the antidote to all of these unhealthy habits? There is one, if husbands and wives are willing to react to angry feelings in the following *healthy* ways:

Healthy Reactions

To begin with, be aware of your emotions. Forget the argument momentarily and concentrate on your emotional reactions. What are you feeling? Embarrassment (because her argument sounds better)? Fear ("He's getting nasty—I hope he doesn't hit me")? Superiority ("I'm ahead on points and she knows it")?

Don't be afraid to admit your emotion. Take a good look at yourself and accept the fact that you are angry. If you are honest, you'll admit that it's high voltage anger, not just a "little" irritation or frustration.

Now investigate how the emotion got there. Ask yourself, "Why am I angry? Why is my spouse getting to me like this?" Try to trace the origin of your emotion. You may come up with a glimpse of some hidden inferiority complex which you've never recognized or a fear or a weakness you didn't want to admit to your spouse.

Share your emotion with your spouse. Just present the facts with no interpretations or judgments. Say something to your mate such as, "Let's stop, because I'm saying things I really don't mean and I don't want this to happen." Whatever you do, don't judge or accuse your spouse. It isn't your spouse's fault that you are angry. Don't blame your spouse, even to yourself.

Decide what to do with your emotion. What's the best thing to do next? Perhaps you will want to tell your spouse, "Let's start again. I think I've been too defensive to listen to you. I'd like to try it again." Or, if necessary, "Would you mind if we dropped the subject of the moment? I'm afraid I'm too touchy to discuss it further right now." (Keep in mind, however, that you had better come back to it later or the problem will continue to grow and rankle the two of you.)

In *Conjoint Family Therapy,* Virginia Satir echoes many of the above ideas and she says, "A person who communicates in a functional (healthy) way can (a) firmly state his case, (b) yet at the same time clarify and qualify what he says, (c) always ask for feedback, (d) and be receptive to feedback when he gets it."[5]

Some other ideas for dealing with an emotional situation in a healthy way are offered by Howard and Charlotte Clinebell in their book, *The Intimate Marriage:* "A couple may find it helpful to ask themselves questions such as these: Is this really an issue worth fighting over or is my self-esteem threatened by something my spouse has said or done? In relation to this issue or problem area, what do I want and what does my partner want that we are not getting? What must I give in the relationship in order to satisfy the needs of my partner, myself in this area? What small next step can we take right now toward implementing this decision, made jointly through the give-and-take of discussion?"[6]

WHAT DO YOU THINK?   #20

"You are having a discussion with your mate. There are several noticeable differences of opinion. Soon voices and emotions begin to rise. You are starting to have some strong feelings toward what is going on and toward the other person. What should you do at this point?"

Describe how to deal with the above situation in an *unhealthy* manner:

Now write a dialogue of two people dealing with the situation in a healthy manner:

He:

She:

He:

She:

Practical Principles for Handling Anger

It helps to know what anger is, causes for anger, different kinds of responses to anger, what the Bible says about getting angry, healthy and unhealthy reactions to anger, etc., etc. But what finally counts is what you *do* with angry feelings when *you* have them. As a summary to this section on anger, here are ten practical principles for facing angry feelings and controlling them. Keep in mind, of course, that the Christian realizes he does not control anger (or any other problem) entirely in his own strength. He relies on the Holy Spirit to guide and empower. And never is the Holy Spirit needed more than when a person feels himself getting good and angry.

According to *The Living Bible* paraphrase of Galatians 5:19,20, when we follow our own wrong inclinations (the flesh) our lives produce evil results. And listed in those "evil results" are hatred and fighting, jealousy and anger . . . complaints and criticisms, the feeling that everyone else is wrong except you.

On the other hand, . . . *when the Holy Spirit controls our lives he will produce this kind of fruit in us: love, joy, peace, patience, kindness, goodness, faithfulness, gentleness and self-control* . . . (Gal. 5:22, *TLB*).

With the background, then, of the apostle Paul's words to the Galatians concerning how to handle anger and other basic emotions, here are ten practical steps you can take:

1. Be aware of your emotional reactions. Ask yourself, "What am I feeling?"

2. Recognize your emotions and admit that you have the feeling. Admitting the feeling of anger does not mean that you have to act it out.

3. Try to understand why you have anger. What brought it about? As mentioned in chapter 6, we are often angry because we are frustrated. We suffer from frustration of our desires, impulses, wants, ambitions, hopes, drives, hunger or will. When you are getting angry, ask yourself, "Does my anger come from frustration?" Then ask yourself, "What type of frustration?" Next, ask, "What or who is the cause of my frustration?" Ask yourself, "What positive solution can I think of?"

Other reasons why we get angry include:

The possibility of harm—physical harm or emotional harm. Our security is threatened and as a defense we become angry.

We become angry due to injustice—to others, ourselves or society. Often, this can be a "noble kind of anger" which is justified. But be careful and don't allow your righteous indignation over injustice become confused with another basic cause of anger which is: selfishness . . . the major cause of anger in most of us. If we are honest about it, we get mad because we aren't getting our own way. We aren't getting what we want.

4. Can you create other situations in which anger won't occur? What did you do to cause the other person to react in such a way that you became angry?

5. Is anger the best response? Write down the consequences of your getting angry. What is a better response? What would kindness, sympathy, understanding of the other person accomplish? Can you confess your feelings to him?

6. Is your anger the kind that rises too soon? If so, take some deep breaths or count to ten. Concentrate on the strengths and positive qualities of the other person instead of his defects.

7. Do you find yourself being critical of others? What does this do for you? Be less suspicious of other persons. Listen to what they say and feel. Evaluate their comments instead of condemning them. They may have something to offer to you. Does your criticalness or anger come from a desire to make yourself feel better? Are your opinions always accurate or could they be improved? Slow down in your speech and reactions toward others. Watch your gestures and expressions as they may convey rejection and criticism of the other person. Can you express appreciation and praise of the other in place of criticism?

8. You may have a time when your anger or criticism is legitimate. When you express it plan ahead and do it in such a way that the other person can accept what you say. Use timing, tact and have a desire to help the other person instead of tearing down.

9. Find a friend with whom you can talk over your feelings and gain some insight from his suggestions. Admit how you feel and ask for his guidance.

10. Spend time praying for the difficulty that you have with your feelings. Openly admit your situation to God. Ask for His help. Memorize the Scriptures that speak of anger, and Scriptures that speak of how we should behave toward others. Memorize and understand them and put them into practice. (Review verses that talk about anger in chapter 6.)

How to Be Christian—and Angry

Yes, it is possible to be angry in a "Christian way." Christian anger, however, must fulfill three conditions:

It must be directed at something wrong and evil.

It must be controlled and not a heated, uncontrolled passion.

There must be no hatred, malice or resentment.

Three brief sentences—easily stated, not so easily lived—especially in marriage where feelings run deep and sensitivity is often at its highest pitch. But it can be done—even a tiny step at a time. It *must* be done if you and your mate are to learn how to handle anger and conflict.

In his excellent book, *After You've Said I Do*, Dwight Small points

CONFLICT CAN BE GOOD... IF

out, "As a reality in marriage, conflict can be creatively managed for good; it is part of the growth process. Don't ever underestimate its positive possibilities! . . . In Christian marriage conflict—with its demand for confession, forgiveness, and reconciliation—is a means God employs to teach humility."[7]

Ask yourself, "Do I really want to change and become more capable of handling anger, frustration and hostile feelings? Do I really want to creatively manage conflict for good?" If your answer is yes to these questions, then read Paul's prayer for the Ephesians (Eph. 3:16–21). Commit yourself anew to Christ and His love and take that love and the power of the Holy Spirit into your marriage—into the nitty-gritty arena where anger and frustration occur in various degrees almost daily. God's mighty power is at work within you and He is able to do far more than you would ever dare to ask or dream of—beyond your highest prayer, desires, thoughts or hopes!

WHAT'S YOUR PLAN?

If you are studying this book with your spouse, best results can be obtained if you complete the following material individually and then discuss your answers together. As you compare ideas, feelings and attitudes, you will achieve new levels of communication and understanding in your marriage relationship.

1. Describe the behavior or attitude that you want to change (for example: anger, anxiety, quarreling, yelling, etc.).

2. List several very personal reasons for giving up this behavior or attitude.

3. Motivation to change is very important. From your reasons for giving up the behavior or attitude, select the most important reason. Write it down.

4. Begin to think about how you should change your behavior if you wish to succeed. Write these down.

5. Adopt a positive attitude. What has been your attitude toward changing this in the past? Describe. Indicate what attitude you are going to have now. How will you maintain this new attitude? Write down your answer.

6. Whenever you eliminate a behavior or attitude that you dislike, often a vacuum or void will remain. Frequently a person prefers the bad or poor behavior to this emptiness so he reverts back to the previous pattern. In order for this not to happen, substitute a POSITIVE BEHAVIOR in place of the negative. Describe what you can substitute for the behavior or attitude that you are giving up.

7. Read Ephesians 4:31,32. List the positive behavior or attitude that this Scripture suggests in place of the negative. Write out the way you see yourself putting this Scripture into action in your life. Describe specific situations and describe how you picture yourself actually doing what the Scriptures suggest. Describe the consequences of thinking or behaving in this new way.

EXAMPLE
Ephesians 4:31,32

Negative Behavior or Attitude to STOP	List the results of this behavior. Give several for EACH one.
Bitterness (Resentfulness, harshness)	
Anger (Fury, antagonism, outburst)	
Wrath (Indignation, violent anger, boiling up)	
Clamor (Brawling)	
Slander (Abusive speech)	

Positive Behavior or Attitude to BEGIN	What do you think would be the results of doing these three commands? List several for each.
Kindness (goodness of heart)	
Tenderheartedness (compassionate)	
Forgiveness (an action)	

Now write out the practical ways in which you see yourself behaving or doing these things suggested in the verse.

List when and how you will begin and the consequences that you expect. Be very specific.

8
The High Cost of Anxiety
(And How Not to Pay It)

As you read this chapter, you will discover . . .
  . . . that worry and anxiety are usually concerned with the past or
      the future, not the present
  . . . that one spouse's anxiety or worry is almost sure to affect the
      other—and their marriage
  . . . that Scripture contains practical advice for coping with anxi-
      ety and worry
  . . . how to deal with pressures that cause worry and anxiety.

Anxiety and worry are common causes of trouble in marriage.
When either marriage partner is tied in knots with fear and anxiety
there is unhappiness. Hours spent in worry add up to discouraging,
out-of-kilter days for both husband and wife, even if only one of
them is the worrier.

Did you ever stop to think that worry has little to do with the
present—except to make it miserable?

Worry is almost exclusively concerned with the past or the future.
You dwell on past mistakes or what someone did to you yesterday

... or what they didn't do or say. And before you know it you're having a terrible day all because you're concentrating on the past. True, it is often necessary to evaluate what happened and it is wise to learn from past experiences. But how much clearheaded evaluating and learning takes place when you worry? And, more important, did worry ever change yesterday?

Or maybe the past isn't what bothers you. It's the future that sends your worry out of control. You look at the bills and the financial obligations you will have to meet in the next six months and it's all too much to cope with. Perhaps you have a nagging health fear that you fret about, or possible future problems with your job. Whatever it is, when worry dominates your thinking you hardly have time to notice today.

No wonder marriages fall into deep trouble when worry consumes large chunks of energy of either the husband or the wife. Healthy, successful marriages need people committed to *today's* joys and problems. How much worry is there in your marriage? In your own life?

Did you ever analyze what you and your spouse worry about most often? Is it the past? What you could have said or should have done? Or is it the future that causes you to worry? Dreading what will happen to your children when they get out on their own? Concern about money for the bills that tie you in knots?

WHAT DO YOU THINK? #21

1. Think back over the last week. Did you spend the time feeling anxious or worried?

2. Were you aware of your mate being worried?

3. If worry was part of the past week, what specifically did you worry about? Do you know what your spouse worried about?

4. Can you list benefits or accomplishments that came as a result of your worry?

___

Defining Fear, Anxiety, Worry

God created man a thinking, emotional being. Because we are human we have the capacity to mull things over, to feel one way or another about a situation. Fear is one of the feelings all people experience from time to time. For example, fear that is based on external, real, physical dangers is healthy fear. It keeps us from being hurt by trucks, guns, hot stoves, etc.

Fear is an emotion and as such it becomes energy or a dynamic force. It is also an impulse to do something. When we refer to fear we think of such words as dismay, timidity, shyness, fright, alarm, panic, terror and horror. When we find that a person has fear we say that he is: afraid, alarmed, nervous, upset, disturbed, scared, faint-hearted, shy, timid, bashful, diffident, frightened or aghast.

What, then, is the difference between fear and anxiety? Anxiety is the feeling of apprehension, tension or uneasiness producing a sense of approaching danger, which does not stem from logic or a reasonable cause. Fear, on the other hand, is an emotional response that is consciously recognized, stimulated usually by some real threat (or at least it seems very real to the person who is afraid).

One way to see it is that fear is *external* and anxiety is *internal*. Anxiety can be defined as "fear in the absence of an adequate cause." Anxiety arises in response to danger and/or threat, yet often the

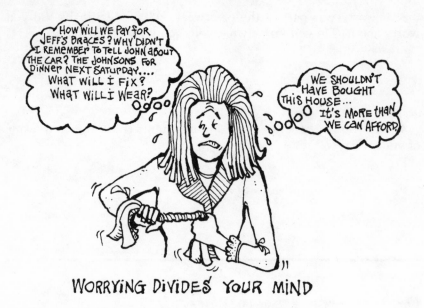

WORRYING DiVIDES YOUR MiND

source of this impending doom is not clear. The Greeks described anxiety as "opposing forces at work to tear a man apart."

We often use the word "worry" as a synonym for anxiety but this is not quite correct. The word "worry" means to fret, or be overly concerned. The person who worries spends great quantities of time thinking and dwelling upon a real or imagined problem. He goes over and over it in his mind. He usually begins thinking the worst about a situation and "crosses many bridges before he ever gets to them." The word "worry" comes from a combination of two words that mean "mind" and "divide." Worry means literally to "divide the mind."

The prophet Habakkuk gives a graphic description of a person involved in worry: *I heard and my inward parts trembled; at the sound my lips quivered. Decay enters my bones, and in my place I tremble. Because I must wait quietly for the day of distress . . .* (Hab. 3:16, *NASB*).

In his book *How to Win over Worry*, John Haggai comments that "Worry divides the feelings, therefore the emotions lack stability. Worry divides the understanding, therefore convictions are shallow and changeable. Worry divides the faculty of perception, therefore observations are faulty and even false. Worry divides the faculty of judging, therefore attitudes and decisions are often unjust. These decisions lead to damage and grief. Worry divides the determinative faculty, therefore plans, and purposes, if not 'scrapped' altogether, are not fulfilled with persistence."[1]

Worry and anxiety weaken and tear down a person. By contrast: *A calm and undisturbed mind and heart are the life and health of the body . . .* (Prov. 14:30, *Amplified*).

Are you consciously controlling worry in your life? Are you discovering ways to face your days with a "calm and undisturbed mind and heart"?

WHAT DO YOU THINK?   #22

1. Can you pinpoint the one thing in your life that causes you the most anxiety and worry? If so, name it.

2. How would you describe this worry?
    Unhealthy   Healthy

3. Explain why you chose the description you did.

How You Can Win over Worry

Practically everyone agrees that anxiety and worry are destructive. But how does a person break out of worry patterns? The Bible gives the Christian practical guidelines for dealing with worry.

For example, Paul reminds the Christian . . . YOU ARE GOD'S CHILD. DEPEND ON YOUR HEAVENLY FATHER FOR HELP.

And now just as you trusted Christ to save you, trust him, too, for each day's problems; live in vital union with him. Let your roots grow down into him and draw up nourishment from him. See that you go on growing in the Lord, and become strong and vigorous in the truth you were taught. Let your lives overflow with joy and thanksgiving for all he has done (Col. 2:6,7, *TLB*).

Don't worry about anything, instead, pray about everything; tell God your needs and don't forget to thank him for his answers. If you do this you will. . . . keep your thoughts and your hearts quiet and at rest as you trust in Christ Jesus (Phil. 4:6,7, TLB).

When you read these instructions they sound so encouraging. Really great. But how do you put them to work to keep you from worrying? In essence Paul is saying:

Don't try to face your troubles on your own. Worry takes over when you look at a dark situation and you begin to fret, "This is awful. There's no way out. I'm sunk." That may (or may not) be true as far as you're concerned, but you're not alone. You can turn to God and tell Him how hard things are and trust Him for help. Depend on His power and strength to get you through.

Remember you have a choice of who "runs the ranch." Do your thoughts control you or do you control your thoughts? For example, when you wake up in the morning do worries take over and begin dictating your mood to you? Or do you say, "Hold it! Worry is not going to help." Get busy thinking about something else. Get busy doing something that demands your attention. Don't let worry "run your ranch." With God's help choose *not* to worry.

Concentrate on reality. Imagining what might happen or daydreaming about the consequences can lead to an extreme state of worry and anxiety. Face up to the actual situation and tell God your needs. As Paul says, *If you do this you will. . . . keep your thoughts and your hearts quiet and at rest as you trust in Christ Jesus.*

Be honest with yourself and accept your problems. Don't be afraid that you are "unspiritual" and "backslidden" because you are discouraged and worried. Don't worry about worrying; that will only make matters worse. Instead, honestly evaluate your feelings. Define your problem. And then follow Paul's advice: *. . . just as you trusted Christ to save you, trust him, too, for each day's problems.* It will help, too, if you thank God for the problem as well as His answer for it . . . even if you don't see a way out just at the moment. Remember what James wrote: *Is your life full of difficulties and temptations? Then be happy, for when the way is rough, your patience has a chance to grow. So let it grow, and don't try to squirm out of your problems* (Jas. 1:2–4, TLB).

Jesus gave His disciples a sound principle for dealing with anxiety and fear . . . FOCUS ON THE SOLUTION RATHER THAN ON THE PROBLEM.

This principle is graphically illustrated in Matthew's account of Peter walking on the water: *And when the disciples saw Him walk-*

ing on the sea, they were frightened, saying, "It is a ghost!" And they cried out for fear. But immediately Jesus spoke to them, saying, "Take courage, it is I; do not be afraid." And Peter answered Him and said, "Lord, if it is You, command me to come to You on the water." And He said, "Come!" And Peter got out of the boat, and walked on the water and came toward Jesus. But seeing the wind, he became afraid, and beginning to sink, he cried out, saying, "Lord, save me!" And immediately Jesus stretched out His hand and took hold of him, and said to him, "O you of little faith, why did you doubt?" And when they got into the boat, the wind stopped. And those who were in the boat worshiped Him, saying, "You are certainly God's Son!" (Matt. 14:26–33, *NASB*).

Peter was fine as long as he stepped out on faith and kept his mind and his eyes on Christ. But when he focused his attention on the wind and the waves (his problems) they became overwhelming. Christ wants us to reach out in faith to Him and, depending on His help and guidance, to use the resources available to us and find workable solutions to our troubles. For example, try these "solution-oriented" ideas:

Think in terms of possible solutions. List your worries and anxieties. Be specific and complete in your descriptions. If you're really worried about the house payment this month don't just write "finances." Instead, put down "money for house payment" and any other pressing money problems you have. Then write a list of possible solutions. Your list may include borrowing, working an extra job, selling the antique clock, or even having a garage sale. Include every possibility you can think of and pray for God's help in choosing how you can move toward a solution.

Actively work on solutions. Thinking up possible solutions isn't enough. Act. For instance, if you feel that you worry far more than the average person and that something must be wrong with you, make an appointment with your doctor. Malfunction of glands, vitamin deficiencies, allergies, lack of exercise and emotional or physical fatigue can sometimes disguise themselves as worry or anxiety. As you look for reasons why you worry, rule out any possible physical causes to start with.

Don't concentrate on things that trouble you. When Peter concentrated on how high the waves were he began to sink. Recognize what increases your anxiety or worry. Stay away from those areas.

Suppose you and your spouse can't discuss politics without tensions building. Or maybe your mate follows the newscasts closely

but you get upset and worried about the troubled world situation. Recognize the situation and work out a solution. When the news comes on maybe you should get busy in another part of the house with an activity you truly enjoy. Or help someone in the family who needs a hand.

One ex-worrier explains, "When I begin to get uptight and start to worry about how my husband and I have different views I get busy and thank God for all the blessings we've enjoyed together. Sometimes I even write out a list of blessings. When I start to 'name them one by one' somehow the worries don't seem important."

It helps to remember that Jesus taught His followers to . . . AC-CEPT WHAT CAN'T BE CHANGED . . . KEEP KEY VALUES STRAIGHT . . . LIVE ONE DAY AT A TIME. See if you can pinpoint these principles in the following words on anxiety spoken by Christ: *For this reason I say to you, do not be anxious for your life, as to what you shall eat, or what you shall drink; nor for your body, as to what you shall put on. Is not life more than food, and the body than clothing? Look at the birds of the air, that they do not sow, neither do they reap, nor gather into barns; and yet your heavenly Father feeds them. Are you not worth much more than they? And which of you by being anxious can add a single cubit to his life's span? And why are you anxious about clothing? Observe how the lilies of the field grow; they do not toil nor do they spin, yet I say to you that even Solomon in all his glory did not clothe himself like one of these. But if God so arrays the grass of the field, which is alive today and tomorrow is thrown into the furnace, will He not much more do so for you, O men of little faith? Do not be anxious then, saying, "What shall we eat?" or, "What shall we drink?" or, "With what shall we clothe ourselves?" For all these things the Gentiles eagerly seek; for your heavenly Father knows that you need all these things. But seek first His kingdom, and His righteousness; and all these things shall be added to you. Therefore do not be anxious for tomorrow; for tomorrow will care for itself. Each day has enough trouble of its own* (Matt. 6:25–34, *NASB*).

Accepting what can't be changed, keeping key values straight, and living one day at a time can take much of the worry and anxiety out of a marriage relationship. Think through what would happen to trouble spots in your own marriage if you . . .

Accept what can't be changed. You've probably read Reinhold Niebuhr's prayer: "O God, give us serenity to accept what cannot be changed, courage to change what should be changed, and wisdom to

distinguish the one from the other." What about making it a personal prayer that you really mean?

Face up to it that no amount of worry, nothing you can say, will really change your marriage partner. On the other hand, accepting your mate and loving him (or her) for what he (or she) is, can free each of you from worry. The changes in you may well be what God will use to help your marriage grow stronger and more satisfying.

In his book, *Are You Fun to Live With?*, Lionel Whiston tells of a man, Pete, who tried for years to change his wife to be more what he felt she should be. But "all he ever got in return was an argument or a brush-off."

Then Whiston goes on to say, "But a recent insight made a great difference to Peter . . . He has found greater joy in loving his family for what they are, not for what they might become.

"Pete still longs for the time when his wife will join him in Christian faith and often asks himself, 'When will my wife change and become a partner with me?' Then he answers, 'I don't know, and in a sense that is not my concern. My job is to love her, enjoy her, and be the finest husband and father that I can be. If God wants to change Arlene, he will. Meanwhile, I'm glad I married her.'"[2]

Keep values straight. What is worth worrying about? Are you worrying about the real issues? As *The Living Bible* puts Christ's words: *So my counsel is: "Don't worry about things—food, drink, and clothes. For you already have life and a body—and they are far more important than what to eat and wear"* (Matt. 6:25).

As a Christian you enjoy God's forgiveness. You have the abundant life—life in God's family. Does remembering that help you take a clear look at your values?

Money may be tight; your clothes may be getting a little worn. You seem to be chalking up more failures than successes. As you work toward solutions for your problems, keep your values straight by remembering that "Christian security has little to do with success or failure. As Christians we believe that Christ loves us totally whether we succeed or fail."[3] He will help us with our needs as we rely on Him and His Word to help us get our values straight in every area of life.

Live one day at a time. Are you worrying about your marriage, or enjoying it? Have you enjoyed your marriage partner today? Or are you too worried about what's coming up tomorrow to get the *now* into focus?

Of course the house needs a new roof and Johnny's teeth should be straightened, and you can't wait much longer to have the brakes on your car relined. Even so, Jesus says, "Don't be anxious about tomorrow. God will take care of your tomorrow too. Live one day at a time." Do you believe that? You'd better. Today's the only day you have.

WHAT DO YOU THINK?   #23

1. Go back through the Biblical principles for dealing with worry. Choose one or two ideas that are especially meaningful to you.

2. Now think of ways you want to use the ideas to help you move from worry to a place of greater freedom and trust in God.

3. Can you think of at least one way trust and confidence in God—instead of worry—will be strengthening to your marriage? Be specific.

Stress Can Be Good for Your Marriage

A final word about problems and stress—the things that make you worry.

Stressful situations can be valuable situations as far as your marriage is concerned. As Dwight Small says, "Life's most trying moments can also be times of communicating at new depths of mutual understanding. It is the experience of couples who have been married for a long while that some of their best times of dialogue have come during setbacks. The loss of a job, sickness of a child, death of a parent—such experiences necessarily bring about a need for cooperation and decisive action. This makes two people sense their need of one another in special ways."[4]

When troubles come, instead of letting worry make you weak and miserable, reach out to God and reach out to your mate, confident that together you can face each day.

WHAT'S YOUR PLAN?

1. Read the following Scripture passage and write down *what* we are to do and *why* we are to do it: *Casting the whole of your care— all your anxieties, all your worries, all your concerns, once and for all—on Him; for He cares for you affectionately, and cares about you watchfully* (1 Pet. 5:7, *Amplified*).

What I am to do:

Why I am to do it:

2. What is the plan for the elimination of anxiety or worry in the following passage? *You will guard him and keep him in perfect and constant peace whose mind [both its inclination and its character] is stayed on You, because he commits himself to You, leans on You and hopes confidently in You* (Isa. 26:3, *Amplified*).

The word "mind" refers to our imagination or thought life. What do you think or dwell upon?

3. Read the following Scripture passage: *Do not fret or have any anxiety about anything, but in every circumstance and in everything by prayer and petition, [definite requests] with thanksgiving continue to make your wants known to God. And God's peace [be yours, that tranquil state of a soul assured of its salvation through Christ, and so fearing nothing from God and content with its earthly lot of whatever sort that is, that peace] which transcends all understanding, shall garrison and mount guard over your hearts and minds in Christ Jesus.*

For the rest, brethren, whatever is true, whatever is worthy of reverence and is honorable and seemly, whatever is just, whatever is pure, whatever is lovely and lovable, whatever is kind and winsome and gracious, if there is any virtue and excellence, if there is anything worthy of praise, think on and weigh and take account of these things—fix your minds on them (Phil. 4:6–8, *Amplified*).

List your anxieties:

List your definite requests:

List some specific things to think of that meet the qualifications of verse 8:

The next time you start to worry, think of Philippians 4:8 and concentrate on what is worthy of reverence, honorable, just, pure, lovely, kind, winsome, gracious. Get together with your spouse and isolate a particular anxiety or worry that each of you has. Make these a matter of prayer and use the verses you have studied above for inspiration to literally forget your troubles and anxieties.

9
How to Cope with Conflict

As you read this chapter, you will discover . . .
  . . . that conflict is part of marriage and should be handled, not
     hidden or ignored
  . . . some major causes for conflict and what to do about them
  . . . ten key principles (with several valuable sub-principles) for
     coping successfully with conflict, according to the teaching
     of Scripture.

Sugar-coated myths picture marriage as the time when you "live
happily ever after" (particularly if you are Christians!). Fighting and

disagreeing, say the myths, are just not part of a healthy, "spiritual" marriage.

But the sugar coating quickly melts away under the heat of married reality. Marriage *does* include conflict, because a marriage is a union of two individuals who have unique viewpoints, frames of reference, and values. No two people can agree on everything all the time. In any marriage there will be conflict from time to time.

What exactly is conflict? For some the word conjures up scenes of battlegrounds and warfare. This is one of the meanings of conflict, but the meaning with which this chapter is concerned is, according to Webster, "Disagreement, emotional tension resulting from incompatible inner needs or drives."

That definition is a challenge for every married couple. How can they handle their disagreements—the tensions that come when the needs and drives of one spouse are at cross-purposes with the other? How do they keep cross-purposes from becoming crossed swords?

Every married couple needs to know how to deal with conflict in a creative, constructive way.

Objectivity, flexibility, willingness to compromise (Is squeezing the toothpaste tube at the bottom rather than in the middle *really* one of the big issues of life?) and the willingness to let the other person be himself, all need to be developed if couples are to enjoy a satisfying and growing marriage relationship.

When conflict comes, it should be faced with the understanding that disagreements do not mean that the entire relationship is on the verge of breaking down. Nor should a disagreement be a trigger for a knock-down, drag-out scrap (verbal and/or physical). Husbands and wives need to know how to "disagree agreeably" or to put it in a little stronger terms, "fight fair." Unfortunately, few couples get any training on how to "disagree agreeably" and "fight fair" before marriage. As a result, their disagreements often turn into spats, heated arguments and quarrels. All of this really isn't necessary. Any couple can cope better with conflict if they use the following ten principles.

Don't Avoid Conflict with the Silent Treatment

Some people use the "silent treatment" as a means of avoiding controversy. They use silence as a weapon to control, frustrate or manipulate their spouse. Or sometimes the husband or wife takes the pathway of silence because it seems to be the least painful. Perhaps one spouse is silent now because in the past the other spouse was not a ready listener. Also, there's always the possibility of a deep hurt that is keeping one marriage partner silent.

But silence never pays off in the long run. "Silence is golden" so the saying goes, but it can also be yellow! Don't hide behind silence because you are afraid to deal with the issue at hand.

Marriage counselors estimate that at least one half of the cases they see involve a silent husband. Men have a tendency to avoid conflict in discussion. Ironically, the issues they avoid are often the ones that indicate where adjustments and changes need to be made—and fast.

Here is a typical pattern that results in the use of silence. When married partners are not communicating because one of them is silent, both of them experience frustration and a rising sense of futility, all of which compounds the silence problem. The more the communicative person tries to talk, the farther the silent person draws into his hostile shell. The person who is trying to talk then feels increasingly useless, inadequate and hurt. The talkative spouse may try shouting, or even violence, in an attempt to drive the silent mate from his refuge. But this is futile because it does nothing more than to drive the silent spouse into deeper silence. When you say to a silent person, "Why don't you talk to me?" or "Please say something—why can't we communicate?" or similar pleas, it usually does nothing more than reinforce that person's silence![1]

How, then, do you encourage the silent person to talk? First, you have to let the silent partner choose the time to speak. Then, when this person does speak, you must communicate in every way you can that you're willing to listen without judging what is said; that you are willing to accept feelings and frustrations. The silent person must find that you really do listen and care. If you create an acceptant, unthreatening climate, the silent spouse will in all likelihood start talking and then communication can begin or be reestablished.

WHAT DO YOU THINK?   #24

1. Circle how you *tend* to respond when controversy arises:
   talk incessantly   clam up

2. List several reasons you think a person might choose to be silent:

3. When would it be best for you to be silent?

Why?

Will your silence solve the problem or improve communication in the long run?

4. Write down several things you can do to encourage a silent mate to be more expressive.

Don't Save "Emotional Trading Stamps"

Always watch yourself to make sure you're not saving up hostility yourself. A husband or wife, for example, could easily save up a lot of hostility when trying to deal with a mate who is dealing out the silent treatment (discussed above). But the worst method of dealing with feelings of irritation or frustration is to deny them and bottle them up. Feelings must be expressed. They shouldn't be allowed to accumulate.

EMOTIONAL TRADING STAMPS
AREN'T WORTH SAVING

Some individuals, however, deal with their emotions like trading stamps. They save up each little irritation as though it were a stamp. They accumulate many stamps and, finally, when something happens that is the last straw, they blow up and "cash in" with all of their pent-up irritations and frustrations. Their emotional trading-stamp book becomes full, and they decide that now is the time to trade it in. In this way they think "they get something back" for all of their trouble. They "redeem their trading stamps," so to speak, and tell themselves, "Well, now at least I feel better."

Are you an emotional stamp saver? If you suspect that you are, now is the time to start doing something about it. It is much better to release your emotions as they *arise*. God created all of us to feel deeply, but we must express what we feel. Our expressions should, and can be done, in a healthy way.

Much of the arguing, quarreling, fighting that occurs between married couples turns into sadistic, emotionally crippling sessions. How do *you* handle your disagreements?

A crucial question is how you handle anger—those strong, even passionate feelings of displeasure that well up within? How does your anger handle you? (At this point you may want to review Chapters 6 and 7 on handling anger.)

Suppose your spouse acts negatively toward you or even gets angry with you. Ask yourself these questions:

Am I really being hurt or affected by this?

Will counter-anger, even if it's justified and rational, really help here?

Is getting angry the most effective thing I can do?

What will my anger accomplish?

How do I respond to or answer another person who is angry? Whatever you do, do not tell the other person, "Now don't get angry." When you say this, it has exactly the opposite effect! Instead, try saying as quietly as you can, "I'm sorry something is making you angry. If it's me, I apologize. What can I do to help?" This suggestion is effective at home, at work—just about anywhere. Strangely enough it sounds vaguely familiar—"like something from the Bible." Solomon, who had quite a bit of marital experience, once wrote, *A soft answer turns away wrath* (Prov. 15:1, *Amplified*).

WHAT DO YOU THINK? #25

1. List several ways you can express anger without hurting yourself or others.

2. State the way in which you wish your mate would let you know he or she is angry.

3. How can you let your spouse know that you would prefer that his or her anger be communicated differently?

If Possible, Prepare the Setting for Disagreement

If you have a major discussion on an important topic coming up, try to arrange for the best time and place. Guard against interruption. You may want to take the phone off the hook, or not answer the door. If you have children, ask them not to interrupt you. If the children do interrupt you, let them know that you are having an important discussion and you will talk to them when you are finished.

Parents do not usually succeed in hiding disagreements and arguments from their children. Let them know that you do disagree sometimes and that all family members will have times of disagreement. Keep in mind that your children will learn their pattern for disagreeing and arguing from watching you. If you can establish healthy patterns for disagreement with your spouse, it can do a lot to help your children learn to disagree in a healthy way—all of which can add to peace and harmony around the house.

Attack the Problem, Not Each Other

Do your best to keep the discussion impersonal. Instead of attacking the problem, too many couples attack each other with innuendos, slurs and other "smart" remarks.

There is an old story about a sheepherder in Wyoming who would observe the behavior of wild animals during the winter. Packs of wolves, for example, would sweep into the valley and attack the bands of wild horses. The horses would form a circle with their heads at the center of the circle and kick out at the wolves, driving them away. Then the sheepherder saw the wolves attack a band of wild jackasses. The animals also formed a circle, but they formed it with their heads out toward the wolves. When they began to kick, they ended up kicking one another.

People have a choice between being as smart as a wild horse or as stupid as a wild jackass. They can kick the problem or they can kick one another. Here are five tips to help you kick the problem—to disagree without kicking your spouse:

. . . back up any accusation or statement that you make with facts.

. . . stay in the present. Complaints over six months old are not permissible. Avoid saying, "I remember when. . . ." There is a sign over one businessman's desk that reads, "Remember to Forget." Every couple needs to place that very sign over their marriage. The apostle Paul said, . . . *I am bringing all my energies to bear on this one thing: Forgetting the past and looking forward to what lies ahead.* . . (Phil. 3:13, *TLB*).

. . . Do not make references to relatives or in-laws.

. . . Do not make references to your mate's appearance. That is, refrain from injecting jabs and cutting remarks about overweight, falling hair, sloppy clothes, etc.

. . . No dramatics, please. No getting highly emotional and exploding into tears. Crying is often a means of manipulating the other person. Threats are also used for manipulation. Some spouses even threaten suicide as an attempt to control their mates. But none of these methods usually help. There are no Oscars for dramatics when married people are trying to work out a disagreement.

SHORT COURSE IN ATTACKING EACH OTHER INSTEAD OF THE PROBLEM

WHAT DO YOU THINK?   #26

What if your spouse attacks you instead of the problem?

1. If an accusation or statement is made which is not backed up with facts, I will say:

2. When a complaint that is over six months old is raised, I will state:

3. If a reference is made to an in-law or relative, I will:

4. If I make a reference to my mate's appearance, I will:

5. If a reference is made to my appearance, I will:

6. When either I or my mate becomes "dramatic," I will:

7. Review your answers to the above six situations. Are your answers positive or negative? Will they help or hurt your mate? Will they make communication more effective next time or will they tend to hinder future communication? If your answers are negative, hurtful, or will tend to hinder future communication, rewrite them!

Don't "Throw Your Feelings" at Your Spouse

Learn how to inform your spouse of your feelings. Don't hurl them like a spear or a rock.

Dr. Howard Clinebell suggests that a ". . . road to productive communication is for both husband and wife to learn the skill of *saying it straight*. Each person can help the other to understand by asking himself, 'Am I saying what I really mean?' This involves learning to be aware of what one is actually feeling and developing the ability to put the feeling clearly into words. Direct rather than devious, specific rather than generalized statements are required. A wife criticizes her husband as he sits at the breakfast table hidden behind his newspaper, 'I wish you wouldn't always slurp your coffee.' What she really means is, 'I feel hurt when you hide in the newspaper instead of talking to me.' Saying it straight involves being honest about negative as well as positive feelings, and being able to state them in a nonattacking way: 'I feel . . .,' rather than 'You are. . . .' Some risk is required in the beginning of this kind of communication, until both husband and wife can trust the relationship enough to be able to say what they really mean.

"James Farmer tells a story about a woman who acquired wealth and decided to have a book written about her genealogy. The well-known author she engaged for the assignment discovered that one of her grandfathers had been electrocuted in Sing Sing. When he said it would have to be included in the book, she pleaded for a way of saying it that would hide the truth. When the book appeared, it read as follows: 'One of her grandfathers occupied the chair of applied electricity in one of America's best known institutions. He was very much attached to his position and literally died in the harness.' The meaning in some attempts to communicate between marriage partners is almost as hidden and confusing. It is usually better to 'say it like it is,' gently if necessary, but clearly."[2]

In the words of the Preacher: *There is a right time for everything: . . . a time to be quiet; a time to speak up* (Eccl. 3:1,7, TLB).

Stay on the Subject

Always try to discover exactly what you are arguing about and stay on that subject. Don't bring in matters that are irrelevant or unimportant. At times you may have to say something like, "Let's stop this conversation and really see what it is we're talking about. You start again and I will listen. Perhaps I have misunderstood something." Take the initiative to do this yourself. Don't wait for your spouse to do so. Always be willing to listen and ask questions.

As you are engaging in an argument or an important discussion, remember to ask yourself, "Is there really as much of a problem or difference of opinion here as I think? Am I seeking a real solution or just looking for problems?" Do you tend to see the dark or the bright side of things? Do you spend a lot of time going over and over problems in your mind? Do you literally create problems in your own mind?

The answer to these questions may lie in whether you are an optimist or a pessimist. The difference is easy to see in this old but still humorous story:

"There were two farmers. One was a pessimist, the other was an optimist.

"The optimist would say, 'Wonderful sunshine.'

"The pessimist would respond, 'Yeah, I'm afraid it's going to scorch the crops.'

"The optimist would say, 'Fine rain.'

"The pessimist would respond, 'Yeah, I'm afraid we are going to have a flood.'

"One day the optimist said to the pessimist. 'Have you seen my new bird dog? He's the finest money can buy.'

"The pessimist said, 'You mean that mutt I saw penned up behind your house? He don't look like much to me.'

"The optimist said, 'How about going hunting with me tomorrow?' The pessimist agreed. They went. They shot some ducks. The ducks landed on the pond. The optimist ordered his dog to get the ducks. The dog obediently responded. Instead of swimming in the water after the ducks, the dog walked on top of the water, retrieved the ducks, and walked back on top of the water.

"The optimist turned to the pessimist and said, 'Now, what do you think of that?'

"Whereupon the pessimist replied, 'Hmmm, he can't swim, can he?' "[3]

Aren't we all like that at times? We can't see the good or the strong points of our spouse because we focus on faults or problems. Perhaps it wouldn't hurt for every husband and wife to memorize Philippians 4:8,9:

Fix your thoughts on what is true and good and right. Think about things that are pure and lovely, and dwell on the fine, good things in others. Think about all you can praise God for and be glad about. Keep putting into practice all you learned from me and saw me doing, and the God of peace will be with you (TLB).

Offer Solutions with Criticisms

If you criticize your spouse, can you offer a clear-cut solution at the same time? To say, "The way you leave your dirty clothes lying around makes our bedroom look like a pigpen" really doesn't help. Saying, "Would it help keep our bedroom neater if I moved the clothes hamper into the bedroom so we wouldn't have to walk so far?" offers a solution to the problem and also communicates displeasure with the status quo.

Another good verse of Scripture for husbands and wives to remember and apply is:

Let us therefore stop turning critical eyes on one another. If we must be critical, let us be critical of our own conduct and see that we do nothing to make a brother stumble or fall (Rom. 14:13, Phillips).

Never "analyze" your spouse during a discussion. Don't play physician or psychiatrist by saying things like, "Now you are saying that because. . . ." Your spouse is not a case study. He or she is part of you—one flesh—your mate!

Never Say, "You Never" or "You Always"

There's nothing like the sweeping statement or the vast generalization to increase the difficulty. Avoid words like "never," "always," "all," "everyone."

Avoid loaded statements such as:

"You're never on time."

"You're always saying things like that."

"All women are emotional."

"All men are like that."

"Everyone thinks you are that way, and so do I!"

Two other excellent ways to decrease difficulty in a conversation are these:

Watch your volume.

Don't exaggerate.

THE EASIEST THING IN THE WORLD IS TO EXAGGERATE...

Most of us tend to raise our voices during family discussions. When we do this, we are really saying, "I can't get through to you in a normal voice because you seem to be deaf to what I say. So I will turn up the volume."

Raising our voice puts our spouse on the defense and can even convey that we have lost control—of our temper, or the situation.

It's easy to add to your problems by exaggerating. We seem to think that the facts as they are do not make any impression upon our spouse, so we try to get our spouse's attention by altering the facts or "dressing them up a little bit."

The sweeping generalization is a typical way that we exaggerate.

She says, "You never finish anything you start around here. You've been working on that fence for the last six months!"

He says, "You're always late. You make us late when we go out to dinner, to the theatre, to P.T.A., to church. We're going to be late for our funeral!"

A verse from Ephesians contains good advice for spouses who exaggerate:

. . . lovingly follow the truth at all times—speaking truly, dealing truly, living truly—and so become more and more in every way like Christ . . . (Eph. 4:15, *TLB*).

Don't Use Criticism to Become a Comedian

While it's true that a joke or dry remark might relieve the tension in some marital disagreements, it's always best to use humor with care. Never try to be funny by criticizing your spouse. The problem might not be serious to you, but it might be very important to your mate.

Questions to ask before using humor are:

"Will this increase tension or relieve it?"

"Can I laugh at myself, or am I just trying to poke fun at my mate?"

"Am I trying to win points for my side with cute remarks?"

When You're Wrong, Admit It; When You're Right, Shut Up

Have the humility to remember that you could be wrong. A lot of people find this sentence difficult if not impossible to say: "I'm wrong—you may be right." Practice saying it by yourself if necessary and then be able to say it when it fits into a disagreement or discussion. When you honestly own up to knowing that you're wrong and the other person is right, you improve communication a thousandfold and deepen your relationship with your spouse.

And when it is appropriate, always ask for forgiveness. James tells us to admit our faults to one another and pray for each other. (See James 5:16 in *The Living Bible*.)

Proverbs 28:13 has good advice: *A man who refuses to admit his mistakes can never be successful. But if he confesses and forsakes them, he gets another chance* (TLB).

Sometimes you will have to admit you're wrong in the face of your spouse's criticism, and this is never easy. It can also be tricky. Be sure that you never play the "I know it's all *my* fault" game with your mate. It is easy to use the line "It's all *my* fault" as a means of manipulating your mate. The idea is that you get your mate feeling apologetic and saying, "Well, I suppose it's partially my fault too. . . ."

If you are really at fault, then be willing to admit it. Saying something like, "You know, I do think that I am to blame here. I'm sorry that I said that and that I hurt you. What can I do now to help or make up for this?"

When you face your spouse's criticism and you know it's correct, keep these proverbs in mind:

If you refuse criticism you will end in poverty and disgrace; if you accept criticism you are on the road to fame (Prov. 13:18, *TLB*).

Don't refuse to accept criticism; get all the help you can (Prov. 23:12, *TLB*).

It is a badge of honor to accept valid criticism (Prov. 25:12, *TLB*).

And when your spouse confesses faults or admits error, be sure to tell him or her of your forgiveness. Even if you were right, take the initiative to forgive *and forget.* Proverbs 17:9 teaches, *Love forgets mistakes (TLB).* Colossians 3:13 says that we should *be gentle and ready to forgive; never hold grudges (TLB).*

In summary, the apostle Peter and Ogden Nash have words of good advice.

Peter tells us, *Most important of all, continue to show deep love for each other, for love makes up for many of your faults* (1 Pet. 4:8, *TLB*).

Ogden Nash once gave this word to husbands (which also is certainly appropriate for wives):

"To keep your marriage brimming with love in the loving cup,
When you're wrong admit it,
When you're right shut up."

WHAT'S YOUR PLAN?

1. Reprinted below are the "Ten Principles for Coping with Conflict." Review them and check off the ones where you feel fairly strong and capable. Go over them again and underline the ones where you feel weak—"in need of more practice."

Ten Ways to Cope with Conflict
1. Don't avoid conflict with the silent treatment.
2. Don't save "emotional trading stamps."

"To keep
your marriage brimming
with love
in the loving cup
When you're wrong
admit it,
when you're right,
shut up."

Ogden Nash

3. If possible, prepare the setting for disagreement.
4. Attack the problem, not each other . . .
   . . . back up accusations with facts
   . . . remember to forget
   . . . no cracks about in-laws or relatives
   . . . no cracks about your mate's appearance
   . . . no dramatics.
5. Don't throw your feelings like stones.
6. Stay on the subject.
7. Offer solutions with your criticisms.
8. Never say, "You never . . ."
   . . . turn down the volume
   . . . don't exaggerate.
9. Don't manipulate your mate with, "It's all *my* fault."
10. Be humble—you could be wrong.

2. Are you an optimist or a pessimist? How does your mate experience you? (circle one).

   "Oh, boy!"   "Oh, no!"

Read and memorize Philippians 4:8,9.

3. List at least three specific changes in behavior you will make, which are based on the "Ten Principles for Coping with Conflict."

4. Get together with your mate and share your findings from doing the above exercises. (A word of caution: apply the principles to *yourself*. Don't infer that "A lot of these are really *your* mate's problem," or you may wind up in a disagreement (conflict) over this chapter on coping with conflict. If you do get into a disagreement, be sure to use the Ten Principles and "fight fair!" Good luck!

10
Communicate to Build
Self-Esteem

As you read this chapter, you will discover . . .
  . . . that building your mate's self-esteem is one of your most important goals in marriage communication
  . . . that it's more important to seek to understand your mate than to worry about your mate understanding you
  . . . that there are ten practical principles for building self-esteem in your marriage partner
  . . . how to plan to use the ten principles for building self-esteem to improve communication in your marriage.

If you have stuck with this book to this point, you have . . .
  . . . discovered that you are already a fairly good communicator and have probably picked up some tips to help you be even better.

. . . or improved on your communication skills in several ways.

. . . or, at least have taken some small steps toward communicating at deeper levels with your spouse.

No matter where you are as husband and wife, you will want to keep communication lines open. A key to communication—perhaps *the* key—is building your mate's self-esteem. A person's self-esteem is his overall judgment of himself—how much he likes his particular person. High self-esteem doesn't mean you are on a continual ego-trip. High self-esteem means you have solid feelings of self-respect and self-worth. You are glad you are you.[1]

Marriage partners with high self-esteem are bound to be happier and communicate better. High self-esteem means an absence or at least a considerable lessening of anxieties, complexes, hangups, and the other problems that prevent good communications. The spouse with low self-esteem is seldom a good communicator. Low self-esteem often drives a person into a shell of silence or compels a person to become a dominating over-talkative, unacceptant dictator in one-way communication—*"my way."*

This final chapter is dedicated to the continuing challenge of building your mate's self-esteem—making him or her feel important, wanted, valuable, successful and, above all, loved. Following are ten practical principles for building self-esteem in your mate.

Make It Safe to Communicate

Strive to establish and maintain a permissive atmosphere in your home. In a permissive atmosphere both marriage partners are free to share openly and honestly what they feel, think and believe. Each family member is allowed to speak the truth in love. The husband, or the wife, does not consciously erect barriers to communication with his or her mate.

Sometimes a spouse tells his mate, "I didn't tell you that because I was afraid of hurting you." In giving this kind of an excuse, a spouse is sometimes hiding behind a pretense of being concerned about his mate's feelings. This kind of cop-out seldom does anything to build the kind of open communication that is needed in a marriage. Perhaps speaking the truth will hurt, perhaps it will not. Too often, marriage partners avoid constructive discussions because they feel that they would have to make changes in their own lives if any communication would take place on that kind of level.

IS IT SAFE TO COMMUNICATE ?

Dr. John Drakeford gives the following guidelines for an open permissive communication in the home:

"1. Look at the positive aspects of openness. When a man and his wife live in such a close relationship they should not have large areas of experience which they hide from each other.

"2. Surely there must come a time when we sit down and say to our mate: 'Honey, you have a right to know who you married. Let me tell you about myself.'

"3. One of the most reprehensible uses of openness is to use it as a means of attack. 'Yes, this is what I did but the reason I did it was that you were so cold to me,' is not honesty, it is attack.

"4. Let us be honest about ourselves without excuse or justification. When we have made a mistake, admit it.

"5. Two parties must play their parts in the process—no one should ever sit in judgment on anybody else."[2]

Dr. Drakeford's five rules are worth following and they parallel closely the principles for coping with conflict given in Chapter 9. But what about times when it seems that openness and honesty may do more harm than good? Aren't there times in a marriage when it is more loving to lie (just a little, perhaps?) than to speak the truth?

Isn't it better to lie on certain occasions if it means that you can avoid unpleasantness in your marriage relationship—if you can avoid hurting your spouse?

We can all think of situations in which it would probably be best not to speak the truth because it will hurt our marriage partner. But does lying really avoid unpleasantness in the long run? Lies—even gentle white lies told to keep the peace—have a way of being discovered and when they are discovered there is even more unpleasantness.

When you consider lying to avoid unpleasantness you should be brutally honest with your motivation. Are you really afraid of hurting your spouse? Or is it yourself that you're worried about? Are you just trying to ease out of an unpleasant situation because it isn't worth the hassle?

Often temptations to lie come when we are confronted with something that we have done. We are tempted to alter the truth or rationalize the facts in order to deflect the blame away from ourselves. This pattern starts when we are small children. When small children are confronted with wrong behavior they find it difficult, if not impossible, to say, "Yes, I did it. I'm sorry."

Have you ever noticed the reaction of other people when you accept responsibility for your actions and are open and truthful about them? To tell the truth, to admit error or wrongdoing, to "let the buck stop with you," often brings reactions from others of amazement if not downright shock!

There may be times when to hold back part of the truth seems to be the best thing to do because the other person may not be ready for all the facts at a certain point in time. But keep in mind when you do this—when you hold back part of the information—you are causing your spouse to think the opposite of what the truth really is. When you do this, you gamble—with your spouse's feelings and certainly with keeping communication lines in good repair. Think it through carefully. Is the gamble really worth it?

Seek to Understand, Not to Be Understood

Spend as much time and effort trying to understand your mate's viewpoint as you do trying to make him or her understand yours. Perhaps there's a good and legitimate reason for your spouse's beliefs, actions or habits. Everyone's background and environment are

different and they bring this background with them to the marriage relationship.

When one spouse sulks, stews or balks because the other "doesn't understand," what is really being said? The real message is, "You don't understand *me!* You don't want to adjust to my ideas and way of doing things. You don't want to give me my way!"

If both spouses start saying, "You don't understand," then there is an even more serious problem—and very little communication. There is, however, a way out of the problem of being "misunderstood." Paul Tournier pinpoints the solution as he says:

"You well know that beautiful prayer of Francis of Assisi: 'Lord!

Grant that I may seek more to understand than to be understood. . . .' It is this new desire which the Holy Spirit awakens in couples and which transforms their marriage. As long as a man is preoccupied primarily with being understood by his wife, he is miserable, overcome with self-pity, the spirit of demanding, and bitter withdrawal. As soon as he becomes preoccupied with understanding her, seeking to understand that which he had not before understood, and with his own wrongdoing in not having understood her, then the direction taken by events begins to change. As soon as a person feels understood, he opens up and because he lowers his defenses he is also able to make himself better understood."[3]

Tournier feels so strongly about the need for understanding one another that he says the husband and wife should become *preoccupied* with it—lost in it—engrossed to the fullest in learning what makes the other one tick, what the other one likes, dislikes, fears, worries about, dreams of, believes in and *why* he or she feels this way.

As is so often the case, Scripture has taught this kind of basic truth for centuries. Long ago the apostle Paul directed the Ephesians to live in a becoming way, . . . *with complete lowliness of mind (humility) and meekness (unselfishness, gentleness, mildness), with patience, bearing with one another and making allowances because you love one another* (Eph. 4:2, *Amplified*).

And Paul had the same thing in mind when he wrote the Philippians and said,

Fill up and complete my joy by living in harmony and being of the same mind and one in purpose, having the same love, being in full accord and of one harmonious mind and intention. Do nothing from factional motives—through contentiousness, strife, selfishness or for unworthy ends—or prompted by conceit and empty arrogance. Instead, in the true spirit of humility (lowliness of mind) let each regard the others as better than and superior to himself— thinking more highly of one another than you do of yourselves. Let each of you esteem and look upon and be concerned for not [merely] his own interests, but also each for the interests of others (Phil. 2:2–4, *Amplified*).

The cry, "You don't understand!" is the childish whine of an immature mate who is playing games with his or her marriage partner. The prayer of St. Francis, "Lord! Grant that I may seek more to understand than to be understood . . ." is the honest plea of the husband or wife who wants to communicate—who wants to build a sound and successful marriage by building up the other partner.

WHAT DO YOU THINK? #27

1. State what ". . . making allowances because you love one another" means to you in regard to your spouse:

2. State what looking upon and being concerned ". . . for the interests of others" means to you in regard to your spouse:

Don't Assume You Know—Ask

Recognize that there is some information you cannot get by any other means than by asking your spouse about it. Never assume that you know what your spouse thinks. Have you ever heard a husband saying, "My wife thinks . . ."? How does he really know? Does he *really* know she thinks or believes that? Or is he just taking it for granted? Has he asked her? Has he ever really discussed the matter?

Assumption about what your spouse knows, thinks or feels is dangerous. True, it is easy to get impressions about what people believe from the non-verbal language they use—their looks, glances and mannerisms. But if you really want to know what your spouse is thinking, start talking about it. Husband-wife communication will automatically improve if both stop assuming and start communicating. Some night soon (or right now) turn off the tube and talk together about the following ideas.

WHAT DO YOU THINK?   #28

1. Write down what you think your mate believes about each of these subjects:

The role of the husband

The role of the father

The role of the wife

The role of the mother

Male and female tasks in the home

Politics

Women's lib

Sex

The importance of a creative outlet for the husband

The importance of a creative outlet for the wife

Recreation together as a couple/family

2. Now compare notes and discuss what you assumed and what is actual fact.

Listen—Don't Interrupt

Much has been said in earlier chapters (4 and 5) about listening, but enough can't be said about this skill, which is so rusty with disuse (or practically nonexistent) in so many marriages.

It may well be true that the first duty of love is to listen. Dr. S. S. Hayakawa says, "We can, if we are able to listen as well as to speak, become better informed and wiser as we grow older, instead of being stuck like some people with the same little bundle of prejudices at sixty-five that we had at twenty-five."

But listening takes discipline. We fail to listen to our spouse because of impatience and a lack of concentration, especially when he or she is saying something that we don't particularly want to hear.

Perhaps it is hardest to listen when your spouse picks a poor time to bring something up. For example, you come home late at night, exhausted, and your spouse is already in bed, asleep (or so you

think). You get ready for bed, wearily crawl in and are just ready for dreamland, when all of a sudden you find out your spouse wasn't sleeping at all. She's been waiting for you and she says, "I'd like to talk to you about something that's been bothering me quite a bit."

Your initial reaction might well be, "Of all the dumb times to bring up something. Why doesn't she do it during the day and not at this ridiculous hour? Can't she see that it's late and I'm beat?"

Granted this kind of timing is hardly the best but before you plead to "let's talk about it tomorrow," think it through. Why has she waited so long to bring something up? Why wait until you're both in bed and it's easy to hide in the darkness? Could there be something you might have done to make it difficult for your partner to talk about what is on her mind? Consider these questions before you react. You might learn something if you pause to listen, too!

There are other common problems concerning not listening and interrupting. For example, there is the "keep the record straight" type. The typical dialogue goes something like this. The husband is talking, starting to tell some mutual friends a story . . .

"We left about the middle of July."

"Oh, no dear, it was actually the twenty-seventh."

"OK, so we left the twenty-seventh about nine o'clock in the morning . . ."

"Oh, I'm sorry, dear, but it was seven-thirty exactly. I remember looking at the clock as I checked the doors."

"Well, we left sometime and drove to San Francisco."

"Are you sure we drove there that first day? Wasn't it . . .?"

It's easy to get the picture here! The wife is "over-listening" but not because she wants to hear what her husband is saying. She wants to keep the record straight!

And then there is the "outguesser" type. This person usually is one step ahead of you and unfortunately he really believes that he is listening. But he never lets you finish what you were going to say. Wives have a tendency to try to outguess their husbands, as in the following example:

"Honey, I was at the store today . . ."

"Don't tell me you forgot the list?"

"No, I wasn't going to say that. I said I went to the store today and I saw John . . ."

"You saw John Richards? How is he doing? Do they like their new home? What about . . ."

"No, I did not see John Richards. As I was going to say . . ."

Or what about the "cross-examiner"? He listens so well that when he responds to what you're saying you feel as though you were going through the third degree . . .

"Say, I just returned from our vacation and we had the greatest time. We stopped at this park and spent two days observing a deer herd."

"Well, what kind of deer were they? Mule or whitetail?"

"Well, I don't know."

"You don't know? Don't you know the difference? Didn't the guide explain the difference between the two? Well, in order to tell the difference you . . ."

Before long you probably wish that you had never seen any deer herd and you certainly wish you had never brought the subject up to your cross-examining friend.

These are just a few of the problems that you may encounter (or cause) because of non-listening.

Listen to what the Word of God has to say about listening:

He who answers a matter before he hears the facts, it is folly and shame to him (Prov. 18:13, Amplified).

A good verse for husbands and wives to commit to memory is James 1:19: every husband and wife should . . . *be quick to hear (a ready listener), slow to speak, slow to take offense and to get angry* (Amplified).

WHAT DO YOU THINK?   #29

1. During the next few days try this experiment. Spend thirty minutes alone with your spouse and set aside everything else. First the wife has five minutes in which she will talk about anything she wants to. During that five minutes the husband must listen, he cannot talk and he must try to think of nothing except what his wife is saying to him. He should not try to daydream or think of what he would like to say in return. At the end of five minutes, switch roles. Now the husband talks and the wife listens. Switch back and forth every five minutes so that each spouse has at least three opportunities to talk and three opportunities to listen. At the end of thirty minutes, discuss your reactions and thoughts concerning this kind of activity. How can you apply this experience to your usual pattern of communicating?

Confucius Say, "Spouse with Horse Sense Never Becomes Nag"

When trying to communicate with your mate, keep in mind the ironic fact that too much talking can be as bad as too little. If you have adequately discussed a problem or a subject, drop it and move on. Do not restate your case and your conclusions over and over again. Too often you can create a bigger problem if you talk too much. Proverbs puts this nicely, if a bit bluntly: *Don't talk so much. You keep putting your foot in your mouth. Be sensible and turn off the flow!* (Prov. 10:19, *TLB*).

A typical form of "too much talking" is nagging—constantly harping or hassling your mate for one reason or another. A technical definition is "critical faulting"—but whatever you call it, nagging usually doesn't work. It irritates and frustrates both marriage partners—the nagger as well as the "naggee."

You may have heard the quip, "The wife who uses good horse

sense never turns out to be a nag." According to a national survey conducted by a leading magazine, the thing that irritates most men more than anything else is the wife's nagging.

On the other hand, men nag just as much as women. You may have said something like this yourself recently: "Nagging is the only way I know of to get my spouse to respond. And it's the same with the kids. If I don't tell them a dozen times and remind over and over again, the job never gets done!"

It's true that spouses and children especially seem to "need to be nagged." But perhaps there is a better way. If you do a lot of nagging, do you enjoy it? Is it really doing the job? If you're not happy with nagging, why continue to use an ineffective method? Consider the possibility that you may have conditioned your spouse and your children not to respond to you unless you nag—repeat and repeat and increase the volume as you do so.

If you have to say things a half-dozen times or more before you get any action your spouse is either:[1] not paying attention;[2] doesn't believe you mean anything the first time you speak.

How then can you gain your spouse's attention and not have to repeat and repeat? Perhaps your husband is sitting there watching the tube and you need to get a message through. Your problem is he's watching the Cowboys and the Redskins and that's an awful lot of opposition for any message—even yours. Use this simple strategy, however, and you'll score every time. Roll out to the left around his recliner, cut straight downfield and wind up standing right in front of the television set. If you really want to put on the pressure, *turn off* the television set. Your spouse's attention is guaranteed.

Or maybe your wife is engrossed in planning the big dinner party for Saturday night and you need to give her the word on servicing the car before you leave for work. The last thing she wants to hear is about what oil needs changing and where the grease has to go. So, go up to her and try looking her right in the eye as you talk to her. Perhaps you may want to put your hand on her shoulder (better yet, put your arms around her waist) and tell her what you have to say. There are all kinds of ways—some of them pleasant—to be something else than a nagger. Be creative and experiment. And keep Solomon's advice in mind: . . . *a nagging wife annoys like constant dripping* (Prov. 19:13, *TLB*). That much-married king also said: *It is better to dwell in a corner of the housetop [on the flat oriental roof, exposed to all kinds of weather] than in a house shared with a nagging, quarrelsome and faultfinding woman* (Prov. 21:9, *Amplified*).

WHAT DO YOU THINK?   #30

1. List five things that you have asked (or nagged) your mate about that he or she has not changed or improved one bit. Why do you want your mate to change in these areas? Would the changes bring his or her behavior or attitude into closer harmony with Scripture? How else could you get your mate to change rather than to "keep mentioning it" (nagging)?

2. List five things that your mate has asked (or nagged) you about but you have not changed either because you could not or did not wish to do so.

3. Of the items listed for question 2, which ones could you have corrected if you had really wanted to do so?

4. Look at the items you have listed in your answer to question 3. Specify in detail your reasons for not making the changes suggested by your mate. Are your reasons valid? Have you honestly prayed about your decision to not make these changes? Would any of these changes bring your life closer to the teaching of Scripture?

5. For each of the items listed in your answer to question 1, put down the reasons why, in your opinion, your mate does not attempt to make the changes that you constantly suggest.

Don't Jump to Conclusions

Almost everyone knows the old joke about putting your brain in gear with your tongue before you start talking, but a lot of people seem to be unable to do this. They are quick to speak, and then spend a lot of time regretting what they said.

As the Scripture advises, *be . . . slow to speak* (See Jas. 1:19) Think first. Don't be hasty in what you say. Control yourself and when you do talk, speak in such a way that your spouse can understand you and accept what you have to say.

Two more pieces of advice from Solomon fit in very well here:

He who guards his mouth and his tongue keeps himself from troubles (Prov. 21:23, *Amplified*).

Do you see a man who is hasty in his words? There is more hope of a [self-confident] fool than of him (Prov. 29:20, *Amplified*).

What these verses both say is that if you want to destroy a mate's self-esteem, just go off half-cocked and leap to conclusions before looking into things and finding out what's really happening. On the other hand, if you want to build your mate's self-esteem take James' advice (which, perhaps, should be part of every couple's marriage vows):

Be quick to hear (a ready listener), slow to speak, slow to take offense and to get angry (Jas. 1:19, *Amplified*).

Jumping to conclusions is a favorite sport in just about any setting, but it's particularly easy to do in a marriage.

She says, "Honey, I was out shopping today and I stopped in this cute little dress shop and I had the best time. . . ." He explodes: "What! You blew a bundle of money on some new clothes? You know we can't afford it!" (Actual situation: she tried on a few dresses and didn't buy a thing.)

Or he says: "Say, I was talking with some of the boys at the office and they're planning to get up this foursome Saturday and I. . . ."

And so she snaps: "You're going golfing when you've got all that trim to paint and the yard is beginning to look like an annex for Jungleland, U.S.A.?" (Actual situation: he turned the boys at the office down because he "had a lot of work to do at home.")

The illustrations go on and on and on. And self-esteem in both marriage partners suffers because of it.

Not only is it important to take your time when you feel yourself going into your "jump to conclusions" crouch . . . but on the positive side it helps to make the right kind of remarks at the right time. As Solomon put it, . . . *a word spoken at the right moment, how good it is!* (Prov. 15:23, *Amplified*).

The illustrations (and opportunities) are endless as far as marriage is concerned. One obvious area where husbands can't say enough at the right moment is when complimenting their little woman's appearance. Instead of waiting for her to pry approval out of you about her hair, dress, cooking, etc., take a little more notice of your wife and pay her sincere compliments without having to have them solicited. A compliment coming from a husband, a spontaneous compliment, is worth a hundred times more in self-esteem value than the typical grunt: "Oh, yes . . . looks very nice. . . ."

As for the wives, they should never forget that their husbands are just as vain as they are (and more so). They also like compliments on their appearance and, again, it's better to do it at a spontaneous moment rather than wait till he is just putting on his new suit. All of us have the built-in resistance to compliments when they're given at those times "when a compliment is expected." Learn to give compliments when they're not expected, and they'll be worth much more on the self-esteem market with your mate.

Disagree? Yes. Disrespect? No!

Always show respect for your mate's opinions even when you disagree. As already mentioned, no husband and wife can agree all of the time. But that doesn't mean they can't respect each other for their opinions and be willing to listen to one another. As Voltaire

said, "I disapprove of what you say, but I will defend to the death your right to say it." You may not want to get that oratorical the next time you and your spouse disagree, but whatever you do, don't come up with such typical gems as:

"You're out to lunch."

"I just can't *believe* you!" (meaning "I don't question your veracity, just your right to belong to the human race").

"Oh, come on, don't get on that junk again."

A well-known TV comedian has gained fame and fortune with the line: "I don't get no respect." Perhaps one reason for his success is that so many husbands and wives identify completely with the idea of "not getting much respect." Paul must have had husbands and wives particularly in mind when he wrote: *Never act from motives of rivalry or personal vanity, but in humility think more of one another than you do of yourselves. None of you should think only of his own affairs, but each should learn to see things from other people's point of view* (Phil. 2:3,4, *Phillips*).

WHAT DO YOU THINK?   #31

1. Think of several instances in which you showed respect for your spouse's ideas, opinions, or beliefs in the last week:

2. Think of several instances in which you may have shown disrespect for your spouse's opinions or ideas or beliefs in the last week:

3. Talk together with your mate about "respect for each other's opinions." If apologies are in order, make them. If gratitude or compliments are in order because both of you do respect one another, don't hold back on that, either! Remember—... *a word spoken at the right moment, how good it is!* (Prov. 15:23, *Amplified*).

Deal in Potential—Not the Past

Don't limit your mate by what he or she has done in the past that hasn't measured up or met completely with your approval. Are you guilty of putting your spouse in a pigeonhole? Check yourself and see if you ever (or often) make comments like these:

"He never understands me."

"She doesn't listen to what I say."

"He just won't change."

"She says one thing and then does another."

"I just can't reach him . . . he's hopeless."

If you've used any comments like these, ask yourself, "Would my spouse make the same statements about me? Do I do what I accuse my spouse of doing?"

The Christian couple will not stereotype or pigeonhole one another if they remember the key truth from the New Testament: God is far more interested in what a person can be than in what a person has been.

"Do you see other people in the process of becoming something better or do you see them as bound by their past—what they have (or haven't) done or said (especially to you)? . . . It is easy to stereotype others. You can place them in neat little pigeonholes like 'sloppy,' 'talk too much,' 'dishonest,' 'undependable,' 'unfair,' etc. . . . Christianity, however, deals in *potential*, and what a person can *become*, not only what he *is*. This is the heart of the gospel. If God had dealt with us strictly on the basis of our past, He would never have sent Christ to die for our sins. But God loved us. He saw us as persons of worth, value, with potential. He forgave, He keeps on forgiving, always looking forward to what we can become if we respond to the opportunity we have in Christ."[4]

Don't Force Your Spouse to Be Your Carbon Copy

If you truly love your mate, you will not demand (subtly or otherwise) that he or she become a modified version of your ideas or a revised edition of yourself. Set your mate free to be an individual with his or her own opinions. Always guard against giving your mate the impression that you love him or her more when he or she agrees with you. Keep in mind that ". . . all of us are self-conscious. Our image of self is directly related to how we feel, what we do, things

DON'T LABEL YOUR MATE

we like. Criticize a person's viewpoint, taste, ideas and you criticize *him*, no matter how much you may mean otherwise.

"Before turning your guns (especially your spiritual guns) on someone's ideas, attitudes, actions, ask yourself a couple of questions: am I trying to help this person or am I really trying to impose my value system on him? Do I respect and like this person for what he is, or am I trying to make him over to suit my idea of what is respectable, likable or spiritual?"[5]

Pray for One Another

Pray for each other privately and, if you can, pray together for each other. There is a lot of talk in Christian circles about husbands and wives "reading the Bible and praying together" but it is questionable how many really do so. To paraphrase the well-known slogan, "If a husband and wife will pray together they will not only stay together but they will communicate much more effectively."

In the Old Testament, the Israelites demanded and finally got a king—Saul—to lead them against the many enemies that surrounded them. Samuel, the last of the judges, reluctantly agreed to find and crown Saul; but again and again he warned the Israelites that they should be sure to follow God and not depend entirely on their new king. In 1 Samuel 12, Samuel makes an impassioned speech to remind the Israelite people of their responsibilities to God and not to get carried away with a recent victory over enemies led by King Saul. The people respond by asking—practically begging—Samuel to continue to pray for them and intercede for them to God.

Samuel responds by saying, . . . *Far be it from me that I should sin against the Lord by ending my prayers for you* (1 Sam. 12:23, TLB).

Husband and wife should spend some time studying this Old Testament passage together. Samuel had spiritual responsibilities for his people, which were given to him by God. When husband and wife take their marriage vows, they are given spiritual responsibility to one another, as well as physical, mental and emotional responsibilities. With all of the challenges and pressures on marriage today, husband and wife should both guard against "sinning against the Lord" (not to mention each other) by failing to pray for one another. As Paul Tournier points out: "It is only when a husband and wife pray together before God that they find the secret of true harmony, that the difference in their temperaments, their ideas, and their tastes enriches their home instead of endangering it. There will be no further question of one imposing his will on the other, or of the other giving in for the sake of peace. Instead, they will together seek God's will, which alone will ensure that each will be fully able to develop his personality. . . . When each of the marriage partners seeks quietly before God to see his own faults, recognizes his sin, and asks the forgiveness of the other, marital problems are no more. Each learns to speak the other's language, and to meet him halfway, so to speak. Each holds back those harsh little words which one is apt to utter when one is right, but which are said in order to injure. Most of all, a couple rediscovers complete mutual confidence, because, in meditating in prayer together they learn to become absolutely honest with each other. . . . This is the price to be paid if partners very different from each other are to combine their gifts instead of setting them against each other."[6]

All of the ideas and suggestions in this book will be of little use to the Christian couple if they neglect prayer, one for another. In fact, many of the ideas and suggestions in this book, especially those that suggest or imply changes that either spouse must make, will be impossible to achieve or use without prayer. God is the One who changes a marriage—not manuals or books!

There is one other guideline to help you and your mate apply this book to your marriage. Better communication depends upon change—changes in both of you. Changing some of your patterns may take a long time, but change is possible through Jesus Christ. To say that you are so set in your ways that you cannot change is to contradict the good news that Jesus Christ can and will make us new creatures.

We all change in proportion to the effort we put forth to try to change. As we let the Word of God sink into our hearts and minds we will change. We will remember what to do because the Scripture is a part of our lives and through Scripture we have a built-in guide for change. How can we learn to communicate, to build self-esteem in each other, to love and understand one another? By reading God's Word and following His rules. We must try our best to find God and we must not wander off from His instructions. We must think much about God's words and store them in our hearts. God's Word will hold us back from sinning against one another by failing to communicate. (See Ps. 119:9,11.)

And as Dwight Small puts it, we should not overidealize the magic power of communication. Small cautions: ". . . that no amount of communication can make marriage perfect, and therefore we should not expect it. God is perfect, the ideal of Christian marriage is perfect, and the means God puts at the disposal of Christian couples are perfect. Yet there is no perfect marriage, no perfect communication in marriage. The glory in Christian marriage is in accepting the life-long task of making a continual adjustment within the disorder of human existence, ever working to improve communication skills necessary to this task, and seeking God's enabling power in it all."[7]

Keep in mind also that communication is a means, not an end. The end of marriage is not communication. The end of marriage is love—love for God and love for one another. Notice the order here. "When married people think only of happiness, they fall short of communicating the highest love of all. They, in fact, idolize each other, taking gratification in possessing and adoring their idol. Such devotion leads them away from God and from the Christian experience of love, since the two are dearer than God is to them. The highest form of love liberates two people from idolatry, keeping them from dominating and possessing each other and from demanding utter devotion as the price of love. Only God is worthy of utter devotion. So a couple is not to live entirely for each other, but must recognize that all love has its source in God. As loving husbands and wives, married partners are servants who mediate God's love, letting their love for each other serve a higher end."[8]

Today everyone realizes that you can have a marriage without love. Some are advocating love without marriage. Neither option is very attractive to the Christian. Love doesn't come automatically in marriage, but love matures in marriage as two people work to communicate.

WHAT'S YOUR PLAN?

1. Sit down with your marriage partner and talk over the principles discussed in this chapter. Make a mutual commitment to try to follow them in the future. Agree to be accountable to one another and devise a plan for regular evaluation of how well you are succeeding.

2. If either one of you violates any of the principles, how will you handle it? List ideas for a procedure that both of you will be able to accept and carry out.

3. Study the "Marriage Communication Guidelines" on the next page. Go through each of the ten guidelines and all of the suggested Scripture verses. Talk about each one. Add other guidelines that you can remember from reading this book, which are not in the list. Then sign your names to the guidelines and put in the date. For the best effect, both marriage partners should sign the same page in a copy of this book. You may want to cut the page from the book and put it up on your bulletin board or other conspicuous spot in the house.

Marriage Communication Guidelines

Marriage Communication Guidelines

Proverbs 18:21; 25:11; Job 19:2; James 3:8–10; 1 Peter 3:10

1. Be a ready listener and do not answer until the other person has finished talking. Proverbs 18:13; James 1:19

2. Be slow to speak. Think first. Don't be hasty in your words. Speak in such a way that the other person can understand and accept what you say.
Proverbs 15:23,28; 21:23; 29:20; James 1:19

3. Speak the truth always but do it in love. Do not exaggerate. Ephesians 4:15,25; Colossians 3:9

4. Do not use silence to frustrate the other person. Explain why you are hesitant to talk at this time.

5. Do not become involved in quarrels. It is possible to disagree without quarreling.
Proverbs 17:14; 20:3; Romans 13:13; Ephesians 4:31

6. Do not respond in anger. Use a soft and kind response.
Proverbs 14:29; 15:1; 25:15; 29:11; Ephesians 4:26,31

7. When you are in the wrong, admit it and ask for forgiveness. James 5:16. When someone confesses to you, tell them you forgive them. Be sure it is *forgotten* and not brought up to the person.
Proverbs 17:9; Ephesians 4:32; Colossians 3:13; 1 Peter 4:8

8. Avoid nagging. Proverbs 10:19; 17:9; 20:5

9. Do not blame or criticize the other person. Instead, restore . . . encourage . . . edify. Romans 14:13; Galatians 6:1; 1 Thessalonians 5:11. If someone verbally attacks, criticizes or blames you, do not respond in the same manner.
Romans 12:17,21; 1 Peter 2:23; 3:9

10. Try to understand the other person's opinion. Make allowances for differences. Be concerned about their interests.
Philippians 2:1–4; Ephesians 4:2

Our Agreement to Follow These Guidelines

Name _____ Date _____
Name _____ Date _____

Endnotes

COMMUNICATION
KEY TO YOUR MARRIAGE

Introduction

1. Richard Lessor, *Love, Marriage and Trading Stamps.* (Argus Publications, 1971), p. 7.
2. Charles Shedd, *Letters to Phillip.* (Spire Books, 1969), pp. 82,83.

Chapter 1

1. J. A. Fritze, *The Essence of Marriage.* (Zondervan, 1969), adapted from p. 24.
2. David Augsburger, *Cherishable: Love and Marriage.* (Herald Press, 1971), p. 16.
3. Dwight Small, *After You've Said I Do.* (Fleming H. Revell, 1968), pp. 11,16.
4. Dwight Small, *After You've Said I Do.* (Fleming H. Revell, 1968), p. 51.
5. Dwight Small, *Design for Christian Marriage.* (Fleming H. Revell, 1959), p. 26.

Chapter 2

1. "What Did St. Paul Want?", Dwight Small. From *His* magazine, May 1973, p. 18.
2. "What Did St. Paul Want?", Gladys Hunt. From *His* magazine, May 1973, p. 14.

Chapter 3

1. Nathan W. Ackerman, M. D., *The Psychodynamics of Family Life.* (Basic Books, 1958), pp. 110–115.
2. James Jauncey, *Magic in Marriage.* (Zondervan, 1966), pp. 110,111.
3. Lionel A. Whiston, *Are You Fun to Live With?* (Word Books, 1968), pp. 126,127.
4. "Spousehold Hints ... His ... Hers", William L. Coleman, from *Moody Monthly,* February, 1973, p. 47.
5. David Augsburger, *Be All You Can Be.* (Creation House Publishers, 1970), pp. 74,75.

Chapter 4

1. Reuel Howe, *Herein Is Love.* (Judson Press, 1961), see p. 100.

2. Adapted from *After You've Said I Do.* Dwight H. Small. (Fleming H. Revell, 1968), See pp. 106,107,112.

3. Adapted from *The Art of Understanding Yourself,* Cecil Osborne. (Zondervan, 1967.) See chapter 9.

Chapter 5

1. John Powell, *Why Am I Afraid to Tell You Who I Am?* (Argus Communications). Adapted from pp. 54–62.

2. Dwight Small, *After You've Said I Do.* (Fleming H. Revell, 1968), p. 244.

Chapter 6

1. William C. Menninger, *Behind Many Flaws of Society.* (*National Observer,* August 31, 1964), p. 18.

2. Spiros Zodhiates, *Pursuit of Happiness.* (Eerdmans, 1966), p. 270.

3. David Augsburger, *Be All You Can Be.* (Creation House), p. 60.

4. John Powell, *Why Am I Afraid to Tell You Who I Am?* (Argus Communications, 1969), p. 155.

5. William C. Menninger, *Ibid.,* p. 18.

6. David Augsburger, *Ibid.,* pp. 31,32.

Chapter 7

1. James A. Hadfield, *Psychology and Morals.* (Barnes and Noble, Inc., 1964), p. 35.

2. Adapted from *Why Am I Afraid to Tell You Who I Am?* John Powell. (Argus Communications, 1969), pp. 91,92.

3. Robert McFarland and John Burton, *Learning for Loving.* (Zondervan, 1969), p. 93.

4. Dwight Small, *After You've Said I Do.* (Fleming H. Revell, 1968), p. 75.

5. Virginia Satir, *Conjoint Family Therapy.* (Science and Behavior Books, Inc., 1967), p. 73.

6. Howard J. Clinebell, *The Intimate Marriage.* (Harper & Row, 1970), p. 99.

7. Dwight Small, *After You've Said I Do.* (Fleming H. Revell), pp. 137,154.

Chapter 8

1. John Edmund Haggai, *How to Win over Worry.* (Zondervan, 1959), p. 17.

2. Lionel Whiston, *Are You Fun to Live With?* (Word Books, 1968), pp. 141,142.

3. Bruce Larson, *Living on the Growing Edge.* (Zondervan, 1968), p. 56.

4. Dwight Small, *After You've Said I Do.* (Fleming H. Revell, 1966), p. 79.

Chapter 9

1. Adapted from Albert Ellis and Robert Harper, *Creative Marriage.* (Lyle Stuart, 1961), pp. 190–191.

2. Howard Clinebell, *The Intimate Marriage.* (Harper & Row, 1970), p. 93.

3. John Edmund Haggai, *How to Win over Worry.* (Zondervan, 1959), pp. 63,64.

Chapter 10

1. Dorothy Briggs, *Your Child's Self-Esteem: the Key to His Life.* (Doubleday and Co.), p. 3.

2. John Drakeford, *Games Husbands and Wives Play.* (Word Publishers, 1970), p. 73.

3. Paul Tournier, *To Understand Each Other.* (John Knox Press, 1962), p. 58.

4. Fritz Ridenour, *How to Be a Christian Without Being Religious.* (Regal Books, 1967), pp. 147,148.

5. Fritz Ridenour, *Ibid.,* p. 126.

6. Paul Tournier, *The Healing of Persons.* (Harper & Row Publishers, 1965), pp. 88,89.

7. Dwight Small, *After You've Said I Do.* (Revell, 1968), p. 81.

8. Dwight Small, *Ibid.,* p. 235.

The publishers do not necessarily endorse the entire contents of all publications referred to in this book.

Other Helpful Reading from Regal Books
1. David Augsburger, *Caring Enough to Confront,* 1981 revised.

2. David Augsburger, *Caring Enough to Forgive,* 1981.

3. David Augsburger, *Caring Enough to Hear and Be Heard,* 1982.

4. H. Norman Wright, *Seasons of a Marriage,* 1982.

5. H. Norman Wright, *More Communication Keys to Your Marriage,* 1983.

More
Communication Keys
for Your Marriage

Contents

1
What Makes a Marriage?

WHY DID YOU MARRY? Can you remember back to that time when your life was filled with dreams, expectations, and hopes for the future? What part did marriage play in those dreams and hopes? How did you look at marriage? What did you expect from your marriage? Your answer might include one or more of the following:

"I wanted to share my life experiences with someone."

"I wanted someone to help make me happy."

"I wanted to spend my life with someone I loved and with someone who loved me."

"I didn't want to spend my life alone."

"I wanted to fulfill what I lacked in my own home."

"I wanted to be faithful to God and love someone He wanted me to love."

"I didn't want to end up alone, especially when I was older. Marriage was that security."

"I wanted the security of a permanent relationship."

All of these are fringe benefits of marriage, but none is strong enough to stand as a foundation for marriage.

Many people are propelled toward marriage without really understanding all they are committing themselves to for the rest of their lives. That is why couples experience surprises and upsets through the duration of their marriage. Marriage is many things:

Marriage is a gift.

Marriage is an opportunity for love to be learned.

Marriage is a journey in which we as the travelers are faced with many choices and we are responsible for these choices.

Marriage is affected more by our inner communication than our outer communication.

Marriage is more often influenced by unresolved issues from our past than we realize.

Marriage is a call to servanthood.

Marriage is a call to friendship.

Marriage is a call to suffering.

Marriage is a refining process. It is an opportunity to be refined by God into the person He wants us to be.

Marriage is not an event but a way of life.

Marriage involves intimacy in all areas for it to be fulfilling. This intimacy must reach into the spiritual, the intellectual, the social, the emotional, and the physical.

I have selected four of these beliefs for you to consider in this chapter. Think about each of these as you reflect on your own marriage relationship. What you believe about marriage and what you expect out of your marriage has a direct effect on communication between you and your spouse.

I believe that (1) marriage is a gift, (2) marriage is a call to servanthood, (3) marriage involves intimacy, and (4) marriage is a refining process.

Marriage is a Gift

Marriage is a gift, *You* may be the finest gift your spouse has ever received! Your spouse may be the finest gift you have received.

A gift is an item which is selected with care and consideration. Its purpose is to bring delight and fulfillment to another, an expression of deep feeling on the part of the giver. Think of the care and effort you put into selecting a gift.

You wonder what the recipient would enjoy. What will bring him/her delight? What will bring happiness?

What will make his/her day bright and cheery? What will show the person the extent of your feeling for him/her and how much the person means to you?

Because you want this gift to be special and meaningful you spend time thinking about what gift to select. Then you begin the search through various stores and shops, considering and rejecting several items until the right one beckons to you and you make the selection. You invest time wrapping the gift. You think of how best to present it to the person so his/her delight and pleasure will be heightened.

There is an excitement and a challenge involved in selecting and presenting a special gift. You not only have given the object, you also have given your time and energy. Gifts which are often appreciated the most are not those which are the most expensive, but are those which reflect the investment of yourself in considering the desires and wants of the other person, and the way you present it and the sacrifice you make.

You are a gift to your spouse. If you consider that you are a gift, how do you live so that your spouse feels that he/she has been given a special gift? Do you invest your time, thought, and energy to your spouse? Does your spouse experience delight, fulfillment, and a feeling of being special? How can you, as a gift, be used in the life of your spouse to lift his/her spirits and outlook on life?

On the receiving end of the gift, how do you react when you receive a special gift which brings you delight? Think of your childhood or earlier years. What was the most exciting or special gift you ever received? Can you remember your thoughts and feelings as you received that gift? How did you treat that gift? Did you take special care of it and protect it from harm and loss? Perhaps you gave the gift a special place of prominence and were carefully possessive of it.

If your spouse is a special gift to you, how do you treat this gift? Are you careful to give your spouse the finest care, attention, protection and place of prominence in your life? Does your partner feel as though he/she really is a gift to you?

A gift is given as an expression of our love. It is not based on whether the recipient deserves it or not. Our giving of a gift is actually an act of grace.

WHAT DO YOU THINK?

1. What is the best tangible gift your spouse has ever given you?

2. What is the best intangible gift your spouse has ever given you?

3. What is the gift you would like to give to your spouse?

4. What would your spouse appreciate?

Marriage Is Servanthood

Marriage is a call to servanthood. This is not a very popular concept and not high on the list of priorities for most marriages. We
would much rather be served than to serve. But our guideline for a
Christian marriage is given to us from the Scriptures. Look at the
following passages:

*"Do not merely look out for your own personal interests, but also
for the interests of others. Have this attitude in yourselves which
was also in Christ Jesus, who, although He existed in the form of
God, did not regard equality with God a thing to be grasped, but
emptied Himself, taking the form of a bond-servant, and being
made in the likeness of men. And being found in appearance as a
man, He humbled Himself by becoming obedient to the point of
death, even death on a cross. Therefore also God highly exalted
Him, and bestowed on Him the name which is above every name"*
(Phil. 2:4–9). Jesus voluntarily submitted to becoming a "bond-
servant," looking out for our interests rather than His own. In the
same way the Apostle Paul tells us to *"be subject to one another in
the fear of Christ"* (Eph. 5:21).

Notice one important point: We must never *demand* that our
partner be our servant or live up to the clear teachings of Scripture.
If we feel that we have to demand it, or even to mention it, then we
become more concerned with meeting our own needs than with being a servant. If a man has to demand that his wife see him as the
head of the family, then—to be blunt—he has lost it! Verses 22–25
say that for a man to be the head he must love his wife as Christ

loved the church and gave Himself for her. This means sacrificial love—servanthood.

The Greek word translated "submit" in Ephesians 5:21 is *hupotasso*. It is also translated "subject" and is used several times in the New Testament. The active form of this verb is a military term. It signifies an externally imposed submission based upon someone's rank or position, such as a private or sergeant would submit to a captain or lieutenant. In Scripture the word emphasizes the rule of Jesus Christ, such as in Romans 8:20 when speaking of "the creation" being subject to Christ. Again, in 1 Corinthians 15:27, on three occasions God is said to have put all things under Jesus' feet, making them subject to Him. This is *hupotasso* in the active voice.

However, the word *hupotasso* has another form, the middle or passive voice. Here subjection is not something which is arbitrarily done to you, but is something you do voluntarily to yourself. In the various marriage texts such as Colossians 3, Ephesians 5, Titus 2, and 1 Peter 3, the word *hupotasso* is in the middle or passive voice. The submission you are called to in marriage is never anything which is externally imposed, but is a definite act on your part which comes from inside you. And it is a mutual submission, not one way.

A great deal has been said in recent years about the husband/wife relationship as described in Scripture. With the feminist movement demanding that women be treated as equals, the Bible scholars have struggled with the true meaning of passages such as Ephesians 5. Some have incorrectly interpreted the word submit in the "military" sense of the word, proclaiming the absolute headship of the husband. Others have swung the other way saying that husbands and wives are equal, and the only kind of marriage that is biblical is one of an equal partnership. As often happens, we struggle with one of many paradoxes in Scripture.

I think perhaps Dwight Small best describes the biblical roles of husbands and wives in his book *Marriage as Equal Partnership*. He states:

> It is good that husband-wife equality is a prominent concern in our time. We are whole-heartedly in favor of extending that equality to every facet of daily living. But there is one thing we must remember. Equality is one principle among others; it doesn't stand alone and unqualified as though it were the only word of God to us. It is only part of the divine equation. It is entirely true, it is not the entire truth. And what humanly seems contradictory to us may be

*IF A MAN HAS TO DEMAND THAT HIS WIFE SEE
HIM AS HEAD OF THE FAMILY, HE'S HAD IT!*

a divine paradox. Thus, in Ephesians 5:21–33 it becomes obvious that husbands and wives are equal in every respect save one—authority and responsibility.

As we've begun to see, this inequality in authority-responsibility is mitigated inasmuch as the husband carries this as his own peculiar burden before the Lord. It is not to be envied, only supported prayerfully. What truly does alleviate all wifely fears is the call to mutual love and Christlike service at the heart of this paradoxical relationship. Its beauty, symmetry, and fairness unfold as we place ourselves within these special conditions under which biblical marriage functions.

Headship is not at all a husband's becoming a master, boss, tyrant, authoritarian—the dominant coercive force. Neither does it imply control or restriction, his being assertive and hers being suppressed. It cannot mean he assumes any prerogatives of greater virtue, intelligence, or ability. It does not mean that he is active and she passive, he the voice and she the silent partner. Nor does it mean that he is the tribal chief, the family manager, the one who has superior rights or privileges. He is not the decision-maker, problem-solver, goal-setter, or director of everyone else in the family's life. Rather he is primarily responsible for their common advance toward freedom and fellowship—creating a partnership of equals under one responsible head.

A truly loving husband will regard his wife as a completely equal partner in everything that concerns their life together. He will assert his headship to see that this equal partnership is kept inviolable. Hers is to be an equal contribution in areas, say, of decision-making, conflict-resolution, emerging family developmental planning, and daily family management. Whether it concerns finances, or child discipline, or social life—whatever it may be, she is an equal partner. Loving headship affirms, defers, shares; it encourages and stimulates. Loving headship delights to delegate without demanding. Yet, throughout the equalitarian process, the husband knows all the while that he bears the responsibility before God for the healthful maintenance of the marriage.[1]

We are on the safe side when we see the definition of subjection in the person of Jesus Himself. He, being free, abased Himself for us. He, being equal with the Father, relinquished that equality to become the Servant for all of us. Subjection, then, means no less than adopting His way of self-denial for the sake of others . . . .

Every Christian is called to servanthood as the expression of his or her new life in Christ. This is emphasized in Paul's reference to Jesus' taking the form of a servant: *"Have this mind among yourselves . . ."* (Phil. 2:5). Servanthood is the identifying mark of every true Christian believer.[2]

To put it simply, a servant's role is to make sure that the other person's needs are met. In a husband-wife relationship, being a servant is an act of love, a gift to the other person to make his/her life fuller. It is not something to be demanded. It is an act of strength and not of weakness. It is a positive action which has been chosen to show your love to each another. Hence, the apostle also said, "Be subject to one another," not limiting the role of servanthood to the wife.

A servant may also be called an *enabler*. The word *enable* means "to make better." As an enabler we are to make life easier for our spouse instead of placing restrictive demands upon him/her. An enabler does not make more work for the partner, nor does he/she hinder the other from becoming all he/she has been designed to become.

A servant is also one who *edifies* or builds up the other person. The English word *edify* is derived from the Latin word *aedes* meaning "hearth" or "fireplace." The hearth was the center of activity in ancient times. It was the only place of warmth and light in the home, and the place where the daily bread was prepared. It was also the place where people were drawn together.

Edifying is often used in the New Testament to refer to building up another person. Three examples of edifying are expressed in the verses below: (1) personal encouragement, (2) inner strengthening, and (3) the establishment of peace and harmony between individuals.

"So let us then definitely aim for and eagerly pursue what makes for harmony and for mutual upbuilding (edification and development) of one another" (Rom. 14:19, AMP).

"Let each one of us make it a practice to please (make happy) his neighbor for his good and for his true welfare, to edify him—that is, to strengthen him and build him up spiritually" (Rom. 15:2, AMP).

"Therefore encourage one another and build each other up, just as in fact you are doing" (1 Thess. 5:11, NIV).

First Corinthians 8:1 sums up the matter of edifying: *"Love builds up"* (NIV).

To *edify* then, means to cheer another person on in life. You are a one-person rooting section for your spouse which can increase your spouse's feelings of self-worth. The result is that your spouse's capacity to love and give in return is enhanced.

Elizabeth Barrett Browning described the essence of edifying when she wrote to the man she would marry, "Make thy love larger to enlarge my worth."

To encourage your spouse is to inspire him or her with renewed courage, spirit, and hope. It is an act of affirmation for who the person is.

Marriage Involves Intimacy

Marriage is a way of life, a celebration of life. A wedding ends but a marriage progresses until the death of one of the partners. The conclusion of the wedding marks the beginning of a marriage relationship which is a call to intimacy. Intimacy is shared identity, a "we" relationship. Its opposite is a marriage in which the individuals are called "married singles"—each partner goes his own way. In shared intimacy there must be a level of honesty which makes each vulnerable to the other. Intimacy is like a multi-stringed musical instrument. The music which comes from a viola comes not from one string but from a combination of different strings and finger positions.

We hear a great deal today about physical intimacy, often referring to nothing more than the physical act of two bodies copulating. However, the basis for true physical intimacy actually results from two other critical areas—*emotional intimacy* and *aesthetic intimacy.*

A physical marriage involves the *marriage of emotions* as well as bodies. Emotions give color to life. Emotional intimacy eludes many couples because one or both make no conscious effort to develop its potential. A man's and woman's emotions may be at different levels and intensities, or a woman's priority may be emotional intimacy whereas the man's priority is physical. When a couple learns to share the emotional level, when they can understand and experience each other's feelings, they are well on the way to achieving true intimacy. Barriers and walls must be lowered for intimacy to develop.

Judson Swihart writes of the tragedy of a marriage lacking emotional intimacy. "Some people are like medieval castles. Their high walls keep them safe from being hurt. They protect themselves emotionally by permitting no exchange of feelings with others. No one can enter. They are secure from attack. However, inspection of the occupant finds him or her lonely, rattling around his castle alone. The castle dweller is a self-made prisoner. He or she needs to feel loved by someone, but the walls are so high that it is difficult to reach out or for anyone else to reach in."[3]

The poem "Walls" describes the devastations of this barrier.

Their wedding picture mocked them from the table,
   these two
whose minds no longer touched each other.
They lived with such a heavy barricade between
   them that
neither battering ram of words nor artilleries of
   touch
could break it down.
Somewhere, between the oldest child's first tooth
   and the
youngest daughter's graduation, they lost each
   other.
Throughout the years, each slowly unraveled that
   tangled ball
of string called self, and as they tugged at stubborn
knots each hid his searching from the other.
Sometimes she cried at night and begged the whis
   pering dark-
ness to tell her who she was.
He lay beside her, snoring like a hibernating bear,
   unaware
of her winter.
Once, after they had made love, he wanted to tell
   her how
afraid he was of dying, but fearing to show his
   naked
soul, he spoke instead about the beauty of her
   breasts.
She took a course in modern art, trying to find herself in
colors splashed upon a canvas, and complaining to
   other
women about men who were insensitive.
He climbed a tomb called "the office," wrapped his
   mind in
a shroud of paper figures and buried himself in
   customers.
Slowly, the wall between them rose, cemented by
   the mortar
of indifference.

One day, reaching out to touch each other, they
   found a barrier
they could not penetrate, and recoiling from the
   coldness
of the stone, each retreated from the stranger on
   the
   other side.
For when love dies, it is not in a moment of angry
   battle,
   nor when fiery bodies lose their heat.
It lies panting, exhausted, expiring at the bottom of a
   wall
   it could not scale.[4]

Another form of intimacy is *aesthetic intimacy,* sharing the experiences of beauty. One couple enjoys sharing music, while another may prefer an oil painting of a mountain scene. Have you discovered this area of intimacy in your marriage yet? Careful and thoughtful questioning, or listening with your eyes may help you make this discovery.

To me one of the most beautiful and restful places on earth is found at the inlet of Jenny Lake in the Grand Tetons National Park. Following a trail along a rushing stream you stroll through woods for several hundred yards. Then you make a sudden hike down a slight hill to discover the inlet and the startling beauty of water, forest, sky, and jagged peaks. I value this place because of its beauty, isolation, and quietness. I have been there early in the morning on a clear, cloudless day, watching the sun creep slowly down the mountainside into the forest, and then brilliantly reflect off the smooth surface of the water.

At other times black clouds frame the rugged horizon and streaks of lightning provide a natural spectacle. I have sat upon a large boulder in a rainstorm with hailstones bouncing off my wide-brimmed hat as I pulled my coat tighter about me for protection. Each occasion provided a different kind of beauty, an experience that added to my reservoir of memories and built my anticipation of the next time. I have enjoyed this special place both by myself and with my wife Joyce.

Sharing and intimacy do not have to come from a series of comments like, "Isn't this beautiful?" or "Look at that!" or "Have you ever seen anything like this before?" Intimacy is standing together quietly, drinking in the amazing panorama and sensing the other's presence and appreciation. Beauty can be shared without a word. Such moments of sharing will be remembered for years and can be referred to again and again in private thought or in conversation.

Intimacy has been described as "we" experiences, a shared identity. In some marriages this "we" relationship does not develop and the result is a parallel marriage. The two individuals think mostly of themselves with little regard for the desires, wishes, or needs of their spouse.

For emotional and aesthetic intimacy to occur there must be communication. And for true communication to occur there must be emotional intimacy. Isn't this a paradox? Where do you begin?

Spiritual intimacy is another basis for true intimacy to occur. As a couple learns to communicate with each other and with God, they learn to trust each other and be more open. Spiritual intimacy comes from developing communication between ourselves and God in the presence of our spouse. It's easy to talk about, but not always easy to achieve.

WHAT DO YOU THINK?

1. What barrier to intimacy needs to be removed in your marriage?

2. Indicate a special time of intimacy you have experienced in the last month.

3. What could you do this week to increase the intimacy in your relationship?

Marriage Is a Refining Process

Joyce and I married at the age of twenty-two, about twenty-four years ago. Much has occurred during these years. A discovery which came early in marriage was the awareness that marriage is a refining process. Two individuals living in such close proximity are going to have to mature and have their rough edges smoothed, or their faults will become intensified and enlarged, and their negative qualities more pronounced.

Daily there are opportunities for growth if we allow it to occur. We encounter both major and minor crises often, some predictable and some like alien invaders from outer space.

What causes a major crisis to become a restrictive, crippling, eternal tragedy rather than a growth-producing experience in spite of the pain?

Our attitude.

Crises and trials can become the means of exciting growth. In the book *Run from the Pale Pony*, William Pruitt uses an analogy to share what has happened in his life. In the foreword of the book he writes:

> About thirty years ago, one of my joys as a boy was to ride a white horse named Prince. That proud, spirited stallion carried me where I wanted to go, wherever I bid him to and at the pace which I chose. I don't have to explain to horsemen the feeling of strength, even authority, which comes from controlling such a powerful animal. Nor need I expand upon the excitement I felt when I galloped him at full speed, or about the quiet pride that came when I twisted him through the corkscrew turns of a rodeo exercise. After all, he was mine and I trained him. Those experiences are part of my heritage.
>
> My cherished white horse was gone and seldom remembered about fifteen years later. It was then that I encountered a completely different kind of horse. When I first became aware of the specter, its shape was too dim to discern. I know only that I had never seen anything like it before. Too, I know that I had not sought any such creature, yet something different was with me wherever I went and that shadow would not go away. I told myself, "Really, now, you're much too busy to bother with something that seems determined to disturb you, get rid of it." And I tried to will it away. No matter what I did

though, the specter followed my every move. Furthermore, the harder I tried to lose it, the clearer the creature's form became to me.

My uneasiness changed to anxiety when I realized that this unwanted shadow had a will of its own. The chill of fear came when I understood that it had no intention to leave me alone. Without further warning, it began to communicate with me openly one day, and in a harsh voice which was almost rigid with animosity, it spat out, "You can no longer go where you want to go when you choose at the speed you pick. That's true because I will give you weakness instead of strength. Excitement and pride? Never again will you have them like before. I plan only confinement and disability for you. And I will be your constant companion. My name is Chronic Illness."

At the time I heard it speak, I shrank back from actually seeing it face to face. It spoke harshly of miseries which were inverse to joys with my white horse named Health and the bitter irony was reflected in the form of a malicious creature. Chronic Illness took the shape of a stunted misshapen pony. Its shaggy coat was pale in color, streaked with ages old accumulation of dark despair. But, unquestionably, the most frightening feature of the animal was its overwhelming glare—its glare-eyed stare which held me helpless. The pony's wild eyes started restlessly from side to side, yet strangely were unblinding. This book is written first of all for those people who have met the pale pony face to face.[5]

There are many possible forms in which the "pale pony" might come—serious physical or mental illness, accident, war injuries, etc. Whatever shape the pony takes, the results can be quite similar. William Pruitt's pale pony was multiple sclerosis. He sensed that the disease was increasingly affecting his life, but his story is the story of hope. He realized that he had a number of years before he would be completely disabled, and realizing that he wouldn't be able to carry on the type of work he was in, he went back to college in a wheelchair. He earned a Ph.D. in economics and began to teach on the college level.

Pruitt's book is not a book about giving up but rather about fighting back and winning. It's a very honest book, telling of the pain and the hurt and the turmoil. But its emphasis is on faith and hope.

The key issue to life's crises is our response. When trouble comes can we honestly say, "God, this isn't what I wanted in my life, I didn't plan for this." But the trouble is there, regardless of our wishes. How will we respond to it?

A verse that has meant so much to me is one which I ask couples in premarital counseling to build their marriage upon: "Consider it all joy, my brethren, when you encounter various trials, knowing that the testing [or trying] of your faith produces endurance" (Jas. 1:2–3). It's easy to read a passage like this and say, "Well, that's fine." It is another thing, however, to put it into practice.

What does the word *consider,* or *count,* actually mean? It refers to an internal attitude of the heart or the mind that allows the trial and circumstance of life to affect us adversely or beneficially. Another way James 1:2 might be translated is: "Make up your mind to regard adversity as something to welcome or be glad about."

You have the power to decide what your attitude will be. You can approach it and say: "That's terrible. Totally upsetting. That is the last thing I wanted for my life. Why did it have to happen now? Why me?"

The other way of "considering" the same difficulty is to say: "It's not what I wanted or expected, but it's here. There are going to be some difficult times, but how can I make the best of them?" Don't ever deny the pain or the hurt that you might have to go through, but always ask, "What can I learn from it, and how can it be used for God's glory?"

The verb tense used in the word *consider* indicates a decisiveness of action. It's not an attitude of resignation—"Well, I'll just give up. I'm just stuck with this problem. That's the way life is." If you resign yourself, you will sit back and not put forth any effort. The verb tense actually indicates that you will have to go against your natural inclination to see the trial as a negative force. There will be some moments when you won't see it like that at all, and then you'll have to remind yourself: "No, I think there is a better way of responding to this. Lord, I really want you to help me see it from a different perspective." And then your mind will shift to a more constructive response. This often takes a lot of work on your part.

God created us with both the capacity and the freedom to determine how we will respond to those unexpected incidents that life brings our way. You may honestly wish that a certain event had never occurred. But you cannot change the fact.

My wife, Joyce, and I have had to learn to look to God in the midst of a seeming tragedy. We have two children; a daughter, Sheryl, who is now twenty-two and a son, Matthew, who is sixteen. Mentally, however, Matthew is at less than a two-year-old level. He is a brain-damaged, mentally retarded boy who may never develop past the mental level of a three-year-old. Matthew can walk but he cannot talk or feed himself; he is not toilet trained. He is classified as profoundly retarded.

We did not anticipate becoming the parents of a mentally retarded son. We married upon graduation from college, proceeded through seminary and graduate school training, and into a local church ministry. Several years later, Matthew was born. We have learned and grown through the process of caring for him. As I look at my life, I know that I have been an impatient, selfish person in many ways. But because of Matthew, I had the opportunity to develop patience. When you wait for a long time for a child to be able to reach out and handle an item, when you wait for three or four years for him to learn to walk, you develop patience. We have had to learn to be sensitive to a person who cannot verbally communicate his needs, hurts, or wants. We must decipher what he is trying to say; we must try to interpret his nonverbal behavior.

Needless to say, Joyce and I have grown and changed through this process. We have experienced times of hurt, frustration, and sorrow. But we have rejoiced and learned to thank God for tiny steps of progress which most people would take completely for granted. The meaning of the name *Matthew*—"God's Gift" or "Gift from God"— has become very real to us.

We might very easily have chosen bitterness over our son's problem. We could have let it become a source of estrangement in our marriage, hindering our growth as individuals. But God enabled us to select the path of acceptance. We have grown and matured. Together. Not instantly, but over the course of several years. There have been steep places to overcome. But there have also been highlights and rich moments of reflection and delight. Matthew has become the refining agent that God is using to change us.

My wife and I discovered a great deal about the way God works. We realized that He had prepared us years before for Matthew's coming, though we hadn't realized the preparation was taking place. When I was in seminary I was required to write a thesis. Not knowing what to write about, I asked one of my professors to suggest a topic. She assigned me the title, "The Christian Education of the Mentally Retarded Child." I knew absolutely nothing on the subject. But I learned in a hurry. I read books, went to classes, observed training sessions in hospitals and homes, and finally wrote the thesis. I rewrote it three times and my wife typed it three times before it was accepted.

Later on, my graduate studies in psychology required several hundred hours of internship in a school district. The school district assigned me the task of testing mentally retarded children and placing them in their respective classes.

While serving as minister of education in a church for six years, I was asked by the church board to develop a Sunday School program for retarded children. My duties included developing the ministry and the curriculum, and training the teachers.

Two years before Matthew was born, Joyce and I were talking one evening. One of us said, "Isn't it interesting that we have all this exposure to retarded children? We've been learning so much. Could it be that God is preparing us for something that is going to occur later on in our life?" That's all we said at the time. I can't even remember which one of us said it. Within a year, Matthew was born. Eight months after that his seizures began. The uncertainty we had felt over the rate of his progress was now a deep concern. Then we learned the full truth and we began to see how the Lord had prepared us.

Where does the call to suffering enter into this whole process?

Romans 8:16–17 says, *"The Spirit Himself bears witness with our spirit that we are children of God, and if children, heirs also, heirs of God and fellow-heirs with Christ, if indeed we suffer with Him in order that we may also be glorified with Him."*
As members of the Body of Christ, we suffer when one member suffers.

In the minor or major crises which will occur in your marriage each person will experience hurt. Hurt shared, diminishes; carried alone it expands. Lewis B. Smedes describes marital suffering in this way. "Anybody's marriage is a harvest of suffering. Romantic lotus-eaters may tell you marriage was designed to be a pleasure-dome for erotic spirits to frolic in self-fulfilling relations. But they play you false. Your marriage vow was a promise to suffer. Yes, to suffer; I will not take it back. You promised to suffer with. It made sense, because the person you married was likely to get hurt he or she was bound to get. And you promised to hurt with your spouse. A marriage is a life of shared pain."[6]

This is a privilege! This is our ministry to one another! This is a reflection of the gift of marriage! How will you respond to this aspect of marriage?

2
Your Inner Conversations

EACH OF US carries on conversations with ourselves daily. This doesn't mean that we are odd or on the verge of spacing out. It's normal to talk to oneself. After you complete this chapter, however, I hope you will be much more conscious of your self talk. You will probably be shocked by the amount of time you spend on inner conversations and how those conversations affect your marriage.

Are you aware that:

- most of your emotions—such as anger, depression, guilt, worry—are initiated and escalated by your self talk?
- the way you behave toward your spouse is determined by your self talk and not by his or her behavior?
- what you say and how you say it is a direct expression of your self talk?

Self talk is the message you tell yourself—the words you tell yourself about yourself, your spouse, your experiences, the past, the future, God, etc. It is a set of evaluating thoughts about facts and events that happen to you. As events are repeated, many of your thoughts, and thus your emotional responses, become almost automatic. Sometimes the words you tell yourself are never put together in clear statements. They may be more like impressions.

Self talk or inner conversation is not an emotion or feeling. It is also not an attitude. However, repeated sets of self talk *become* attitudes, values, and beliefs. Attitudes are with us for a long period of time and may be inactive. Self talk represents the evaluating thoughts that we give ourselves at the present time. Your expressions of anger, ways of showing love, how you handle conflict, are motivated by conscious and subconscious self talk. Your self talk may be based upon some of your attitudes. A positive attitude toward life would tend to generate positive self talk and a negative attitude, negative self talk. Self talk is different from our beliefs, yet it is often *based* on our beliefs.

Most people believe that outside events, other people, and circumstances determine their emotions, behaviors, and verbal responses. Actually, however, your thoughts are the source. What you think about these things and about people will determine the emotions you feel and the behaviors and verbal responses you express.

As an example of *your beliefs* affecting your self talk, consider these typical beliefs about marriage:
1. A spouse should make me happy.
2. A spouse should meet all of my needs.
3. A spouse should know what my needs are without having to tell him/her.
4. A spouse should be willing to do things according to my way of doing them.
5. A spouse should not respond in an irritable or angry way to me.

WHAT DO YOU THINK?

Assume that none of the above beliefs were true in your marriage. What do you think you would be saying to yourself? Write out your response for each one.

1.

2.

3.

4.

5.

Another example of the results of self talk can be seen in two different groups of people: those with a failure identity and those with a success identity. Each identity appears to be tied into the person's self talk. Positive self talk statements would include the following: "I have value and worth as a person"; "I have accomplished much of what I have tried in the past"; "Trying a new venture is worthwhile"; "If something is new, I see it as a challenge and an opportunity for me to grow."

A failure identity can come from statements like "I'm not as capable as others"; "I will probably fail"; "I can't accomplish what I try"; "If I try I might fail and others will see my weaknesses."

Let's consider for a moment this exchange between a husband and wife and discover the self talk that prompted it.

Saturday morning, 11:00 A.M.

Wife: It's about time you got up. It looks like you're going to waste the entire day!

Husband: (looking a bit startled) What's with you? I'm just taking my time getting up and enjoying a day off.

Wife: That's just it. You're around here so rarely and half the day is shot! By the time you get dressed and cleaned up lunch will be over and nothing has been accomplished!

Husband: Who said I was getting dressed and cleaned up? The only thing I want to accomplish is a cup of coffee, the paper and the football game on TV!

Wife: What? Then the whole day is shot to . . . I don't get a day off. There's a whole list of work to be done here. When *are* you going to do it?

Husband: What? I suppose you've been saving up a list of work projects again. Why don't you give me some notice ahead of time? If I wanted to work today, I could go into the shop and get overtime plus some peace and quiet!

What is happening in this conversation? First of all, each person has an unspoken expectation for Saturday. One for work and one for pleasure. Many problems such as this could be eliminated if individuals clarified their expectations in advance. Let's look at the wife's self talk at this point. She was expecting her husband to accomplish a number of tasks on Saturday. She got up at 6:30. Note her inner conversation and the progression.

7:30 "I hope he gets up pretty soon. I'd like to get started on these projects. With the kids away today we can get a lot done."

8:15 "Boy! I don't hear a sound. Well, I'm going to start work in the yard. He'll probably hear me and then he can join me."

9:15 "What time is it? 9:15! I don't believe it! He's sleeping away the morning. Who does he think he is? How thoughtless! I ought to go in there and wake him up!"

10:00 "Just because he has no work at the plant or at church he thinks he's entitled to sack out. What about me? When do I ever get to do this? He ticks me off! He probably knows I want him to take care of those chores he's been putting off. He just wants to ignore them and me! Boy, is he going to hear from me. I'll let him sleep but he's going to pay a price for it!"

10:45 "And I was going to cook his favorite meal and dessert tonight. Fat chance of that. How could he be so insensitive? Look at all I do for him!"

What type of emotions do these statements arouse? What kind of behaviors do you think these statements prompt? What kind of communication is happening?

Suppose, instead, the wife chose self talk such as the following:

"I wish he would get up. I think I'll check and see if he's just resting or sleeping."

"I'm not sure he's going to get up in time to do much today. I'd better revise my list and then ask him if he could help me with these two chores after lunch."

"I am a bit upset with him but I have to admit I didn't tell him I wanted him to work today. Next time I'll talk it over with him before the weekend."

"I could serve him breakfast in bed when he wakes up. That'll knock his socks off! When's the last time I did that?"

Two different styles of self talk. The choice is ours whether to make our self talk positive or negative.

Many of your thoughts are automatic. You don't sit around thinking about what you are going to think next. Thoughts slide into our consciousness so smoothly that you don't even sense their entrance. Many of them are stimulated from past experience, attitudes and beliefs. You build up storehouses of memories and experience, retaining and remembering those things which you concentrate upon the most.

Whether they are automatic or consciously thought out, what are your thoughts like? Are they negative or positive? Most people who worry, are depressed, irritable, or are critical toward others have automatic thoughts which are negative.

A characteristic of negative thoughts is that they are generally wrong. They do not reflect reality. Often they reflect our insecurity, our feelings of inadequacy, and our fears. These alien invaders are not usually welcome guests. They are generally exaggerated negative conclusions about our future, our spouse, our marriage, our everyday life, and ourselves.

WHAT DO YOU THINK?

If you have negative thoughts, and give into them without countering and evaluating them, the results will be negative. Consider the examples of thinking errors listed below which we either consciously conjure up or which jump into our mind. As you read each one, indicate in the space provided whether you have this type of thought. Then write an example of your most recent one. Try to remember what you said to your spouse based upon your thoughts. *Personalizing*—Thinking that all situations and events revolve around you. "Everyone at my spouse's business party thought I looked out of place."
Example:

What I said:

Magnifying—Blowing negative events out of proportion. "This is the worst thing that could have happened to me."

Example:

What I said:

Minimizing—Glossing over the positive factors. Overlooking the fact that everything went well such as hosting a successful dinner. This could include explaining away or discounting a compliment.
Example:

What I said:

Either/or thinking—"Either I'm a successful spouse or a total failure."
Example:

What I said:

Taking events out of context—After a delightful day with your spouse, focusing on one or two rough spots. "The day was really a loss because of . . ."
Example:

What I said:

Jumping to conclusions—"My spouse isn't paying me as much attention. His/her love for me is fading."
Example:

What I said:

Over-generalizing—"I never can please him/her. I constantly blow it as a married partner." Or "He/she can never do anything right. He/she will always be this way."
Example:

What I said:

Self blame—Blaming the total self rather than specific behaviors that can be changed. "I'm no good as a marriage partner."
Example:

What I said:

Magical—"My marriage is all messed up because of my lousy past."
Example:

What I said:

Mind reading—"My spouse thinks I'm unattractive and fat."
Example:

What I said:

Comparing—"Comparing yourself with someone else and ignoring all of the basic differences between the two of you. "My husband is much smarter than I am."
Example:

What I said:

Here are some examples of a few of these statements and how to counter them.

Wife: "I'll never be able to satisfy my husband. I've made too many mistakes these first three years of marriage."

Thinking Error: *Over-generalization*

Response: "I don't know that I won't be able to satisfy him. I can grow and develop as a person. I can change. Where's the evidence that I'll *never* be able to? Here is what I will attempt today—"

Husband: "My work isn't exciting or challenging at all. My life isn't fulfilling anymore."

Thinking Error: *Minimizing* (disqualifying the positive)

Response: "My work may not be exciting but there is a purpose to it. Have I focused on that? Have I thought of how this job affects others? Just because my work is not challenging, who says the rest of my life can't be fulfilling? What can I do at this time to enrich my life?"

Wife: "I'll probably mess up this new recipe. Then my husband will get angry at me and won't speak to me the rest of the evening."

Thinking Error: *Jumping to conclusions*

Response: "I don't have to be a perfect cook. I can make it better the next time if it doesn't turn out too well. If he becomes angry, I can let him know that I'm disappointed too, but it's not the end of the world."

Husband: "What's the point in doing that for her? She wouldn't like it or she probably won't even notice it."

Thinking Error: *Mind reading*

Response: "I have no way of knowing. I can at least try. I need to give her a chance to respond. I might be surprised. If she doesn't care, it's not the end of the world."[1]

COUNTERING AUTOMATIC
THOUGHTS IS BRINGING
YOUR THOUGHTS TO TRIAL
AND EXAMINING THE
EVIDENCE.

How to Control Your Thoughts

There are several basic ways of controlling your automatic thoughts and giving yourself an opportunity to produce more positive communication. The first is to become aware of these thoughts by keeping track of them. Writing them on a piece of paper or 3 × 5 card is one way to accomplish this.

Another way to eliminate automatic thoughts is to learn to counter or answer them. Countering is bringing your thoughts to trial and examining the evidence. But you can do this only if you are aware of them. You need to catch the thoughts that come into your mind, and then, when you are aware of them, respond with a conscious thought. You need not settle for either your automatic thoughts or those you consciously work up. You can choose precisely what you will think about.

Here are some typical thoughts that will probably enter your mind at one time or another:

"My spouse will never change. He/she will always be that kind of a person."

"I can never meet my spouse's needs."

"If I bring up that subject, my spouse will just get mad again."

"If I share what really happened, I'll never be trusted again."

"Why bother asking him/her to share his/her feeling? He/she will only clam up again."

"He hates me."

"I just know there's an affair going on."

"He's so inconsiderate! Why doesn't he grow up!"

"I must have everything perfect in my house."

WHAT DO YOU THINK?

What thoughts come into your mind? List them below.

1.

2.

3.

4.

5.

6.

When a thought comes into your mind, what do you do with it? A negative or angry thought, when not challenged, intensifies and expands. In 1 Peter 1:13 we are told to "gird your minds for action." "Gird" requires mental exertion. Peter says that we are to eliminate or cast out of our minds any thoughts that would hinder growth in our Christian life. This in turn will affect our married life.

WHAT DO YOU THINK?

What would you do to change the thoughts you listed above? What do you do to change your own thoughts? Question and challenge them.

On paper answer these three questions:
1. Which of the automatic thoughts listed above are true?
2. How do I know whether they are true or false?
3. What are some alternative ways of thinking?

Remember, in answering your automatic thoughts, there are different interpretations for each situation. Some interpretations are closer to fact than others; therefore, you should develop as many interpretations as possible. Often we confuse our thoughts with facts, even when the two do not necessarily relate. Questioning your negative and automatic thoughts will help you create a new form of thinking.

Here is a list of twenty questions which can be very helpful in learning this new art of challenging our thoughts.

1. *What is the evidence?* Ask yourself the question, "Would this thought hold up in a court of law? Is it circumstantial evidence?" Just because your husband missed calling you when he was late for dinner one day does not mean that you cannot count on him for anything. Just because you tripped walking into your Sunday School class and everyone laughed does not mean that you will trip again or that they think you are a clod.

2. *Am I making a mistake in assuming what causes what?* It is often difficult to determine causes. Many people worry about their weight, and if they gain weight they make the assumption that "I don't have any willpower." But is that the only reason? Could there be other causes such as glandular imbalance, using eating as a means to deal with unhappiness, etc.? We do not know the causes of obesity for certain. The medical profession is still studying the problem.

3. *Am I confusing a thought with a fact?* Do you say, "I've always failed before so why should this be any different?" Calling yourself a failure and then believing your name-calling does not mean that the label you've given yourself is accurate. Check out the facts with yourself and with others.

4. *Am I close enough to the situation to really know what is happening?* You may have the thought, "My wife's parents do not like me and would probably like her to leave me." How do you know what they are thinking? Is your source of information accurate? How can you determine the facts?

5. *Am I thinking in all-or-none terms?* Many people see life as black or white. The world is either great or lousy. Men are either all good or all bad. All people are to be feared. Again where did you get this idea? What are the facts?

6. *Am I using ultimatum words in my thinking?* "I must always be on time or no one will like me." That is an unfair statement to make about yourself or anyone else.

7. *Am I taking examples out of context?* A woman overheard one instructor talking to another instructor about her. She thought the instructor said she was rigid, pushy, and dominant. Fortunately, she checked out the conversation with one of the instructors and discovered that she had been described as having high standards and determination. The words were spoken in a positive context, but because of her tendency to think the worst, distortion occurred.

8. *Am I being honest with myself?* Am I trying to fool myself or make excuses or put the blame on others?

9. *What is the source of my information?* Are your sources accurate, reliable, trustworthy? And do you hear them correctly? Do you ask the persons to repeat what they say and verify it?

10. *What is the probability of this thought occurring?* Perhaps your situation is so rare an occurrence that there is little chance of your worry coming true. One man had the thought that because he missed work for two days he would be fired. After he challenged the negative thought he said, "Well, I've worked there for several years and have a good record. When was the last time anyone was fired because he missed two days' work? When was the last time anyone was fired?"

11. *Am I assuming every situation is the same?* Just because you didn't get along at the last two jobs doesn't mean that you will not get along at your new one. Just because you messed up a recipe once doesn't mean you will mess it up the next time.

12. *Am I focusing on irrelevant facts?* Of course your spouse is imperfect and there are problems in the world, and people are physically and mentally sick, and there is crime, etc. What can your sitting around worrying about them or becoming depressed over them do to eliminate these problems? How else could you use your thinking time in a more productive manner?

13. *Am I overlooking my strengths?* People who worry or who are depressed, definitely overlook their positive qualities. They do not treat themselves as a friend. They are hard on themselves and focus upon their supposed defects instead of identifying their strengths and praising God for them. It is important not only to list your strengths but also recall times in your past when you were successful.

14. *What do I want?* This is a question I ask people over and over again in counseling. What goals have you set for your marriage? For your worry? What do you want out of life? How do you want your life to be different? How do you want your communication to improve?

15. *How would I approach this situation if I were not worrying about it?* Would I tend to make it worse than it is? Would I be as immobilized by our communication problems as I am now? Imagine how you would respond if you believed that you had the capabilities of handling it.

16. *What can I do to solve the situation?* Are my thoughts leading to a solution of this problem or making it worse? Have I written down a solution to the problem? When was the last time I tried a different approach to the problem?

17. *Am I asking myself questions that have no answers?* Questions like, "How can I undo the past?" "Why did that have to happen?" "Why can't he/she be more sensitive?" or "Why did this happen to me?" Often questions like these can be answered with the question "Why not?" What if something terrible happens? "So what if it does?" Why spend time asking yourself unanswerable questions?

18. *What are the distortions in my own thinking?* The first step in overcoming errors is to identify them. Do you make assumptions or jump to conclusions? What are they? The best way to deal with an assumption is to check it out. Look for the facts.

19. *What are the advantages and disadvantages of thinking this way?* What are the advantages of worrying? List them out on a piece of paper. What are the advantages of thinking that people don't like you? What is the benefit of any type of negative thinking?

20. *What difference will this make in a week, a year, or ten years?* Will you remember what happened in the future? Five years from now who will remember that your shirt was buttoned wrong? Who really cares? We believe that our mistakes are more important to other people than they really are. If someone chooses, ten years from now, to remember something you said or did that bothered them, that's their problem, not yours.[2]

To create new interpretations, write down all possible interpretations. List as many as possible—both automatic and conscious thoughts. Challenge each thought and write down new interpretations. Then act on your new interpretations if action is needed.

WHAT DO YOU THINK?

There is yet another way to evaluate and control your automatic or self talk. Take an event that occurred recently in your marriage. Using the chart below, in the column briefly state the "facts and events" that occurred. Then write all of the "inner conversation" statements you made. Write positive, negative, or neutral after each one.

After you complete this, simply describe the emotions and feelings that were activated by your self talk. Then tell what you actually said. Go to the next column when you complete the first.

The next column is a "videotape check." Look at what you wrote under *A* and ask yourself, "If I had made a videotape of this event, would the tape back me up on my description of the facts?" Video-tapes record facts—not beliefs or opinions.

Then, *B*, evaluate your self talk. Was your self talk based on fact and objective reality? Under *C*, how would you like to feel the next time a similar situation arises? Remember that these feelings will come from what you *say* to yourself. Then tell what you think you will say based on your new emotional responses.

Then, under #2, write out "What I learned from this experience."

1. Evaluate a recent experience.

A Recent Event	*Videotape Check*
A. Facts and events	A. Evaluate the facts
B. My inner conversation	B. Evaluate your self talk
C. My emotional consequences	C. How would you like to feel about this?
D. What I said in verbal conversations	D. What will you say next time?

2. What I learned from this experience:

Power to Change

What does Scripture say about our inner conversations or self talk?

In the book of Lamentations, Jeremiah is speaking of his depression. His symptoms are very intense and he is miserable. He thinks constantly of his misery which further depresses him. He *chooses* to think this way. *"Remember my affliction and my wandering, the wormwood and bitterness. Surely my soul remembers and is bowed down within me"* (3:19–20).

He then begins to change his self talk and says, *"This I recall to my mind, therefore I have hope"* (3:21).

Self talk generates and creates mental pictures in our mind. As mental pictures begin to emerge in our mind our imagination has now been called into action. As we run mental pictures through the panoramic screen of our mind our self talk is expanded and reinforced. Note what others have said about the role of imagination in our life.

> Imagination is to the emotions what illustrations are to a text, what music is to a ballad. It is the ability to form mental pictures, to visualize irritating or fearful situations in concrete form. The imagination reinforces the thoughts, the thoughts intensify the feelings, and the whole business builds up.
>
> The imagination is far stronger than any other power which we possess, and the psychologists tell us that on occasions, when the will and the imagination are in conflict, the imagination always wins. How important therefore that we should vow by the Saviour's help never to throw the wrong kind of pictures on this screen of our minds, for the imagination literally has the power of making the things we picture real and effective.[3]

With practice you can learn to turn your thoughts off and on. To do so you must put things in their proper perspective. The more a person practices control the greater the possibility of immediate control. We do not have to act in accordance with our self talk or our feeling.

The Scriptures have much to say about thinking and the thought life. The words *think, thought,* and *mind* are used over 300 times in the Bible. The book of Proverbs says, *"As he thinks within himself, so he is"* (Prov. 23:7).

Scriptures indicate that our mind is often the basis for the difficulties and problems that we experience. "Now the mind of the flesh [which is sense and reason without the Holy Spirit] is death—death that comprises all the miseries arising from sin, both here and hereafter. But the mind of the (Holy) Spirit is life and soul-peace. . . . [That is] *because the mind of the flesh—with its carnal thoughts and purposes—is hostile to God"* (Rom. 8:6–7, AMP).

God knows the content of our thoughts. *"All the ways of a man are pure in his own eyes, but the Lord weighs the spirits—the thoughts and intents of the heart"* (Prov. 16:2, AMP). *"For the Word that God speaks is alive and full of power—making it active, operative, energizing and effective; it is sharper than any two-edged sword, penetrating to the dividing line the breath of life (soul) and [the immortal] spirit, and of joints and marrow [that is, of the deepest parts of our nature] exposing and sifting and analyzing and judging the very thoughts and purposes of the heart"* (Heb. 4:12, AMP).

A Christian does not have to be dominated by the thinking of the old mind, the old pattern. He has been set free. God has not given us the spirit of fear, but of power, and of love, and of a sound mind (see 2 Tim. 1:7). Soundness means that the new mind can do what it is supposed to do. It can fulfill its function.

What can you do? Let your mind be filled with the mind of Christ. There are Scriptures that place definite responsibility upon the Christian in this regard. In Philippians 2:5 *(KJV)*, Paul commands, *"Let this mind be in you, which was also in Christ Jesus."* This could be translated, *"Be constantly thinking this in yourselves, or reflect in your own minds the mind of Christ Jesus."* The meaning here for the words "this mind be" is "to have understanding, to be wise, to direct one's mind to a thing, to seek or strive for" (see Wuest's Word Studies in *The Greek New Testament* for explanation).

The main thrust here is for the Christian to emulate in his life the virtues of Jesus Christ as presented in the previous three verses. *"Complete my joy by being of the same mind. . . . Do nothing from selfishness or conceit, but in humility count others better than yourselves. Let each of you look not only to his own interests, but also to the interests of others"* (Phil. 2:2–3, RSV).

In verses 6 through 8 another example of Christ is given—that of humility. This humility came about through submission to the will of God. The mind of Christ knew God and submitted to Him. A Christian following Jesus Christ must give his mind in submission to God. Remember in 1 Peter 1:13, we are told to gird up our minds. This takes mental exertion, putting out of our minds anything that would hinder progress. Thoughts of worry, fear, lust, hate, jealousy, and unwillingness are to be eliminated from the mind. This means negative and unrealistic self talk. *"Finally, brethren, whatever is true, whatever is honorable, whatever is right, whatever is pure, whatever is lovely, whatever is of good repute, if there is any excellence and if anything worthy of praise, let your mind dwell on these things"* (Phil. 4:8).

Remember, your inner conversations will determine your outer conversations!

WHAT DO YOU THINK?

1. How do I treat myself? (Describe.) How will I treat myself this week?

2. Have I ever thought of myself as being a parent to myself? (Describe.)

3. What kind of parent messages do I give myself? (List five.)

4. Do I often treat myself with scorn and disrespect? If so, what are some of my "scornful" and "disrespectful" thoughts?

5. Do I sometimes punish myself? What are my self-punishing thoughts? (List.)

6. Do I expect and demand too much of myself? Again, what am I telling myself along this line?

7. Does the way I treat myself reflect on my concept of God? How would a loving God talk to me about the thoughts I've listed above?

8. Does God treat me in the same manner that I treat myself? If not, how does His treatment differ from mine?

9. What do the following Scriptures say about how I should view myself? (Read them and write your responses to each one.)
　　　Psalm 139:14–16

Ephesians 2:10

Philippians 1:6

1 Peter 2:9

1 Corinthians 4:2–5

2 Corinthians 12:9

Luke 1:37

Psalm 1:1

Philippians 4:6–7

1 John 1:9

Isaiah 40:31

Psalm 32:8

10. What are ten positive thoughts I have about my spouse?

11. What are five positive thoughts I will focus on each day this week concerning my spouse?

12. List several comments I make to my spouse and identify the self talk which generated the thought.[4]

———————————————————————

3
Messages from the Past

ARE YOU FREE to communicate the way you want to? Are your thoughts and words a reflection of the way you feel now, or are they locked into a pattern because of past influences?

In America the creed of independence is so strong that we feel a need to achieve our own individual independence. "I am my own person"; "I have risen above my life experiences and my past." It sounds good, but most of us are not nearly as independent and free as we would like to believe we are. Our outer conversations come from our inner conversations. But where do the inner conversations originate?

For many of us, unresolved relationships and issues of the past are still guiding our lives and hampering communication. Some of us even suffer because of a half-resolved and half-buried past. Because we react and respond to others on the basis of unresolved past relationships, we actually perpetuate those difficulties.

Some of us carry wounds from the past, some carry scars. Some of us have buried our painful memories, hoping those memories never resurrect.

As we grow older our storehouse of memories increases. Our personalities and general make-up are the results of those memories. Many of our feelings of joy, hurt, anger, or delight are tied into how we remember events and experiences.

You and I will remember the same event in a very different way. For example I may remember the enjoyment and delight of a day in the mountains hiking to a lake. You may remember the ten-hour drive, arising at 4:00 A.M. and feeling exhausted for three days. We both experienced the same events but different aspects made an impression.

How we remember an event, and its significance, influences today's responses. Our emotions are closely tied to our memory. Henri J. M. Nouwen said, "Remorse is a fitting memory, guilt is an accusing memory, gratitude is a joyful memory, and all such emotions are deeply influenced by the way we have integrated past events into our way of being in the world. In fact, we perceive our world with our memories."[1]

Much of the suffering in marriages today is caused by memories. The forgotten anniversary, a bitter fight, the discovery of an affair, and numerous other events continue to fester and simmer in our minds. Sometimes we try to hide these memories in the recesses of our minds. A usual response to an undesirable memory is to repress or forget it. Who wants to remember the pains of the past? Let's live as though they did not occur.

Hiding them, however, prevents them from being completely healed. Thus they continue to act as an anchor which we drag along with us as we limp through life. When we bury memories and wounds we bury them alive. And their resurrection comes when we least suspect it. Painful memories must be dredged up and faced for healing to occur.

Buried memories of the past surface anew when we encounter problems in our marriage, and the past may determine how we deal with those problems. Some marry hoping that the marriage will serve as a blotter to eradicate the past. They soon learn, however, that the past sticks with them. Marriage does not change our past—it works in just the opposite way. Marriage can reveal past hurts, and all our efforts to keep those memories hidden may eventually result in a crumbling marriage.

Where Memories Begin

Where do our memories begin? How might they influence us and our attempts to communicate with our spouses today?

What is the earliest memory you can recall? One of my earliest memories is a series of images which come to mind when I think of a trip I took with my parents across the United States at the age of four.

What are the five earliest memories you can recall?

What is the earliest positive memory you can recall? One which comes to mind was a fishing trip at a creek with my brother and a cousin. We pulled in fish after fish and it was a delightful experience.

What is the earliest painful memory you can recall? A painful memory for me was a spanking I got with a switch because I had misbehaved.

Childhood memories are more than remembrances. Feelings and attitudes from even the earliest of years can determine our present-day responses. Some can enable us to move forward in our life. Others interfere. Bottled-up unpleasant memories conflict with your adult life. Dr. Hugh Missildine describes these memories as the "inner child of the past." This child still seeks to control your life. Part of your discomfort arises because many of the feelings are not unreasonable for a child, but they seem undesirable and unreasonable for an adult.

There are times when we ask "Why do I *say* what I do?" "Why do I *act* the way I do?" "What is wrong with me?" "Why do I feel this way?" We may become angry at ourselves for these feelings. We may even criticize ourselves for these inner feelings. But attempts to deny or repress them only create a greater discomfort. Because we don't share this struggle with others, the difficulty is compounded.

Many of your memories fall into the category of unresolved childhood conflict—your "child of the past." Who usually responds to a child? His or her parents. But what do you do when you're an adult and your parents are not around or are dead? Who parents your "child" then? You do. Whether you realize it or not, you have assumed the attitudes and beliefs of your parents so you respond to yourself and to others the way they did, even though these attitudes are not your own. Thus your communication is not really your own. You respond to life partly as a mature adult and partly as your child of the past.

In becoming your own parent you cling to old patterns from the past because they are familiar. And you give in to them even though they hurt because, to live in the unfamiliar present means breaking free of the familiar. And it takes effort to break away from the past.

Our past emerges more clearly when we marry. Dr. Hugh Missildine has suggested that marriage involves four people and not *two!* There are the two adults who act in the present and the two children who respond because of their family background and memories. This certainly complicates a marriage, to say the least! Without realizing it we carry into marriage hidden aspects of our childhood nature. We all do this even though we have heard the admonition from Scripture again and again: "*When I was a child, I talked like a child, I thought like a child, I reasoned like a child; now that I have become a man, I am done with childish ways and have put them aside*" (1 Cor. 13:11, *AMP*).

During courtship we try to emphasize our mature adult qualities to impress the other person. But once we are married we relax. We make our new home into a place of comfort and soon feel familiar in our surroundings. Now it becomes an atmosphere wherein we can allow patterns from the past to emerge. Haven't you heard husbands and wives say, "He wasn't like this before we married"? Or "I never saw this side of her before"?

A wife's memory may be of a home that was a showplace. She remembers her mother telling her for years that a good wife keeps an impeccable home. So she never allows her home to be messy. She wants to be a good wife, doesn't she? Her husband, however, sees home as a place of cluttered refuge where neatness and order do not exist! Why? He too has messages and images from the past, and perhaps he is following the example set by his own father. Many of us consciously or unconsciously attempt to duplicate the familiar patterns of our childhood.

The child in us had numerous expectations. How we communicated in our childhood home will be brought into our marriage. In many cases the difference in communication patterns and styles between husband and wife is as complicated as two foreign nations getting together. Dr. Missildine takes this point a step further. "Generally, in order to achieve the 'at home' feeling within our marriage, we treat ourselves in the same way our parents treated us. The old 'at home' emotional atmosphere of childhood is copied as precisely as possible, including any painful attitudes that may have characterized our family life in the past. We frequently even invite our spouse to treat us the way our parents did—unknowingly seeking their approval and depending on their evaluation of us in the same way that we once sought the approval and love of our parents. This is, in a way, what is happening when your spouse refuses, perhaps by default or abdication, to assume responsibility or 'acts like a baby.' "[2]

If we could realize that each of us has both an adult part and a child part within us which is (hopefully) still in a growth stage, we may become a bit more accepting of one another.

WHAT DO YOU THINK?

How can we discover how our past has influenced us? How can we discover our past patterns of response?

1. Evaluate your life by completing your own family history.

a. List what you feel are/were the positive qualities of your father.

b. List what you feel are/were the negative qualities of your father.

c. Describe how you feel/felt about your father.

d. What emotions does/did he express openly to you and how?

e. Describe how you and your father communicate/communicated.

f. Describe the most pleasant and unpleasant experiences with your father.

g. What messages did your father give you about yourself? Were they positive or negative? Please describe.

h. Describe how your father punished or criticized you.

i. In what ways are you different from your father?

j. List what you feel are/were the positive qualities of your mother.

k. List what you feel are/were the negative qualities of your mother.

l. Describe how you feel/felt about your mother.

m. What emotions does/did she express openly and how?

n. Describe how you and your mother communicate/communicated.

o. Describe the most pleasant and unpleasant experiences with your mother.

p. What messages did your mother give you about yourself? Were they positive or negative? Please describe.

q. Describe how your mother punished or criticized you.

r. In what ways are you different from your mother.

2. Describe on the following chart (by drawing a line graph) the history of your personal relationship with your father from infancy to the present time.

Very
Close

Close

Distant

| Birth–5 | 5–10 | 10–15 | 15–20 | 20–present time |

What made the relationship close?

What made the relationship distant?

3. Describe on the following chart (by drawing a line graph) the history of your personal relationship with your mother from infancy to the present time.

Very
Close

Close

Distant

| Birth–5 | 5–10 | 10–15 | 15–20 | 20–present time |

What made the relationship close?

What made the relationship distant?

4. Indicate on the following chart (by drawing a line graph) the history with sibling of the opposite sex closest in age to you. (If there is none the opposite sex, use the same sex.)

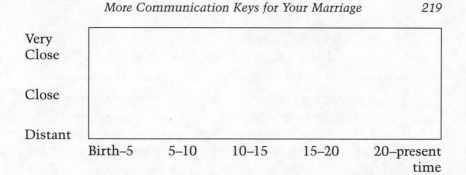

	Birth–5	5–10	10–15	15–20	20–present time
Very Close					
Close					
Distant					

5. Describe the relationship your parents had as you grew up. Did they openly express feelings? Describe. Did they ever argue or fight? Describe. Was one domineering? Describe. Describe the kinds of difficulties that you sensed between your parents. How did you feel about their relationship?

6. What were you most afraid of as a child (criticism, failure, rejection, competition, darkness, getting injured)? Tell as best you can about the circumstances when you were most likely to have this fear. Give examples.

7. Did you have any Christian training? Describe the role that God has played in your life. What concerns, fears, or problems have you had in relation to God? When were you first aware of them? What have been the most serious concerns for you?

8. List ten adjectives that describe you.

1. _____ 6. _____
2. _____ 7. _____
3. _____ 8. _____
4. _____ 9. _____
5. _____ 10. _____

Which of these adjectives are characteristic of each of the following?

Spouse_____
Father_____
Mother_____
Brother_____
Sister_____
Friend_____

9. Where on the following line would you place yourself currently in relationship to your parents?

_____

completely   completely
dependent   independent

10. Write out your earliest memory.

_____

One of our tasks as adults is to identify our thoughts and feelings and discover their origin. Recognizing them may be the easiest task; accepting or modifying them will be difficult. Many of these memories (thoughts and feelings) are the bases for how we feel about ourselves. Many of us carry around distorted views of ourselves. These too stem from childhood, continuations of our past which may have been created by longtime parental attitudes. But blaming our parents for who and what we are today has no value. All parents are fallible, we all make mistakes. Most parents do the best they can. We are now responsible for how we continue to treat ourselves.

Communication Difficulties—Past and Present

Communication difficulties can be traced to our memories and unresolved childhood patterns. Have you ever wondered why one person is always demanding, asks his/her spouse to perform perfectly, has excessively high standards the other must conform to, and is short on compliments and long on demands and commands? This person may be a perfectionist—you will observe it in his/her behavior and communication. Let's look at this person to see the relationship between the past and the present.

A perfectionist is difficult to live with. If you are this individual, let me illustrate what you probably do. You are demanding of yourself and possibly of your spouse. You exert tremendous energy to accomplish an ever elusive goal. Everything must be in its place; colors must match; every item has to be properly lined up on the table; you must say the right phrase; be punctual; etc. You may give great attention to every little detail and become upset when you cannot regulate all of your life or the life of your partner. The problem is you are never satisfied with your own or with your mate's performance.

You experience success but still feel empty and dissatisfied. You may feel like a "successful failure." Many individuals are successful and proficient, they can rest in what they have accomplished and feel good about their attainment. Often what they do benefits and serves others. They are satisfied. The perfectionist, however, strives for his own benefit and does not find satisfaction. His cry is, "I must do better, better, better!"

A perfectionist probably received parental messages which included: "You can do better"; "That's not good enough"; "Always do better than others"; "You'll receive love if you perform"; "Beat the next guy." We remember comments, words, withheld praise, double messages, sad faces, frowns, signs of disappointment, requests for more this, more that, etc. And thus the treadmill of striving is perpetuated.

The perfectionist has an endless goal of pleasing his parents. They may no longer be around but their parental message is still a recurring childhood memory. This colors the perfectionist's inner conversations and thus how he responds outwardly. Those around him must also perform. "If I must be perfect, so must they. I must urge them on, criticize, correct, make them perfect as I must be perfect. Never let up on them. Everyone can do better." What happens when others slack off and are not perfect? The perfectionist becomes anxious because the lack of perfect behavior in others arouses his own feelings of self-belittlement. His feeling is that no one ever succeeds, including himself. His striving is a desire to escape this constant feeling of "I could have done better."

In relationships, the message is, "You could have done better." There is always the elusive promise of future acceptance if only a better job is done. But it never really occurs. The perfectionist's communication patterns reflect his feelings. By continuing to use the same belittling expressions and statements he undermines himself and his relationships.

We do not need a list of achievements to prove ourselves as persons of worth. When we think of our worth as an achievement rather than a gift we end up on a treadmill. We need not fear losing our worth, because God's estimation of us is not based upon our qualifications. He created us in His image as persons of value and worth. If we feel our worth has to be achieved, then we must be constantly concerned about any threat to our performance.

The perfectionist's fear of failure is a fear of the sense of worthlessness. He has learned to focus more on what he lacks than on what he has. But when we can believe that our worth is a gift from God we are free to risk, for our worth remains stable whether we achieve or not. We are free then to attempt new ventures which could actually enhance this gift of worth. God's act in our life is an emancipation. We are free from the infringement of fearful hesitation and perfectionistic striving.

WHAT DO YOU THINK?

1. In what ways do you need to be declared free?

2. What slave/master messages still bind you?

3. What do you need to ask God to free you from?

Some of us came from yet a different home environment which affects our life and our marriage. Our parents may have thought that the best way to express their love to us was through indulgence. As a child we were given, given, given! Even before we asked, we received. Even if there was no interest or need on our part, material items, attention, and services were provided. A child in this type of home atmosphere has little opportunity to learn satisfaction from his own efforts. The child is almost kept in a dependent passive state and does not learn to take initiative. Instead, he learns to expect others to provide for him and entertain him. You would probably label this person selfish or self-centered.

What kind of messages does this child receive? He believes that others will and should provide for him. He doesn't have to do much to receive attention, affection, gifts, etc. He demands whatever he wants and feels little need to provide anything in return. He is generally passive with high expectations of others. How will these childhood messages and memories affect marriage? Watch and see.

An overindulged partner expects his/her spouse to be a mind reader, and when the spouse isn't, he/she complains—not always outwardly but in his inner conversations. He feels frustrated, annoyed, restless, and hurt. When the complaints do come they may sound like this:

"My wife ought to know I like . . ."

"My wife should know how I'm feeling . . ."

"My husband ought to do most of the housework for me so I could go out . . ."

"Why should I tell him? If he truly loves me he should know what I want."

This person is a taker but not a giver. Intimacy and emotional involvement in marriage cannot develop. He has no concern over disappointing his partner. He resists any efforts on the part of his partner to become a contributing member of the marriage. He will find many ways of escaping giving.

These are just two brief illustrations of how our childhood is still with us. There are many other ways in which these patterns emerge.

Changing the Effect of Our Memories

How can the influence of our memories be changed? How can our childhood messages be altered?

Blaming our circumstances or our parents is not the solution. Our parents were human and fallible. We may feel resentment, anger, and bitterness toward them because of what they either did or did not do. But in making them our scapegoat we simply rid ourselves of the responsibility for the way we are today. We *can* do something about the *continuation* of parental attitudes and memories which continue to influence us. For these we *are* responsible. Perhaps if we become a better parent to ourselves we can become a more mature child to our parents.

Nor can we expect our parents to change in order to make our life different. Many of us move through life never having our needs for approval, acceptance, or recognition met by our parents. And we never will. No other person can make up in a few days or even months what we feel we lacked for years and years. To continue to strive to meet parental expectations or to rail against their lack of love is futile. The solution is to come to the place where we can say, "It's alright for this to have occurred. It was painful but I can go on in my life without the influence of the past. It is okay for them to be them and for me to become all that I can."

Joyce Landorf has written one of the most insightful books of our time on this topic, *Irregular People*. An irregular person is a very significant person in our life, possibly a sibling or a parent. This individual is emotionally blind to us and cannot give us what we feel we need from him or her. The irregular person continues to wound us, reinforcing some of the negative messages we've already incorporated into our life. The affirmation we want will not be coming.

In her book, Joyce shares a letter she received from Dr. James Dobson concerning her irregular person. He writes:

> Joyce, I am more convinced every day that a great portion of our adult effort is invested in the quest for that which was unreachable in childhood.
>
> The more painful the early void, the more we are motivated to fill it later in life. Your irregular person never met the needs that he should have satisfied earlier in your life, and I think you are still hoping he will miraculously become what he never has been. Therefore, he constantly disappoints you— hurts you and rejects you.
>
> I think you will be less vulnerable to pain when you accept the fact that he cannot, or will he ever, provide the love and empathy and interest that he should. It is not easy to insulate yourself in this way . . . but it hurts less to expect nothing than to hope in vain.

A GREAT PORTION OF OUR ADULT EFFORT IS INVESTED IN THE QUEST FOR THAT WHICH WAS UNREACHABLE IN CHILDHOOD.

I would guess that your irregular person's own childhood experiences account for his emotional peculiarities, and can perhaps be viewed as his own unique handicap. If he were blind, you would love him despite his lack of vision. In a sense, he is emotionally "blind." He's blind to your needs. He's unaware of the hurts behind the incidents and the disinterest in your accomplishments, and now Rick's wedding. His handicap makes it impossible for him to perceive your feelings and anticipation. If you can accept him as a man with a permanent handicap—one which was probably caused when *he* was vulnerable—you will shield yourself from the ice pick of his rejection.[3]

Here is part of the answer to freeing us up so that we don't become an irregular person to someone else. Our first step is to accept this person as he/she is, and not to expect the person to change.

The second step is to remember that this person has probably experienced the same negative treatment at some point in life. Now you have the opportunity to break the cycle. The Bible says: "*Remember ye not the former things, neither consider the things of old. Behold, I will do a new thing; now it shall spring forth; shall ye not know it? I will even make a way in the wilderness, and rivers in the desert*" (Isa. 43:18–19, KJV).

Lloyd Ogilvie suggests that "the sure sign that we have an authentic relationship with God is that we believe more in the future than in the past. The past can be neither a source of confidence nor a condemnation. God graciously divided our life into days and years so that we could let go of yesterdays and anticipate our tomorrows. For the past mistakes, He offers forgiveness and an ability to forget. For our tomorrows, He gives us the gift of expectation and excitement."[4]

Forgiveness—the Key to a New Life

"Is it fair to be stuck to a painful past? Is it fair to be walloped again and again by the same old hurt. Vengeance is having a videotape planted in your soul that cannot be turned off. It plays the painful scene over and over again inside your mind. It hooks you into its instant replays. And each time it replays, you feel the clap of pain again. Is it fair?

"Forgiving turns off the videotape of pained memory. Forgiving sets you free. Forgiving is the only way to stop the cycle of unfair pain turning in your memory."[5]

Can you accept your parents for who they are, what they may have done, and for the messages they gave you? This means forgiving to the point that you no longer allow what has occurred in the past to influence you anymore. Only by doing this can you be free—free to develop yourself, to experience life, to communicate in a new way, free to love yourself and your spouse.

Lloyd Ogilvie asks the question: "Who's your burden? Whom do you carry emotionally, in memory, or in conscience? Who causes you difficult reactions of guilt, fear, frustrations, or anger? That person belongs to God. He's carrying him or her too, you know! Isn't it about time to take the load off, face the unresolved dynamics of the relationship, and forgive and forget?"[6]

Not forgiving means inflicting inner torment upon ourselves. When we reinforce those parental messages we make ourselves miserable and ineffective. Forgiveness is saying, "It is all right, it is over, I no longer resent you nor see you as an enemy, I love you even if you cannot love me back."

Then we need to ask for a renovation of our memory. We cannot forget but we can remember factually and not emotionally.

Perhaps Webster's definition of forget would give us some insight into the attitude and response we can choose. Forget means "to lose the remembrance of . . . to treat with inattention or disregard . . . to disregard intentionally: overlook: to cease remembering or noticing . . . to fail to become mindful at the proper time."

Scripture gives us our guiding pattern for this process.

- Don't keep score anymore. "[Love] *does not act unbecomingly; it does not seek its own, is not provoked, does not take into account a wrong suffered"* (1 Cor. 13:5).
- Develop a greater love for the Word of God which will allow you *not* to be offended. *"Those who love Thy law have great peace, and nothing causes them to stumble"* (Ps. 119:165).
- Refuse to hang onto a judgmental attitude. *"Do not judge lest you be judged yourselves. For in the way you judge, you will be judged; and by your standard of measure, it shall be measured to you. And why do you look at the speck in your brother's eye, but do not notice the log that is in your own eye? Or how can you say to your brother, 'Let me take the speck out of your eye,' and behold, the log is in your own eye? You hypocrite, first take the*

log out of your own eye, and then you will see clearly enough
to take the speck out of your brother's eye" (Matt. 7:1–5).

As you learn to forgive you will be able to accept your past for
what it was and go on.

Resignation is surrender to fate.

Acceptance is surrender to God.

Resignation lies down quietly in an empty universe.

Acceptance rises up to meet the God who fills that universe
with purpose and destiny.

Resignation says, "I can't."

Acceptance says, "God can."

Resignation paralyzes the life process.

Acceptance releases the process for its greatest
creativity.

Resignation says, "It's all over for me."

Acceptance asks, "Now that I'm here, what's
next, Lord?"

Resignation says, "What a waste."

Acceptance asks, "In what redemptive way will
you use this mess, Lord?"

Resignation says, "I am alone."

Acceptance says, "I belong to you, O God."[7]

Recalling Positive Memories

Negative memories and parental messages are a part of life. But
what are the good memories? They are there but perhaps they have
lain dormant. During difficult times and distress, good memories
can bring hope and positive response. Can you recall specific times
when you experienced trust, love, forgiveness, acceptance, and
hope?

Perhaps we, like the children of Israel, need to be called back to
positive memories. Moses reminded the people to *"remember how*
the Lord your God led you all the way in the desert. . . . Observe
the commands of the Lord your God, walking in his ways and rever-
ing him" (Deut. 8:2,6, NIV). *"Do not mistreat strangers, remember*
that once you were a stranger" (see Exod. 22:21). Isaiah urged the
people to *"remember the former things long past. For I am God,*
and there is no other . . . like Me" (Isa. 46:9).

Remembering who we are in the sight of God can, in time, become a stronger memory overshadowing the negative memories from the past. God asks us to remember, to refocus our attention, to challenge our negative way of responding to life and correct it. How is this done?

First, *change the direction of your thought life and remembrances.* "Be anxious for nothing, but in everything by prayer and supplication with thanksgiving let your requests be made known to God. And the peace of God, which surpasses all comprehension, shall guard your hearts and your minds in Christ Jesus. Finally, brethren, whatever is true, whatever is honorable, whatever is right, whatever is pure, whatever is lovely, whatever is of good repute, if there is any excellence and if anything worthy of praise, let your mind dwell on these things" (Phil. 4:6–8).

Second, *identify your parental attitudes and your present reaction to them.*

Third, *identify the belittling comments which you make to yourself and challenge them.*

Fourth, *if you are a perfectionist, as you see yourself striving a little too hard, force yourself to stop sooner.* Lower expectations and reduce your efforts. At the same time keep telling yourself that you have done enough. That you are worth more than your efforts and results. Recall the values and worth you have because of God's view of you. The overindulged person's efforts, on the other hand, need to be increased. Spend more time meeting the needs of others. Become a giver.

Fifth, *commit yourself to treat yourself in a new, positive way, and not as you have treated yourself in the past.*

The more we incorporate the biblical perspective of ourselves into our consciousness, the easier it will become to overcome hurtful memories and crippling messages. For it is God that does it in us.

Who are we? How does God see us? He sees us as being worth the precious blood of Jesus. *"Or do you not know that your body is a temple of the Holy Spirit who is in you, whom you have from God, and that you are not your own? For you have been bought with a price: therefore glorify God in your body"* (1 Cor. 6:19–20). *"Knowing that you were not redeemed with perishable things like silver or gold from your futile way of life inherited from your forefathers, but with precious blood, as of a lamb unblemished and spotless, the blood of Christ"* (1 Pet. 1:18–19). *"And they sang a new song, saying, 'Worthy art Thou to take the book, and to break its seals;*

for Thou wast slain, and didst purchase for God with Thy blood men from every tribe and tongue and people and nation" (Rev. 5:9).

God knows us through and through! He is fully aware of us. *"And the Lord said to Moses, . . . 'you have found favor in My sight, and I have known you by name'"* (Exod. 33:17). *"Before I formed you in the womb I knew you, and before you were born I consecrated you"* (Jer. 1:5). *"I am the good shepherd; and I know My own, and My own know Me, . . . and I lay down My life for the sheep. . . . My sheep hear My voice, and I know them . . . and they shall never perish"* (John 10:14–15,27–28).

Dr. James Packer writes, "There is tremendous relief in knowing that His love to me is utterly realistic, based at every point on prior knowledge of the worst about me, so that no discovery now can disillusion him about me, in the way I am so often disillusioned about myself, and quench His determination to bless me . . . He wants me as His friend, and desires to be my friend, and has given His Son to die for me in order to realize this purpose."[8]

The times in our lives when we are at peace with ourselves, not bound by the past, are the times when we feel as though we belong. We feel wanted, desired, accepted, enjoyed. We feel worthy: "I count." "I am good." We also feel competent: "I can do it."

These feelings are essential for they work together to give us our sense of identity. But the times of feeling complete may be all too infrequent. Now is the time to remember our roots, our heritage.

We are created in the image of God. He wants His work to be complete in us. When we relate to His Son Jesus Christ by faith, we have the potential for a sense of inner wholeness (see Col. 2:10).

In our relationship to God we can be assured that we belong to Him. Dr. Maurice Wagner suggests that "we never outgrow the need for a parent even though we may be parents ourselves." We are responsible to God, and we relate to Him as our heavenly Parent. There is deep emotional satisfaction in relating to God as Father. For He is a Father as a father should be.

Perhaps the greatest security to be found is in the sense of parental acceptance. We read, "He [the Father] hath made us accepted in the beloved [Christ]" (Eph. 1:6). We did absolutely nothing to earn that acceptance; we submitted to Him, and He made us accepted to Himself! "God so loved the world, that He gave His only begotten Son" (John 3:16). He made us accepted because He loved us!

He is pleased to call us His sons. That gives us a position

with Him in His family. We know we are somebody to God; we have been redeemed from being a nobody!

In our relationship with the Son of God we are assured of worthiness. Being forgiven all sin, we lose our sense of guilt and the associated feelings of being a nobody, a bad person.

We also have a secure sense of competence as we relate to the Holy Spirit as our Comforter, Guide, and Source of strength. He is with us daily to face our situations with us, and He is in sovereign control of the situations that He allows us to experience.

He imparts the ability to live a godly life and maintain a relationship with God in spite of the undertow of habit and the emotional insecurities we derived from our childhood. He is our competence, making it possible to live the Christian life and hold onto the sense of being somebody in God.[9]

This is the beginning for new growth—new memories. New messages to ourselves. New self talk. New outward communication and new relationships. It is possible!

WHAT DO YOU THINK?

1. Identify any memories or messages from the past which you want to release. Describe how you will do this.

2. Which passage of Scripture from this chapter will assist you the most with your communication? Describe how this will occur.

3. Describe the memories you wish others to have of you.

4. What do you need to do at this time for them to have these memories?

_____

4
Communicating the Real You

Now THAT YOU REALIZE how your past molds your present thinking, how do you begin to communicate the real you?

Communication is the process of sharing yourself both verbally and nonverbally in such a way that the other person can understand and accept what you are sharing. Of course, it means you also have to attend with your ears and eyes so that the other person can communicate with you.

Communication is accomplished only when the other person receives the message you send, whether verbal or nonverbal. Communication can be effective, positive, and constructive, or it can be ineffective, negative, and destructive. While one spouse may intend the message to be positive, the other spouse may receive it as negative.

The Word of God is the most effective resource for learning to communicate. In it you will find a workable pattern for healthy relationships. Here are just a few of the guidelines it offers:

- *"But speaking the truth in love, we are to grow up in all aspects into Him, who is the head, even Christ"* (Eph. 4:15).

- *"A man who refuses to admit his mistakes can never be successful. But if he confesses and forsakes them, he gets another chance"* (Prov. 28:13, *TLB*).
- *"For we all stumble in many ways. If any one does not stumble in what he says, he is a perfect man, able to bridle the whole body as well"* (Jas. 3:2).
- *"Let him who means to love life and see good days refrain his tongue from evil and his lips from speaking guile"* (1 Pet. 3:10).
- *"Some people like to make cutting remarks, but the words of the wise soothe and heal"* (Prov. 12:18, *TLB*).
- *"A wise man controls his temper. He knows that anger causes mistakes"* (Prov. 14:29, *TLB*).
- *"Gentle words cause life and health; griping brings discouragement. . . . Everyone enjoys giving good advice, and how wonderful it is to be able to say the right thing at the right time!"* (Prov. 15:4,23, *TLB*).
- *"Timely advice is as lovely as golden apples in a silver basket"* (Prov. 25:11, *TLB*).
- *"A friendly discussion is as stimulating as the sparks that fly when iron strikes iron"* (Prov. 27:17, *TLB*).
- *"Pride leads to arguments; be humble, take advice and become wise"* (Prov. 13:10, *TLB*).
- *"Love forgets mistakes; nagging about them parts the best of friends"* (Prov. 17:9, *TLB*).
- *"Let all bitterness and wrath and anger and clamor and slander be put away from you, along with all malice. And be kind to one another, tenderhearted, forgiving each other, just as God in Christ also has forgiven you"* (Eph. 4:31–32).

Communication which is effective depends not so much on what is said but on why and how it is shared. Much of the conversation between married couples is simply conveying information—"I had a rough day at work today"—which is really the least important purpose of marital communication.

Why do we seek to really communicate with one another? For some of us it is a way of achieving empathy with our spouse. We want to know that our partner feels what we are feeling. We want someone to share our positive feelings and our joys, as well as our negative feelings and sorrow. Romans 12:15 exhorts us to do this.

Sometimes, rather than merely conveying information, we desire to draw the other person into our life. When we are encouraged to talk about what happened to us at work, at home, or at church, we feel accepted by our spouse.

Another reason for sharing is to ventilate anger and pain. Not only do we need to express our emotions, we also need someone to listen and accept us. We need a sounding board; however our listener needs inner security and emotional stability in order to be a sounding board.

The foregoing are a few of the reasons why we share with one another, but they all boil down to one basic need—we want to be affirmed and supported by the person we love. This kind of support reinforces our own beliefs or feelings about ourselves. We need positive (not negative) feedback that says, "You are adequate, lovable, good, nice to be around, etc." Marcia Lasswell and Norman Lobenz in their outstanding book *No-Fault Marriage* suggest four levels of support.

Support Level 1 is what we all desire. This is when one spouse is in total agreement with his partner's goals, ideas, or beliefs. Many people feel this is the only type of support that has any value. It is the easiest to give because supporting what one agrees with does not make an overwhelming demand on your love or concern.

Support Level 2 is when you do not agree with what your spouse wants to do, but you will provide support to whatever extent you can. This support is based upon respect for one's partner.

Support Level 3 is sort of a hands-off position. You disagree with your spouse and cannot give any kind of support. But you do not create problems or obstacles for him.

Support Level 4 is really *no* support. Not only do you disagree with your spouse but you attempt to prevent him from doing what he wants to do.

WHAT DO YOU THINK?

1. Give an example of a time when you experienced each support level and tell how you felt.

Support Level 1:

Support Level 2:

Support Level 3:

Support Level 4:

2. In what area of your life would you like Level 1 support from your spouse?

3. How could you express this particular concern to your spouse?

4. In what area of his/her life would your spouse like Level 1 support from you?

What Do Your Words Mean?

When a couple marries, two distinct cultures and languages come together. If each of you does not define your words, then assumptions and misunderstandings will occur. A husband tells his wife that he will be home early tonight. What is his definition of "early"? What is his wife's definition? Or when a wife responds to her husband's request, "I'll do it later," what does that loaded word "later" mean? The wife may mean, "I'll do it in three days." Her husband may interpret it as, "She'll do it in three hours."

Nonspecific commitments such as, "I'll think about it," create disagreements and frustration. The response, "Yes, I'll try," is also insufficient. Nothing may happen but the spouse can still say, "But I'm trying." A definite and specific commitment is much more acceptable.

"I will call you if I see that I will be late for dinner."

"I will help clean up the family room starting this Saturday."

"I will help you in disciplining John by . . ."

"I will have dinner ready by the time you arrive home from the office."

"I will begin praying with you, and we will pray together at least three days a week."

A significant question for couples to ask each other is, "To what extent do we both mean the same thing by the words we use?" Two people can speak Spanish and not mean the same thing. Two people can speak German and not mean the same thing. Two people can speak English and not mean the same thing. Our own experience, mind set and intent give meaning to our words. Have you ever experienced one of the following situations?

"Could I talk to you for a minute?" your spouse asks. You say yes assuming your partner means "a minute." Forty minutes later your spouse is still talking and you are becoming agitated and restless.

"Could you please pick up one or two things at the market on the way home for me?" your spouse asks. After you agree you discover that "one or two things" involves four different stops at locations scattered away from your main route home.

You're on your way home with your spouse and he/she asks, "Could you stop at the store just for a minute. I need one item." Thirty minutes later you are still waiting in the car.

Even when we raise our voices when we communicate means something different to each person. Yelling may be a normal form of expression for one person, whereas to the other it means anger and being out of control.

A husband responds to his wife's question of "How did you like the dinner?" with "Fine." To him the word means "Great; very satisfying. I like it a lot." But to his wife it means he had little interest in what he was eating. If the situation was reversed she would use several sentences and lots of adjectives to describe her delight. He uses a single word. But both people may mean the very same thing.

One of the most vicious and destructive communication techniques is silence. It can be devastating. Each of us needs to be recognized and acknowledged. But when our partner retreats into silence our very presence, existence, and significance are ignored by the most significant person in our lives. In fact, many people would consider such silence an insult!

Silence can communicate a multitude of things: happiness, satisfaction, a sense of contentment, and well-being. But more often than not it communicates dissatisfaction, contempt, anger, pouting, sulking, "who cares," "who gives a darn," "I'll show you," etc. When silence prevails there is little opportunity to resolve issues and move forward in a relationship. "Talk to me," we beg and our spouse gets angry or continues to withdraw through silence. Too many of us use silence as a weapon.

But think about the meaning of silence for a moment. What is silence? It is really a form of communication and if we respond accordingly we may get our spouse to open up. "What do you think about the question I've asked you?" you might say. Or, "Your silence is telling me something. I wonder what you're trying to communicate to me through it?" Or "I'd like to talk to you about your silence and what it does to me. But first I would like to hear what you think about your silence."

Another approach might be, "I've noticed that there are times when it is difficult for you to talk with me. Is there something I am doing that makes it so difficult for you to share with me that you would rather be silent?" If your spouse responds with an answer to this, just let him talk. Do not attempt to defend yourself. Thank him for sharing his feelings with you. If he has not told you what it is that he wants you to do differently, ask him for a suggestion.

What Do Your Nonverbals Say?

We sing, we cry, we talk, we groan, we make simple or extended sounds of happiness, joy, despair, or anger. This is verbal communication. We touch, gesture, withdraw, frown, slam doors, look at another person. These are forms of nonverbal communication.

Are you aware of the effect your nonverbal communication has upon your spouse? We use gestures, body movements, and eye expressions constantly, but often our awareness of them is minimal. Frequently our words convey a message of approval or permission, but our nonverbals express a conflicting message of disapproval. This means the listener *hears* approval and *sees* disapproval. The result is confusion. Often the listener ignores the spoken message and responds to the nonverbal. Or if he does respond to the words, the speaker becomes irritated and the listener wonders why the speaker is upset.

Body movements provide a basis for making some reasonable assumptions but not for drawing absolute conclusions. It is important, therefore, that couples learn to do the following:

1. Become aware of the nonverbal messages *you* send your spouse.
2. Become skillful in correctly interpreting the nonverbals which your spouse sends you.
3. Develop a fluency in your nonverbal skills.
4. Learn how to bring your nonverbal communication and your spoken communication into harmony.

Nonverbal communication is similar to a code. We need to learn to decipher it, modify, refine, and enhance it. Tone of voice and inflection add another element to the communication process. The mixture can be rather complicated.

WHAT DO YOU THINK?

1. Let's consider what some nonverbal or voice behaviors might mean. Look at the following list and try to give two or three meanings to each behavior.

a. A child nods his head up and down.

b. A person turns her head rapidly in a certain direction.

c. A person smiles slightly.

d. A person's lower lip quivers slightly.

e. A person speaks in a loud, harsh voice.

f. A person speaks in a low, monotonous voice.

g. A person suddenly opens his eyes wide.

h. A person keeps her eyes lowered as she speaks to you.

i. A person speaks in a very halting or hesitant voice.

j. A person yawns during a conversation.

k. A person shrugs his shoulders.

l. A person is sitting rigid and upright in her chair.

m. A person has his arms folded tightly across his chest.

n. A person wrings her hands.

o. A person holds his chair tightly with his hands.

p. A person's breathing is quite irregular.

q. A person starts to turn pale.

r. A person keeps fiddling with his shirt collar.

s. A person slouches in her chair.

t. A person is constantly squirming.

u. A person inhales quickly.

v. A person continuously moves her legs back and forth.

w. A person hits his forehead with his hand.

2. If you would like to know more about the nonverbal behaviors in your family, conduct the following experiment. Make a list of as many of your own nonverbal behaviors as you can think of. Ask each member of the family to do the same project. After you have made your list, indicate in writing what you think each behavior means to the other members of the family. Ask them to do the same. Then discuss your responses together.

3. There are many ways to strengthen your communication skills. Here are some suggestions for both husband and wife:

a. Describe in writing what your spouse does when he/she is telling you by nonverbals that he/she cares for you, loves you, thinks highly of you, etc.

b. Describe in writing your partner's nonverbals when he/she is telling you he/she respects or approves of something you are doing or intend to do.

c. Describe in writing what your spouse does nonverbally when you think he/she does not approve of what you are doing or saying.

d. Describe in writing what you do when you tell your spouse by nonverbals that you care for, love, and think highly of him.

e. Describe in writing your nonverbals when your spouse is telling you he/she respects or approves of something you are doing or intend to do.

f. Describe in writing what you do nonverbally when you think he/she does not approve of what you are doing or saying.

Spend thirty minutes sharing your answers with each other. Give a visual demonstration or example with each statement. This could prove to be very enlightening and entertaining as well.

4. Each of you might keep a written list of the many nonverbals your spouse exhibits over a week's time. At the end of the week sit down and discuss what you saw and what you thought these nonverbals meant. Ask your spouse to clarify uncertain or incorrect meanings.

A wife might share her observations with her husband in the following manner: "Honey, I noticed that there were three mornings this week when the corners of your mouth were turned down and you were rubbing your hands together much of the time. There were also mornings when you were short with the kids and appeared a bit grumpy. When I see these nonverbals it tells me that you are having a grumpy morning. Am I right?"

Or "I've noticed that when you are doubtful about something another person says, you raise and lower your eyebrows and move your head a bit from side to side. Are you aware of this?"

How Do You Ask Questions?

The effective use of questions is a tremendous skill for clarifying communication. Avoid questions that begin with "why" because they often create confusion and defensiveness. Questions such as "Why did you do that?" "Why are you so late?" "Why do you always do that?" often produce frustrating answers like *"Because!"* or "I don't know."

A "what" question with its variations—"Who?" "Which?" "When?" "Where?" and "How?"—is far better.

Notice the difference between these two interchanges.

"Why are you unsure of what to say?"

"I don't know. I just am."

"What is it that you are unsure of?"

"I think that I am not certain of . . ."

Using a "what" question does not guarantee a response but there is a greater chance of it happening than if you ask "why?"

A "why" question can bring a halt to the communication process. A "what" question is more likely to continue the interchange.

Here is a list of some "what" questions and their uses:

Husband: "I'm not sure I want to go to that church function."
    Wife: *"What* is it that you are not sure about?"

    Wife: "I can't get all these projects done this week, John."
Husband: "All right. What is preventing you from getting them done or at least starting?"

    Wife: "Let's work on that next month instead of now."
Husband: "No. In what way will our situation be different next month?"

Husband: "Boy, I just don't know about that."
    Wife: "What is it that you don't know about? Or if you did know, what do you think your answer would be?"

Husband: "I don't think we will be able to go to your parents this holiday."
    Wife: "Well, what changes or circumstances would it take for us to be able to go?"

    Wife: "I don't believe that at all!"
Husband: "What is it you don't believe?"

    Wife: "Let's do that this summer."
Husband: "How will our finances be any different then?"

Go back over all of these examples. Substitute the question "why" for each one. What kind of response would "why" elicit as compared to the response which was given?

Are You Visual, Feeling, or Auditory?

Communication means different things to different people. In counseling married couples who are having "communication" problems, it soon becomes apparent that each person has a different communication style. As I mentioned earlier in this chapter, when a couple marries, two different cultures and languages come together. For a relationship to blossom, each must learn the other's language. And each must be willing to use the other's language without demanding that the other person become like him/her.

When people communicate they process their information in different ways. Some people are more *visual,* some are more *auditory,* and some are more *feeling* oriented. Some people think by generating visual images in their minds; some respond from the feeling level; others talk to themselves and hear sounds. (No, they aren't wacky!)

You may be primarily a visual person. You see the sentences that you speak in your mind. Another person responds best to what he hears. The feeling person has a heightened sense of touch and emotion or intuition. He responds on the basis of his feelings.

Each of us has a dominant mode of perception. We have been trained to function primarily in that mode. *But it is possible for a person to learn to function and communicate in the other modes as well.* What are you like? Are you primarily a visual, auditory, or feeling person? What is your spouse? Are you aware of your differences and similarities? Can you communicate or do you usually pass one another in the night?

An easy way to understand the way in which you and your spouse communicate is to pay attention to the words, images and phrases you both use.

What do these phrases say to you?

"I *see* what you are saying."

"That *looks* like a good idea. *Show* me more about it."

"I would like to know your *point of view.*"

"Let's *focus* in on just one subject."

These phrases reflect a visual bias. The person thinks and speaks on the basis of strong visual pictures. Other people see vague pictures, and some no pictures at all.

"I hear you."

"Boy, that *sounds* great to me."

"*Tell* me that again."

"That's coming through *loud and clear.*"

"Let's *hear* that again."

These phrases come from a person who is basically auditory. Sounds are of primary importance to him.

"I *sense* that you are upset with me."

"This gun has a good *feel* to me."

"My *instincts* say this is the right thing to do."

These are phrases coming from a person who responds in a feeling mode. Perhaps you have been in a group where a new idea has been shared. If, at that time, you had been aware of these three modes of responding you may have heard, "That idea *feels* good," "That idea *looks* good," and, "That *sounds* like a good idea." They all mean the same thing but are presented via three different processes.

What does all this have to do with husband-wife communication? Just this! If you learn to use your spouse's style of speaking *(perceptual mode)* he or she will listen to you. It may be a bit of work and take you a while to become skillful at it but it can work. Too often we expect our spouse to cater to us and do it our way. But if we are willing to take the initiative and move into his/her world first, then we establish a common ground for communication.

There are occasions when you may feel that your spouse is resisting your idea or suggestion. It could be that you have failed to communicate in a way that he/she can understand. If you ask a question and do not receive the right response, switch to another way of asking the question. "How does this sound to you?" No response. "Does this look all right to you?" No response. "How do you feel about this issue?" A response!

A wife asks her husband to complete a chore. He responds by saying, "Write it down," or "Make me a list." If in the future she makes a list or note and gives it to him at the same time she tells him, she may get a quicker response.

Once you are able to communicate with your spouse in his mode, your spouse may be willing to move into your world. If you learn to see, hear, and feel in the same way that your spouse sees, hears, and feels, communication is bound to improve. We all use all three modes, but one is better developed in each of us than the others.

IF YOU ASK A QUESTION AND DO NOT RECEIVE THE RIGHT RESPONSE, SWITCH TO ANOTHER WAY OF ASKING THE QUESTION.

I have found these principles essential in communicating with my clients in the counseling office. As I listen I try to discover their perceptual mode so that I can enter into their world with them. I listen also to their tone of voice and phrases. I study their nonverbals. Some couples are loud, expressive, gesture a lot, use many nonverbals. Others come in and are somewhat quiet, reserved, very proper, and choose their words carefully. I need to communicate as they do first so that eventually they are willing to listen and move the direction I would like them to move.

Basically I am a visual person, but I have learned to use all three modes. I still prefer the visual, however. If someone brings me a letter or something he has written and says, "Listen to this," my first response is, "Oh, let me see it." I prefer reading it myself rather than listening to it being read. It registers more with me and I digest it more quickly. When I discover some new exciting material that I would like to share with my students, my first inclination is, "How can I diagram this and use it on charts and overhead transparencies so others can see it?" I am more conscious of my tendency to use "visual" words. But not everyone else responds the way I do. Thus I need to broaden my responses to include the auditory and feeling modes. By doing this, others can understand me and I can better understand them as well—and so can you.

WHAT DO YOU THINK?

What can you and your spouse do to develop your communication?

1. Become more sensitive to the words and phrases others use. Listen to a friend or colleague, or listen to someone on TV or radio. Can you identify the person's perceptual mode?

2. Make a list of the various phrases you use during the day. What is your dominant mode?

3. Make a list of the various phrases your spouse uses. What is his or her dominant mode? Practice using that style. You may need to expand your vocabulary so that you are better able to speak your spouse's language. Unfortunately there is no Berlitz language course to teach you this new language. It is something you will have to teach yourself.[1]

5
The Gift of Listening

ONE OF THE GREATEST gifts one person can give to another is the gift of listening. It can be an act of love and caring. Too often conversations today between married couples are dialogues of the deaf. If a husband listens to his wife, she feels, "I must be worth hearing." If a wife ignores her husband, he thinks, "I must be dull and boring."

Have you had the experience of being really listened to? Look at these verses from the Word of God that talk about how God listens:

- *"The eyes of the Lord are toward the righteous, and His ears are open to their cry. The face of the Lord is against evildoers, to cut off the memory of them from the earth. The righteous cry and the Lord hears, and delivers them out of all their troubles. The Lord is near to the brokenhearted, and saves those who are crushed in spirit"* (Ps. 34:15–18).

- *"I love the Lord, because He hears my voice and my supplications. Because He has inclined His ear to me, therefore I shall call upon Him as long as I live"* (Ps. 116:1–2).

- *"Call to Me, and I will answer you, and I will tell you great and mighty things, which you do not know"* (Jer. 33:3).

The Word of God also gives us directives concerning how *we* are to listen:
- *"He who gives an answer before he hears, it is folly and shame to him"* (Prov. 18:13).
- *"Any story sounds true until someone tells the other side and sets the record straight"* (Prov. 18:17, TLB).
- *"The wise man learns by listening; the simpleton can learn only by seeing scorners punished"* (Prov. 21:11, TLB).
- *"Let every man be quick to hear* (a ready listener)*"* (Jas. 1:19, AMP).

What do we mean by listening? What do we mean by hearing? Is there a difference? Hearing is basically to gain content or information for your own purposes. Listening is caring for and being empathic toward the person who is talking. Hearing means that you are concerned about what is going on inside *you* during the conversation. Listening means you are trying to understand the feelings of *the other person* and are listening for his sake.

Let me give you a threefold definition of listening. Listening means that when your spouse is talking to you:

1. You are not thinking about what you are going to say when he/she stops talking. You are not busy formulating your response. You are concentrating on what is being said and are putting into practice Proverbs 18:13.

2. You are completely accepting what is being said without judging what he/she is saying or how he/she says it. You may fail to hear the message if you are thinking that you don't like your spouse's tone of voice or the words he/she is using. You may react on the spot to the tone and content and miss the meaning. Perhaps he/she hasn't said it in the best way, but why not listen and then come back later when both of you are calm and discuss the proper wording and tone of voice? Acceptance does not mean you have to agree with the content of what is said. Rather, it means that you understand that what your spouse is saying is something he/she feels.

3. You should be able to repeat what your spouse has said and what you think he/she was feeling while speaking to you. Real listening implies an obvious interest in your spouse's feelings and

opinions and an attempt to understand them from his/her perspective.

Failing to listen may actually increase the amount of talking coming your way. Joyce Landorf explains:

> Your wife may be a compulsive talker. Was she always that way, even before you were married? Or did she just seem to get that way with time? Some women talk at the moment of birth and a steady stream follows each moment of their lives forever after, but others have developed a nonstop flow of talk for other reasons. Many times a compulsive talker is really shouting to be heard by someone. The more bored you look, the more you yawn, the more you watch the dog or TV, the harder she talks. She just talks all the more to compensate. You may have stopped listening a long time ago, and she knows that better than anybody.
>
> Do you think this has happened to you? When was the last time that you asked these questions of your wife? "How do you feel about . . . ?" and/or "What happened here at home today?" Do you ever intersperse her remarks with, "You may be right, Hon." If your wife feels you are not willing to listen to her, she has two options: to talk louder and harder; or to talk less and withdraw. Either way, it's very hard on the marriage.[1]

You can learn to listen, for it is a skill to be learned. Your mind and ears can be taught to hear more clearly. Your eyes can be taught to see more clearly. But the reverse is also true. You can learn to *hear* with your *eyes* and *see* with your ears. Jesus said: *"Therefore I speak to them in parables; because while seeing they do not see, and while hearing they do not hear, nor do they understand. And in their case the prophecy of Isaiah is being fulfilled, which says, 'You will keep on hearing, but will not understand; and you will keep on seeing, but will not perceive; for the heart of this people has become dull, and with their ears they scarcely hear, and they have closed their eyes lest they should see with their eyes, and hear with their ears, and understand with their heart and turn again, and I should heal them'"* (Matt. 13:13–15).

Let your ears hear and see.

Let your eyes see and hear.

The word *hear* in the New Testament does not usually refer to an auditory experience. It usually means "to pay heed." As you listen to your spouse you need "to pay heed" to what he or she is sharing. It means tuning into the right frequency.

Because of my retarded son, Matthew, who does not have a vocabulary, I have learned to listen to him with my eyes. I can read his nonverbal signals which carry a message. Because of Matthew I have learned to listen to what my counselees cannot put into words. I have learned to listen to the message behind the message—the hurt, the ache, the frustration, the loss of hope, the fear of rejection, the feeling of betrayal, the rejection, the joy, the delight, the promise of change. I reflect upon what I see on a client's face, his posture, walk, pace, and tell him what I see. This gives him an opportunity to explain further what he is thinking and feeling. He *knows* I'm tuned in to him.

Three Components of Communication

Every message has three components: (1) the actual content, (2) the tone of voice, and (3) the nonverbal communication. It is possible to express many different messages using the same word, statement, or question simply by changing our tone of voice or body movement. Nonverbal communication includes facial expression, body posture, and actions.

The three components of communication must be complementary in order for a simple message to be transmitted. One researcher has suggested that successful communication consists of 7 percent content, 38 percent tone of voice, 55 percent nonverbal communication.

We often send confusing messages because the three components are contradicting each other. When a man says to his wife with the proper tone of voice, "Dear, I love you," but with his head buried in a newspaper, what is she to believe? When a woman asks, "How was your day?" in a flat tone while passing her husband on the way to the other room, what does he respond to, the verbal or nonverbal message?

A husband, as he leaves for work, comes up to his wife, smiles, gives her a hug and a kiss, and states in a loving voice, "I really love you." After he leaves she feels good. But when she notices the newspaper in the middle of the room, pajamas on the bed, dirty socks on the floor, and the toothpaste tube with the cap off lying in the sink, her good feeling begins to dissipate. She has told her husband how important it is to her that he assume responsibility for cleaning up after himself because it makes extra work for her when he doesn't. But he has been careless again. She believed him when he left for work, but now she wonders, "If he really meant what he said and really loves me, why doesn't he show it by assuming some responsibility? I wonder if he really does love me." His earlier actions contradicted his message of love, even though the message may have been sent properly.

Concerning nonverbal communication, Dr. Mark Lee writes:

Marital problems may grow out of unsatisfactory nonverbal communications. Vocal variables are important carriers of meaning. We interpret the sound of a voice, both consciously and subconsciously. We usually can tell the emotional meanings of the speaker by voice pitch, rate of speech, loudness, and voice quality. We can tell the sincerity or insincerity, the conviction or lack of conviction, the truth or falsity of most statements we hear. When a voice is raised in volume and pitch, the words will not convey the same meaning as when spoken softly in a lower register. The high, loud voice, with rapid rate and harsh quality, will likely communicate a degree of emotion that will greatly obscure the verbal message. The nonverbal manner in which a message is delivered is registered most readily by the listener. It may or may not be remembered for recall. However, the communicator tends to recall what he said rather than the manner of his speech.[2]

There are many types of listening. Some people listen for facts, information, and details for their own use. Others listen because they feel sorry for the person. They feel a sense of pity. Some people listen to gossip because they revel in the juicy story of another person's failures or difficulties. There are occasions when people listen out of obligation, necessity, or to be polite. Some who listen are nothing more than voyeurs who have an incessant need to pry and probe into other people's lives.

Some listen because they care. Why do you listen? What are your motives? Any or all of the above? Listening which springs from caring builds closeness, reflects love, and is an act of grace.

Sensitive listening and hearing are open mine shafts to intimacy. Too often the potential for listening lies untapped within us like a load of unmined gold. All of us have barriers which inhibit our listening. Some are simple and others complex.

Obstacles to Listening

In order for caring listening to occur we need to be aware of some of the common listening obstacles to communication.

Defensiveness is a common obstacle. We are busy in our minds thinking up a rebuttal, an excuse, or an exception to what our spouse is saying. In doing this we miss the message. There are a variety of defensive responses.

1. *Perhaps we reach a premature conclusion.* "All right, I know just what you're going to say. We've been through this before and it's the same old thing."

2. *Or we may read into his/her words our own expectations, or project onto another person what we would say in the same situation.* David Augsburger writes, "Prejudging a communication as uninteresting or unimportant lifts the burden of listening off one's shoulders and frees the attention to wander elsewhere. But two persons are being cheated: the other is not being given a fair hearing, and the listener is being deprived of what may be useful information. I want to cancel all advance judgments—prejudgments—and recognize them for what they are, prejudices. I want to hear the other in a fresh, new way with whatever energies I have available."[3]

Two other defensive indicators may be 3. *rehearsing our responses* or 4. *responding to gun-power words.* Rehearsing a response (as well as other defensive postures) is not what the Scripture is calling us to do as a listener. *"He who answers a matter before he hears the facts, it is folly and shame to him"* (Prov. 18:13, AMP).

Gun-power words hook you into a negative defensive response. They create an inner explosion of emotions. Gun-power includes, "That's crude"; "That's just like a *woman* (or man)"; "You're *always* late"; "You *never* ask me what I think"; "You're becoming just like your mother." Not only do we react to gun-power words but we may consciously choose to use some which makes it difficult for our spouse to listen. What are the gun-power words that set you off? What is your spouse's list of gun-power words? Certain selected words can cut and wound.

Not all defensiveness is expressed. Outwardly we could be agreeing but inside we are saying just the opposite. If your spouse confronts you about a behavior or attitude you display that is creating a problem, do you accept the criticism or defend yourself?

Look at the guidance of Scripture:

- *"If you refuse criticism you will end in poverty and disgrace; if you accept criticism you are on the road to fame"* (Prov. 13:18, *TLB*).
- *"Don't refuse to accept criticism; get all the help you can"* (Prov. 23:12, *TLB*).
- *"It is a badge of honor to accept valid criticism"* (Prov. 25:12, *TLB*).
- *"A man who refuses to admit his mistakes can never be successful. But if he confesses and forsakes them, he gets another chance"* (Prov. 28:13, *TLB*).

Another listening barrier may be attitudes or biases we hold toward certain individuals. These could include people who speak in a certain tone of voice, ethnic groups, the opposite sex, people who remind us of someone from our past, etc. Because of our biases we reject the person or the personality without listening to what the person has to say. In effect we are saying, "If you're————(and I don't like people who are————) I don't need to listen to you."

Our own personal biases will affect how well we listen more than we realize. For example, it may be easier for us to listen to an angry person than a sarcastic person; or some tones or phrases are enjoyable to listen to, whereas others may be annoying; repetitive phrases which another uses (and may be unaware of) can bother us; excessive gestures such as talking with the hands or waving arms can be a distractor.

Some people are distracted in their listening because of the sex of the person who is speaking. Our expectations of what a man shares and doesn't share and what a woman should or should not share will influence us.

We may listen more or less attentively to someone who is in a position over us, under us, or in a prestigious position.

We may assign stereotypes to other people, and this influences our listening to them.

One person hears with optimism and another with pessimism. I hear the bad news and you hear the good news. If your spouse shares a frustration and difficult situation with you, you may not hear him because you don't like complaining; it bothers you. Or you may hear him as a person who trusts you enough to share.

Our own inner struggles may block our listening. We have difficulty listening when our emotional involvement reaches the point

GUNPOWER WORDS CAN HOOK YOU INTO
A NEGATIVE, DEFENSIVE RESPONSE.

where we are unable to separate ourselves from the other person. You may find it easier to listen to the problems of other people rather than your own spouse's. You are hindered by your emotional involvement. Listening may also be difficult if you blame yourself for the other person's difficulties.

Hearing what someone else is saying may bring to the surface feelings about similar problems we are facing. Our listening may be hindered if we are fearful that our own emotions may be activated too much. A man may feel very ill at ease as his emotions begin to surge to the surface. Can you think of a time when in listening to another person you felt so overwhelmed with feelings that you were unable to hear?

If someone has certain expectations for you, you may be hindered in listening to that person. If you dislike the other person you probably will not listen to him very well. When people speak too loudly or softly you may struggle to keep listening.

Do you know what the hindrances are to your listening? Who is responsible for the obstacle? Your partner or you?

You can overcome the obstacles. The initial step is to identify the obstacle. Of those listed, which obstacle do you identify as yours? Who controls this barrier? You or the one speaking? Perhaps you can rearrange the situation or conditions so listening would be easier. You may need to discuss as a couple what each of you can do to become a better listener and what you can do to make it easier for your spouse to listen to you.

Another obstacle which hurts the listening process is similar to defensiveness—it is interrupting. You may erect this barrier because you feel the other person is not getting to the point fast enough. Or you may be thinking ahead and start asking for information which would be forthcoming anyway. Your mind wanders and races ahead. You say, "Hold it. I've got a dozen ideas cooking because of what you said. Let me tell you some of them . . . " It is easy for our minds to wander, for we think at five times the rate we can speak. If a person speaks at 100 words a minute and you listen to 500, do you put your mind on hold or daydream the rest of the time? We process information faster than it can be verbalized, so we can choose to stay in pace with the speaker or let our minds wander.

You may find yourself facing yet another obstacle—overload. Perhaps you have used up all the space available in your mind for information. Someone else comes along with a new piece of information and you feel you just can't handle it. You feel as though you are being bombarded from all sides and you don't have enough time to digest it all. Thus it becomes difficult to listen to anything. Your mind feels like a juggler with too many items to juggle.

Timing is another common obstacle. Have you ever heard comments such as these, "Talk? Now? At 2:30 in the morning?" "Just a minute. There's only thirty-five seconds left in the final quarter of the game." "I'd like to listen but I'm already late for an appointment."

Physical exhaustion presents another obstacle. Both mental and physical fatigue make it difficult to listen. There are times when you need to let your partner know that this is not a good time, but tell him/her when you *will* be able to listen.

Have you heard of selective attention? Another way of expressing this obstacle is *filtered listening,* screening the information being shared. If we have a negative attitude we may ignore, distort, or reject positive messages. Often we hear what we want to hear or what fits in with our mind set. If we engage in selective listening we probably engage in selective retention. That means we remember certain comments and situations and forget those which we reject. David Augsburger describes the process this way:

> Memory is the greatest editor of all, and it discards major pieces of information while treasuring trifles. When I try to work through an unresolved conflict that is only an hour old, I find my memory—which I present as though it were complete, perfect and unretouched—is quite different from my partner's—which I can see is partial, biased and clearly rewritten. We both have selective memories.
>
> Selectivity is an asset. It saves us from being overloaded with stimuli, overwhelmed with information, overtaxed with demands from a humming, buzzing environment.
>
> Selectivity is also a liability. If I deny that it is taking place there will be much that I don't see, and I won't see that I don't see. If I pretend I saw it all, understood it all, recall it all, there will be many times when I will argue in vain or cause intense pain in relationship with my inability to hear the other whose point of view is equally good, although probably as partial as my own. We each—even at our best—see in part, understand only in part, and recall only a small part.[4]

Steps to Better Listening

How can you become a better listener?

Understand what you feel about your spouse. How you view your spouse affects how you listen to him or her. A partner's communication is colored by how you view him. This view may have been shaped by your observations of his past performance or by your own defensiveness.

Listen with your ears, your eyes, and your body. If your partner asks, "Are you listening to me?" and you say, "Yes" while walking away or fixing dinner or doing the dishes, perhaps you aren't really listening. Concentrate on the person and the message, giving your undivided attention. Turn off the appliance or TV when there is an important matter to talk about; set aside what you are doing and listen.

There are several responses that you could make to indicate to your spouse that you are listening and catching all of what he is saying.

1. *Clarifying* is one of these responses. This response reflects on the true meaning and the intention of what has been said. "I think what you're saying is that you trust me to keep my promise to you, but you are still a bit concerned about my being away just before your birthday."

2. *Observing* is another skill. This response focuses upon the non-verbal or tonal quality of what your partner has said. "I noticed that your voice was dropping when you talked about your job."

3. Another response is called *reflective listening.* A reflective statement attempts to pick up the feelings expressed. Usually a feeling word is included in the response, such as, "You seem quite sad (joyful, happy, delighted, angry, etc. about that."

4. *Inquiring* is yet another helpful response. An inquiry draws out more information about the meaning of what was said. A very simple response would be, "I would like you to tell me more if you can."

Be patient, especially if your spouse is a slow or a hesitant talker. You may have a tendency to jump in whenever you can find an opening, finish a statement, or hurry him along. You cannot assume that you really know what is going to be said. You cannot read your partner's mind.

In conclusion, here are Ten Commandments for Better Listening:

    I. *On passing judgment.* Thou shalt neither judge nor evaluate until thou hast truly understood. "Hold it right there,

I've heard enough to know where you stand and you're all wet."

II. *On adding insights.* Thou shalt not attribute ideas or contribute insights to those stated. "If you mean this, it will lead to there, and then you must also mean that."

III. *On assuming agreement.* Thou shalt not assume that what you heard is what was truly said or what was really meant. "I know what you meant, no matter what you say now. I heard you with my own ears."

IV. *On drifting attention.* Thou shalt not permit thy thoughts to stray or thy attention to wander. "When you said that, it triggered an interesting idea that I like better than yours."

V. *On closing the mind.* Thou shalt not close thy mind to opposing thoughts, thy ears to opposite truths, thy eyes to other views. "After you used that sexist language I didn't hear another thing you said."

VI. *On wishful hearing.* Thou shalt not permit thy heart to rule thy mind, nor thy mind thy heart. "I just knew you were going to say that, I had it figured all along."

VII. *On multiple meanings.* Thou shalt not interpret words except as they are interpreted by the speaker. "If I were to stop breathing, would I or would I not expire?"

VIII. *On rehearsing responses.* Thou shalt not use the other's time to prepare responses of your own. "I can't wait until you need a breath! Have I got a comeback for you."

IX. *On fearing challenge.* Thou shalt not fear correction, improvement or change. "I'm talking faster and snowing you because I don't want to hear what you've got to say."

X. *On evading equality.* Thou shalt not overdemand time or fail to claim your own time to hear and be heard. "I want equal time. I want you to feel equally heard."[5]

Listen to your spouse in love. When you listen in love you are able to wait for the person to share his/her thoughts, feelings and what he or she really means.

WHAT DO YOU THINK?

1. List three steps you will take to enhance your listening ability.

2. What topic would you like your spouse to listen to with full attention?

3. Describe an experience in which you feel that God really listened to you. Have you shared this experience with your spouse?

4. Describe how you listen to the Lord.

6
Limiting Communication Potential

THERE ARE MANY communication patterns which limit the growth of closeness or intimacy. Sometimes couples simply do not have much to talk about, they have a limited repertoire. This is usually because one person—or both—never learned how to converse. Perhaps he/she never learned to allow others to talk, so he/she tends to dominate conversations. Or perhaps he/she never learned how to express emotions and feelings. Also, some are so limited in education or life experience that their range of topics for discussion is narrow. There are other reasons for poor communication.

Barriers to Communication

Sometimes we put up barriers to communication.

Avoiding topics is a common evasive technique. This is when we clearly and openly refuse to talk about a given subject or subjects. We may sidetrack the conversation when the other implies that it is coming up, or we may stop it cold when it does come up:

Wife: What happened at the doctor's office today?

Husband: Nothing.

Wife: You mean to say he told you nothing about your health?

Husband: I don't wish to talk about it. (And, in fact, he does not discuss the topic further.)

Content shifting is when a person changes the subject before any conversation occurs about it. He/she may completely ignore the question:

Wife: What happened at the doctor's office today?

Husband: I've been wondering, how Joe did in school today? Did he get his mathematics test back?

The person who changes topics is attempting to avoid responsibility. He prevents a confrontation by shifting attention to someone else. He may even make counter-accusations. Switching topics is unfair and is destructive to the process of healthy communication. There are three ways to deal with this difficulty.

1. Insist on sticking to the subject at hand but let your spouse know that you are willing to discuss the topic he brought up at a later time. "I'm willing to discuss that later on, but let's continue discussing (the first subject)."

2. Ignore the change in topic and ask for a constructive solution to the situation you are discussing.

3. Respond to your spouse's choice of subject, but come back to the original topic later on. This shows that you are concerned for your spouse's feelings, but it also indicates that the topic which you have raised must be discussed.

Another barrier to communication is *under-responsiveness*—a person says too little in response to a question. A woman who has been having pains in her legs, has a heart condition and arthritis is questioned by her husband. The doctor suspects it's phlebitis.

Husband: What happened at the doctor's office today?

Wife: Not much. He looked at my leg and ankle.
Husband: Is that all?
Wife: He took my blood pressure. (Etc., etc.)

Quibbling occurs when a person tries to clarify or dispute an irrelevant detail. In this example both partners get involved in the quibbling.

Wife: What happened at the doctor's office today?
Husband: I didn't go to the doctor's office today.
Wife: You did too.
Husband: No, I went yesterday.
Wife: I thought it was today.
Husband: No.
Wife: Are you sure?
Husband: Positive.

Quibbling often occurs in disputed versions of some past event. Each of us remembers different events with different meaning.

Wife: You came home at 1:30 that night!
Husband: Oh, no! It was 11:30. I remember you were still watching that program.
Wife: No. I looked at the clock. Besides, you know you don't remember well.

A strange form of communication distraction occurs when a person talks about something whose relationship to the immediate focus of the discussion is not clear. The discussion may involve *irrelevant examples* or ideas.

Wife: What happened at the doctor's office today?
Husband: Yes, I went to the doctor today. He said my blood pressure was a little high. I had a good lunch, turkey and stuffing. Gravy was not too good though. My heart is okay. Says I'm too fat. Need more exercise.

Topic overkill is when a person speaks excessively on a topic. A husband discusses a football game at great length. His wife indicates that she is familiar with the game; she is also finished with the subject!

Husband: That was some pass to Jones in the end zone. He was wide open. No one around. What a play!
Wife: Yes, I saw it, you know!

> *Husband:* The pass was overthrown slightly but that guy Jones got it anyway. Good hands—and he runs fast. A very crucial play.
> *Wife:* (Silence.)
> *Husband:* It was fourth down, too, just fifteen seconds left before the half . . . (etc., etc.)

Over-responsiveness involves a person speaking too long on a subject. What he says goes beyond what is called for in response to the partner's talk. The partner doesn't have a chance to respond to specific points, may remember only a portion of what is said, and may wish he hadn't asked about it in the first place!

> *Wife:* Harry, how do I recognize the Smith's house when I get to Pine Street?
> *Husband:* Well, it's halfway down the first block, on the left side. I think the drive is on the right, with a walk made out of bricks. Yes, it's painted dark green and has a mailbox in front with their name on it.
> *Wife:* Are there other green houses on the street?
> *Husband:* No, just that one.
> *Wife:* Oh, that's all I needed to know.

Defective Communication Patterns

In addition to barriers to communication described above, there are such things as defective communication patterns which can also hinder the development of a marriage.

Interruptions frustrate a partner and indicate that he/she is not listening. It is important to wait and listen while the other person is talking.

> *Husband:* Well, I think that the best solution would be for you to—
> *Wife:* No, I can't go along with . . .

Fault finding can be deadly! As each person blames the other, both become angry and intimacy is blocked.

> *Wife:* You shouldn't have gotten so angry at me when I was late.
> *Husband:* Well, I wouldn't have if you had been on time.

It doesn't help to argue about whose fault it was. It is a better use of energy to discover a solution which will satisfy both.

Trying to establish "the truth" is often futile for each one has a different view of how something happened. Neither person will change the other's memory and the ensuing argument will probably just anger both of them.

Wife: You did not come home early, it was late!
Husband: I was home on time. It was only . . .

Sidetracking breeds quarrels. It is important to not be defensive and to focus upon one issue at a time.

Husband: I'm tired of seeing dirty dishes on the sink all the time.
Wife: Well, your desk is always messy too, you know.

Then there is the *overload of complaining*. It is better to work on one issue at a time.

Wife: Well, you leave the tub full of water, clothes on the floor, the beds unmade, dishes in the sink, etc.

Placing *guilt* on the other person implies that the spouse is horrible and insensitive. Anger expressed in this guilt-producing manner creates dissension.

Wife: You just don't care about my feelings. You hurt me and you don't even care . . .

Giving ultimatums will push a spouse into a corner. He can either give in and lose face or act strong and tell you to go ahead and carry out your threat. Both breed resentment.

Husband: You do that, and I'll leave, or I'll . . .

Gun-power words such as *always* and *never* elicit a defensive response. The person being accused will remember *one* occasion when he did respond in the proper manner. A useless time-consuming argument will probably be the end result.

Wife: You never come home when you say you will.

Name-calling or *labeling* implies that the person cannot change. It is a surefire way to create anger.

Husband: You're just insensitive and undersexed.

A better way is to share with your spouse the specific behavior that you would like to see changed.

Justifying isn't always necessary. You don't have to justify or give reasons for your likes and dislikes. If you don't like something, just say you don't. Giving reasons often perpetuates a problem because now the person can attack your reasons as well as your actions. In giving your reasons you hand over control to your spouse.

> *Wife:* I don't want to go to the mountains for our vacation. As we've discussed before, I don't like heights.
> *Husband:* Why not?
> *Wife:* I don't know, I just . . .

Mind reading occurs when you tell your spouse you know what he or she is thinking. We feel resentful when someone presumes to be an authority on what we are like internally.

> *Wife:* You think I spend too much money.

Confusing messages create mistrust in any relationship. When you verbally agree but your body language conveys the opposite, what is a person to believe?

> *Wife:* Okay, if that's what you want (signs and rolls eyes).

WHAT DO YOU THINK?

1. Which of these communication difficulties occur frequently in your own relationship?

2. What will you do specifically to change any of these patterns?

3. What Scriptures would help you develop a new pattern of communication?

Critical Communication Times

There are two extremely critical times for communication between a husband and wife. Both times involve only four minutes! That's all. They are the first four minutes upon awakening in the morning and the first four minutes when you're reunited at the end of the day. These eight minutes can set the tone for the day and the evening. This is a time when couples can share their love and concern, their interests, and can affirm one another, or, they can be angry, curt, critical, or indifferent and adversely affect the rest of the day or evening.

Examine the patterns which you have established in your marriage. Do you say the same things to each other morning after morning and evening after evening? Think about the way you have responded to each other each morning for the past week and compare your responses with this list.

The Silent Partner—"Don't expect me to talk until I've had my third cup of coffee," he groans as he rejects his wife's attempts at friendliness. He is unaware of his grumpy attitude and places his faith in a magic chemical guaranteed to soothe his disposition.

The Commander—He awakens giving orders. His spouse feels as though she should salute. "Okay, we have ten minutes to get into the kitchen. I want scrambled eggs, crisp bacon, and half a grapefruit. Come on, get up. You take a shower first. I'll give you eight minutes. Then I'll shave, etc., etc."

Compulsive Groomer—She leaps out of bed as the alarm rings, and rushes to the bathroom. Her spouse is not allowed to see her or touch her until she has combed her hair, brushed her teeth and rinsed her mouth. It's probably a syndrome that originated in a TV commercial.

Efficiency Expert (her)—"You know, George, I tell you every morning, if you'd wake up at seven instead of seven-thirty, you'd have five minutes for your hot shave, seven minutes to shower, six minutes to shine your shoes, eight minutes to dress and four minutes to comb your hair. Then you could come to the kitchen just as I'm putting the eggs on the table. Now, why don't you listen? I tell you this every morning."

Efficiency Expert (him)—"You know, Helen, if you get up twelve minutes earlier, you could have the coffee ready by the time I was through shaving. Then while I showered and dressed, you could

make my lunch and finish making breakfast. We could chat for three minutes and I'd be in the car by seven-fifteen."

Affectionate Aficionado—"Come on, honey, don't pull away; you know I enjoy making love in the morning. The kids can wait a few minutes for breakfast." Not a bad way to start the day if both partners have the same urge and make time for sex without disrupting other routines. Obviously, if a couple awaken and embrace, four minutes of kissing and fondling is very likely to launch the day positively.

Trivia Trapper—"Good morning, I'll be home at five today. Have dinner ready because I have a meeting at seven. I left some clothes for the cleaners on the chair by the window. Don't forget to renew our subscription to *Time*, and have the mail sorted by the time I get home, please . . . " A guaranteed way to make your spouse feel like a hired hand.

Panic-Stricken Pessimist—"Oh, this is Wednesday. What a terrible day it's going to be. I have a deadline to meet (or three kids to drive three different places) and I haven't even started. I hate Wednesdays!" Tuesdays, Mondays, or even Sundays can also be equally cursed.

The Complainer—"Jean, did you know I've been up all night? These sheets are filthy; why weren't they changed? And there's dust all over the nightstand. When are you going to learn how to clean?" On the other hand, Jean might open the day with: "Jim, did you know I didn't sleep a wink? It's all those rotten bills we haven't paid. Why can't we balance our budget? Haven't you asked for a raise yet? I'm going crazy thinking about money, and I need a new dress for the Carsons' party."[1]

Discuss together your morning routine. Is this a time when you want closeness and intimacy, or would you prefer quiet and privacy? Try making your routine something that is satisfying to both of you and which brings you feelings of love and affirmation.

The second important time of the day has a significant impact on a couple's relationship. What happens during the first four minutes when you and your spouse are reunited at the end of the day? Is it a time of factual reports about the news, the weather, the kids' misbehavior, or other bad news? Is it a time of silence?

Some spouses complain that the family dog gets more attention than they do! And it may be true. Dogs are talked to, caressed, patted; they get their ears rubbed and their back and chin scratched. Not a bad way to greet your spouse! Touching, asking feeling questions, expressing happiness in seeing the other person should make the evening better.

A positive greeting between husband and wife can have a positive impact on other family members as well. Here are several steps to take to enhance your evening.

1. When you see each other at the end of the day give each other your undivided attention and listen with your eyes as well as your ears.

2. Don't come in with a task-oriented checklist of "Did you do . . . ?" Your spouse may end up feeling like the hired hand.

3. Touch, kiss, hug, hold—whatever is pleasing to both of you.

4. Don't make your first statement to your spouse a complaint. It will put a damper on his anticipation of seeing you.

5. Create a relaxing time. Don't immediately hit your spouse with a list of chores to do. Don't breeze in and head directly for the phone, workbench or hobby.

6. Prepare yourself mentally to greet your spouse. Spend time thinking of what you will say and do. Rehearse it in your mind. At least one night a week plan a surprise greeting—something you rarely do or have never done before.

7. Attempt to look appealing to your spouse. A quick combing of the hair or swish of mouthwash will be appreciated.

8. You could phone one another before you leave work for the day. During this time you could discuss who has the greatest need to be met when you arrive home. Some days a wife may need a half-hour relief from the kids to restore her sanity. Both of you may need a half-hour to clear your mind (after the initial four minutes) before you're human again. You might even discuss how you would like to be greeted as you reunite at the end of the day.

Communication Rules and Guidelines

All of us have rules we abide by in communication and in resolving conflict. But seldom do we define or verbalize them. Some rules are positive and healthy. Others are negative, detrimental, and continue to perpetuate communication problems.

If married couples would take the time to develop specific guidelines for communication and agree to follow them, communication could become a very positive experience. These guidelines help especially when there are differences of opinion.

A few years ago as I was working with a couple in premarital counseling, I discovered that they were having a bit of a struggle in the area of conflict. I suggested they develop a communication covenant to follow in their conversations. The next week they returned with several guidelines. I sent them out with the assignment to detail the steps involved in implementing each guideline. They returned with their list and then we spent some time refining and revising it.

Here is their unedited covenant. Would these guidelines work for you in your marriage?

Communication Covenant

This covenant will be read together each Sunday and then we will ask one another in what way can we improve our application of this covenant in our daily life.

1. We will express irritations and annoyances we have with one another in a loving, specific, and positive way rather than holding them in or being negative in general.
   A. I will acknowledge that I have a problem rather than stating that you are doing such and such.
   B. I will not procrastinate by waiting for the right time to express irritations or annoyances.
   C. I will pinpoint to myself the reason for my annoyances. I will ask myself why is it that I feel irritation or annoyance over this problem.
2. We will not exaggerate or attack the other person during the course of a disagreement.
   A. I will stick with the specific issue.
   B. I will take several seconds to formulate my words so that I can be accurate.
   C. I will consider the consequences of what I say before I say it.
   D. I will not use the words always, all the time, everyone, nothing, etc.
3. We will attempt to control the emotional level and intensity of arguments. (No yelling, uncontrollable anger, hurtful remarks.)
   A. We will take time-outs for calming down if either of us feel that our own anger is starting to elevate too much. The minimum amount of time for a time-out will be one minute and the maximum ten minutes. The person who feels he needs a greater amount of time in order to calm down will be the one

to set the time limit. During the time-out each person, by themselves and in writing, will first of all define the problem that is being discussed. Secondly, the areas of agreement in the problem will be listed and then the areas of disagreement will be listed, and then three alternate solutions to this problem will be listed. When we come back together the person who has been most upset will express to the other individual "I am interested in what you have written during our time-out and I am willing and desirous of you sharing this with me."

    B. Before I say anything I will decide if I would want this same statement said to me with the same words and tone of voice.

4. We will "never let the sun go down on our anger" or never run away from each other during an argument.

    A. I will remind myself that controlling my emotional level will get things resolved quicker and make one less inclined to back off from the problem.

    B. I am willing to make a personal sacrifice.

    C. I will not take advantage of the other by drawing out the discussion. If we have discussed an issue for 15 minutes then at that time we will then take a time-out and put into practice the written procedure discussed under #3.

5. We will both try hard not to interrupt the other person when he/she is talking. (As a result of this commitment, there will be no need to keep reminding the other person of their responsibility, especially during an argument.)

    A. I will consider information that will be lost by interrupting the other person.

    B. It is important that the person talking should be concise and to the point.

    C. I will remember that the person that was interrupted won't be able to listen as well as if I had waited for my turn.

    D. I will put into practice Proverbs 18:13 and James 1:19.

6. We will carefully listen to the other person when he/she is talking (rather than spending that time thinking up a defense).

    A. If I find myself formulating my response while the other person is talking I will say, "Please stop and repeat what you said because I was not listening and I want to hear what you were sharing."

    B. If we are having difficulty hearing one another then when a statement is made we will repeat back to the other person what we heard them saying and what we thought they were feeling.

7. We will not toss in past failures of the other person in the course of an argument.

    A. I will remind myself that a past failure has been discussed and forgiven. True forgiveness means it will not be brought up to the other person again.

    B. I will remind myself that bringing up a past failure cripples the other person from growing and developing.

    C. If I catch myself bringing up a past failure I will ask the other person's forgiveness and I will then state what it is that I am desirous that the other person will do in the future and I will commit myself to this behavior.

8. When something is important enough for one person to discuss, it is that important for the other person.

    A. If I have difficulty wanting to discuss what the other person desires to discuss I will say to them, "I know this topic is important to you and I do want to hear this even though it is a bit difficult for me."

    B. In implementing this agreement and all the principles of communication in this covenant we will eliminate outside interferences to our communication such as the radio on, television, reading books on our lap, etc. We will look at one another and hold hands during our discussion times.

DATE
SIGNED (HUSBAND)
SIGNED (WIFE)

As I have shared these guidelines with others, some people have said, "Well, they worked that out when they were engaged. Just wait until the realities of marriage sink in."

Thirteen months after their marriage I saw the couple for their last session as I do with all couples. Halfway through I asked them if they remembered the covenant they had developed previously. They said, "Oh yes, we take it out quite often for review. In fact we went through it two weeks ago and rated ourselves and each other on a scale of 1–5 for each item to see how we were doing. Then at the bottom of the covenant we wrote 'This is what I will do this next week to enhance the application of this covenant.'"

I had no further questions.

WHAT DO YOU THINK?

1. Select three items from this covenant which would help you in your communication.

2. List three of your own guidelines you would like to implement.

3. What passages from Scripture would you like to apply to your communication process?

Many couples communicate as though life is a contest. They challenge each other, compete, and continually resist each other. In our society we are taught to be competitive. We believe there are winners and losers, and it is best to be a winner (at all costs). There are many winners, however, who have won the battles but lost the war. The best way to handle another person's point of view is not to fight it but to try and find some point of agreement with it. This allows you to move along *with* the person instead of confronting him head on. The attitude needed is, "How can we both achieve some of what we want?" Life is *not* a contest! But often husbands and wives make it that way!

How can you prevent a discussion from deteriorating into a knock-down-drag-out, either verbally or physically? Consider a situation in which a husband and wife are talking about changing their vacation plans. They have been vacationing at the same spot for seven years and the husband is very comfortable with the choice. His wife would like some variety and a more active time. During the past seven years they spent their vacation time eating, fishing, doing a bit of sightseeing and a lot of loafing. Joan has broached her new suggestion to Rick.

Joan: "Well, Rick, what do you think of this suggestion?"

Rick: "Boy, it's new to me. I don't know. It comes as sort of a shock. I've been satisfied with where we've been going and I thought you were. I need to think about this."

Joan: "That's good, Rick, because we should think about it. I know you've been satisfied and so have I. Perhaps we could talk about what it is that we've enjoyed so much and what new possibilities may be available in a new vacation spot. Perhaps we'll find some overlap."

Joan accepted Rick's resistance, but she brought the attention back to her suggestion. Now they can begin to evaluate.

A second step is to agree with any feelings your spouse has expressed. Rick stated that he was a bit shocked. Joan could say, "I can appreciate your feeling shocked (or angry, fearful, confused, rejected, etc.). I can understand that you'd feel that way. I'd probably have similar feelings." Whether you feel that way or not you can validate the other person's feelings. You are not agreeing with facts or ideas. And you can share if you do have similar feelings.

Joan could also express curiosity or interest in what Rick has said. "I'm interested in what you have enjoyed so much about our vacations." Or, "Tell me some more about your feelings of shock. I'm interested in how you think and feel."

Suppose Rick and Joan continue to discuss and Rick begins to share more of his objections.

Rick: "Well, I've really enjoyed the low-key aspect of where we go. It's not busy and it doesn't take three days of driving to get there. We've met some people there who come back each year and I really enjoy seeing them."

Joan: "If I understand you, this place has become a place of relaxation for you, sort of a hideaway with selected people you enjoy."

Rick: "Yeah, I guess that's it. I'm not sure what a change would be like. This is comfortable and I'm not sure a new place would be as relaxing."

At this point Joan could ask Rick what other information it would take for him to consider a change. Very often we tell our spouses only what we want them to know in order to convince them of our new idea.

There is one other principle to follow: acknowledgement and persistence.

Rick: "Why don't we talk about this another time? Or perhaps when we do we could think about it for the following year and follow through with our plans for the same place this July."

Joan: "I can understand that you'd prefer to go to the same place, but I'd like to discuss the possibility of a new location for *this* year."

Rick: "I don't know. Let's table the discussion for now."

Joan: "I can agree to that but let's set a time to discuss it again for this year."

Rick: "Why don't we just wait and see for awhile . . ."

Joan: "I can understand that you'd rather not set a time, but I'd rather we set a time now to talk about this year's vacation."

In this last conversation Joan is acknowledging Rick's reluctance but presses ahead in spite of it. By being carefully persistent, eventually the other person may agree to setting a time to discuss this year's vacation. This approach can work very well when one person tends to wait to delay discussions and decisions.

In conclusion, here are a number of communication guidelines. Read through them and then complete the "What Do You Think?" portion at the end of the chapter.

1. Greet your spouse after a period of being separated (even if only for a few hours) with a smile, pleasant talk such as a happy greeting, touching and kissing, a compliment, humor, or recounting one of the day's interesting or "success" experiences.

2. Set aside a period of transition between work—or any potentially stressful activity—and other parts of the day. This transition time is designed to provide a "decompression period" so that any pressures, frustrations, fatigue, anger, or anxiety that may have been generated will be less likely to affect marital communication. Some men pray as they drive home, committing the day's activities to the Lord. Others visualize how they are going to respond to each family member. Some couples take twenty minutes when they arrive home to sit in a dimly lighted room and listen to a favorite record with very little talking.

3. Never discuss serious subjects or important matters that involve potential disagreement when you or your spouse are overly tired, emotionally upset, sick, injured, or in pain.

4. Set aside a special agreed-upon time every day to take up issues involving decision making, family business, disagreements, and problems. This "Decision Time" should allow for the relaxed and uninterrupted discussion of all decision-making and problem-solving activities. No other activities should be involved, such as eating, driving, or watching television. Take the phone off the hook. It may also help to set a time limit.

5. Some couples have found it helpful to save all complaints about their marriage, disagreements, and joint decisions for the scheduled Decision Time when these matters are taken up. Jot down items as they arise. When you pose a problem or lodge a complaint, be specific as to what you want from the other person. Do you want anger, defensiveness, resistance, and continuation of the problem? Or openness, cooperation, and a change on the part of the other person? The way you approach the problem will determine your spouse's response.

Example: "You are not involved enough with the children."

Better to say: "I appreciate the time you spend with the children and so do they. I know you have a lot going on but we would all appreciate your evaluating your schedule so you could spend more time with them."

Example: "You are never affectionate."

Better to say: "I enjoy the times when you touch me. I would appreciate it if you would touch me and hold me several times a day and also let me know if you like something I'm doing."

Recognition and praise of what another person has done is necessary to his sense of self-worth. It also opens the door for a person to accept a constructive suggestion.

6. In the decision sessions, try to reach a specific solution.

7. Set aside a scheduled time for noncontroversial marital conversation, every day if possible. Among the topics that could be discussed are: the experiences you each have had during the day or at other times; noncontroversial plans or decisions that involve individual partners; the couple or the family.

8. Each person should have a special "topic turning signal" to signal his or her spouse to change the conversation from a controversial topic. The signal should be an agreed-upon neutral word or phrase.

9. Do not blame your partner. Save matters of complaint and proposed change for the Decision Time.

10. Stay on the topic being discussed until each of you has had a say.

11. Avoid talk about what happened in the past or what might happen in the future if it is potentially controversial.

12. Be specific in what you talk about. Define your terms and avoid overstatement and generalities.

13. Acknowledge the main points of what your partner says with such words as "I see," "I understand," "Yes," "Um-hm."

14. Try to keep the nonverbal aspects of your communication con-

sistent with the verbal message. Don't express compliments with scowls, or an indifferent tone of voice and a pleasing facial expression.

15. Be as accurate as you can in describing objects or events for your partner. Remember you are describing it from your perspective.

16. Praise your spouse for the things he/she says that you like. Use words that you think will be appreciated.

17. Discuss topics with your partner that you know he/she will like to talk about. If your partner fails to discuss topics to your liking, do not hesitate to suggest that you would like to discuss the desired subjects further.

18. Never exaggerate in order to make a point. If you really want to persuade your spouse, write the subject down and save it for the next Decision Time.

19. Don't mind read or make presumptive statements about what your partner has said.

20. Don't quibble about minor or trivial details.

21. Respond fully but not excessively when your turn comes.

22. Repeat what you think your partner said if you have trouble understanding him or if you think you did not hear what he/she intended.

23. Help each other to follow the rules. Praise your spouse for rule-consistent talking.

WHAT DO YOU THINK?

1. Go back through the list and put your initials by each guideline that you would like to apply in your marriage. After your spouse has done the same, share your selections. Discuss the steps you will take to implement these principles in your marriage. Set a date to evaluate how these guidelines are working.

7
How Are Men and Women Different?

"OH, HE THINKS just like a man!" Betty says in exasperation. "He never seems to really understand what I'm talking about."

Her husband John says, "Look, I try to talk logic to her but she's on another wavelength. Why can't she be logical? In fact, I find most women are like that! They beat around the bush!"

Have you ever heard comments like these? Perhaps you have made similar statements because you have difficulty understanding how your partner communicates. I have heard some people say that they feel like they have married someone from a foreign country. Their spouse's language is completely foreign to them.

How different are men and women in their style of thinking? In the way they communicate? Or are there any differences? What do you think?

Look below at the list of differences between men and women that has been compiled from various sources. Think about each statement. Do you agree with them?

Male/Female Differences

1. Men and women are very different by nature in the way they think, act, respond, etc. These differences can be complementary, but very often lead to conflict in marriage.

2. A woman is an emotional-feeler; a man is a logical-thinker.

3. For a woman language spoken is an expression of what she *feels*; for a man language spoken is an expression of what he's *thinking*.

4. Language that is heard by a woman is an emotional experience; language that is heard by a man is the receiving of information.

5. Women tend to take everything personally; men tend to take everything impersonally.

6. Women are interested in the details, the nitty-gritty; men are interested in the principle, the abstract, the philosophy.

7. In material things, women tend to look at goals only; men want to know the details of how to get there.

8. In spiritual or intangible things, the opposite is true. Men look at the goals; women want to know how to get there.

9. Men are like filing cabinets. They take problems, put them in the file and close the drawer. Women are like computers; their minds keep going and going and going until the problem is solved!

10. A woman's home is an extension of her personality; a man's job is the extension of his personality.

11. Women have a great need for security and roots; men can be nomadic.

12. Women tend to be guilt-prone; men tend to be resentful.

13. Men are stable and level off; women are always changing.

14. Women tend to become involved more easily and more quickly; men tend to stand back and evaluate.

15. Men have to be told again and again; women never forget!

16. Men tend to remember the gist; women tend to remember details and distort the gist.

WHAT DO YOU THINK?

1. Go back through the list and indicate whether you agree or disagree with each statement. If you disagree, change the statement to read in such a way that you could agree with it.

2. Share your response with your spouse and discuss how you see each other.

3. If a person believes these statements, how would it affect the way he responds to members of the opposite sex?

4. If there are distinct differences between men and women, are these differences because that is the way men and women are created, or are these differences learned and developed?

Actual Differences

Are the differences listed really true? And if they are, is that bad or good? Some people have very definite beliefs about men and women. And those beliefs color the way they behave and respond to others, including their spouse. Let's take a look at some of the actual proven differences between men and women. Genesis 1:27 says: *"Male and female He created them."* Right from the beginning, the Bible says, there was a difference. God wanted male and female to be different. So, first of all, there are numerous physical differences between men and women.

Dr. David McClelland of Harvard concludes that literally thousands of studies show that significant sex differences exist. In all human societies men are larger and stronger than women. The average man is 6 percent taller than the average woman. Also men average about 20 percent more weight than women. This is caused by greater body bulk, mainly from larger muscles and bones. Large muscles in males permit them to lift more weight, throw a ball farther or run faster than most women. Even at birth the male has more strength to lift his head higher and for longer periods of time than do females. At puberty the difference in male strength is accentuated, largely due to testosterone.

Men have a higher metabolic rate. They produce more physical energy than women and thus need more food to keep the body performing to its full potential. Women are usually a few degrees cooler than men, and may therefore require less food to maintain a constant weight. Men's blood is richer than women's with an average of 300,000 more red corpuscles per cubic millimeter.[1]

Does this mean that men are physically superior to women? Some people draw that conclusion (especially men!). But recent research indicates that women actually possess certain biological advantages when they are compared with men.

- 130–150 males are conceived for every female, but by the time of birth there are only 106 boys to every 100 girls.
- 25 percent more boy babies are born prematurely than girl babies.
- During the first year the mortality rate among boys is almost one-third higher than among girls.
- Circulatory and respiratory infection and digestive diseases affect boys in greater numbers than girls.
- Boys have more genetic defects than girls.

But what about psychological differences? This is the area that affects communication between men and women. People tend to take extreme views on this particular issue. Some say men and women are totally different mentally, and others say there are no psychological or mental differences between the sexes. There are some differences between the sexes but they may not be as extensive as some would like to think. In some areas men and women are very much alike and in some areas they are different.

WHAT DO YOU THINK?

1. Before you proceed in your reading make a list of the ways you and your spouse are different because of sex. Make a specific list of your unique qualities and your spouse's unique qualities.

2. Indicate which of these you think you could change and how you would make these changes.

Stanford University researchers Dr. Carol N. Jacklin and Dr. Eleanor E. Maccoby released a study in 1974 *(The Psychology of Sex Differences)* in which they reviewed and summarized over 2,000 books and articles on the subject. Several conclusions regarding male/female differences were presented:

> Males have superior verbal ability, males excel at visual-spatial tasks, and males are better at math. In addition, the researchers believed that the evidence was sufficient to reject eight myths about sex differences. They concluded that the sexes do not differ in (1) sociability, (2) self-esteem, (3) motivation to achieve, (4) facility at rote learning, (5) analytic mindedness, (6) susceptibility to environmental influences, or (7) response to auditory/visual stimuli. These characteristics are not biological in nature.[2]

Some other differences have been noted as well. Women are more likely than men to express their emotions and display empathy and compassion in response to the emotions of others. Men as a whole are more skillful than women at visually perceiving spatial or geometric features of objects. Females tend to be more anxious than males about risking failure. When they fail they are more likely to blame themselves. When males fail, they tend to blame others.

Culture plays a large part in our determination of what is masculine and what is feminine. Too many men live by these Ten Commandments of Masculinity (by Warren Farrell).

1. Thou shalt not cry or expose other feelings or emotion, fear, weakness, sympathy, empathy or involvement before thy neighbor.
2. Thou shalt not be vulnerable, but honor and respect the "logical," "practical," or "intellectual"—as thou defines them.
3. Thou shalt not listen, except to find fault.
4. Thou shalt condescend to women in the smallest and biggest of ways.
5. Thou shalt control thy wife's body, and all its relations.
6. Thou shalt have no other egos before thee.
7. Thou shalt have no other breadwinners before thee.
8. Thou shalt not be responsible for housework—before anybody.
9. Thou shalt honor and obey the straight and narrow pathway to success: job specialization.
10. Thou shalt have an answer to all problems at all times.[3]

As I have conducted marriage enrichment seminars with thousands of couples across the country over the past ten years, many wives have shared the same concern: "Men do not share their emotions sufficiently." These women say they do not know what their husbands are feeling or if they are feeling. The husbands avoid being known. (This appears to be true in their relationships with other men as well as women. See David Smith's excellent book *The Friendless American Male*, Regal Books.)

Many men do not have a sufficient vocabulary to express their emotions. As they were learning to be men they learned to value expressions of masculinity and to devalue what they labeled "feminine" expressions. These men are locked up emotionally. They are not comfortable sharing their failures, anxieties or disappointments. An indicator of being a man is "I can do it by myself. I don't need any help." Unfortunately this leads to the inability to say "help me" when help is desperately needed. Masculinity means not depending on anybody. Dependence is equated with being a parasite. These men resist being dependent. This often shows up in the man's obsession with his work, his inability to relax and play—unless he is in a highly competitive situation, and his struggle with weekends and vacations.

Many men think that all feelings are "weaknesses." Sympathy and empathy are awkward for them. Fear is one of the most difficult emotions for them to admit.

Some men (and some women) use their intellect to defend against their feelings. They may dissect, analyze, and discuss their emotions, but they do not spontaneously share them. Men and women have the same emotions. Men do NOT have different emotions than women. We simply differ in our expression of them. Many men are seen as totally cognitive or logical. Many women are seen as totally relational and feeling oriented. Could it be that we are actually both? Could it be that there are various forms of logic? Not everyone goes directly from *A* to *B* to *C*. Some leave *A* and make several side trips before coming back to *B* and then take several other side trips before arriving at *C*. Some go through this process in a few short words, others add descriptive adjectives and paint a beautiful mental picture. Consider Dr. Ross Campbell's discussion of the difference between emotional and factual communication.

> We can start by realizing that there is a difference between cognitive (that is, intellectual or rational) communications and emotional (that is, feeling) communications. Persons who communicate primarily on a cognitive level deal mainly with factual data. They like to talk about such topics as sports, the stock market, money, houses, jobs, etc., keeping the subject of conversation out of the emotional area. Usually

they are quite uncomfortable dealing with issues which elicit feelings, especially unpleasant feelings such as anger. Consequently, they avoid talking about subjects which involve love, fear, and anger. These persons have difficulty, then, being warm and supportive of their spouses.

Others communicate more on the feeling level. They tire easily of purely factual data, and feel a need to share feelings, specially with their spouses. They feel the atmosphere between husband and wife must be as free as possible from unpleasant feelings like tension, anger, and resentment. So, of course, they want to talk about these emotional things, resolve conflicts with their spouse, clear the air, and keep things pleasant between them.

Of course no one is completely cognitive or completely emotional.

/___/___/___/___/___/___/___/___/___/___/

Emotional   Cognitive

1. Indicate where you are on this graph by placing your initials near the appropriate mark.

2. Indicate where each of your family members is on the chart, using their initials.

3. Indicate where you think they would place you on the chart. Mark your initials and circle them. . . .

A person on the left side of the graph, who shares more feelings, is not less bright or less intellectual. This person is simply aware of his/her feelings and is usually better able to do something about them. On the other hand, a person on the right side of the graph, who displays less feelings, does not have less feelings; the feelings are simply suppressed and buried, and this person is less aware and often blind to his feelings.

A surprising fact is that the so-called cognitive person (on the right) is controlled by his feelings just as is the so-called emotional person but he doesn't realize it. For example, the stiff, formal intellectual has deep feelings also, but uses enormous energy to keep them buried so he won't be bothered with them. But unfortunately they do bother him. Whenever someone (like an "emotional" wife, or child) is around asking him for affection and warmth, he is not only unable to respond, he is angered that his precious equilibrium has been disturbed.[4]

One belief which some men hold is that being masculine automatically means being logical, analytical, or scientific. The word *logical* means "capable of reasoning or of using reason in an orderly cogent fashion." Therefore intuition or the ability to sense or feel what is happening is not available to many men, for that seems feminine. They believe that logic and intuition cannot work together.

Warren Farrell raises an interesting question: "Must a person who expresses emotions think without logic or does it ultimately free one to think logically?"[5] Isn't it possible that a person who is in touch with his emotions and expresses them freely may see things accurately and make decisions logically and perceptively as well? Feelings are not to be feared but experienced and expressed. They are to be accepted as one of God's gifts and used to add greater depth to life. Feelings are to be used as an inner release.

Herb Goldberg, in his enlightening book *The Hazards of Being Male,* describes the destructive consequences for a man who does not express his emotions.

1. He is vulnerable to sudden, unpredictable behavior.

2. He denies his feelings and needs and then becomes resentful because intimates take him at face value and don't read his hidden self correctly.

3. He becomes prone to emotional upsets and disturbances.

4. He becomes prone to countless psychophysiological disorders.

5. The defenses against feeling force him further and further away from relationships.

6. His inability to ask for help means that when his defenses begin to shatter, he begins to withdraw further or turns to drugs or alcohol.[6]

Lack of emotional acceptance and expression is one of the contributions to a male mid-life crisis (See *Seasons of a Marriage* for a complete discussion). A man was not created to deny his emotions. No one was. Neither were we created to just express our emotions and not use the cognitive ability God has given us. Some people's communication reflect a life devoid of correct thinking and feeling.

In His creative act God has given all of us different temperaments, talents, spiritual gifts, skills, and motivations. Our culture and upbringing, however, can create a filter which keeps us from experiencing our full creation. Soon we begin to be molded to this world. But

Paul tells us, "*Do not be conformed to this world, but be transformed by the renewing of your mind, that you may prove what the will of God is, that which is good and acceptable and perfect*" (Rom. 12:2).

Even if women are more prone to express their emotions and empathy, does the Word of God say that this is the way it was meant to be? Culture might tell us that emotions are female traits, but God's Word does not agree. Jesus expressed anger. He wept. He felt distress and was deeply depressed! In the Word of God we are called to experience various attitudes and demonstrate outward expressions of Christian growth and character. In the Sermon on the Mount Jesus says blessed are those who are sorrowful, who possess a gentle spirit, who show mercy, whose hearts are pure, and who are peaceful. We are called to manifest the fruit of the Spirit which is love, joy, peace, patience, kindness, goodness, faithfulness, gentleness, and self-control.

> Jack Balswick, a Ph.D. in sociology, argues that the strongest evidence that innate temperamental differences exist with each sex is the general similarity of behavior for males and females in most cultures. While the sexes differ in physiology and in temperament, much of what we call male or female behavior or attitudes is social conditioning (nurture) rather than the result of biology (nature). Much behavior that is now explained as biologically either male or female may just as easily be explained by social conditioning.[7]

If we have learned certain patterns of behavior in the past, the good news is that we can also unlearn them and begin to respond in a new way. The result will be a change for the better in our ability to communicate.

Look back at the original list of items which were purported to be differences between men and women. Words like *always* or *never* are too absolute. They simply perpetuate a stereotype.

WHAT DO YOU THINK?

1. Do any of those statements describe you? If so, how do you feel about this *tendency* in your life?

2. How does this tendency affect your marriage? Specifically, the communication process?

3. Is this a tendency that you would like to change? If so, why?

4. How does your spouse feel about this tendency?

You may find that your own tendencies do not fit what has been suggested as a female or male characteristic.

Build Your Vocabulary

If you do not know how to share your feelings and emotions, obtain a synonym finder or thesaurus and begin to expand your vocabulary. When it comes time to share, give three or four descriptive sentences instead of a one-line summary. Your description should include at least one feeling or emotional word.

I mention the one-line summary because in the groups of married couples I mentioned earlier a major complaint of the women is: "Men never give sufficient details. They give us the summary." As one woman expressed it, "Jim is on the phone for twenty minutes talking to a friend. When he gets off and I ask him what they said, he gives me a one-line summation. I don't want the condensed version. I want the whole novel-length story! One day he came home and told me he had just run into one of our closest friends and the man's wife had had their baby early that morning. I asked him, 'Well, was it a boy or girl? How large was it? What time was it born? etc.' He said all he remembered is that they had their baby. He didn't remember all those trivial details!"

Another woman in a seminar suggested that "men tend to view communication like a telegram. Women view it as a meal to be savored." Men tend not to share many details in certain areas or about certain topics. But listen to us as we talk about what is important to *us!* Our work, our hobbies, our recreation, etc. Men can be just as detailed and precise as anyone else when they want to. And they can express themselves in detail with emotion as well. I have heard the communication of men that has moved me to tears. Each year I read dozens of novels and many of the authors are men. They paint word pictures in my mind that are a combination of facts, feelings, and descriptive adjectives. We *are* capable.

A man who is more of a cognitive responder not only can build his vocabulary, he can begin to think out loud in the presence of his wife. He can say to her, "I'm going to just brainstorm out loud and what I say may not make complete sense or have continuity but I'm willing to try and describe my day differently for you." And as he does this his wife has the opportunity to listen and take in. She should not criticize, correct, or make any value judgments about what he is saying.

A simple way to learn how to expand what we say is the *XYZ* method: *X* is the actual event you want to describe; *Y* are your feelings about the event; *Z* are the consequences or results of the event.

Instead of coming home from work and saying, "I bought a new car today." Period. Try expanding on the topic: "Guess what I did. Boy, am I excited! I finally did something I've always wanted to do but was afraid to. I saw this new car on the lot that was just what we'd talked about three months ago. I saw the price, offered them $400 less, and bought it. I feel great. In fact I feel like a kid again, and it's a car we can afford! How would you like to take a ride with me tonight?"

Remember to share more than the event. People who care about you want to know your inner feelings as well as your thinking. If you make a decision about something, don't just share the decision. Share with your spouse the process that led you to make that decision.

What can a wife do to help her husband share his feelings?

A wife can do a number of things to help her husband become more expressive, but the changes, if they do occur, will take time. You are battling years of conditioning, so beware of making demands that he can't meet as yet.

Barbara, a forty-year-old mother and accountant, said, "When I wanted John to share, I wanted his feelings when I wanted them. My requests came across as demands. And one day he told me so. I learned to be sensitive to his days and moods and whenever he began to share some of his frustrations I listened and listened well. He didn't want a dialogue or someone to solve his problem. He wanted to vent, and I wanted to hear!"

Some of the suggestions that follow may sound familiar, others

quite new. Remember, if what you're doing now isn't working, why keep using the same approach? A new approach used in a loving, consistent manner may help build the intimacy you're looking for.

Help your husband acknowledge that he has feelings inside of him, and that by learning to share these the relationship will bloom. One husband said, "After fifteen years of marriage, I wondered why our relationship was so stale. And then I realized it wasn't the relationship, it was me! When Jan asked me questions or wanted to talk, I gave her thoughts and facts, but no feelings. She could have gotten the same from a computer. We decided to take fifteen minutes a day to share. She agreed to summarize her three-minute descriptions into three or four lines. I agreed to share whatever I said with feeling words. It took us a while to learn this new style, but what a difference it has made! I share—she listens—and we feel closer."

Try direct questions that encourage a direct response.

"I'd like to know the most interesting experience you had at work today (or this week)."

"When have you felt angry, sad, excited, happy, or whatever this week and what caused it?"

"I feel there's a portion of you I don't know. If I had to describe how you feel about your work, what would I say?"

"You really seem to enjoy your woodworking. What do you enjoy so much about it?"

"When you were a little boy, what were your greatest delights and your greatest fears?"

By asking thought-provoking questions about topics fairly comfortable to him—like work, hobby, childhood—you make it easier for him to communicate. These questions vary in their degree of comfort. Sometimes it's easier to pose a factual question first, then lead into how he feels about it. Most husbands find it easy to describe facts about work. But it may take them time to discuss the joys, frustrations, or boredom of their job.

One wife asked her husband: "Honey, you know I enjoy hearing more details and feelings from you. Often it appears that you seem hesitant to talk to me about them. Is there something I do to make it difficult for you to share these with me?"

Another wife was more direct: "John, you know I like to hear the details, your feelings, the inner workings of who you are. I need this, and the times you have shared with me were fantastic. You're so articulate and have such depth. You probably feel I pressure you, or even nag you, into opening up to me. I know you don't like it when

I do slip into that trap. I want you to know that I'm not trying to nag. But I do appreciate your sharing more with me."

Develop an atmosphere of trust so he will eventually be able to express the entire gamut of feeling arising in him. If you ask your husband how he feels about his job and he says he hates it and wants to quit, your own feelings of insecurity may cause you to respond, "You can't! Think of us and our children!" And your husband won't be as open with you again. You don't have to agree with his feelings; the goal is not to debate, but to build communication and thus intimacy.

Thank him for sharing. Let your husband know how much it means to you and ask if there's anything you can do to make it easier for him. Before he leaves for work in the morning ask what it is that you can pray about for him that day. This gives you something specific to talk about at the end of the day.

Often watching a movie together can open the emotional side of a person. A film can bring out feelings in a person who would ordinarily suppress them. Emotions brought to the surface through the film seem "safe" because in a sense they are not "real." Discussing the movie later, using factual and feeling questions, may lead to a unique discussion.

What then is the answer to some of the complaints and concerns which men and women bring up about one another? The answer is, *adjust, change,* and *reinforce* any changes which occur.

Let's look once again at some of the items of the original list of male/female differences. But note the changes which are more accurate. Some of the statements have been combined.

1. Men and women may be a bit different in the way they communicate and relate to others. These differences, if quite strong, can be complementary and they can change.

2. Both men and women think and feel internally. Men tend to verbalize thoughts and ideas whereas women tend to express emotions and feelings more than men.

3. Language spoken and heard for some men and women may be either an emotional experience or a thinking experience. But how would you know? You really wouldn't unless you asked questions and discussed it with your spouse. What about you? What kind of an experience is it for you? Have you shared this with your spouse?

4. Men or women may tend to take statements personally or impersonally. You might not know because they may keep it hidden inside. If you think your partner tends to take situations or state-

ments personally, check it out with him—ask and discuss. If he does take something personally, could it be because of something you have said?

5. In material or spiritual matters, it varies with the individual whether he/she is more concerned with the ultimate or the process of getting there.

6. Are men like filing cabinets and women like computers? Could it be that the difference is really in how much we verbalize? How we deal with problems may be due to two important factors discussed earlier in this book: the resolution of past issues, and our self talk.

7. For many women her home is an extension of her personality, but so is her work. For most men their job is not only an extension of their personality but the source of their identity.

8. All men and women have a need for security and roots. Perhaps women express this need more. For many homemakers their home is the source of security and rootedness. Men may appear to be nomadic if a job change occurs because their work has such a high degree of significance for them. Thus to another person they appear not to care about the roots of the home and family. Many men say that the fact that they do love and care for their family is the reason they strive to get ahead in their job and take advancement opportunities.

9. Both men and women have a wide variety of emotions available to them. Some individuals become tied into experiencing one emotion more than others because they reinforce its occurrence. A person becomes used to expressing anger, fear, or sorrow.

10. Women are not always changing and men are not the stable sex per se. A man or woman can be either. Often we tend to evaluate people on the basis of their verbal expressions and are led to believe in a stereotyped view. Those who are impulsive with few inner controls—whether men or women—are the ones who become too involved too soon.

11. We tend to remember what is most important to us. Some events and items hold greater significance than others. If we can remember details at work we can learn to remember details at home or socially if we choose to do so. There are also times when the details of an event are just not that important to us, and that's all right! We need to discuss why some details are so important to a person in order to understand his perspective. Distortions occur because a topic or event is not that important to the speaker or the

listener. We may not have been listening, we don't understand our
past, or our self talk is interfering with our current communication.

WHAT DO YOU THINK?

1. Write a paragraph describing how your mother communicated,
how your father communicated, and in what way you are like them.

2. Ask your spouse to describe how you communicate.

3. What specific changes will you make this week in your communication with your spouse?

8
Do You Really Want Your Spouse to Change?

W E ARE STRANGE creatures. For years we search for just the right person to be our mate—someone who is attractive, loving, considerate, and all those other qualities we hold dear. At last we find the right one and we hasten to tie the knot. Then are we satisfied? Not exactly. Our reforming tendencies soon emerge and the struggle begins. Our mate may not *want* to change, and, if the truth were known, he or she would like *us* to change![1]

Are we abnormal in wanting to change another person? Do all couples desire change in their relationship and their partner? Yes, indeed. The desire for change is a natural response when we are committed to another person. Too often couples do not realize that desiring change in each other is an act of caring.

The question before us, however, is: Am I willing to change as much as I want my partner to change? Perhaps God is asking *you* to be a pacesetter in change as an example to others, for your own benefit and for the glory of God. Look at what Scripture says to each of us. We are called to be people who change! *"Not that I have now attained [this ideal] or am already made perfect, but I press on to lay hold of (grasp) and make my own, that for which Christ Jesus, the Messiah, has laid hold of me and made me His Own. I do not consider, brethren, that I have captured and made it my own [yet]; but one thing I do—it is my one aspiration: forgetting what lies behind and straining forward to what lies ahead, I press on toward the goal to win the [supreme and heavenly] prize to which God in Christ Jesus is calling us upward"* (Phil. 3:12–14, AMP).

"Like newborn babies you should crave—thirst for, earnestly desire—the pure (unadulterated) spiritual milk, that by it you may be nurtured and grow into [completed] salvation" (1 Pet. 2:2, AMP).

But what about trying to change others? Isn't that wrong? Isn't it unethical or selfish to expect another person to change his actions or his attitude? Too often we adopt a hands-off philosophy and assume a pious spirituality. "I will accept my spouse exactly as he or she is and not make any attempt to change him," we say. Or "I just want to change the relationship, not the other person." If you take this attitude, why do you read books on marriage and communication such as this one! Our desire to change is seen in the vast multitude of marriage books published in the last decade. Look at the thousands of people who attend Marriage Enrichment Seminars! If people didn't want to change themselves and their mates, why invest all this money, time, and energy? "But I just want to *improve* my marriage," you reply. That's fine, but improvement necessitates change on someone's part.

So what is our response as a married person to be? Total blind acceptance of our spouse and our marriage as it is? Or could God use us as a positive factor to bring about change?

We are called upon to be enablers or encourages. Would a desire to bring about change fit the role of being an enabler or encourager? *If we were to evaluate the desired change in light of the Scripture would we discover that this change we are called to make is from the Word of God?*

What is it you want to change in your relationship? Is it something specific or something general? Is it an attitude or behavior? Usually we want our spouse to change his or her attitude. It is easier for people to change their behavior, however, than their attitude. If a change actually occurs, all you will see is a change in behavior.

That change in behavior may or may not reflect a genuine change in attitude.

What happens when we honestly want change but feel that we should not or cannot do anything to make it happen? We learn to cope. But there is a cost to coping. Too often we do not anticipate this cost and its effect upon our own life and the relationship. There are several ways to cope, some active and some passive.

Passive Coping

There are two passive ways to cope—resignation and martyrdom.

Resignation: "I give up," Joan says. "I just have to accept the fact that Jimmy is always going to leave his clothes all over the house. I haven't found any way to change his sloppy habits, and now other people are telling me I just need to accept him as he is. I'm going to have to learn to live with the fact that I'll always have to pick up after my husband."

The acceptance which we see here in Joan is coming from a feeling of impotence. "I'm stuck and I better learn to live with it." When we resign ourselves to accepting another person's undesirable behavior, we admit that we are powerless. Soon this begins to erode our sense of self-esteem. And when you start thinking less of yourself, how do you think that affects your view of your spouse? You're right! You begin to think less of him or her also. You begin to care less for the person and you may begin to withdraw. Resignation can be destructive in a relationship. Soon you will begin to feel a sense of loss for what the relationship could have been.

Martyrdom: A martyr accepts the behavior of others that he feels he is unable to change. But he uses this acceptance to show others how good *he* is. He frequently reminds his mate (and other people as well) of the sacrifice he is making in putting up with his mate's behavior. This becomes a sore spot in the relationship and the mate learns to tune the martyr out. The martyr in turn withdraws and in time begins to question the relationship itself.

Active Coping

There are also two rather active responses to our inability to bring about change.

Revenge: We proclaim "Vengeance is mine" in small insignificant ways which may go unnoticed at first. A spouse who is tightly controlled and dominated by his/her partner may begin to lie about his/her activities when on his/her own. A spouse who is restricted financially by the frugality of the other partner may use some of the budgeted money secretly for his/her own use. Other responses are more than obvious and quite direct. Revenge is a subtle response against both our spouse and our marriage. It stems from our anger over not being able to change the relationship. But revenge is counterproductive. Does it bring about the change we desire? Does it move us closer to our mate? Not likely. Our expressions of revenge may bring about the very same response in our mate.

Withdrawal: This is a declaration that "if I can't change you, then I choose not to be involved with you at all!" There are degrees of withdrawal ranging from the most extreme of divorce or separation to living together as "married singles" sharing only the same house. Caring, love, and commitment become foreigners in a land of pretense for the sake of others. Couples pay a great price of emotional hurt in a "withdrawal within a relationship." Withdrawal is a costly option.

WHAT DO YOU THINK?

Listed below are the four typical coping responses we have just discussed. Think back to the home in which you were raised. Indicate which of these (if any) were modeled for you in your parents' relationship. Then indicate the result.

Coping response   *Result*

1. Resignation

2. Martyrdom

3. Revenge

4. Withdrawal

Now indicate which responses you have used with your own mate in different (or maybe the same) situations. Indicate the consequences and then how you felt afterwards.

Situations	*How I Coped*	*Consequences*	*My Feelings*

How do you now respond when change does not occur?

What are some of the reasons we want other people to change? The usual ones are: "I don't like what he/she does." "It creates more work for me." "It's for his own good." "I have to complete the work his parents never finished." "I just want to improve our relationship."

Are these really the reasons? No, they are not. Are the changes for the person's own good? Are the changes really for the good of the relationship? Or are they for *our* own good? What is the reason?

Real Reasons We Want Change

Here are some of the *real* reasons that lie behind our desire for change. They may surprise you! Underlying all of these reasons is our need to belong, to be accepted, to be loved, to feel we are special to another person.

We seek renewal. Sometimes we lose the feelings of affirmation we originally had, thus we ask for a change in the relationship to renew those positive feelings we once experienced in our relationship. We want to recapture good feelings about ourselves, and we want our spouse to change in some way so things can again "be the way they once were." We want renewal. A wife may want to recapture the first year of marriage. "I want him to take the afternoon off once a week as he did twenty years ago. We would go for a walk or ride bikes or lie on the floor in front of the fireplace and read or talk. I guess I want him to court me again."

We want more. We may feel that we have not received sufficient affirmation of our self-image and we want more. Our need for positive input from others will vary according to events and circumstances and our own individual development. When we want more it may mean quality or a different approach. "My husband is attractive. He touches me, compliments me now and then, but often I hint for the compliments. I would like him to think for himself and create new compliments. I want to be loved and pursued ten times the amount I am now. In fact, I'd settle for a 50 percent increase! And I don't want to tell him how to do it either!"

We need variety. A different expression of affirmation is needed if we feel our spouse has taken us for granted or our relationship has become routine. If our partner affirms us in the same old ways, it is not enough. His or her love and concern needs to be expressed in some new way so we are convinced of our spouse's sincerity. "My wife is very loving and affirming. But she is so predictable. I like all that she does but it's almost like she's been programmed a certain way. I want some surprises. I'd like her to say new things to me, to be different in her sexual responses too. I guess I should be satisfied. So many men don't receive what I do, and yet . . ."

We want to be seen in a different light. We also want our partner to affirm us for more than one aspect of who we are. One woman said, "I want to be seen not just as a competent homemaker. I'd like my husband to see that I have value as a teacher, as a creative thinker, but he can't seem to grasp that." New affirmation gives us the feeling of being even more valued and special. Concern for the other person and the relationship may be tied in to all of these other reasons.

These are only four reasons people seek change. There are others. Some very insecure people cannot tolerate differentness. Others have a need to dominate and must be in control of change.

How does the biblical mandate to exhort one another or encourage one another apply to the marriage relationship? The Word of God gives us examples of our response to one another (italics have been added).

"And when [Apollos] wished to cross to Achaia [most of Greece], the brethren wrote to the disciples there, urging and encouraging them to accept and welcome him heartily" (Acts 18:27, AMP).

"I entreat and advise Euodia and I entreat and advise Syntyche to agree and to work in harmony in the Lord" (Phil. 4:2, AMP).

"Let the word [spoken by] the Christ, the Messiah, have its home (in your hearts and minds) and dwell in you in [all its] richness, as you teach and admonish and train one another in all insight and intelligence and wisdom [in spiritual things, and sing] psalms and

hymns and spiritual songs, making melody to God with [His] grace in your hearts" (Col. 3:16, *AMP*).

"But we beseech and earnestly exhort you, brethren, that you excel (in this matter) more and more" (1 Thess. 4:10, *AMP*).

"Therefore encourage (admonish, exhort) one another and edify— strengthen and build up—one another, just as you are doing" (1 Thess. 5:11, *AMP*).

Who determines what we are to exhort another person to do? Who determines what we are to teach another or encourage another person to do?

The word *exhort* in these passages means to urge one to pursue some course of conduct. It is always looking to the future. Exhorting one another is a three-fold ministry in which a believer urges another to action in terms of applying scriptural truth, encourages the other with scriptural truth and comforts the other through the application of Scripture. *Encourage* is to urge forward or .persuade in Acts 18:27. In 1 Thessalonians 5:11 it means to stimulate another to the ordinary duties of life. Therefore, what are we to exhort another person to do?

To answer this you need to look at your motives for change. When you begin to understand what your motives really are, you may discover that it isn't really necessary for your spouse to change. Perhaps your needs can be fulfilled in other ways which allow your partner not to have to change. If you can discover why you want your spouse to change, you may discover what you want change in your own life. The key is to understand your own motives.

WHAT DO YOU THINK?

Indicate any changes you would like your spouse to make. Select the reason from the "Real Reasons We Want Change."

Changes   *Reason*

A Strategy for Change

When you ask your spouse to change some behavior of his/hers that you do not like, he/she will interpret the proposed change in one of four ways: (1) as a destructive change; (2) as a threatening change; (3) as having no effect upon him/her; or (4) as a change that would help him/her become a better person. Thus it is important in requesting a change to present the suggestion in such a way that your spouse sees it as an opportunity for growth. How can this be done?

First of all, *you must give him information.* Each person has a different need for and capacity for handling information. For most individuals, the more information you provide about a desired change the less the resistance. Why? Because there is more opportunity for him to see the request for change as a step toward growth. "John, I appreciate your interest in the children and their education. I'd like you to help me in two areas with them—David needs your assistance with some of his projects and I need your help in talking to his teacher. I understand that this may take some time, but your opinions and knowledge can help David more than I can. If we both talk to the teacher we'll both be able to share our ideas and also present a united front to both the teacher and David." A person needs to know what you expect of him, why you expect it, and what may be the results.

Involving your partner in exploring various alternatives for change will also lessen resistance. Your spouse will be less defensive if he/she has a chance to express his/her ideas and make suggestions. "Jan, you know that we've been able to talk a bit more lately about how the home is kept and also our scheduling difficulties. I'm wondering if we could explore some possible alternatives that might work. This doesn't mean we're going to just accept whatever idea is shared, but just that we get some more ideas to work with. What do you think?"

Start out slowly so that it's easier to do. Is the change requested an overwhelming and gigantic step? Or have you broken the request down into small increments which can actually be accomplished? If so, there may be a better response. If the requested change is for increased communication, starting out sharing for fifteen minutes one night a week is reasonable. The goal may be thirty minutes a night, four nights a week, but that is too much to expect at first. Having the garage cleaned and kept clean is a typical request. But developing a specific smallstep plan to accomplish this over a four-month period of time may be workable.

Intimacy is a final factor. Resistance is a normal response when one partner mistrusts and fears the other. If motives or intentions are questioned, how can a suggested change be seen as anything but damaging? If trust and intimacy exist, a spouse may see the request as one way to achieve even greater intimacy in the marriage. A wife who has responded favorably to her husband's previous suggestions for change will be open if:

1. Her husband acknowledges her change in a positive way. He doesn't say, "Well, it won't last," or "It's about time," or "I can't believe it."

2. He doesn't mention her change or lack of change in front of others to embarrass her.

3. He is open to changes himself.

4. She knows he loves her whether she changes or not.

5. She sees his request for change as something that will enhance her life.

Resistance to Change

Why do we resist change? Why is it difficult to comply with the requests of others? Too often the reasons we give are covers for the real source of resistance.

If a spouse doesn't respond positively to a request to change, his resistance can take many forms.

Some people simply stop listening as an expression of their unwillingness to change. They cut off the conversation, leave the room, or busy themselves with some task. A man may stay late at the office or a woman may say she has to leave early for an appointment in order to prevent further discussion.

On the other hand, some people agree with the request, but *they do not follow through on it* because they have no intention of doing so. This is a stall tactic to get the person making the request to back off! But after numerous requests with no follow-through, the spouse becomes suspicious and angry.

Or perhaps the person counters with, "Why don't *you* change?" a resistance tactic which *throws the request back to the person making it.* This completely turns the request around and the result will probably be an argument.

Why are we so reluctant to change?

One simple reason for not changing is habit. Day in and day out we maintain a fairly predictable routine. Inside of us we have a selection of comfortable responses which make us feel secure. We don't have to think about or work at new ways of responding. But the habits that make us feel secure may be an irritant to others. Habit is probably the most frequently used form of resistance. Why? Because it works so well.

Have you ever used these excuses or heard them used? "I've always done it this way." "After twenty-eight years, it's too late to change now." "Why change? I'm comfortable. This way works." "How do I know the new way is better? I don't have to think about this one. I just do it."

Perhaps you live with someone who is messy. The person does not: pick up after himself; put items away; hang up his clothes when he comes home from work; change into old clothes before he does a messy chore; pick up the paper and magazines he dropped on the floor; clear his own dishes away from the table.

You may have tried to correct this individual by begging, pleading, threatening, letting the mess accumulate for days or even weeks, but nothing has worked. Probably your mate was accustomed to having people pick up after him while he was growing up. If this is the case, perhaps he developed the belief that he is special and deserves to be waited on. If he was waited on and picked up after for many years and now his spouse is saying, "Pick up after yourself," the message he is receiving is, "You no longer deserve to be catered to." Thus his self-esteem is under attack. The way he thinks about himself has been challenged. This is the real reason why he resists. If he changes he will have to change some perceptions he holds about himself.

Habits can be changed. A habit of twenty-five years can change as quickly as one of ten years or one year once the source of resistance is discovered. And the change is easier than most people realize.

There are others who plead ignorance as their resistance. "I didn't know that's what you wanted"; "I don't know how to do that. What do you think you married? Superman?" Ignorance can be an effective tool because it puts the person making the request on the defensive. He begins to question whether he *did* tell his mate what he wanted or whether he is expecting too much.

Control is another resistance frequently used. If someone asks me to change I may not comply because of my fear of losing control. I want to stay in control of me and even you. The resistance to change comes about because of what that change would communicate about who is in control of the situation. We don't like others determining how we are to behave. The request may not be a control issue but we interpret it in that manner.

Uncertainty or anxiety is an honest resistance response. "How will this change affect me?" "Will I be capable?" "Will people still respond to me in the same way?" "What if I can't do it to please you?" We anticipate some threats and fears coming into play. *We feel our self-esteem being challenged and threatened, and this again is the key: Any perceived threat to our self-esteem is going to be resisted. Will I still receive affirmation? Will I be as secure?*

Do you really think that all your requests for change should meet with instant applause and compliance? If your partner resists your request for change do you become angry, despondent, perplexed, stubborn? Can you see value in resistance? Probably not. But consider the possibilities.

If your requests are resisted, perhaps this will cause you to consider why you want the change, how intensely you want it, and how committed you are to pursuing the change. What does your commitment level to this change tell you about your own needs at this time?

Perhaps the resistance will assist you in being more specific concerning what it is you wish changed. Have you considered your mate's resistance as a unique form of communication? He could be telling you something new about himself—what he values, what elements are involved in his self-esteem. If the person's resistance is too strong, you may be convinced to try another approach.

How to Promote Change

How can we motivate others to change? We have been told for years that we cannot change others, only they can change themselves. That's true. But how can we help to create the conditions under which another person would desire to change? Let's look at the main means which are used to bring about change.

First of all, here are several ineffective but frequently used means of bringing about change.

The first of these is the show me tactic: "If you loved me you would . . ." Have you ever been asked to change as a demonstration of your love for your mate? Have you ever asked your mate to change for this reason? The response we usually get or give is: "If you loved me, you wouldn't ask!"

Next, some try to trade off: "Look I'll change _____ if you'll change _____." This is like saying, "I've got a deal for you!"

Frequently people resort to the demand: "You better do this or else I will . . ." This is a risky approach and can backfire. It also sounds like power play.

For centuries people have used power and coercion to bring about change. Threats, demands, and rewards are frequently used, including giving or withholding verbal or physical affection, and even abuse. Power can work, but what are the consequences? None of us likes to be dominated by another person.

Another approach is to make people worry, feel uncomfortable, or ill at ease about what they do. If we can create guilt or anxiety we think we can bring about change. But the change is usually not real or lasting. Instead of bringing about the change we seek, the other person may actually withdraw from us. We don't like to be around people who make us feel uncomfortable. It is difficult to develop intimacy between people when either power or discomfort is used as a means of bringing about change.

But there are legitimate and effective methods that can be used to promote change. *One approach is to provide new information* that will help the other person move to a new behavior. This approach is based upon believing that our mate will examine new data and make a rational decision to change. Hopefully the person will discover that what he is currently doing will not achieve his goals as well as using the new approach. The information approach may be effective, but it is quite slow. The person must clearly see the consequences of the new suggestion and the ways it will enhance his feelings of self-worth.

Another approach is called the growth approach. If the person can see little or no risk involved to himself and his self-image, he may be open to change. "If I don't have anything to lose, I may try it." The key is to eliminate risk! Which means the person needs to be assured that his self-image will remain intact or even be enhanced. This is the ideal. There will always be some degree of risk however.

Of all strategies for change *the most intimate is trust.* Trust is paramount if you wish to bring about change. If you have a solid basis of trust already established, your requests may find a response. If there is no pattern of trust, it may take a while to build it. And if trust has been destroyed you may never rebuild it. Trust and credibility (yours!) are at stake.

To build trust, and to request change based on this trust, requests for change should be very simple and trivial to begin with. Think of

how safe the other person feels now. How safe and secure will he need to feel before he responds to your request?

If your mate is going to change he must see that you are trustworthy and that you seek the best for him. And all you can do is *request* change. It is up to the other person to *decide* to change and do it. Before you begin, are the changes you request in harmony with the pattern of living as stated in Scripture? Or do the changes reflect your own insecurities? Remember, "We try to change people to conform to our ideas of how they should be. So does God. But there the similarity ends. Our ideas of what the other person should do or how he should act may be an improvement or an imprisonment. We may be setting the other person free of behavior patterns that are restricting his development, or we may be simply chaining him up in another behavioral bondage."[2]

Change can occur if *you* will do the following:

1. Examine and clarify your reasons and desires for change. Examine your need.

2. Evaluate the requests in light of Scripture. Is this a change which Scripture calls upon us to make?

3. Understand how your partner sees him/herself and what his/her self-esteem is built upon.

4. Present changes in a way that enhances his/her self-esteem.

5. Consider your own willingness to change. Are you willing to stand by your mate and encourage, edify, and build him/her up? Are you open to change and is that openness obvious to others? A yes answer to these questions is vital.

6. Reinforce, reinforce, and reinforce! If your mate makes a requested change and you ignore it or take it for granted, he/she will feel violated, let down, and will revert back to his/her previous behavior. We all need feedback and reward for making a change. Then our self-esteem remains intact. Changes are fragile and must be strengthened. When I *experience* affirmation as a person for my new behavior I feel like making it a part and parcel of my life-style. If I feel uncertain with this new behavior, then I will return to the certainty of the old. And the new experience and reinforcement needs to be strong. Otherwise, I remember my old experience which is a natural part of my life and is not easily overcome. The reinforcement must come at a time when it can be linked to the new behavior. This means right after it occurs.

7. Be persistent and patient. Don't expect too much too soon and don't become a defeatist.

WHAT DO YOU THINK?

1. List a change you would like to see in your relationship with your spouse.

2. What changes would you like your spouse to make and what changes will you make?

3. In what way is your spouse's current behavior tied into his self-esteem?

4. Describe how you will present your request so that your partner will feel that this is going to enhance his self-esteem.

9
Anger and Communication

WHO MAKES YOU ANGRY? You do! Situations and other people cannot make you angry. No matter what your spouse does, he or she does not make you angry. You create your own anger.

Anger, like other emotions, is created by your own thoughts. If your spouse fails to follow through with a commitment he has made to you, you may become angry. Your anger comes from your thoughts about the meaning or significance you have given to his failure to follow through.

What Creates Anger?

There are many ways we create our own anger. But we do create our own anger. We may label our partner in some way because of what he has or has not done by thinking (or even verbalizing): "You jerk"; "You selfish person"; "You inconsiderate clown." We label a person in anger because of something he/she has done. But in doing so we tear him/her down. His/her good points are discounted. All you see is this one event and any others similar to it, passing over the things you love about him/her.

Sometimes we become angry when our self-esteem is threatened. Perhaps your spouse insulted or criticized you. You may not feel loved or liked and that feeling makes you angry.

Anger can also be generated by mind reading. In your mind you create your own reasons for why your spouse did what he or she did and you project those reasons onto him.

"That's his mean nature. He's just like his father."

"She just wants to argue for the heck of it."

"Anyone who acts like that must not have any love or compassion."

But mind reading never works. You cannot know for certain the thoughts and motivation of another person. Mind reading only creates additional conflicts.

Inappropriate should/shouldn't statements create highly flammable fuel for your anger. Whenever you say, "My spouse shouldn't (or should) have done that" you create the setting for anger. What you are doing is interpreting a situation a certain way and saying it should have been different. When you insist on holding onto the "shoulds," you keep yourself festered and upset. It would have been nice if the other person had performed as you wanted, but he didn't. Your anger won't change the past and probably will do little to alter the future. Consider the following two situations:

Situation 1: The house is a mess. Especially the kitchen. John's wife is gone and he decides he is going to treat his wife by cleaning the living room, family room, and kitchen. He vacuums, sweeps, dusts and washes dishes for two hours. "Wait until she sees this. Will she be surprised! She'll go wild with appreciation." So he hopes.

Sometime later his wife, Janice, arrives home with bags of groceries and clothes. She staggers into the house and drops the bags in the living room.

"John, would you bring in some of the groceries for me please? There are so many and I'm beat. Wait until you see the great prices I found on clothes at Penney's. And guess who I saw . . ."

And so it goes for the next hour. Janice never mentions one word about the clean rooms. And after her whirlwind entrance the house soon looks like a hurricane had swept through. By now John is doing a slow burn. His anger has reached the boiling point. Is it her behavior that creates John's anger? Or is it his own thoughts? Let's enter his mind to see what he is thinking.

"She should have noticed all this work I did for her."

"She should have thanked me."

"She shouldn't have been so insensitive and inconsiderate."

"What a lousy way to treat me."

"She shouldn't have messed up these rooms."

"Just wait until she wants me to help her! Fat chance."

John's thoughts are making him feel hurt and angry. He *could* have thought:

"I wish she would notice the work I've done."

"Perhaps I did all this for what I would get out of it instead of just helping her."

"I can get along without her noticing. If not, I'll just ask if she noticed anything. I could let her know I have a better understanding of what housework is like."

"Next time I'll find a creative way to let her know her work has been done for her."

This series of thoughts is much more realistic and less emotionally charged. Changing "should" statements to "I wish . . ." or "It would be nice if . . ." will help us use our minds to control our emotions so we can maintain the ability to reason.

Situation 2: Curt was frustrated when he came in for counseling. He was livid with anger at his wife. "You bet I'm angry," he said, "and I've got a right to be. If you had to live with that hypocritical woman you'd be angry too. Oh, she puts on a great performance. She responds with love, kindness, patience, and fairness with everyone else. But at home it's just the opposite! Everyone at church sees her as a saint! Ha! At home she's constantly griping, complaining, running me down, and comparing me to others. If there's fault to be found with me, she'll find it. She makes life miserable for me and I'm burned up. And don't tell me I don't have a right to be angry. I'm ready to take a walk on her!"

Curt had many expectations for Susan which (from his point of view) were not being fulfilled.

As we talked we discovered that Curt not only had expectations but felt he had a right to demand that she fulfill those expectations. Curt was telling himself that:

1. It is wrong and terrible to be treated by my wife in this way, especially when she demonstrates Christian love to others.

2. I am correct in demanding that she treat me differently than she does.

3. She owes me love and a submissive attitude since she is my wife.

4. She is terrible to treat me this way.

5. She should change her response to me.

Curt's self talk and expectations were creating his anger. As we continued to explore his feelings we discovered that he felt like he was wasting his life with Susan and he wasn't sure that she could change. He believed that (most of the time) he was loving, kind, and considerate with Susan and thus she should respond in like manner.

Curt had three causes for his anger: (1) expectations; (2) a list of shoulds and oughts for Susan; (3) a pattern of self talk which fed his anger.

WHAT DO YOU THINK?

1. If you were counseling Curt what suggestions would you give him for dealing with the above three causes?

2. What new statements would you ask him to make in his mind which would help with his anger?

The *American Heritage Dictionary* describes anger as a strong, usually temporary displeasure, but does not specify the manner of expressions. You can be just as angry while keeping silent as you can while yelling at someone.

The words *rage* and *fury* are used to describe intense, uncontained, explosive emotion. Fury is thought of as being destructive, but rage can be considered justified by certain circumstances.

Another word for anger is *wrath*—fervid anger that seeks vengeance or punishment. *Resentment* is usually used to signify suppressed anger brought about by a sense of grievance. *Indignation* is a feeling which results when you see the mistreatment of someone or something which is very important to you.

A simple definition of anger is "a strong feeling of irritation or displeasure."

What can you do with your anger? There are several steps you can take to lessen anger and reduce inner tension.

Identify the cause. Your anger is a symptom, the tip of the iceberg. Underlying thoughts or other feelings are creating your sense of irritation.

1. What are your thoughts? Are you applying labels to your spouse? Are you trying to mind read? Are you operating on the basis of "shoulds" or "should nots"?

2. Are you feeling hurt over some situation?

3. Is there something that you are afraid of? Identify your fear.

4. What are you frustrated over? Frustration is one of the biggest causes of anger. If you're frustrated you probably have some unmet needs and expectations—probably unspoken.

Evaluate the reason for your anger. Is your anger directed toward your partner because he did something intentionally and knowingly to hurt or offend you? How do you know it was intentional?

Write out your responses to these questions: How is your anger helpful or useful? Is it going to help you build your relationship or reach the goal that you want?

Apply Nehemiah 5:6–7. In order to reduce your anger you need some practical application of Nehemiah 5:6–7. *"Then I was very angry when I had heard their outcry and these words. And I consulted with myself [or thought it over], and contended with the nobles and the rulers and said to them, 'You are exacting usury, each from his brother!' Therefore, I held a great assembly against them."*

One way to "consult with yourself" is to make a list of the advantages and disadvantages of feeling and acting in an angry manner. Consider the short-term and long-term consequences of the anger. Look over the list and decide what is the best direction to move.

Another approach is to identify the hot thoughts and replace them with cool thoughts. Hot thoughts are the anger-producing thoughts. David Burns describes a situation in which a couple had disagreements over the husband's daughter from a previous marriage. Sue, the wife, felt that Sandy, the daughter, was a manipulator and led John around by the nose. No matter what Sue suggested he ignored her. As Sue pressured him, John withdrew from her. Sue became more and more upset and angry. Then Sue made a list of her hot thoughts and substituted cool or calm thoughts.

Hot Thoughts	Cool Thoughts
1. How dare he not listen to me!	1. Easily. He's not obliged to do everything my way. Besides he is listening, but he's being defensive because I'm acting so pushy.
2. Sandy lies. She says she's working, but she's not. Then she expects John's help.	2. It's her nature to lie and to be lazy and to use people when it comes to work or school. She hates work. That's her problem.
3. John doesn't have much free time, and if he spends it helping her, I will have to be alone and take care of my kids and myself.	3. So what. I like being alone. I'm capable of taking care of my kids by myself. I'm not helpless. I can do it. Maybe he'll want to be with me more if I learn not to get angry all the time.
4. Sandy's taking time away from me.	4. That's true. But I'm a big girl. I can tolerate some time alone. I wouldn't be so upset if he were working with my kids.
5. John's a schmuck. Sandy uses people.	5. He's a big boy. If he wants to help her he can. Stay out of it. It's not my business.
6. I can't stand it!	6. I can. It's only temporary. I've stood worse.[1]

WHAT DO YOU THINK?

1. List some of the hot thoughts you experience.

2. Write out a replacement or cool thought.

3. What do you become angry at the most?

What You Need to Know About Anger

The Scriptures teach a balanced perspective on anger. We are to be angry at times, but for the right reasons. We are always to be in control of the intensity and direction of our anger. It is not supposed to dominate us or run out of control. Revenge, bitterness, and resentment are not to be a part of our life. We are to recognize the causes and our responsibility for our anger. We are never to deny our anger or repress it, but eliminate it in a healthy manner.

What happens outside of us—external events—do not make us angry. Our thoughts do, whether they are automatic thoughts or ones we choose to think. Realizing that you are responsible for your anger is to your advantage. You have an opportunity to take control of your thoughts and your emotions.

In most situations your anger will work against you and not for you. It can cripple you and make you quite ineffective. Anger can limit your capability to discover creative solutions. If no real solution is available, at least you can free yourself from being dominated by the situation and give up resentment. Can joy, peace, and contentment reside side-by-side with your anger?

If you're angry at your spouse it could be that you believe that he/she is acting in an unfair or unjust manner. By looking at your expectations and beliefs you can lessen your anger. What we label unfair or unjust may be *our* evaluation alone.

Much of your anger may be your way of protecting yourself from what you see as an attack against your self-esteem. If someone criti-

BOTTLED UP OR REPRESSED FEELINGS
ARE LIKE PLUGGING UP A STEAM VENT
OR BOILER.

cizes you or disagrees with you or doesn't perform according to your expectations, your self-esteem may be threatened. Why? Because of what others have done? No. Because of your negative thoughts.

You and I have three choices for our anger: (1) we can turn it inward and swallow it, absorbing it like a sponge; (2) we can ventilate it; or (3) we can stop creating it. Let's look first at what happens when we swallow it.

Turning anger inward against yourself can give you hypertension, high blood pressure, ulcerated colitis, or depression. Joseph Cooke describes what happened to him when he internalized his anger.

Squelching our feelings never pays. In fact, it's rather like plugging up a steam vent in a boiler. When the steam is stopped in one place, it will come out somewhere else. Either that or the whole business will blow up in your face. And bottled-up feelings are just the same. If you bite down on your anger, for example, it often comes out in another form that is much more difficult to deal with. It changes into sullenness, self-pity, depression, or snide, cutting remarks. . . .

Not only may bottled-up emotions come out sideways in various unpleasant forms; they also may build up pressure until they simply have to burst forth. And when they do, someone is almost bound to get hurt. . . . I remember that for years and years of my . . . life, I worked to bring my emotions under control. Over and over again, as they cropped up, I would master then in my attempt to achieve what looked like a gracious, imperturbable Christian spirit. Eventually, I had nearly everybody fooled, even in a measure my own wife. But it was all a fake. I had a nice-looking outward appearance; but inside, there was almost nothing there. . . .

And way underneath, almost completely beyond the reach of my conscious mind, the mass of feelings lay bottled up. I didn't even know they were there myself, except when their pale ghosts would surface now and then in various kinds of unsanctified attitudes and reactions. But they were there nevertheless. And the time came when the whole works blew up in my face, in an emotional breakdown.

All the things that had been buried so long came out in the open. Frankly, there was no healing, no recovery, no building a new life for me until all those feelings were sorted out, and until I learned to know them for what they were, accept them, and find some way of expressing them honestly and nondestructively.[2]

Bottled-up or repressed anger may emerge in some nondirective ways. When it does, the angry person does not have to admit anger or take responsibility for it. This nondirective expression is usually referred to as passive-aggressive. The person's behavior can manifest itself in several ways. Forgetting is very common: "Are you *sure* you asked me?" or "Are you *sure* that was the time we agreed upon?" If you are the one who asked the question, you begin to wonder and doubt yourself. Actually, you have been set up!

Sarcasm is a "nice" way to be angry. A person is given two messages at one time—a compliment and a put-down. "You look so young I didn't recognize you." "Your new suit is sure radical but I like it."

Being late is another frustrating experience for the one against whom the anger is directed. This behavior may emerge unconsciously—the person is on time to some events but late to others.

Passive-aggressive behavior is unhealthy because: (1) it can become an ingrained pattern of behavior which can last a lifetime; (2) it can distort a person's personality; (3) it can interfere with other relationships.

Another choice is to ventilate all your anger. This may help *you* feel better but the results may not be very positive. And the person on whom you vent your anger certainly won't feel better!

A third choice is to stop creating your anger and/or to control the expression of your anger. How? By changing your thought life.

"Conscious delay" is a procedure which can be used to hold back angry responses or any negative response which has been generated in the mind. It is possible to edit negative thoughts (which is not the same as denying or repressing them) so that you will express yourself or behave in a positive manner. It is not hypocritical nor is it dishonest to edit your thoughts. Ephesians 4:15 states that we are to speak the truth in love. A literal translation of this verse means that we are to speak the truth in such a way that our relationship is cemented together better than before. Totally blunt, let-it-all-hang-out honesty does not build relationships. By editing, you are aware of your thoughts and feelings and you are also controlling them. You are actually taking the energy produced by the anger and converting it into something useful which will build the relationship.

How is it possible to edit my thoughts when I begin to become angry? First of all, make a list of some of the behaviors of your spouse which you respond to with anger.

1. My spouse is usually late, as much as fifteen or twenty minutes. Whenever this happens I become angry.

2. My spouse frequently overspends the monthly household allotment and does not tell me about it.

3. My spouse leaves clothes and dishes around the house consistently and expects others to pick them up.

4. Often when I set up an outing or a date for us (even well in advance) my spouse has already planned something for that time and does not tell me in advance.

WHAT DO YOU THINK?

1. What are some things that make you angry? How do you usually think when these things occur?

2. What is your self talk?

3. What are some of the possible explanations for the way your spouse is behaving?

4. Are you guilty of the same problem or a similar problem? Have you attempted to be constructive and positive in any of your discussions with your spouse about this problem? Will what you are about to say or do reduce the chance of your spouse repeating the same behavior?

5. What are three alternate statements you could make to your spouse to replace your usual response?

Write the above questions on a piece of paper and carry it with you. As you find yourself starting to get angry, take a brief time-out and look at your list.

The Word of God has much to say about anger and uses a number of words to describe the various types of anger. In the Old Testament, the word for anger actually meant "nostril" or "nose." In ancient Hebrew psychology, the nose was thought to be the seat of anger. The phrase "slow to anger" literally means "long of nose." Synonyms used in the Old Testament for anger include *ill-humor* and *rage* (Esth. 1:12), *overflowing rage* and *fury* (Amos 1:11), and *indignation* (Jer. 15:17). Anger is implied in the Old Testament through words such as *revenge, cursing, jealousy, snorting, trembling, shouting, raving,* and *grinding the teeth.*

Several words are used for anger in the New Testament. It is important to note the distinction between these words. Many people have concluded that the Scripture contradicts itself because in one verse we are taught not to be angry and in another we are admonished to "be angry and sin not." Which is correct and which should we follow?

One of the words used most often for anger in the New Testament is *thumas* which describes anger as a turbulent commotion or a boiling agitation of feelings. This type of anger blazes up into a sudden explosion. It is an outburst from inner indignation and is similar to a match which quickly ignites into a blaze but then burns out rapidly. This type of anger is mentioned twenty times (see for example Eph. 4:31 and Gal. 5:20). We are to control this type of anger.

Another type of anger mentioned only three times in the New Testament, and never in a positive sense, is *parorgismos.* This is anger that has been provoked. It is characterized by irritation, exasperation, or embitterment. "*Do not ever let your wrath—your exasperation, your fury or indignation—last until the sun goes down*" (Eph. 4:26, *AMP*).

"*Again I ask, Did Israel not understand?—Did the Jews have no warning that the Gospel was to go forth to the Gentiles, to all the earth? First, there is Moses who says, "I will make you jealous of those who are not a nation; with a foolish nation I will make you angry"* (Rom. 10:19, *AMP*).

Acceptable Anger

The most common New Testament word for anger is *orge*. It is used forty-five times and means a more settled and long-lasting attitude of anger which is slower in its onset but more enduring. This kind of anger is similar to coals on a barbecue slowly warming up to red and then white hot and holding this temperature until the cooking is done. It often includes revenge.

There are two exceptions where this word is used and revenge is not included in its meaning. In Ephesians 4:26 we are taught to not *"let the sun go down on your anger."* Mark 3:5 records Jesus as having looked upon the Pharisees *"with anger."* In these two verses the word means an abiding habit of the mind which is aroused under certain conditions against evil and injustice. This is the type of anger that Christians are encouraged to have—the anger that includes no revenge or rage.

Rage interferes with our growth and our relationships. Rage produces attacks (verbal or physical), tantrums, and revenge. It can destroy other people first and then ourselves.

Resentment is another loser. It breeds bitterness and can create passive-aggressive responses. Resentment can actually destroy us and, in time, other people as well.

Since we are rational creatures we can choose how we will respond to external events. In fact we have more control than we give ourselves credit for. Often, however, our past experiences, memories, and patterns of response tend to hinder us from exercising this control, but we can overcome these influences.

What is indignation and where does it fit into our system of responses? Indignation creates constructive actions to change injustice, to protect ourselves and others.

In his book on anger, Richard Walters compares the effects of all three: rage, resentment, and indignation.

> Rage seeks to do wrong, resentment seeks to hide wrong, indignation seeks to correct wrongs.

Rage and resentment seek to destroy people, indignation seeks to destroy evil.

Rage and resentment seek vengeance, indignation seeks justice.

Rage is guided by selfishness, resentment is guided by cowardice, indignation is guided by mercy.

Rage uses open warfare, resentment is a guerrilla fighter, indignation is an honest and fearless and forceful defender of truth.

Rage defends itself, resentment defends the status quo, indignation defends the other person.

Rage and resentment are forbidden by the Bible, indignation is required.[3]

Rage blows up the bridges people need to reach each other, and resentment sends people scurrying behind barriers to hide from each other and to hurt each other indirectly. Indignation is constructive: it seeks to heal hurts and to bring people together. Its purpose is to rebuild the bridges and pull down the barriers, yet it is like rage and resentment in that the feeling of anger remains.[4]

Dr. Walters' description of the characteristics of indignation is different from rage and resentment in attitudes and purposes. Indignation concentrates on real injustice to other people and/or yourself.

With indignation there is realism. Energy is exerted only if there is a possibility of accomplishment.

Unselfishness is a component of indignation. When we are indignant about something we give or are willing to give, we admit our mistakes and even endure suffering.

An additional element is love. Out of a sense of love and concern for others, indignation arises and is expressed. A person feeling indignation is a person under control. He knows what he is doing and what he wants to express, and his responses are appropriate. Is this the way you respond to your spouse when you are angry? It is difficult to be indignant and not full of rage if we are not endeavoring to live the teachings of Scripture. If there is no fruit of the Spirit in our lives (Gal. 5), what place would indignation find?

Before you express your indignation there are two things you should do: (1) pray about your purpose, your attitude, and your words; (2) write out what you would like to say and visualize yourself saying it.

Before you express your indignation, forgive the other person. Regardless of how the other person responds you then have nothing to lose! Why? Because you are not trying to win!

"Good grief," you say to your spouse. "Anyone with any sense would have brought in the rugs and towels we had airing when he saw a dust storm coming. What's the matter with you, John? Don't you ever think?"

A better way to respond to this anger-producing incident would be to say: "John, you left the rugs and towels out during the dust storm. I'm bothered because it's caused me additional work. I wish next time we have any kind of a storm and I'm not around you would check outside and bring in what might be damaged."

There are four healthy reasons for controlling anger.

The first is that the Word of God tells us to control it. Note the reasons given in these verses.

"Do not be quick in spirit to be angry or vexed, for anger and vexation lodge in the bosom of fools" (Eccles. 7:9, AMP).

"He who is slow to anger is better than the mighty, and he who rules his own spirit than he who takes a city" (Prov. 16:32, AMP).

"He who has no rule over his own spirit is like a city that is broken down and without walls" (Prov. 25:28, AMP).

"The beginning of strife is as when water first trickles [from a crack in a dam]; therefore stop contention before it becomes worse and quarreling breaks out" (Prov. 17:14, AMP).

"Good sense makes man restrain his anger, and it is his glory to overlook a transgression or an offense" (Prov. 19:11, AMP).

"Cease from anger and forsake wrath; fret not yourself; it tends only to evil-doing" (Ps. 37:8, AMP).

"Make no friendships with a man given to anger, and with a wrathful man do not associate, lest you learn his ways and get yourself into a snare" (Prov. 22:24–25, AMP).

These are just a few of the passages.

A second reason is the effect that anger has on our bodies. Our heart rate increases, bowels and stomach tense up, blood pressure increases, lungs work harder, our thinking ability lessens. A continual pattern of anger can make our bodies wear out more quickly. Stifled anger can create irreversible damage.

A third reason concerns the sharing of the gospel. How will others respond to our faith if we are known more for our anger than for our love?

The last reason for avoiding anger is that it interferes with our own growth and development of relationships with others.

What If My Spouse Is Angry At Me

"My biggest problem," John said as he sat quietly near me, "is that I don't know what to do or how to act when Jean is angry with me. I either withdraw and crawl into a cocoon or I explode viciously. Neither response solves the problem!"

You and I will always live around people who become angry with us. Here are some suggestions for handling their anger.

1. Give the other person permission in your own mind to be angry with you. It is all right. It isn't the end of the world and you can handle it.

2. Do not change your behavior just to keep your spouse from being angry with you. If you do you are allowing yourself to be controlled. If your spouse becomes angry it is his responsibility to deal with it.

3. Do not reward the other person for becoming angry with you. If the person yells, rants and raves, and jumps up and down and you respond by becoming upset or complying with what he/she wants you to do, you are reinforcing his/her behavior. If he/she is angry but reasonable, respond by continuing to state your point in a caring logical manner.

4. Ask the person to respond to you in a reasonable manner. Suggest that your spouse restate his/her original concern, lower his/her voice, and speak to you as though you had just been introduced for the first time.

5. If your spouse is angry you do not have to become angry also. Read back over the Scriptures we listed and apply them to your life.

If anger interferes with your communication, there are ways you can change the pattern.

Identify the cues that contribute to the anger. It is important to determine how and when you express anger. What is it that arouses the anger? What keeps the anger going? What is it that *you* do in creating the anger and keeping it going? Focus only on your part and don't lay any blame on your partner.

One way to accomplish this is by the use of a behavioral diary. Whenever anger occurs each spouse needs to record the following:

1. The circumstances surrounding the anger such as who was there, where it occurred, what triggered it, etc.

2. The specific ways you acted and the statements you made.

3. The other person's reactions to your behaviors and statements.

4. The manner in which the conflict was eventually resolved.

Establish ground rules for "fair fighting." (See the chapters on communication for information on ground rules.) Each of you will need to make a firm commitment to follow through in keeping these rules.

Develop a plan of action for interrupting the conflict pattern. This plan should involve immediate action to disengage from the conflict. It should also be a way to face and handle the problem at a later time. Interrupting the conflict is an application of Nehemiah 5:6–7: "I [Nehemiah] *was very angry when I had heard their outcry and these words. And I consulted with myself, and contended with the nobles and the rulers.*"

Even the neutral expression of the phrases, "I'm getting angry," "I'm losing control," "We're starting to fight," "I'm going to write out my feelings," is a positive step. Upon hearing one of these statements, the other spouse could say, "Thank you for telling me. What can I do right now that would help?"

A commitment from both of you not to yell or raise your voices and not to act out your anger is essential. We call this "suspending" the anger. Agree to return to the issue at a time of less conflict. Most couples are not used to taking the time to admit, scrutinize, and then handle their anger.

The interruption period could be an opportune time for you to focus upon the cause of your anger.

David Mace suggests two more positive ways to control your anger.

> This does not mean you do not have a right to be angry. In an appropriate situation, your anger could be a life-saver. Anger enables us to assert ourselves in situations where we should. Anger exposes anti-social behavior in others. Anger gets wrongs righted. In a loving marriage, however, these measures are not necessary. My wife is not my enemy. She is my best friend; and it does not help either of us if I treat her as an enemy. So I say, "I'm angry with you. But I don't like myself in this condition. I don't want to want to strike you. I'd rather want to stroke you." This renouncing of anger on one side

prevents the uprush of retaliatory anger on the other side, and the resulting tendency to drift into what I call the "artillery duel." If I present my state of anger against my wife as a problem I have, she is not motivated to respond angrily. Instead of a challenge to fight, it is an invitation to negotiate.[5]

Ask your partner for help. This step is the clincher. Without it, not much progress can be made. The anger may die down, but that is not enough. Both partners need to find out just why one got mad with the other. If they do not, it could happen again, and again, and again. Your request for help is not likely to be turned down. It is in your partner's best interests to find out what is going on, and correct it if a loving relationship is going to be maintained. When the request for help is accepted, the stimulus that caused the anger is usually completely neutralized and the negative emotion dissolves away. Then the work can begin right away, if possible, or at some agreed upon future time. The whole situation can thus be calmly examined, and some solution found. In fact, conflicts between married people are not really destructive. Rightly used, they provide valuable clues that show us the growing edges of our relationship—the points at which we need to work together to make it richer and deeper.[6]

De-cue your spouse. If you have certain behaviors that tend to provoke anger from your spouse, you should eliminate those behaviors so that your spouse has no reason to retaliate. Minor or even defensive behaviors can be a trigger. Leaving clothes on the floor, a hair dryer on the sink in the bathroom, bringing up the past, banging pots and pans are triggers which are easy to change. If a spouse cowers and this elicits abusiveness, he/she can leave the room before the abuse occurs. In determining the cues it may be important to talk through some of these episodes to discover specific triggers and then to seek alternatives.

Change the faulty thinking pattern that affects the relationship. Here again the problem of expectations and assumptions arises. The faulty beliefs will need to be exposed and challenged. Some common themes are:

"You won't love me if I tell you how I really feel."
"You won't love me if I disagree with you."
"It's better just to hide how I feel."
"It's better just to fake it and go along with what he wants."
"Even if I do speak up, you'll win anyway."

"He should know what I need."

"All anger is wrong so I'm not going to express any."

"I'm not going to lower myself and get angry like he does."

Analyze and challenge the assumptions and eliminate any mind reading.

Redirect your focus from "who is right or wrong?" to "what are the behaviors involved and how do they affect our relationship?"

The Effect of Blame

Blame is one of the major cripplers of a relationship. It discourages the healing of hurts and erects even greater walls. When marital discord occurs, each of you usually tries to remove your own guilt. You may look, therefore, for a scapegoat rather than evaluate your own part in the problem. If you can succeed in placing blame, then your own sense of responsibility is lessened. One person attacks, the other person counterattacks. Eventually both become proficient combatants. Each of you struggles under the pain of self-criticism.

Most husbands and wives do not need to refine their blaming skills. Rather, they need to find new ways to avert placing the blame.

There are several practical steps you can take:

1. Instead of blaming or attacking your spouse, share your own inner hurt and feelings. Hurt is usually where the blame is coming from.

2. When you have calmed down sufficiently enough to share complaints in a constructive manner, discuss some of the principles of communication or conflict resolution.

3. It is sometimes difficult, but very necessary, to distinguish between the person and his negative behaviors. This eliminates labeling the person as "bad" or "destructive."

4. If your spouse suggests that you intentionally behaved in a negative manner, you could pose the question. "How would you respond if you knew that what happened was unintentional?" The person's accusation suggests that he is more of an expert on you than he really is. Give him an opportunity to put himself in your shoes.

The Prayer of an Angry Person
Loving God, I praise You for Your wisdom, for Your love, for Your power. Thank You for life, with its joys and mysteries. Thank You for emotions—including anger.

Forgive me when I am led by my anger instead of being led by You. Make me aware of the things I do that produce anger in others—help me change those things. Show me how to clean up the offenses I commit toward others, and give me the courage to ask forgiveness.

Help me to be able to look past the anger of another person and see Your creation in them, and to love them. Teach me how to forgive; and give me the humility to forgive gracefully.

Arouse me to oppose justice and other evils. Show me how to channel my energy that might otherwise be wasted in anger into constructive action in Your service.

You ask me to minister to persons around me. Help me understand what that means. Wake me up. Help me recognize that every moment of my life is an opportunity for Your love to flow through me.

Thank You heavenly Father, for Your love. Thank You for sending Christ so that we might have life and have it to the full, and for sending the Holy Spirit to comfort and guide us through the uncertainties and confusion of everyday living.

In Christ's name, Amen.[7]

WHAT DO YOU THINK?

1. What specific changes do you want to make with your anger?

2. Describe the plan you will implement this week to bring about these changes.

3. Go back through this chapter and list the specific points which will help you the most.

_____

10
My Parents, Your Parents, and Us

COMMUNICATION between husband and wife is one thing. But what about communication between you and your parents— yours and your spouse's? And how does your in-law/parent relationship affect your marital communication?

By now you have grasped the importance of past relationships and experiences. The old relationship with your own parents and the new relationship with your in-laws will have a definite effect on your marriage. Positive and healthy relationships with our in-laws and parents are possible. Let's consider some of the areas of potential conflict or harmony.

Each partner brings to the marriage different customs, traditions, and life-styles. In the homes in which we were raised there were housekeeping practices, cooking styles, and family customs which may differ from those of our spouse. We may believe that the way our parents did things was the right way. Christmas holiday customs are a common example. The husband may have been raised in a home where the tree was trimmed the week before Christmas, the presents were opened on Christmas Eve, and a turkey dinner was eaten in early afternoon on Christmas Day. His wife's family may have trimmed the tree on Christmas Eve, opened the gifts the next morning, and sat down to a ham dinner in the evening.

What about those this-is-the-way-we-always-did-it customs that are part of our background and which bring uncomfortable feelings and even conflict if we are asked to change them? Who should compromise? Which family tradition should you adopt? Should a newly married couple always fit into the established family customs of their parents? Or should they begin to develop their own? If you *always* go to your wife's parents' home for Christmas, what would happen if you wanted to go to your parents' or to a friend's home? Do you always have pumpkin pie for Thanksgiving? What happens if you suggest a change? Who makes the gravy for the turkey dinner? And whose recipe is used for the dressing? These sound like small items but they can become major problems if they are part of a family's traditions. Can anyone rationally hold that the practices of one family are "right" and the other's are "wrong"? And how do you communicate to your parents or in-laws that you want to change some customs or start new ones?

One of the major reasons couples come for counseling is because of conflict with their in-laws. There is hurt, bitterness, and misunderstanding. Often one partner feels caught in the middle between his parents and his spouse. Sometimes one or both spouses have not left home psychologically. After marriage, however, a couple's primary allegiance is to each other and not to his or her parents!

There are several factors which can affect the relationship between couples and in-laws.

The ages of the couple in comparison with the ages of the parents are a possible source of conflict. A very young couple who had not made a break from home before marriage by living elsewhere or attending college in another location is faced with this adjustment. At the same time he/she is faced with the adjustment of learning to relate to another person in a marriage relationship.

Most parents of young couples are middle-aged and still involved in their own careers and achievements. They have interests and rewards apart from their married children. If they have assisted their children into adulthood, they may be looking forward to responding to their children now as adults on an equal basis.

But some parents *demand* attention from their children, such as those with a declining income, few outside interests, chronic illness, or very old age. If the parents divorce, their relationship with their grown children may also be affected.

WHAT DO YOU THINK?

1. Are you or your parents in any of these categories? If so, describe the effect it has had on you and your marriage.

2. How have any of these affected your communication?

3. What needs to be done to remedy the situation?

A person's birth order in the family can influence his relationships with his in-laws. If one spouse is the oldest child in a family and the other the youngest, this difference may affect their marriage relationship and also the expectations of their parents and in-laws. The parents of the youngest child may be somewhat reluctant to let go of their last child. The parents of the oldest child may have higher expectations for their son-in-law or daughter-in-law.

WHAT DO YOU THINK?

1. Where are you in the birth order of your family?

2. How is this affecting your marriage?

Couples and parents often have unrealistic expectations of what a relationship should be between themselves. One set of parents may have imagined a close, continuing relationship between themselves and their new son-in-law or daughter-in-law. They assume they will all get together every weekend, call every third day, and enjoy all Thanksgivings and Christmases together. They are also certain that the young couple will never live more than five miles away so they can have constant contact with their grandchildren. And they expect at least four grandchildren, the first within two years!

But what if you have other plans? What if you plan on not having any children, or living 2,000 miles away, and writing your parents once a month? These expectations need to be openly discussed as soon as possible.

What happens when one person comes from a family with close and warm relationships and the other does not? The latter may not want to establish a close relationship with his in-laws. Or the opposite might be true. The person who had little or no warm, close times at home may seek a close relationship with the in-laws. The one whose family was close may want to break away!

A newly married couple's choice of where they live can influence their relationship with in-laws. Couples who live with their parents are only asking for increased conflicts. The young couple will feel restricted in many ways. The wife, particularly, will feel out of place in her mother-in-law's home. When a couple lives with one set of parents, the other in-laws may get jealous and want to do some "controlling" of their own.

What about the life-style and goals of the couple and their parents? Highly affluent, work-oriented parents often have a difficult time restraining themselves from exerting pressure on their married children who may have a different standard of living. The problem is intensified if the couple consistently criticizes their parents' standards.

What differences and similarities do you see in your life-style and goals and those of your parents and in-laws?

And then there is the area of grandparents and grandchildren. Some parents look forward to becoming grandparents and have their own ways of pressuring a couple to "produce." Other grandparents resent being grandparents, it makes them feel old. If a child does not look like the grandparents, is not the sex they were hoping for, or does not behave according to their expectations, conflicts may arise. A frequent complaint in this area is the way grandparents treat their grandchildren when they come for a visit. Some grandparents overindulge or spoil their grandchildren, making discipline that much harder for the parents when the children come back home. And what if the grandchildren prefer one set of grandparents over the other and want to spend time with them and not with the others?

All of these issues affect communication. Perhaps you are struggling with some of these issues right now. Or you may be breathing a sigh of relief and saying, "We're fortunate. We have never had any difficulty." But what will happen when your own children marry. What if problems such as these do occur? What can you do now to prevent these problems from arising when your own children marry and have children?

Here are some typical adjustment difficulties which can occur. How would you communicate with your spouse or your in-laws in order to resolve these problems?

Case 1. A husband judges and criticizes his wife's housekeeping. He keeps referring to how his mother did it and uses her example as a standard. Or a wife continues to refer to her relationship with her own father as a model of what a dad does with children.

Case 2. John's parents constantly criticize him and his wife. They have an opinion for everything, especially how to raise the children. These unsolicited comments are beginning to frazzle John and Betty's nerves. How could they constructively confront John's parents with the problem?

Case 3. Harry's parents are very demanding in a manipulative way. They want attention and have many expectations regarding Harry and Tina's time. When they don't get their way they try to make Harry and Tina feel guilty. Here is a portion of their conversation with Harry. How would you respond to some of these statements?

Mom: Hello, Harry, this is Mom.

Harry: Hi, Mom, how are you doing?

Mom: Oh, all right I guess. (She sighs.)

Harry: Well fine, but how come you're sighing?

Mom: Oh, well, I guess I haven't been doing so well. Anyway are you coming over this weekend? I was hoping to see you. You know it's been several weeks since you and Tina have been over.

Harry: I'm sorry you're not feeling well, Mom. No, we won't be coming over this weekend. We have some other things that we have already planned to do.

Mom: Well, what's more important than seeing your dad and mom? Aren't we important to you anymore? Well, we sure are disappointed. We were positive that you would be over, and I already have a turkey for dinner. Did you know that? You know your brother and sister come over to see us all the time. We don't even have to ask them! A good Christian son wants to see his parents often. If you really loved and cared for us, you would want to come and see us.

Case 4. The husband says: "Every year we have to spend our vacation with my wife's parents. We've done this for the past eight years! And it's not the most relaxing experience either. I feel stuck but what else can we do? They *expect* us to come! I'd like to see some other parts of this country."

Case 5. Another common problem is that of parents who feel they must contact their son or daughter every day. For example, a wife was really bothered because of constant mothering by her mother-in-law. Each day the mother would call and want to know how her son was doing at his job, whether he was gaining or losing weight, eating the right food, whether he had stopped smoking yet, etc. This was a situation in which the mother-in-law needed to stop making the phone calls in order for the wife to feel better. How would you handle the situation?

Here are some possible ways to handle the situations just described.

Case 1. If the wife's cooking (or housekeeping, driving, ironing, etc.) is being compared with her mother-in-law's, she might say something like, "Honey, one of the things I would really appreciate and would make me feel better is for you to let me know when something I've cooked for you pleases you. I do feel hurt when I hear about your mother's cooking all the time. I want to develop my own cooking skills, but I need positive feedback from you."

Or the husband might say, "Honey, I would really appreciate it if you could let me know when I have done something that helps you as you work with the kids. I really become discouraged when I keep hearing about how your dad always did such and such when you were growing up." Both of these statements contain positive and specific comments that are the proper ways to share concern and complaints.

Case 2. This can be a delicate situation which most of us would prefer avoiding. We are afraid of the outcome although we dislike the constant criticism. We are concerned over the potential hurts and anger of our parents if we confront them. Remember that you are confronting them because you care and want a better relationship. If you do not confront them and request a change, in all likelihood your relationship will die. Here are some ways you might confront them.

"I would really appreciate your sharing some positive things about what's going on with you."

"When you have a complaint, I would really appreciate it if you would also suggest something positive that you feel we are doing."

"When we are disciplining the children, I would appreciate your not saying anything about what we are doing in front of them. I am always open to positive suggestions but please share them with me later, when they are not around."

Case 3. Here is the actual entire conversation that Harry had with his mother. This may be a totally different way of responding for you, but Harry's persistence and nondefensive responses were effective.

Mom: Hello, Harry, this is Mom.

Harry: Hi, Mom, how are you doing?

Mom: Oh, all right I guess. (She sighs.)

Harry: Well fine, but how come you're sighing?

Mom: Oh, well, I guess I haven't been doing too good. I don't know what's wrong. Anyway, are you coming over this weekend? I was hoping to see you. You know it's been several weeks since you and Tina have been here.

Harry: I'm sorry you're not feeling too well, Mom. No, we won't be coming over this weekend. We have some other things that we have already planned to do.

Mom: Well, what's more important than seeing your mom and dad? Aren't we important to you anymore?

Harry: I can understand that you want to see us, Mom, and you are important, but we won't be coming over this weekend.

Mom: Well, we're sure disappointed. We were positive that you'd be over, and I already have a turkey for dinner. Did you know that?

Harry: No, Mom, I didn't.

Mom: Both your father and I are disappointed. Here we were expecting you two to come and we have the turkey already bought.

Harry: Mom, I can tell that you're disappointed, but we won't be able to be there this weekend.

Mom: You know your brother and sister come over to see us all the time. We don't even have to ask them!

Harry: That's true, Mom. They do come over more, and I'm sure they're a lot of company. We can plan for another time and work it out in advance.

Mom: A good Christian son wants to see his parents often.

Harry: Does my not coming over make me a bad Christian son?

Mom: If you really loved and cared for us, you would want to come and see us.

Harry: Does my not coming to see you this weekend mean that I don't love you?

Mom: It just seems that if you did, you would be here.

Harry: Mom, not coming over doesn't mean I don't care for both of you. I love you and Dad. But I won't be there this time. I'm sure you can use the turkey now or freeze it. Now, let me check with Tina and look at our schedule and see when we could all get together.

Case 4. Vacations with in-laws can be a problem. One spouse can become irritated and may come away very upset after a lengthy visit. A solution might be to engage in some enjoyable activity elsewhere while his mate visits her own parents alone. This may seem to contradict what people have been taught or what seems to be right. But if the extended stay does not promote better relationships between in-laws and does not have a positive effect upon the marriage, this may be the only solution. I am not suggesting that a spouse never visit his in-laws. But many couples have found the answer to be infrequent visits for brief periods of time.

Another possible solution is to shorten the entire visit. If one person would like to visit his/her parents for a month and the other feels uncomfortable with being there that long, or being separated from his/her spouse for that long, they could compromise. Make the visit for only two weeks. It might also be best not to visit in-laws or parents every year on your vacation. This could create a tradition which you may find difficult to change later on. It also limits your possibilities of enjoying other vacation experiences.

Case 5. Constant contact initiated by the parents may reflect many needs on their part—loneliness, control, a need to be needed,

TYPICAL ADJUSTMENT DIFFICULTIES

etc. A couple needs to be in agreement as to the approach to take to resolve this particular conflict. They could agree on a goal and then communicate this goal to his mother: "Mom, we do enjoy hearing from you but there really is no need for you to call each day. Why don't we arrange our calls in this way: If we need something or something is wrong we'll be sure to call you. We also would like you to have the opportunity to develop other relationships and not be so dependent on us. You know that you are always invited for dinner on Sunday. Why don't you plan to see us on Sundays and call us just on Wednesdays? That way we can stay in touch on a regular basis. In case of emergency you know you can always call."

Principles from Scripture

The ideal pattern for any relationship is found within Scripture. In any situation or relationship we need to visualize the Word of God in practice in our lives. Begin by asking yourself, "How do I see myself actually doing what this passage says to do?" Then visualize several practical scenes. If you are going to develop healthy in-law relationships, this process is a must.

WHAT DO YOU THINK?

The Word of God abounds with examples of how we are to live in relation to others. Consider the following passages and apply them to yourself and to your extended family. After each passage write out how you see yourself responding to your in-laws or parents.

1. *"Let all bitterness and wrath and anger and clamor and slander be put away from you, along with all malice. And be kind to one another, tenderhearted, forgiving each other, just as God in Christ also has forgiven you"* (Eph. 4:31–32).

2. *"Pursue peace with all men, and the sanctification without which no one will see the Lord. See to it that no one comes short of the grace of God; that no root of bitterness springing up causes trouble, and by it many be defiled"* (Heb. 12:14–15).

3. *"Blessed are the peacemakers, for they shall be called sons of God"* (Matt. 5:9).

4. *"If possible, so far as it depends on you, be at peace with all men"* (Rom. 12:18).

5. *"Walk . . . with all humility and gentleness, with patience, showing forbearance to one another in love"* (Eph. 4:1–2).

One of the goals of our family relationships is harmony with unity. As people get in the habit of being open, honest, and truthful with one another, deeper relationships develop. But hard work is involved.

Paul wrote, *"Make my joy complete by being of the same mind, maintaining the same love, united in spirit, intent on one purpose"* (Phil. 2:2). We might define these mandates as follows:

"Being of the same mind"—intellectual unity

"Maintaining the same love"—social unity

"United in spirit"—emotional unity

"Intent on one purpose"—volitional unity

Here are some specific steps you can use to improve your in-law relationships. It is vital that both you and your spouse discuss and apply these together.

Take a positive, optimistic view of your in-law relationships. There are many stereotypes about in-laws, but we need to move beyond these biased perspectives.

Mothers-in-law are not always a curse; often they are a blessing.

Couples do not always find it impossible to live with or near their in-laws; some do so and enjoy it.

Men are not more frequently annoyed by their in-laws than are women. There are actually more conflicts between the husband's wife and his mother!

Keeping quiet about in-law problems is not the best way to deal with them. It is far more preferable to clear up differences as they arise.

A person does not have to feel helpless about his in-law relationships; there is much that can be done to make them satisfactory. We must become willing to take risks, however.

Recognize the importance of your partner's family early in your marriage. Any attempts to ignore in-laws just increases friction.

Evaluate which customs from your family background you want and what new ones you would like to try or to establish. Then communicate these to your parents and in-laws. You may want to change customs every few years. Let parents and in-laws know that you will do this. Remember that as married adults *you* have as much say about what to do on Thanksgiving and Christmas as your parents and in-laws do. Perhaps you have simply not yet exercised your freedom of choice.

Consider the needs of your in-laws at this time in their lives. Often the reason people behave in the way they do is because they are trying to fulfill some particular need. But their behavior may not accurately reflect what their needs really are, and thus we are confused. Have you ever considered that the suggestions coming from your in-laws may reflect some of their own needs? They may not really be attempts on their part to control your lives or interfere.

A young woman shared this experience. Whenever her mother would come over to her home she would constantly check the house for dust and dirt. One day after this woman had worked for hours cleaning the house and scrubbing the floor, her mother came for a visit. As the mother sat in her daughter's kitchen, her eyes spotted a six-inch section of woodwork next to the tile which her daughter had missed. She mentioned this to her daughter. The daughter could feel the anger slowly creeping up through her body and her jaw tensed and her face became red.

Her mother noticed this reaction to her comment and said, "Honey, I can't really be of much help to you in anything else, but this is one thing I can help you with." As she shared, the daughter realized that her own mother felt inadequate and useless around her and this was her only way of attempting to feel useful and needed. Both mother and daughter now have a better understanding of each other.

Most parents-in-law need to feel useful, important, and secure. They still like attention. What could you do to help them fulfill these needs? Have you ever asked your in-laws outright what you could do to help them feel useful? It may take just a few simple actions and the expression of concern on your part to help your in-law feel important and loved.

Treat your in-laws with the same consideration and respect that you give your friends. If your in-laws are Christians, can you see them not just as in-laws but as fellow members of the Body of Christ? Can you see them as brothers or sisters in Christ? If they are not Christians, can you see them as individuals for whom Christ died? Can you remember that God's love is an unconditional commitment to imperfect people? See their potential in the same way God sees them.

When your in-laws show an interest in some area of your life and give advice, respond just as you would if a friend were giving you some advice. If it is good advice, follow it and thank them for their concern. If it is not what you want to do, thank them for their suggestion but continue doing what you had planned to do in the first place.

Some couples say, "But you don't know my in-laws or my parents! They won't give up! They keep on and on, and if one approach doesn't work they will try another, or they will try to divide my spouse and me on the issue!" Perhaps they will, but honest and firm assertiveness on your part will be helpful. They probably continue to press because it has worked for them in the past. If you remain firm and consistent, they will learn that you have the right to respond to their advice and suggestions as just that—advice and suggestions, not absolute laws.

Give your in-laws the benefit of doubt. If they seem overly concerned with your affairs, it could be that they are really concerned with your welfare. They may not be trying to interfere in your life. Could your past experience or self talk be influencing your current response?

Look for positive qualities in your in-laws. Too often we tend to focus on the faults and weaknesses of others and overlook their positive traits.

When you visit your in-laws (and when they visit you), keep the visits reasonably short. Be sure you have plenty to do when you are there. Be as thoughtful, courteous, and helpful as you can be. Consider them as you would your friends. Don't view parents and in-laws as built-in baby-sitters.

Give your in-laws time to adjust to the fact that you are now married. Your mother-in-law has been close to your spouse for many years. Recognize that the process of separation should be as gradual as possible.

If you want to give advice to your in-laws, it is usually best to wait until they ask for it. If you offer a suggestion to them, remember that they have the right to accept or reject it. After all, don't you want the same right?

Don't discuss your disagreements and your spouse's faults with your family. If you do you may bias them against your spouse, thus making it more difficult for all parties involved to achieve a better relationship.

Don't quote your family or hold them up as models to your spouse. He/she will probably feel defensive and seek to defend his/her own parents' ways of doing things, even if you are correct in your statements. If you desire your in-laws to do something differently, ask your spouse how he/she feels about his/her parents. Perhaps he/she can share some insights about their behavior that you cannot see. Remember that both families have their idiosyncrasies and eccentricities. This is called being human!

WHAT DO YOU THINK?

1. What have you done in the past to let both your own parents and your in-laws know they are important to you?

2. During the past two weeks, what have you done to express your positive feelings toward your parents and your in-laws?

3. What additional things could you say or do that would let your parents and in-laws know they are important to you?

4. What have you learned about the kind of relationship your parents or in-laws expect from you and your spouse? (Such as how often to visit or call, their involvement in disciplining your children, etc.)

What should you do about their expectations in the future?

5. In the past, how have you helped your parents or in-laws meet their own needs and develop a greater meaning in life?

How can you help them in the future?

6. If your parents or in-laws have had serious difficulties in the past, how did you respond to them?

How can you be more helpful in the future?

7. In the past, what have you done with your parents or in-laws to make it easier for them to demonstrate love toward you and your immediate family?

How can you improve this in the future?

8. What have you done in the past to assist your parents or in-laws to receive love from you?

What have you done to demonstrate your love to them?

Endnotes

MORE COMMUNICATION KEYS FOR YOUR MARRIAGE

Chapter 1

1. Dwight H. Small, *Marriage as Equal Partnership* (Grand Rapids: Baker Book House, 1980.) pp. 29,30,48.

2. Ibid., p. 63.

3. Judson Swihart, *How Do I Say I Love You?* (Downers Grove, IL: InterVarsity Press, 1977), pp. 46–47.

4. Source unknown.

5. William Pruitt, *Run from the Pale Pony* (Grand Rapids: Baker Book House, 1976), pp. 9–10.

6. Lewis B. Smedes, *How Can It Be All Right When Everything Is All Wrong?* (San Francisco: Harper & Row, 1982), p. 61.

Chapter 2

1. Adapted from Gary Emery, *A New Beginning: How You Can Change Your Thoughts Through Cognitive Therapy* (New York: Simon & Schuster, 1981), p. 54.

2. Ibid. p. 59–63.

3. Alexander White, as quoted by Hannah Hurnard, *Winged Life* (Wheaton, IL: Tyndale House Publishers, 1975).

4. Adapted from Jerry Schmidt, *Do You Hear What You're Thinking?* (Wheaton, IL: Victor Books, 1983), pp. 23–24.

Chapter 3

1. Henri H. M. Nouwen, *The Living Reminder* (New York: Seabury Press, 1977), p. 19.

2. W. Hugh Missildine, M. D., *Your Inner Child of the Past* (New York: Simon and Schuster, 1963), p. 59.

3. Joyce Landorf, *Irregular People* (Waco, TX: Word Books, 1982), pp. 61–62.

4. Lloyd John Ogilvie, *God's Best for My Life* (Eugene, OR: Harvest House, 1981), p. 1.

5. Lewis B. Smedes, "Forgiveness: The Power to Change the Past" *Christianity Today*, January 7, 1983, p. 26.

6. Ogilvie, *God's Best for My Life*, p. 9.

7. Creath Davis, *Lord, If I Ever Needed You It's Now* (Palm Springs, CA: Ronald H. Haynes, 1981), p. 88.

8. J. I. Packer, *Knowing God* (Downers Grove, IL: Inter-Varsity Press, 1973), p. 37.

9. Maurice E. Wagner, Ph.D., *The Sensation of Being Somebody* (Grand Rapids: Zondervan Publishing House, 1975), pp. 164–167.

Chapter 4

1. Adapted from Jerry Richardson and Joel Margulis, *The Magic of Rapport* (San Francisco: Harbor Publishing, 1981).

Chapter 5

1. Joyce Landorf, *Tough and Tender* (Old Tappan, NJ: Fleming H. Revell Co., 1975), pp. 76–77.

2. Gary Collins, ed., *Make More of Your Marriage* (Waco, TX: Word Books, 1976), From an article by Dr. Mark Lee, "Why Marriages Fail—Communication," p. 75.

3. David Augsburger, *Caring Enough to Hear* (Ventura, CA: Regal Books, 1982), p. 46.

4. Ibid., pp. 41–42.

5. Ibid., pp. 55–58.

Chapter 6

1. Leonard Zunin, M. D., *Contact: The First Four Minutes* (New York: Random House, 1972), pp. 136–137.

Chapter 7

1. David Smith, *The Friendless American Male* (Ventura, CA: Regal Books, 1983), p. 37.

2. Ibid., p. 43.

3. Warren Farrell, *The Liberated Man* (New York: Random House, Inc., 1974).

4. Ross Campbell, *How to Really Love Your Child* (Wheaton, IL: Scripture Press Publications, 1977), pp. 19–20.

5. Farrell, *The Liberated Man*, pp. 328–329.

6. Herb Goldberg, *The Hazards of Being Male* (New York: The New American Library, 1975), p. 39.

7. Smith, *Friendless American Male*, p. 48.

Chapter 8

1. Many of the concepts in this chapter came from Michael E. McGill, *Changing Him, Changing Her* (New York: Simon & Schuster, 1982).

2. James G. T. Fairfield, *When You Don't Agree* (Scottdale, PA: Herald Press, 1977.

Chapter 9

1. David Burns, M. D., *Feeling Good: The New Mood Therapy* (New York: The New American Library, Inc., 1980), p. 152.

2. Joseph R. Cooke, *Free for the Taking* (Old Tappan, NJ: Fleming H. Revell Company, 1975), pp. 109–110.

3. Richard P. Walters, *Anger, Yours and Mine and What to Do About It* (Grand Rapids: Zondervan Publishing House, 1981), p. 17.

4. Ibid., p. 139.

5. David R. Mace, "Marital Intimacy and the Deadly Love-Anger Cycle," *Journal of Marriage and Family Counseling*, April, 1976, p. 136.

6. Ibid.

7. Walters, *Anger*, pp. 150–151.

Chapter 10

Some material from this chapter has been adapted from *How to Be a Better Than Average In-Law* by Norman Wright (Wheaton, IL: Victor Books, 1981).

The Secrets of a Lasting Marriage

Contents

Introduction

A<small>N OLDER COUPLE</small> you know, or see frequently as you go about your daily activities, has something very special to teach people today. I don't know their names or circumstance, and you may not either, but my experience in marriage counseling assures me they are there, in or near your life.

They may walk together, around the block or at the mall or the beach, arm in arm or holding hands. They may exchange knowing glances and half-smiles while in conversation with others. You may catch her smoothing an unruly wisp of his hair. He has an old-fashioned way of opening doors for her.

They so accurately anticipate what each other is saying or thinking that they often don't complete the sentences they start. A smile or a nod indicates the point is made. It's a kind of telepathy born of having spoken volumes to each other, and having learned each other's style of communication.

The couple I'm describing has been married thirty or forty or fifty years or even more.

They have a love that lasts.

Love that doesn't last gets so much more attention these days that you may think there are very few couples like this left. But the reason I'm confident you known one or more is that I've known them myself. And I think it's high time that a society in which half of the new marriages end in divorce get acquainted with this couple.

We need desperately to learn what kept them together through the years, some of which were very difficult. They stuck together through hard financial times, and wars, and sickness, and loss. Looking into their eyes you can sometime see remnants of pain, but somehow—unlike many modern marriages—it didn't create a wound between them that could not be healed.

In my work with couples, I believe I have found some characteristics of this couple's relationship that other marriages can use. So in this book we will be looking not at what makes marriages fail, but what makes them last. In the process I will challenge you, the reader, to call on every available resource, including the power of

God and His Holy Spirit, to look at your own marriage in this positive light.

A great deal is at stake. You and your spouse can find greater joy by developing a love that lasts. As many current studies show, the children we used to say would "bounce back" from divorce, but who actually often suffer permanent damage, can be saved a great deal of pain when couples discover a love that lasts. Homes can be happier when they are characterized by long-term marriages. Opportunities for personal and interpersonal growth are so much greater in this kind of marriage.

As Christians, discovering a love that lasts is important for another reason that is often overlooked. We need to love forever because that's how God loves. *Whole marriages give glory to God, while broken marriages communicate the wrong message about Him.*

When the aged apostle John wrote to early Christians, he reflected profoundly on this topic of love. He said it is demonstrated in its highest degree by God's sending His own Son, Jesus, into the world. Then John states: *"Love is made complete among us . . . because in this world we are like him"* (1 John 4:17, *NIV*, roman added).

God started a vast circle of love in sending His Son. But as heavenly a concept as that is, think of this—John says that *this circle is completed by human love!* When two people give to each other in the way God gives to us, they demonstrate something of the love of God. And of course the reverse is true: When two believers fail to love, it's a bad reflection on the God who taught them to love.

Paul applied this principal to the Church when he urged Christians to "keep the unity of the Spirit through the bond of peace" (Eph. 4:3, *NIV*). Then follows that famous list of "ones"—one body, Spirit, hope, Lord, faith, baptism—and *one God and Father* (see vv. 4–6). Christian unity is based on the unity of God. Unlike pagan deities, God is One. And Christians who live as one body in the Church reflect that oneness. And when we are divisive, we still reflect a picture of the God we serve—although it is a very wrong picture. Divided, factious Christians give the impression they're getting their orders from differing gods!

In a similar way, Christian union in marriage is based on the unity of God. When a couple allows its immaturity or in-laws or selfishness or differing views of money management or child rearing or a host of other issues to drive it apart, it's not just a "this worldly" problem. The two are demonstrating that they may have a problem with God as well. Because despite the differences God has with us, He never gives up on His long-term love for us!

This book shows how you and your spouse can also develop a love that doesn't give up.

In chapter 1 we'll talk about the nature of that kind of love, and about the power of commitment. Chapter 2 helps you recall the love that brought you and your spouse together, and shows how to keep from falling out of love. Getting down to practical, if not brass, tacks, chapter 3 answers the question of what makes a marriage work. Chapter 4 is designed to inspire in each of you a vision of what your marriage might be. And chapter 5 challenges you to probe your thought life to root out the kind of negative and false thinking that defeats so many marriages.

In chapter 6 we deal with the sticky wicket of change—transitions that can be either friends or foes. Working through individual differences is the focus of chapter 7, and rediscovering the positive steps that have previously worked in your marriage is the topic of chapter 8. Chapter 9 is about the all-important topic of the spiritual connection between you and your mate, and chapter 10 allows several of those couples I mentioned, whose love has lasted through the years, to tell you what worked for them.

So read on—if you care deeply not just about the first blush of love when it is beautiful and so very tender, but also about the maturing of a relationship into a love that lasts.

1
A Love That Lasts

THE WONDER and the promise of a love that lasts were once related to me in the writings of an older man. Listen to the message he gave to all of us as he wrote:

I couldn't even describe what I thought love was when I was first married. Forty years is a long time to be together with one person. It's almost half of a century. All I knew then was that I wanted a love that would keep us together forever. Jean really felt those love feelings a lot of people talk about. I'm not so sure I did. But I knew that I loved her. I just knew it. Jean described me as a "logical lover." I liked that. I still do. That's me all right. We learned it's all right to be different in the style of love we had and how we expressed it, as long as we were adaptable enough to learn to put it into a package that the other person liked. I didn't do that the first twenty years and that's what created what we now call our valley of "love recessions." Sometimes the wick of our candle of love got kind of low. But it never went out. We learned to work at our love and make it stronger. And it works, no matter what anyone says.

Now that we're almost in our seventies we don't know how many more years we'll have to love one another. But we'll make the most of them. I'm not a poet or much of a reader, never have been, but I found a statement that puts into words some of my thoughts better than I can. Maybe this will have a message to the next generation right behind us.

"It is love in old age, no longer blind, that is true love. For love's highest intensity doesn't necessarily mean it's highest quality. Glamour and jealousy are gone; and the ardent caress, no longer needed, is valueless compared to the reassuring touch of a trembling hand. Passers-by commonly see little beauty in the embrace of young lovers on a park bench, but the understanding smile of an old wife to her husband is one of the loveliest things in the world."

That sums it all up.[1]

A lasting love is possible, and it's also necessary. Commitment and love go hand in hand. Just as commitment is a choice, so also is love. Love is not just something that happens. It must be cultivated so it can grow.

Romance Versus Infatuation

As I work with young couples in premarital counseling, I push them to evaluate whether what they are calling love is really love. If it's infatuation, then both it and the relationship will die. There is a blindness to infatuation that makes people see what they want to see. Later they discover what they thought they saw is not what they got. When their infatuation dies, it's like stepping out of a plane without a parachute. The trip down is long and painful.

The longer we are married the more we understand (hopefully!) about the kind of love that binds us together when we are at our best and at our worst. As a personal friend put it, "There are many times when we look at each other and there is no physical or passionate response. That's OK. It's been there before and it will be there again. We're not threatened when it's not because we know that we love each other. That's permanent, lasting. And we think it's also a gift from God. And for that we rejoice."

When couples begin their lives together there is usually a sense of romantic or passionate love. That's good. For many people that's how it begins. It can be the overture that comes before the main event—lasting love. Romance and passion are easy; love is work. The difference is, "Romance is based on sexual attraction, the enjoyment of affection and imagination. Love is based on decisions, promises, and commitments."[2]

There is a benefit to romantic or passionate love. Dr. Neil Warren suggests that:

> . . . passionate love performs a powerful service as long as it lasts. It focuses the total attention of two people on each other long enough for them to build an enduring structure for their relationship. The passionate love experience will never

hold the two of them together forever. But building "enduring structures" for a relationship takes a lot of time and effort, and if two people are not attracted to one another physically, the hard work might never get done. That's another function of passionate love—the life-changing experience of being accepted and valued. When two people find themselves totally engrossed in each other, they often experience a dramatic boost in their self-esteem. For in the process of discovering that someone else finds them attractive, they begin to see themselves as attractive, too. Passionate love focuses a bright, positive light on each of the persons involved, and both of them fall in love not only with each other, but also with themselves.[3]

It does help to have some natural physical attraction or emotional response.

The Friendship of Marriage

What kind of love helps a marriage last? You may be surprised, because I'm not going to begin with *agape*, which is what most people expect. I'm starting with another kind of love—friendship love. Why? Because in a national study of hundreds of couples who had fulfilling marriages, couples were given thirty-nine factors that would best explain the success of their marriages and why they were successful whereas others were not. Both husbands and wives were asked to put these factors in order of importance for their marriages. The fascinating fact was that the top seven selected by both husbands and wives were the same. But the first and second choices reflect the type of love we're considering here. They were "My spouse is my best friend" and "I like my spouse as a person."[4]

This love is *phileo* love. *Philos* is a biblical word for friendship love. Whereas romantic love cannot sustain a relationship, companionate or friendship love can. A friend is someone you like to be with. You enjoy his or her company; you like his or her personality; you can play and work together. You have shared interests. It's not that you are loved only because of what you share, but by sharing you develop a different kind of love. It means companionship, communication, and cooperation. One writer describes it as "companionate love."

This may be defined as a strong bond, including a tender attachment, enjoyment of the other's company and friendship. It is not characterized by wild passion and constant excitement, although these feelings may be experienced from time to time. The main difference between passionate and companionate love is that the former thrives on deprivation, frustration, a high arousal level, and absence. The latter thrives on contact and requires time to develop and mature.[5]

I have seen numerous marriages over the years fall apart not only because this type of love was nonexistent, but because the couples weren't even sure how to develop it. When *phileo* or companionate love has developed, couples will have this to stabilize their relationships when the romantic love fades. Unfortunately, some with certain personality proclivities are almost addicted to the "high" or excitement of romantic love, and when it diminishes, they fall apart or bail out to seek new and exciting relationships.

Requirement: Friendship
What does friendship love entail? It's an unselfish dedication to your partner's happiness. It's when the fulfillment of his or her needs becomes one of your needs. It's learning to enjoy what he or she enjoys, not just to convince him or her that you're the right person, but to *develop* the enjoyment yourself as you share the enjoyment together.
I love trout fishing. Because of my wife's unselfish friendship-love, she developed a liking for trout fishing, too. Now she even has her own set of waders and a float tube. Recently she asked me to take her to Alaska for salmon fishing sometime!
I have genuinely learned to enjoy art and fine paintings from Joyce. We both learned, and it brought us closer together. Friendship means you do some things together, but you're also comfortable with having your own individual interests and you encourage each other in these. There is a balance between togetherness and separateness.

Requirement: Intimacy
Friendship-love involves a certain level of intimacy in which there is openness, vulnerability, and emotional connection. You also share goals, plans, and dreams, and work together.[6]
A marriage that lasts is a marriage that has a husband and wife

who are friends. In fact, a marriage that begins with friendship as the initial relationship, with romance developing later, is the ideal basis for a marriage. As a friendship develops over the years, the real evidence is there when you choose each other for just the joy of the other person's company. Some couples have said they are friends, but sometimes I wonder if they would be if their sexual or household dependencies didn't exist.

Requirement: Practice

Friendship in marriage means that you practice it. Friendship is part of God's intention for marriage. There is a vow of trust. You don't become selfishly competitive, but wish your partner the best. You share each other's happiness and rejoice in it almost as much as the other does.

A friend doesn't automatically approve of everything we do or say, and that's all right. Friends don't attempt to control each other, because they respect each other too much. Friends try to understand the other's preferences. They can disagree and it doesn't damage the relationship. To be a friend you have to be able to take the other person's point of view. Becoming a friend necessitates changing old habits and beliefs.

Recently I read an interesting book on peer marriage. The word "peer" means one that is of equal standing with the other. The author felt there were several requirements to be fulfilled in order to have deep friendship in a marriage. Friendship in marriage means learning to express your romantic side in a way that meets your spouse's needs. It also means that both husband and wife are able to be a caregiver and a care receiver.

Counterfeit Loves

There are many expressions of love in marriage, some genuine and some counterfeit. Dr. Les Parrott effectively describes the counterfeit styles of love in his book *Love's Unseen Enemy* (Zondervan Publishers). Each style has several characteristics.

Pleasers

Unfortunately, some people equate marital love with being a pleaser. Pleasers are persons who are dominated and guided by their emotions. They do the right things for the wrong reasons. They do loving things rather than *being* loving persons.

Pleasers have this overwhelming need to please. It's as though they live to make people happy. As you watch them, they appear to be conscientious and caring. They go out of their way to make others—especially their partners—feel comfortable. They're especially good at remembering to do the little things others overlook. They're approachable and agreeable, and when asked to do something they usually do more than they're requested to do, and they do it with a warm smile.

But these acts of love aren't voluntary; they're compulsive. Such people feel personally responsible for the happiness of others. If their partners are unhappy, they feel guilty. They're driven to do too much so they will feel better. In a marriage they may end up feeling used. And . . . most pleasers tend to be women.

Pleasers are the givers of life. Hundreds of husbands and wives constantly give and give and give, but not because of love. It is either because of guilt or because they meet some of their own needs by giving. They need to give to others in order to feel good about themselves. It is like being hooked on helping. They become "helpaholics."

Pleasers try to avoid being receivers. When they must receive, they feel uneasy and guilty, and they begin thinking of ways to repay.

Pleasers have a performance mentality. They must do things right away, and they want to look good. They need approval from their partners in order to keep their guilt under control. They live for the applause. They also live with a fear of failure, and unfortunately this can drive them to comply with unrealistic requests for their help. Saying no to anyone is unheard of, because they view that as a personal failure. But this is not a healthy, biblical way to love another person.

Pleasers believe they're responsible for their spouses' well-being and happiness. It reminds me of a rescuer, a self-appointed lifeguard. But the ones they tend to rescue aren't drowning.

To pleasers, self-denial is not a means to an end, but an end in and of itself. But this makes loving behavior no longer loving. They turn into martyrs and, in the process, may drive others away. This in turn makes them feel more guilt so they try harder, which pushes others away even more. I've seen this happen again and again in marriages, and yet pleasers can't understand the negative effect of their behavior.

Pleasers are some of the great conflict avoiders of the world. They defer, give in, say yes when no is more appropriate, and allow wrong to continue. But they do have limits. If pushed or cornered into conflict, they either give in and blame themselves or erupt like a volcano because they're so unskilled in resolving conflicts.

In marriage, pleasers live for their partners' affections, holding on to any small measure they can get. But they also expect their partners to know what they want or need without ever telling them. Can you even imagine pleasers expressing what they need to their partners? Not really! Any withdrawal or diminishing of intimacy on the part of their partners is a disaster.

Time after time I have seen the same scenario played out in my office. The pleasing spouse sits there and says, "I just don't understand it. I love him so much, and I tried to please. . . . Yet it seems that the more I try to please, the more I seem to push him away from me." It's true. The partner felt smothered and constricted.

One husband married to a pleaser told me, "It makes me sick. I wish she had more backbone and would stand up to me. Let's have some conflict. I'm tired of having a 'yes' person for a spouse." Pleasers tend to create some of the very problems they wish to avoid.

The Controller

Another counterfeit pattern is the *controller*. In many ways, this is the opposite of a pleaser. They both have a strong need for acceptance, but they certainly try to get it in different ways. Pleasers yield power to others in their desire to be loved, but controllers take over and take charge to gain the respect of others. A pleaser has an overabundance of sympathy but very little objectivity. The controller, being just the opposite, has a great amount of objectivity but doesn't know the first thing about sympathy. Controllers are very analytical. Even though this helps them understand the needs of others, the purpose is usually to gain control over them. Controllers can usually be identified by seven characteristics of how they relate to others.

1. *Their need to be in control is obvious.* They use two means to gain control. Fear expressed through intimidation is typical, and they are very adept at discovering and using weaknesses in other people. The other tool is to quietly silence their partners—by a word, a rolling of the eyes, or a gesture. Any mistake is noticed and used to guide the erring spouse into line with the controller's agenda.

2. *Controllers are very self-reliant.* For them, teamwork in a marriage is not possible. Totally independent, they create their own vacuums of loneliness, for their style of independence alienates them from others.
3. *Emotion is absent from their lives.* This helps to create marriages in which their partners end up starving for closeness and intimacy (see point 7). The emotional bonding that is necessary for a healthy relationship fails to happen. And all too often, controlling kills their spouses' love.
4. *They are inept at expressing loving behavior.* What may appear to be graciousness, politeness, kindness, or even being very sociable has a purpose in mind—to take control of the other person. Having love as an end result has no real meaning, but *using* love as a means to an end makes sense to them. If they show interest in another person, it's for a purpose. Their partners end up feeling used.
5. *Rules, rules, and more rules is their way of life.* And the more rigid they are the better. There is a right way to do things—it's their way, and it's the only way. They know what's best for others and will orchestrate their lives.
6. *Their style of communication is demanding in words, intent, and tone.* They're bottom-line people who cut right to the heart of a matter.
7. *Controllers won't open up and reveal their inner lives and feelings* for fear of losing their position of power or control. This makes it very difficult to develop intimacy in a marriage, especially when an overly dominant controller's partner is overly submissive. Even the submissive partner becomes fearful of being open and vulnerable, because he or she could be attacked and overwhelmed by the other person. There is a lack of mutuality in the marriage.

Agape Love in Marriage

Another form of love, agape, can increase our gratitude as well as our constant awareness and remembrance of God's agape love for us. An attitude of thankfulness for all of life develops. We're able to see and concentrate upon the positive qualities and attributes of our spouses, which we might overlook or take for granted. Our mindsets and attributes can be refocused because of the presence of agape love. An attitude of appreciation causes us to respond with even more love toward our spouses.

Manifestations of Agape Love

Agape love manifests itself through several characteristics. First, it is an *unconditional* love. It is not based upon your spouse's performance, but upon your need to share this act of love with your spouse. If you don't, your spouse may live with the fear that you will limit your love if he or she does not meet your expectations.

Sometimes you have to learn to love your partner unconditionally. Here is what one husband said about how he learned to love in this way:

> When I married my wife, we both were insecure and she did everything she could to try to please me. I didn't realize how dominating and uncaring I was toward her. My actions in our early marriage caused her to withdraw even more. I wanted her to be self-assured, to hold her head high, and her shoulders back. I wanted her to be feminine and sensual.
>
> The more I wanted her to change, the more withdrawn and insecure she felt. I was causing her to be the opposite of what I wanted her to be. I began to realize the demands I was putting on her, not so much by words but by body language.
>
> By God's grace I learned that I must love the woman I married, not the woman of my fantasies. I made a commitment to love Susan for who she was—who God created her to be.
>
> The change came about in a very interesting way. During a trip to Atlanta I read an article in *Reader's Digest.* I made a copy of it and have kept it in my heart and mind ever since.
>
> It was the story of Johnny Lingo, a man who lived in the South Pacific. The islanders all spoke highly of this man, but when it came time for him to find a wife the people shook their heads in disbelief. In order to obtain a wife you paid for her by giving her father cows. Four to six cows was considered a high price. But the woman Johnny Lingo chose was plain, skinny, and walked with her shoulders hunched and her head down. She was very hesitant and shy. What surprised everyone was Johnny's offer—he gave eight cows for her! Everyone chuckled about it, since they believed his father-in-law put one over on him.
>
> Several months after the wedding, a visitor from the U.S. came to the islands to trade and heard the story about Johnny

Lingo and his eight-cow wife. Upon meeting Johnny and his wife the visitor was totally taken back, since this wasn't a shy, plain, and hesitant woman but one who was beautiful, poised, and confident. The visitor asked about the transformation, and Johnny Lingo's response was very simple. "I wanted an eight-cow woman, and when I paid that for her and treated her in that fashion, she began to believe that she was an eight-cow woman. She discovered she was worth more than any other woman in the islands. And what matters most is what a woman thinks about herself."

This simple story impacted my life. I immediately sent Susan flowers. (I had rarely if ever done that before.) The message on the card simply said "To My Eight-Cow Wife." The florist (who was a friend of mine) thought I had lost my mind and questioned if that was really what I wanted to say.

Susan received the flowers with total surprise and bewilderment at the card. When I returned from the trip I told her that I loved her for who she is and that I considered her to be my eight-cow wife, and then I gave her the article to read.

I now look for ways to show her that I am proud of her and how much I appreciate her. An example of this involved a ring. When we became engaged I had an antique engagement ring that I inherited from a great-great-aunt. Susan seemed very pleased and I never thought any more about it. But I had come out cheap, and that's how she felt. After twenty years of marriage, she shared with me how she felt about the hand-me-down wedding ring. We had our whole family get involved in learning about diamonds. Susan found what she liked. It was not the largest stone nor the most expensive. I would have gladly paid more. I bought it and gave it to her for Christmas. "To My Eight-Cow Wife, with all my love!" But what this did for our relationship is amazing.

First, it changed me! My desires began to change. My desire is now for Susan to be all that God has designed her to be. It is my responsibility as her husband to allow her that freedom.

It also changed her. Susan became free. She learned who she is in Christ. She has gained confidence and self-assurance. She is more aware of her appearance, her clothes, hair, makeup, because she is free to be who she is.

Susan rarely buys clothes for herself. Last year for Christmas I told her this year I would buy her an outfit or some type of clothing each month. This has boosted her confidence in her appearance. She looks great because she wants to!

Susan really is an Eight-Cow Wife of whom I am very proud. We have been married now since 1971.[7]

Agape love is given *in spite of how the other person behaves*. It is a gift, rather than something that is earned. You are not obligated to love. This form of real love is an unconditional commitment to an imperfect person. And it will require more of you than you ever realized. But that's what marriage is all about.

Agape love is also *a transparent love*. It is strong enough to allow your partner to get close to you and inside you. Transparency involves honesty, truth, and sharing positive and negative feelings. Paul Tournier shared the story of a woman whose mother gave her this advice: "Don't tell your husband everything: To maintain her prestige and keep her husband's love, a woman must retain a mystery for him." Tournier commented, "What a mistake! It fails to recognize the meaning of marriage and the meaning of love. Transparency is the law of marriage and the couple must strive for it untiringly at the cost of confessions which are always new and sometimes very hard."[8]

Agape love has a *deep reservoir to draw from*, so no matter what occurs, the love is felt and provides stability during times of stress and conflict.

Agape kindness is *servant power*. Kindness is love's willingness to enhance the life of another.

Chuck Swindoll describes this willingness:

Anne Morrow was shy and delicate. Butterfly like. Not dull or stupid or incompetent, just a quiet specimen of timidity. Her dad was ambassador to Mexico when she met an adventurous young fellow who visited south of the border for the U.S. State Department. The man was flying from place to place promoting aviation. Everywhere he went he drew capacity crowds. You see, he had just won $40,000 for being the first to cross the Atlantic by air. The strong pilot and the shy princess fell deeply in love.

When she became Mrs. Charles Lindbergh, Anne could have easily been eclipsed by her husband's shadow. She wasn't, however. The love that bound the two together for the next forty-seven years was tough love, mature love, tested by triumph and tragedy alike. They would never know the quiet comfort of being an anonymous couple in a crowd. The Lindbergh name didn't allow that luxury. Her man, no matter where he went, was news, forever in the limelight . . . clearly a national hero. But rather than becoming a resentful recluse or another nameless face in a crowd of admirers, Anne Morrow Lindbergh emerged to become one of America's most popular authors, a woman highly admired for her own accomplishments.

How? Let's let her give us the clue to the success of her career.

"To be deeply in love, of course, is a great liberating force and the most common experience that frees . . . Ideally, both members of a couple in love free each other to new and different worlds. I was no exception to the general rule. The sheer fact of finding myself loved was unbelievable and changed my world, my feelings about life and myself. I was given confidence, strength, and almost a new character. The man I was to marry believed in me and what I could do, and consequently I found I could do more than I realized."

Charles did believe in Anne to an extraordinary degree. He saw beneath her shy surface. He realized that down in her innermost well was a wealth of wisdom, a deep, profound, untapped reservoir of ability. Within the security of his love she was freed—released—to discover and develop her own capacity, to get in touch with her own feelings, to cultivate her own skills, and to emerge from that cocoon of shyness a beautiful, ever-delicate butterfly whose presence would enhance many lives far beyond the perimeter of her husband's shadow. He encouraged her to do her own kind of flying and he admired her for it.

Does that imply she was a wild, determined, independent wife, bent on "doing her own thing," regardless? Am I leaving that impression? If so, I'm not communicating clearly. Such would be an inaccurate open portrait of Anne Morrow Lindbergh. She was a butterfly, remember . . . not a hawk.

Make no mistake about it, this lady was inseparably linked in love to her man. In fact, it was within the comfort of his love that she gleaned the confidence to reach out, far beyond her limited, shy world.

We're talking roots and wings. A husband's love that is strong enough to reassure yet unthreatened enough to release. Tight enough to embrace yet loose enough to enjoy. Magnetic enough to hold, yet magnanimous enough to allow for flight

. . . with an absence of jealousy as others applaud her accomplishments and admire her competence. Charles, the secure, put away the net so Anne, the shy, could flutter and fly.[9]

Agape love is the readiness to move close to another and allow him/her to move close to you. Agape is trying to be content with those things that don't live up to your expectations.

Agape love must be at the heart of a marriage. It's a self-giving love that keeps on going even when the other person is unlovable. This love will keep the other types of love alive. It involves kindness and being sympathetic, thoughtful and sensitive to the needs of your loved one, even when you feel he or she doesn't deserve it.

Think about this:

Love means to commit yourself without guarantee, to give yourself completely in the hope that your love will produce love in the loved person. Love is an act of faith, and whoever is of little faith is also of little love. The perfect love would be one that gives all and expects nothing. It would, of course, be willing and delighted to take anything it was offered, the more the better. But it would ask for nothing. For if one expects nothing and asks nothing, she can never be deceived or disappointed. It is only when love demands that it brings on pain.[10]

Agape's Power

Since agape love is the heart of the marital love relationship, let's think some more about this wonderful gift.

Agape love is a healing force. To demonstrate the power of this love let's apply it to a critical area that affects marriage—irritability. Irritability is a barrier, and it keeps others at a distance if they know it is present within us. It is the launching pad for attack, lashing out, anger, sharp words, resentment, and refusal of others' offers to love us.

Agape love is unique in that it causes us to seek to meet the needs of our mate rather than demanding that our own needs be reciprocated. Our irritability and frustrations diminish because we are seeking to fulfill another rather than pursuing our own needs and demanding their satisfaction.

The Need to Express Agape

No matter how deep your love for your spouse may be, it will be unknown to him/her unless it is openly and consistently expressed in a manner that registers with your partner. Far too many marriage partners are silent and passive in their expressions of love. God has called us to be vessels of love pouring out generously to our partners. Marriage is God's creative gift to us, providing us the opportunity to express love to its fullest in the safety and security of an abiding relationship. And we are only able to love because He first loved us. His love is so extensive that it can heal the loveless experiences of the past. We no longer need to be dominated by hurtful memories. Instead, we can live and love knowing the adequacy of Jesus Christ in our lives.[11]

So liberating is this miracle of loving and being loved that it is something of which a husband and wife will take great joy in reminding one another. Indeed, one of the most important tasks for a couple to fulfill is this work of telling one another their love, which at heart is the wonderful reminder that they each are loved by God. This will not always be a pleasant or an easy task: Sometimes, to be sure, when a wife says, "I love you," it is something that a husband does not want to hear, at times something that he almost cannot bear to hear. He is tired of hearing it. He doesn't want to think about what it means. He does not want to let go of whatever it is that is preventing him from accepting it. He doesn't have the time or the energy to make a response. He doesn't want to be bothered with it. It is one more responsibility he can do without. He is not in the mood to be loved, let alone to love anyone else.

Still in spite of all resistance, the words of love are important. It is important that they be heard, and it is important that they be spoken, out loud, no matter how painful this hearing and this speaking might be. It is a marvelous thing when love comes bubbling up like tears in the throat as one is gripped by a sudden stabbing realization of the other's beauty and goodness, of how incredibly precious they are.[12]

Do you know how love is expressed? It is expressed through the ears. It is expressed with the eyes. When you give attention, you give affection. It is expressed in time scheduled and availability offered. It's the assurance that each will be there for the other.[13]

We have all been called to be people of love. Love is actually a commandment from God. Again and again in Scripture Jesus calls us to love:

Jesus replied: "'Love the Lord your God with all your heart and with all your soul and with all your mind.' This is the first and greatest commandment. And the second is like it: 'Love your neighbor as yourself.' All the Law and the Prophets hang on these two commandments" (Matt. 22:37–39, NIV).

Conclusions About Agape

Because love is a commandment, there are three conclusions that can be drawn from it.[14]

Loving others is a moral requirement. It is our responsibility to love even if others don't love us. This is an important principle when the love in your reservoir is low.

Love is an act of the will. We choose to love in our hearts and minds. You choose to think a certain way about your spouse. Love means choosing what is right and best to do rather than what you may want or feel like doing. It is this choice that will keep many marriages alive.[15]

Love is not determined by our feelings. Nowhere in Scripture does it say to love others if you feel like it. We can't command our feelings. They come and go. They're like the tide in the ocean; they come in and then recede. Don't allow your feelings to be your guide. I've had a number of spouses say, "My feelings of love for that person are gone." The shock on their faces is evident when I say "great." Now they can learn true love if they haven't already. And it does happen.

The Glue of Commitment

What I'm going to say now is going to sound contradictory, but here it is. The glue that will keep marriage together is *not* love.

There is a word that is becoming foreign in meaning and application to our culture in general—it's the word "commitment." Oh, I hear many who say they can commit to someone or something, and their commitment is in place when everything is going well. But it's when things get tough that the true level of commitment is evident.

Is Marriage a Contract?

Some psychologists, marriage counselors, and ministers have suggested that marriage is a contract, and many people are quick to agree. But is this really true? Is marriage really a contract?

In every contract there are certain conditional clauses. A contract between two parties, whether they be companies or individuals, involves the responsibility of both parties to carry out their parts of the bargain. These are conditional clauses or "if" clauses. If you do *this*, the other person must do *this*, and if the other person does *that*, you must do *that*. But in the marriage relationship there are no conditional clauses. Nowhere in the marriage ceremony does the pastor say, "If the husband loves his wife, then the wife continues in the contract." Or, "If the wife is submissive to her husband, then the husband carries out the contract."

In most contracts there are escape clauses. An escape clause says that if the party of the first part does not carry out his or her responsibilities, then the party of the second part is absolved. If one person does not live up to his or her part of the bargain, the second person can get out of the contract. This is an escape clause. In marriage there is no escape clause.

Marriage is not a contract. It is an unconditional commitment into which two people enter.

The Meaning of Commitment

Commitment means many things to different people. For some, the strength of their commitments varies with how they feel emotionally or physically. But the word "commit" is a verb and means "to do or to perform." It is not based primarily on feelings. It is a binding pledge or promise. It is a private pledge you also make public. It is a pledge carried out to completion, running over any roadblocks. It is a total giving of oneself to another person. Yes, it is risky, but it makes life fulfilling.

Commitment means giving up the childish dream of being unconditionally accepted by your partner who will fulfill all your needs and make up for all your childhood disappointments. It means expecting to be disappointed by the other, learning to accept this, and not using it as a reason to pull the plug.[16]

Perhaps a better way to describe this is to compare it to bungee jumping. If you've ever taken the plunge, you know that when you take that step off the platform you are committed to following through. There is no more time to think it over or change your mind. There is no turning back.

A friend of mine shared with me what has made his marriage last. He said, "Norm, we each had a commitment to each other and to the marriage. When our commitment to each other was low, it was the commitment to the marriage that kept us together."

Commitment to another person until he or she dies seems idealistic to some. When it suits us and we're not inconvenienced by it, we keep it. But when certain problems occur, it's not valid.

Commitment is more than continuing to stick it out and suffer with a poor choice of a spouse. It's not just maintaining; it's investing. It's not just enduring; it's working to make the relationship grow. It's not just accepting and tolerating negative and destructive patterns on the part of your spouse; it's working toward change. It's sticking to someone regardless of circumstances. A wife once shared this story with me in a letter:

> In 1988, I was diagnosed with Epstein Barr Virus (Chronic Fatigue Syndrome). It really changed my life, which had been filled with excitement and vibrancy. My husband, Kelly, has stood with me and become my protector through these past years of adjustment. He has taken care of our family when my strength would not allow me. He has held my hand through depression, including ten days in the hospital. He has insisted I get needed rest, even if it put more of a burden on him. He has paid the price of any hopeful cure we have found, no matter the cost. He has been more than a husband; he has been my best friend—a friend that has stayed closer than any family member. He was my "knight in shining armor when I met him" and he has proven to be so throughout our fourteen-and-a-half years of marriage. I sometimes tell him that he has been "my salvation," because I don't know that I would still be going on if it weren't for his strength. I don't know that I would still walk with the Lord if it were not for his encouragement. Knowing him has been the greatest experience in my life.

Commitment Through Change

Keep in mind there will be ups and downs throughout the life of your marriage. There will be massive changes, some predictable and others intrusive. They hold the potential for growth, but are risky at the same time. Many marriages die because too many choose to ignore the inescapable fact that relationships and people change.

A wife shared the following with the congregation at her son's church:

> Since we have been married fifty years, you can just imagine how much change we have gone through: three wars, eleven Presidents, five recessions, going from the model A to

the moon, from country road to the information superhighway. While these changes around us have been great, the personal changes that God has enacted within us through each other have been even greater. Although we often couldn't see how God was working in our lives at that time, we look back now and realize that our marriage has been a school of character development. God has used my husband in my life, and he's used me in his life to make us more like Christ. So what are the lessons that we've learned about how God uses marriage to change us? There are many. Through fifty years of marriage we've learned that differences develop us, that crises cultivate us, and that ministry melts us together.

First, God has used our differences to help us grow. There have been many, many crises that God has used to develop us and to grow us. The first one was the big, big one—the crisis of being separated as soon as we got married. Ours was a wartime romance. We met at church, dated two months, got married after three weeks of engagement, and just after two months of marriage, we didn't see each other for the next two years, for Jimmy was shipped to the South Pacific during World War II. When he returned two years later, we were total strangers, but we were married to each other!

How would you have handled that situation?

How do you handle change? How do you handle the difficult, sudden, and painful changes? You've got to be willing to face the fact that change exists—you will change, your marriage will change, your partner will want you to change, and you will want him or her to change.[17]

Donald Harvey, author of *The Drifting Marriage*, says,

Making a commitment to marriage as an institution is not meant to be a sentencing. Its intent is to offer security and stability. All couples have conflicts. Every marriage has to make adjustments. Feeling secure in a mate's commitment to the marriage allows the opportunity for dealing with conflicts and for needed adjustments to occur. This is what makes marriage resilient.

A marriage can endure many affronts, whether from within or without, if the commitment to marriage as an institution is strong. It takes this kind of commitment for growth to occur.[18]

The Security of Commitment

I like what Neil Warren has said about one of the advantages that commitment provides for a relationship:

> Commitment significantly eases the fear of abandonment. It is this fear that is central to so many persons. It is often the most potent fear of all.
>
> When we were young and unable to take care of ourselves, we worried about becoming lost in a crowd, forgotten while waiting to be picked up at school, or left alone by dying parents. Fears like these persist throughout our lives. We shudder at the very thought of abandonment.
>
> That's why a spouse's promise to remain devoted means so much. Your partner will be loyal through every kind of circumstance. That frees you in a radical way. It allows you to be yourself at the deepest of levels, to risk and grow, to be absolutely authentic without any fear of being abandoned.[19]

I think the following comments by a wife illustrate lifelong expression of love and commitment. After many years together, one partner in every marriage could experience in one way or another what this person did.

> Real life death scenes aren't like the movies. My husband, too tall for a regulation bed, lay with his feet sticking out of the covers. I stood clinging to his toes as though that would save his life. I clung so that if I failed to save him from falling off the cliff of the present, of the here and now, we'd go together. That's how it was in the netherworld of the intensive care unit. . . .
>
> It seemed that the entire world had turned into night. Cold and black. No place you'd volunteer to enter. Doctors tried to be kind. Their eyes said, "This is out of our hands. There's nothing more we can do."
>
> A nurse with a soft Jamaican lilt placed a pink blanket over my shoulders. Someone whispered, "It's just a matter of minutes."
>
> Just a matter of minutes to tell each other anything we had ever forgotten to say. Just a few minutes to take an accounting of our days together. Had we loved well enough?[20]

There will always be unasked and unanswered questions because of our imperfections. But love and commitment that are renewed and expressed lessen the need to ask. Perhaps one husband's description of commitment sums it up best of all:

> Commitment is dangerous. It can be exploited. If my wife takes my commitment for granted, she may rest too easily on her laurels. Perhaps commitment should be not simply to each other as we are but to the highest potentialities we can achieve together. Commitment then would be to marriage not simply as a status but as a dynamic process. Let me commit myself to a lifelong adventure, the adventure of living with this woman. The route of this adventure has been only dimly charted by those who have gone before. Because I am unique and my partner is unique, our marriage will also be unique. We commit ourselves to undertaking this adventure together, and to following wherever it may lead. Part of the excitement of marriage is not knowing in advance what either the joys or the sorrows will be. We can be sure, however, that we will be confronted with countless challenges. Commitment provides the momentum for going forward in the face of those challenges.[21]

Well, that's a start on understanding what makes marriages last—love and commitment. Perhaps we should call these requirements the framework for a marriage. Now we need to consider the day-to-day elements that help to keep the framework in place. That's what our journey is all about for the remainder of this book.

2

How to Keep from
Falling Out of Love

A WIFE shared with me, "I knew there would be disappointments and that John had flaws. During the first two years these became more evident, and each time they emerged I just took the attitude of 'I knew this beforehand. I'm just discovering them now. It's all right. I couldn't handle a perfect man anyway, because he's got to live with me. And I've got lots of flaws.' I guess that's what love is all about . . . loving a flawed person. I guess God knows all about that, too, doesn't He?"

Certainly He does. Yet God stays in love with us.

And for human beings to remain in love and have it continue to grow year after year, it is helpful to understand the steps involved in the death of love in a relationship. In fact, it isn't that difficult to predict which marriage relationships are most likely to have one person fall out of love with his or her partner. I have seen numerous people who have claimed to have "fallen out of love" with their spouses. This was usually something that had evolved over a period of years, until the person was apathetic and indifferent. One author describes "falling out of love" as marital dissatisfaction.[1]

Marital dissatisfaction can be described as the gradual loss of emotional attachment towards one's spouse. This encompasses diminished caring, emotional distancing, and over time, an increasing sense of apathy and indifference toward the other.[2] Those who are "socially committed" because of morality or the opinions of others choose to remain married, whereas others divorce quite readily. Often those who have less commitment to their partners as persons choose to exit from the relationships.

What happens to love in a marriage? There seems to be a process involved in the death of love that follows a pattern of five phases.

Phase I—Disillusionment

I think that almost everyone who marries eventually experiences some degree of disillusionment. The higher the level of expectations, the more idealistic the dreams, the less prepared a person is for the onset of this phase. When you don't expect or anticipate it, the devastation is worse.

Each phase carries with it the same pattern of *feelings, thoughts,* and ultimately, *behavior.* In this initial phase a person experiences disappointment that moves to disenchantment with marriage itself. During this time, spouses tend to compare their partners now with the way they were before they were married. Over the years I've heard many wives complain about the change they noticed in their husbands even during the first month. They said their husbands were open, feelings-oriented, communicative, and highly attentive during their courtship, but that within a month all that had disappeared.

Sometimes the partner has in fact changed, but sometimes it's only the perception spouses have of their partners' behavior. What they used to see as positive traits are now viewed as negative. As one husband said, "I knew she was organized and neat, but not to this extent. She's so rigid and perfectionistic, it's hard to live with her in the same house now."

When the feelings occur, *thoughts* that feed the disaffection process begin. At this phase, it's usually an increased awareness that the relationship isn't going as well as expected. This can lead to doubts about the persons they married as well as their decisions to marry them. Spouses use a number of coping strategies at this time. Some speak up, but many people tend not to say anything. Others use denial to cope. I've heard people make statements like the following:

"I told myself it just wasn't true. It was all in my head. It wasn't happening."

"I'm a peace-keeper anyway, so I didn't say anything. I just buried it. I thought it would get better. It didn't."

"For six years I kept all my feelings in. Then I discovered that just reinforced the problems."

The thoughts lead to various ways of *blaming.* Some try to change themselves. They feel some self-improvement would make a difference. They love more, try to be more attractive, or try to please even more than they have.

Some people tend to turn the responsibility outward and blame their partners, but many, especially women, blame themselves for the positions they're in. And when you take the responsibility for the problem you do the same for the solution. Unfortunately, women tend to do this more than men. This is consistent with our experience over the past thirty years that women are more likely than men to want to do something about marital problems. When husbands or wives attempt to "please" their partners in this way, they are conveying the message that when and if there are problems in the marriage, they'll take care of them. They assume the responsibility and this just perpetuates the problem.[3]

Phase II—Hurt

Hurt is the best way to describe the second phase of the death of love, which can overlap the first phase. The feelings in this phase include loneliness, being treated unfairly and unjustly, and a sense of loss. Often the person doesn't identify this as a loss or perceive what the loss involves. Now the thoughts expand to include more negatives such as the following:

"My spouse just doesn't understand me. That's unfair. He/she should understand."

"My needs are not being met by my spouse and they should be."

"I must not be very important to my spouse or he/she would be acting differently."

Frequently persons suffering in this phase begin to think about what the relationship is costing them and what they are getting out of it. Usually they feel they have ended up with the short end of the stick.

This is where the "old nature" of man begins to kick in. We all have a bent or inclination toward negative thinking. It's one of the effects of the fall of man. You begin to use a wonderful gift that God has given you—the imagination—in a negative manner. We all talk to ourselves. That's a given. But too often, unfortunately, the content is negative.

Man has struggled with this since Genesis 6:5: *"The Lord saw that the wickedness of man was great in the earth, and that every imagination and intention of all human thinking was only evil continually" (AMP).* Scripture again and again points out the importance of our thoughts and how they need to be controlled. *"As he thinketh in his heart, so is he"* (Prov. 23:7, *KJV*). We also find that

"The thoughts of the righteous are right: but the counsels of the wicked are deceit" (Prov. 12:5, *KJV*). *"Search me, O God, and know my heart! Try me and know my thoughts!"* (Ps. 139:23, *RSV*). *"Gird your minds for action"* (1 Pet. 1:13 *NASB*). *Gird* means mental exertion or putting out of the mind anything that could be hindering the Christian life.

There's a strong interrelationship between thoughts, feelings, and behaviors. Most of our emotions or feeling responses come from our thought lives; what we dwell upon, that we think about, can stimulate feelings. The words *think, thought,* and *mind* are used more than 300 times in Scripture. Often, a person's thoughts generate both feelings and behaviors, then the behavior becomes a reinforcer of the feelings and thoughts. And then the cycle repeats: The feeling intensifies or reinforces a particular thinking pattern and thus the behavior. Perhaps we see this pattern more in the marital relationship than elsewhere. Chuck Swindoll put it so well, as he usually does:

> Thoughts, positive or negative, grow stronger when fertilized with constant repetition. That may explain why so many who are gloomy and gray stay in that mood, and why others who are cheery and enthusiastic continue to be so, even in the midst of difficult circumstances. Please do not misunderstand. Happiness (like winning) is a matter of right thinking, not intelligence, age, or position. Our performance is directly related to the thoughts we deposit in our memory bank. We can only draw on what we deposit.
>
> What kind of performance would your car deliver if every morning before you left for work you scooped up a handful of dirt and put it in your crankcase? The fine-tuned engine would soon be coughing and sputtering. Ultimately, it would refuse to start. The same is true of your life. Thoughts about yourself and attitudes toward others that are narrow, destructive, and abrasive produce wear and tear on your mental motor. They send you off the road while others drive past.[4]

To counter negative thoughts about our spouses, it would be helpful to consider once again words of Scripture, such as the following:

"Do not be conformed to this world but be transformed by the renewal of your mind" (Rom. 12:2, *RSV*).

"Set your minds on things that are above, not on things that are on earth" (Col. 3:2, *RSV*).

We all need a transformation of the mind to have the mind of

Christ. Dr. Lloyd Ogilvie, former pastor of the First Presbyterian Church of Hollywood—and as of March 1995, chaplain of the United States Senate—said, "Each of us needs to surrender the kingdom of our mind to God." Right on.

In this hurt phase there are certain behaviors that tend to occur. To solve hurt feelings, another person (a confidant) is sought out in order to gripe and complain about how dissatisfying the marriage or spouse is. Attempts are made to change the relationship and make it better, as well as attempts to change one's partner. Personally I believe we can and need to help one another change (this is addressed elsewhere in this book). But when you approach it from a position of hurt, you usually use an approach that either reinforces the basic problem or makes it worse.

Phase III—Anger

The third phase is *anger*. It too can overlap with the previous phase as a husband or wife travels the road to the loss of love. The disillusionment diminishes and the hurt turns into anger. Hurt and anger frequently go hand in hand.

But anger doesn't have to kill a marriage. It can actually show that we still care about our partner and the relationship. It can be a sign that we're alive and well and want to have something better in the relationship. Anger causes us to assert ourselves in situations where we should. And if it's presented correctly it can actually be an invitation to negotiate.

This is the time when the phrase "I think I'm falling out of love" begins to emerge. As the disappointment and hurts continue, they tend to obscure the love that was there when the relationship began.

The feelings of this stage can best be described as resentment, indignation, or bitterness. And these feelings can deaden feelings of love. Why is it that Scripture tells us to never let these gain a foothold in our lives regardless of what the other person has done?

An abundance of thoughts reinforce the cycle. Trust is just about gone. A spouse is now looking at the accumulation of hurts, and feeling their combined impact. The focus is on what the partner has done or hasn't done, and blame is a consistent thought. As the spouse thinks about the other, negative thoughts outweigh the positive.

"He doesn't love me. He wants a maid and sex partner, not a wife."

"Why did I ever think she would love me? She doesn't ever say it or show it. Sometimes I could just throttle her. She's bankrupting me as well."

"Sometimes I wish he'd have an accident driving home. He deserves it."

"I didn't marry her for her to have an affair every six months. She thinks I don't know, but I do. How can she be loving to others when she's an iceberg to me?"

With feelings and thoughts like this, you can imagine what behaviors might happen at this time. By now the feelings are usually being expressed to the errant spouse—not in a way that draws the two closer, but in a way that tends to alternate them. Expressions of hurt, anger, and disappointment are usually presented in a critical way, and mingled with an air of disgust. It's not uncommon to avoid the partner; sexual involvement is either cut off or becomes a mechanical duty. There is a physical and emotional withdrawal from both the partner and the marriage. As one wife said, "How is it possible to physically respond to someone you've started to loathe? I can't even sleep in the same bed with him because I'm so angry at him."

This is a dangerous time in a person's life, for hurt and anger makes us vulnerable to seeking need fulfillment elsewhere. In the death of love, emotional desperation is usually present, and this is a major cause for affairs. This lack of need fulfillment and intimacy creates an intense vacuum. It contributes to alienation as well as resentment. One writer describes the process in this way:

> Affairs begin not just for sexual reasons but to satisfy the basic need we all have for closeness, goodness, kindness, togetherness—what I call the "ness" needs. When these "ness" needs are not met on a regular basis in a marriage, the motivation may be to find a person who will be good to us, touch us, hold us, give us a feeling of closeness. Sexual fulfillment may indeed become an important part of an extramarital relationship, but the "ness" needs are, for most men and women I know, initially more important.[5]

When resentment exists, there is a feeling of ill will toward the other, a desire to make the spouse pay, and a rationalization or justification of what is being done. "If my partner isn't fulfilling my needs or making me happy, I will find satisfaction elsewhere. He (or she) is to blame for this." I've heard this excuse time and time again.

But there are other and better options. I've seen many marriages even at this stage turn around and become what each partner wanted to begin with.

Sometimes our anger isn't because of what our spouse has done or didn't do. It's because of our own expectations. Often these are intermingled with what is known today as *entitlement*. This says that the degree of your need or desire justifies your demand that your partner supply that need. It's like saying, "I want it so bad that I'm entitled to have it." It confuses personal desire with obligation on your partner's part. It's almost saying that our partners have no right to say no. Have you ever thought about this? Our expectations breed entitlement. Have you ever considered what your expectations are for your partner? Are they reasonable and are they attainable? Anger can be reduced when both expectations and our thoughts are rearranged. Consider this everyday household situation that could lead to a deadening of feelings between partners. This came from my client Joan's own words:

Let me give you an example of what's been going on for months in one way or another. The other day I spent several hours cleaning the house. I slaved over each room until they were spotless. All I wanted was for Dave to notice. Later on I realized not only was I expecting it, I deserved it. And when all he did when he came home was mess up two rooms, flop in front of the TV and ask, "Where's dinner? I'm hungry," I blew! I was ticked. Later on I wrote in my journal and not only did I figure out what went wrong. I got some insight into what I could do differently the next time. I wrote down what my thoughts were. "He should have noticed all the work I did today. He should have thanked me for what I did. I deserved it. He shouldn't have been so insensitive and inconsiderate. He's so sloppy. And he'll probably want sex tonight. He can just wait." As I wrote, I didn't like what I had thought, but there it was.

Then when I wrote what I could do differently, I really liked what I created. And again it started with my thought life. Some of them were as follows: "I wish he would notice all my work. I wonder why it's so important for him to notice and then praise me. Am I doing this for him or for me? Perhaps I could find a different way to get him to notice what I do around the house. Perhaps I could bring in our camera or video and ask him if he would like to take a picture of a fantastically clean house and the housekeeper who created this wonder!" I also wrote out a statement that I am going to read several times on those days that I clean. It goes like this: "I want Dave to notice what I've done today. If he doesn't, that's all right. I can handle that, too. My happiness and sense of satisfaction doesn't depend on his response. I didn't clean it just for him. I did it because it needed to be done. I feel good about what I've done and the results. If he notices, that's just icing on the cake. I don't have to be upset over it."

This worked for Joan. Eventually Dave did notice, because she gave him a note that simply said, "I feel even closer to you than usual whenever you notice what I've done around the house." Change does happen.

Phase IV—Ambivalence

The fourth phase of love's loss is *ambivalence.* The feelings reflect a sense of turmoil, because they shift back and forth between despair and hope for both the marriage and the partner. We're indecisive and unsure about what to do. This state is also reflected in our thoughts as well. We wonder, *What will it take for this marriage to work?* and *Would it be best to just get out of this? I don't see it going anywhere.* We consider other options to staying with this person, but we are also aware of and think about how the divorce would affect us and others.

All these feelings and thoughts lead to a set of behaviors that could include counseling over what to do. Sometimes friends and relatives are made aware of what is occurring, and there may be consideration of another who might be a better choice for a spouse than the current partner. Once again, remember that these phases can overlap and it can all add up to a state of confusion.

Phase V—The Death of Love

The final phase is what all this has been leading up to: disaffection or "the death of love." The only feelings left are those that reflect the death of what each hoped would be a happy and fulfilling relationship. Indifference, detachment, and apathy exist and that's about it. I've heard this expressed in many ways.

"I've had it. I have no more energy. Nothing I did worked and now it's over."

"I have nothing left to feel with. I'm numb. I never thought it would end up like this. But ten years is enough time to invest in a bankrupt situation."

"I can't even get angry at her anymore. There's nothing left and I'm moving on."

"I don't care what she says she'll do now. It's too late. I don't even want to try anymore. I've been rejected way too much."

The *thoughts* are reflective of the feelings. There is very little desire to be or try to be at all close to the spouse. In terms of our partners ever meeting our needs, it's a closed book as far as we're concerned. Nothing our spouses do will work, and besides, it's too late. We behave basically in an avoidance pattern. There's no interest in any physical contact. The couple lives under the same roof, but they live separate lives for the most part. They're married singles and any counseling undertaken at this point is for the purpose of getting out of the relationship.[6]

It may help to see this pattern in chart form.

What Kills Love in a Marriage: Five Phases

I. Disillusionment
    A. Feelings—Disappointment
    B. Thoughts—Doubts or denial
    C. Behavior—Blame

II. Hurt
    A. Feelings—Loneliness, sense of loss, "it's unfair"
    B. Thoughts—"My needs aren't met, my spouse doesn't understand me, I must not be important"
    C. Behavior—Complain to others, try to change spouse

III. Anger (accompanied by "I think I'm falling out of love")
    A. Feelings—Resentment, indignation, bitterness (a "bitter" bank develops)
    B. Thoughts—Focused on what spouse has or hasn't done—constant blame
    C. Behavior—Expresses feelings; critical, physical and emotional withdrawal; vulnerable time; affair prone

IV. Ambivalence
    A. Feelings—Sense of turmoil, unsure, indecisive about what to do
    B. Thoughts—Wonder what to do. "What about divorce?"
    C. Behavior—May seek counseling, tells friends and relatives
V. The Death of Love
    A. Feelings—Indifference, detachment, apathy
    B. Thoughts—Indifference, detachment, apathy. "Nothing will help."
    C. Behavior—Separate lives or divorce

Why Love Dies

Fortunately, not all couples experience this pattern. Why do some love relationships die and others live on? Are there any patterns or predictors that can be used to help avoid those behaviors that are so destructive? I hear this question frequently from young couples. It's a good question and there is good news. There are answers that can be used to prevent this from happening as well as to reverse the process. God does have a future for all marriages, but it must be a cooperative effort between the three of you: God, husband, and wife.

This entire book is actually about keeping love alive. So let's consider some specifics that are based both on my research and my own counseling experience.

Control Tactics

One of the main contributing factors to the death of love is a lack of mutuality in the marriage. This can involve a variety of behaviors, including overt acts of controlling one's spouse through disregard of his or her unique personality qualities, opinions, faith, desires, activities, or lifestyle. It can involve forcing one's partner to do something against his or her will. It may include criticism, blame, and put-downs. These are all control tactics. Control comes in many forms and disguises. Perfectionists have a tendency to want to control others.

A wife married for ten years described her life:

    Carl is just so critical and particular but not in a loud or angry way. He never raises his voice. But he looks at me, shakes his head, or rolls his eyes to show his disgust over what I've done. If not that, I get what I call the "soft lecture."

He doesn't raise his voice, get angry, or sound firm. Rather, he talks in a soft, patient condescending tone of voice implying, "How could you have been so stupid?" Sometimes I get the silent treatment and some sighs. That's the signal for me to figure out what I've done wrong.

There have even been times, believe it or not, when he has taken the fork out of my mouth because I'm eating too much, turned off the TV because I shouldn't be watching that program, or corrected my volume of talking in public. I'm tired of it. I'm tired of going along with what he's doing. I can't deny who I am and I can't live trying to figure out how to please him. Besides, I've heard this so much I've begun to doubt myself. I've even thought, Maybe he's right. Maybe I need to do what he says. Maybe I am creating the problems. But fortunately I came to my senses.[7]

Some couples have observed that the control tactics of their partners became the deciding factor in the demise of their relationships. If you happen to be married to a controller or a perfectionist, see chapter 11 of the book *How to Change Your Spouse (Without Ruining Your Marriage)* (Servant Publications, 1994).

The Lack of Empathy

When one is a controller, one of the key ingredients of mutuality in marriage will be missing—empathy. Regard for others and the ability to enter into their feeling worlds are parts of empathy. With empathy you show you are interested in your partner's world as well as your own. Empathy means entering the private world of your partner and becoming comfortable with it. It also means moving into that world for a time without making judgments.

Empathy conveys an exceptionally important message to another person. It says, "You count. You're important and significant." It both validates and encourages the development of the partner's self-esteem. But controllers don't usually care about their partners' feelings.

The Lack of Intimacy

In any marriage in which one partner is dominant and the other is passive or submissive, one of the necessary foundations for the survival of the marriage is lacking—emotional intimacy. (The word "submissive" in this context is not the healthy, biblical definition, but refers to submission based on fear, inadequacy, and insecurity. It's the "keeping peace at any cost" response.)

Dominant persons are not about to open their lives and become vulnerable, because it would lessen their sense of power or control. And submissive partners learn not to reveal much, because it will probably be used against them in some way. Not only does the controlling partner restrict you from expressing who you are, you don't want to express yourself because of the repercussions.

Power and Intimacy

(*Power*—the capacity to influence another.)

Style of Marriage	P	N	Level of Intimacy
		I	
More or less equal	O	T	Deep levels can develop.
Dominant-submissive	W	I	Intimacy is avoided.
Warfare	E	M	Intimacy is impossible.
Fused	R	A	Intimacy is shaky and condi-
		C	tional.
		Y	

The *more or less equal* style of a marriage relationship indicates a balanced power distribution. It is a complementary relationship. Both partners think of themselves as competent, and each sees the other person as competent, too. Each person has specific areas of expertise in which his or her views have greater weight than the other, but this is not threatening.

Some relationships are *explosive.* Both husband and wife have the freedom to initiate action, give advice, criticize, etc., but most of their behaviors are competitive. If one states that he has achieved a goal or progressed in some way, the spouse lets it be known that she, too, has attained similar success. Both make it a point to let the other know of his or her equal status.

When conflicts in such a relationship become fairly open and consistent, the relationship is in a *warfare* state. The couple does not have balance for the relationship because both are vying for the dominant position and exchanging the same type of behavior.

Finally, there is the *fused* relationship, in which each person shares some power. But in order to have power, they each give up some of their individual identity. Separateness does not exist because it seems dangerous, and consequently there is an unhealthy type of closeness. Sometimes individuals like this will say, "We are so close that we think alike, we feel alike, and we are completely one."[8]

And this contributes to another major reason for the death of love in a marriage—the lack of emotional intimacy. As we work with couples in premarital counseling, through the various tests and evaluation tools that are used, we can now predict the probability of this problem occurring in advance, and take corrective steps. Sometimes this happens because people have shut down emotionally due to the pain of childhood abuse. In other cases, especially with men, the development of the emotional side of their lives is basically stunted. They haven't been encourage to develop it.

The lack of intimacy can mean the absence of emotional connectedness, no emotional support, the absence of significant communication, no romance, etc. When couples marry, one of their desires and one of the characteristics of such a relationship is the opportunity to fling open all the doors and share their innermost feelings. And this should be present. It's one of the reasons people marry, as well as an ingredient that keeps a couple together. Over the past twenty-five years of conducting marriage seminars across the country, I have found that the number one frustration wives reflect about their marriages is this lack of emotional intimacy. Usually it is because their husbands do not show their feelings.

"Nothing Happens"

One of the constant problems that I've heard from couples year after year is, "We never resolve our problems. It's not that we don't talk about them, it's just that nothing happens. They just go on and on." When this happens it's usually because of not understanding and accepting individual differences that then are reflected in a communication process that goes nowhere and accomplishes little. Constant unproductive attempts as well as the avoidance of conflict will soon move to emotional distancing and, ultimately, disaffection.

These are some of the major reasons for the death of love. Perhaps you've identified with some, but hopefully what has been described in this chapter has not been totally characteristic of your experience. If it is, your question is more than likely, "What can I do about it?"

What Can Be Done?

Some couples seek out counseling because an objective person can be helpful. But often couples are able to bring about needed changes by their own efforts. How can one person make it happen? The following suggestions have been used by many to build their marriages.

The initial step is to *assume that both your partner and the marital relationship can change.* This may mean going counter to your thoughts as well as your feelings. If you're at the place of saying "It just isn't possible," assume that a miracle is going to occur in the future and begin living your life as though you expect it to happen. What I am suggesting is probably something that you haven't tried fully yet—but what you have been doing hasn't worked, has it? So you don't have that much to lose, do you?

The second step is to *have in your mind a small but reasonable change you would like to see happen in your relationship.* Keep in mind that for the marital relationship to change, it will be necessary for both you and your partner to change. And contrary to a popular damaging myth, it *is* possible to change your spouse. (Hopefully it will be for the best, but all too often it's negative.)

It is also biblically sound to work for change in your partner. Scripture says that we are to urge, encourage, entreat, advise, teach, admonish, and exhort one another (see Acts 18:27; Phil. 4:2; Col. 3:16; 1 Thess. 4:10; 5:11). Sometimes another person doesn't even realize that the change you are requesting is to his or her advantage. There are definite, specific, and positive ways for you to assist your partner in change. (Again, see *How to Change Your Spouse [Without Ruining Your Marriage]*.)

Another step closely aligned to the previous one is to *change your perception of your partner.* Eliminate negative, degrading perceptions you have about your spouse. Focus on the qualities, strengths, and potential you believed were there years ago. You may find your highly developed negative thoughts intruding, but they can be eliminated.

Then *identify the extent of your anger and resentment pool.* To restore love, resentment and bitterness must be addressed and released. The longer you hold on to them, the more work will be involved in letting them go. One author suggests that those experiencing the death of love for their partners usually have a "bitter bank."[9]

This is an accumulation of the bitterness that has been collected over the years. But most are not that aware of it, because they have concentrated so much energy on blaming their partners. Their emotions are dominated by this bitterness. And all the time and energy that have gone into the bitterness keeps them from taking constructive, positive steps.

Often at this stage people have given up hope that their partners will ever change, and the next best thing, in their opinion, is to fantasize about life without their partners. They think about how much better life would be without their partners, and many (especially Christians) fantasize about them dying, because that's easier and more acceptable than divorce. The time and energy used in this way keep them from making positive changes in their lives and reinforces their feelings about the futility of the relationships. This is what bitterness can do.[10] Bitterness and resentment need release. For most people, writing their anger in journals or nonmailed letters to their partners and then reading the words aloud in a room by themselves is a healthy step.

One final step is a very necessary part of releasing resentment. Not only is it important to express and give up feelings of resentment, it is also essential that you *project a positive response to your spouse.* Emptying the container of resentment is only half the battle. You need to fill that void with feelings and expressions of love, acceptance, forgiveness, and friendship.

A number of my clients have stated that they have neither positive nor negative feelings toward some individuals. They're blasé. But what they have really developed is a state of emotional insulation. Neutrality must be replaced by positive, productive feelings.

Writing Away Your Resentment

I often recommend an exercise that develops a positive response to a resented spouse as a means of finding and eliminating the last vestiges of resentment. Take a blank sheet of paper and write your spouse's full name at the top. Below the name write a salutation, as in a letter: Dear _____.

Under the salutation, write on the left side of the page, "I forgive you for . . . " Then complete the sentence by writing down everything that has bothered you over the years. For example, "I forgive you for always trying to control my life."

Next, stop to capture the immediate thought that comes to mind after writing the statement of forgiveness. Does the thought contradict the concept of forgiveness you have just expressed? Do you feel an inner rebuttal or protest of some kind? Is there any anger, doubt, or caustic feeling that runs against your desire to forgive? Write all these contradictory thoughts underneath the "I forgive you for . . . " statement. Don't be surprised if your thoughts are so firm or vehement that it seems that you have not done any forgiving at all. Continue the exercise by writing the "I forgive you for . . . " statement, followed by your immediate thoughts, even if they are contradictory.

Keep repeating the process until you have drained all the pockets of resentment. You will know you have reached that point when you can think of no more contradictions or resentful responses to the statement of forgiveness you have written. Some people finish this exercise with only a few contradictory responses. Others have a great deal of resentment and use several pages to record their feelings.

The following is a typical example of how a husband forgave his wife for her coldness and critical attitude toward him, and for her extramarital affair. Notice how his protests and contradictions to forgiveness become progressively less intense. Finally his resentment drains away to the place where he can simply say "I forgive you" and feel no further need for rebuttal.

> Dear Liz, I forgive you for . . . *I'm hurt and angry. I've put up with you for years.*
>
> Dear Liz, I forgive you for . . . *How do I know I can trust you after what you did?*
>
> Dear Liz, I forgive you for . . . *How do I know you're going to be any different? I can't take your coldness anymore.*
>
> Dear Liz, I forgive you for . . . *I'm really hesitant to open myself up to you anymore. I want to love you, but I've been rejected so much. I'm afraid of being rejected again.*
>
> Dear Liz, I forgive you for . . . *I would like to forgive you at times. I don't like these feelings I have. It's a bit better as I write this. I feel*

> *a bit funny and awkward*
> *as I do this.*

Dear Liz, I forgive you for . . . *I wish this had never*
> *happened.*

Dear Liz, I forgive you for . . . *I know I've blamed you and I*
> *feel you're responsible. But*
> *maybe I contributed to the*
> *problems in some way.*

Dear Liz, I forgive you for . . . *My anger is less, and maybe*
> *some day it will go away.*

Dear Liz, I forgive you for . . .

Dear Liz, I forgive you for . . .

Jim wrote this letter to Liz one day, then three days later he repeated the exercise. In his second letter, after writing eight contradictory thoughts, Jim was able to conclude with several "I forgive you . . . " statements with no rebuttals.

After completing your own version of this exercise, spend time in prayer asking God to help you completely release your anger and change your heart toward your partner. Then try to visualize your partner sitting in an empty chair, verbally accepting your forgiveness. Take as long as you need for this step, because it is very important. When you have finished the exercise, destroy your list of statements, without showing it to anyone, as a symbol that *"old things are passed away; behold, all things are become new"* (2 Cor. 5:17, *KJV*).

Feeling and Behaving

Perhaps you're at a place where the hurt has been so painful that you're reluctant to try to rebuild your love. As one wife said, "Why should I reach out to him again? If I do and he doesn't respond, I'll just be hurt all over again. Sometimes enough is enough." If this is how you feel, admit it and accept your feelings. But stay away from the danger of believing that before you try again you need to wait until your feelings change. It just doesn't work that way. Nor does Scripture teach this.

If we behave in a loving manner it is more than likely that our feelings will begin to change. The principle is quite simple and all it takes is a decision on your part to do it. Invite the Holy Spirit to empower you. When you behave toward your spouse as if your loving feelings were alive and well (which can stimulate your partner's feelings), then the possibility of reviving your love for your spouse is possible.

The next step may create some tension within you, but it is a necessary step. It's called forgiveness. Forgiveness is many things. It is no longer being chained to the hurt you've experienced with your spouse. It is no longer using the wonderful gift of memory as a weapon. It is no longer hurting others as we have been hurt. It is making yourself vulnerable and open to being hurt again. It is as Lewis Smedes said:

> . . . a new vision and a new feeling that is given to the person who forgives. . . . True forgivers do not pretend they don't suffer. They don't pretend the wrong does not matter much. . . . You will know that forgiveness has begun when you recall those who hurt you and feel the power to wish them well.[11]

Applying the various principles found throughout this book will help you in this process of restoring your love. (If your spouse is the one who has lost his or her love for you, the best resource for you to read is *Rekindled* by Pat Williams [Revell, 1985].)

In keeping with the principle of acting in a loving, caring manner, the next step is to realize that you have been choosing to allow your partner to dominate and control you. You may be surprised by this statement, but it's true. You've been allowing your spouse's responses or lack of the same to dictate what has been happening to your feelings, thoughts, and behaviors. You've let him/her do this. Now is the time to determine to respond in a positive, loving way regardless of what he/she does about it.

The formula for change and reactivating love feelings is quite simple—increase the positive and reduce the negative beliefs, thoughts, and behaviors. If there is something you want from your partner, be sure that it's stated in such a way that he/she will hear it and consider your request. (See *How to Change Your Spouse* by Gary Oliver and this author, chapter 3.)

Several other specific guidelines can be followed that may seem odd but are necessary. Consider this: You've probably been blaming your spouse for numerous things, and this has taken its toll upon your love feelings. But what if you could no longer blame him or her? What other reasons could you find for what is happening in your relationship? What other reasonable explanations could you discover? One wife shared her experience of doing this.

When I had this suggestion I really resisted it. It didn't seem right or logical. And I guess a part of me didn't want to give up making him accountable. But I realized I didn't have much to lose. So I came up with this list:

1. It could be he really doesn't know how to do or give what I want and resists trying because who wants to fail?
2. I assumed he wasn't willing to learn what I want. I accused him of that.
3. I hate to admit it, but some of my approaches probably turned him off. I pushed him further away.
4. Perhaps he doesn't know how important this is to me and I can share it in a way he understands better.

I hope all this works. Even if it doesn't, I won't feel so upset and I can say that I was willing to try something new.

People have asked me over the years, "How long, Norm? How long will this take?" No one can give you a time frame. I've seen the love return in months, but in some cases it takes years. Prayer and opening our lives completely for God to work within and on us is at the heart of the process. Change and restoration are possible. That's good news.

3
What Makes a Marriage Work

THEY SAT IN MY OFFICE, young and a bit anxious. They were both age twenty-two and fresh out of college. They had been engaged for three months, and the wedding was just six months away. The first question I asked them was: What are you expecting out of premarital counseling? What is it you want?

Their reply was similar to one I've heard from many couples over the years, but it had a different twist to it. They said, "We want to know what we need to do to make our marriage work and to stay married for the rest of our lives. We know about the importance of commitment and love. We believe in that. But what else can we do?" I've heard this before.

But then they added, "Since you've been counseling for many years and have listened to hundreds of couples, is there any way you could share with us now at this stage in our life and marriage what it takes married couples thirty-six years to learn? We've heard many older couples say they wished they knew back when they were first married what they know now after thirty or forty years of marriage. That's what we want to know now so we'll have a better chance at having a lasting and productive and fulfilling marriage. What do we need to know and what can we do?"

Couple Styles

Since they had asked an important question, I decided to answer them with a question as well. I said, "Let me describe three different couples for you, and after I do I'd like to ask you a question to help answer your own question."

The Validating Couple
"The first couple work at their communication," I continued. "Occasionally they argue and disagree like all couples, but they deal

with their differences before anger gets out of hand. They don't get into shouting matches but instead have 'conferences' in which each one has the opportunity to share his or her opinion.

"As they try to work toward understanding their partner, their goal is to work out a compromise. They can listen and hear their partner and can problem solve. There is a lot of mutual sharing. This type of couple has been called a validating couple because even when they don't agree with their partner's view or feelings, they accept them as valid."

The Volatile Couple

"The second couple," I continued, "is the kind you would hear fighting if they lived next door. They quarrel loudly, interrupt one another, and defend fiercely their own viewpoints. There is a lot of passion. They argue and debate minor issues that others would let pass. They don't really try to understand and empathize with their partner—their goal is to persuade. Rather than listen, they interrupt. They want to win.

"But couples like this are also very affectionate and loving in the same intense way. There's usually more laughter and affection than the validating couples experience. They express more positive feelings as well as negative ones, and they do this with ease. They are able to resolve their differences. They see themselves as equals, and believe marriage should emphasize strengths and individuality, not suppress them. Couples like this are called *volatile*."

The Avoidant Couple

"The last couple," I concluded, "enjoys being together, and rarely do they fight. When disagreements arise, they tend to use time and distance to resolve the conflict. Rather than resolving differences, they tend to minimize their differences. And when they are discussed, nothing much seems to occur. They agree to disagree and avoid discussions they know will end up with nothing resolved. They don't put pressure on the other person to persuade them.

"Issues are resolved by avoiding or minimizing. They would rather focus on the positive—on what they love and value in marriage— and they accept the rest of the stuff. There isn't that much sharing or companionship in this kind of marriage. They like separateness and autonomy in their relationship. To an outsider, their interaction might appear shallow. They reflect some of the characteristics of what I call 'married singles'! All this is why they are called an *avoidant* couple."

Which Style Is the Most Stable?

I then asked the couple the question "Having shared these three descriptions of couples, which would you say is a stable relationship?

They thought a minute and said, "Even though we're more like the second one, the volatile, it sounds like the first one, the validating couple, is the more stable one. The others could end up with some real problems."

I replied, "It's true the other two could get into serious difficulty. A *volatile* couple could end up being consumed by the constant quarreling. And unfortunately in some cases it could lead to violence. Some of the feelings they experience could really hurt their partner."

An avoidant marriage could end up without the emotional connectedness the couple needs to hold their marriage together. And unresolved negative feelings could cause the relationship to deteriorate. They could become quite lonely, because neither fully knows nor understands his or her partner. Neither knows what's at the source of the partner's feelings, and when a major conflict does have to be faced some day, we might wonder whether they will have the skills they need to resolve it.[1]

Actually, the answer to the question of which type of marriage is the most stable is that all three of them can be stable. What makes the difference isn't so much the style of marriage you have as much as what happens within it. It's the amount of positive interaction you have. For your marriage to be stable you need at least five times as many positive as negative moments together! It's not whether you don't fight in a marriage, it's your ability to resolve the conflicts and have a high degree of positive rather than negative interaction.[2] If you have the five-to-one ratio, your marriage can last.

Volatile couples may vent a lot, but they spend more time being loving and positive. *Validators* have some tension but much more fun, love, and warmth. Even if *avoidant* couples don't show as much passion as others, they express less criticism and negatives. Your background, temperaments, and personalities have a lot to do with the style of marriage you develop. Positive thoughts and expressed feelings nourish both the marriage and the partners.[3]

Perhaps you are as surprised as the young couple in my office to hear that it's not so much the style of the marriage that determines

its stability as the amount of positive interactions compared to negative. But it's true.

What about you? Does the positive overpower the negative or is it
equal or less? Perhaps it would be beneficial for you to keep track
for awhile. You might be surprised.

Accentuating the Positive

Perhaps you're like the couple in my office. I knew that they didn't
want to leave what I said alone because they asked, "Norm, un-
doubtedly what you just shared with us is based on research. What
was it that was described as positive and what was negative? I think
it would help us to know the specifics."

They were right. Stable couples suggest numerous ways to express
positive interactions in a marriage. And time and time again the
Word of God admonishes us to behave in a positive and encouraging
way. *"And become useful and helpful and kind to one another, tenderhearted (compassionate, understanding, loving-hearted), forgiving one another [readily and freely], as God in Christ forgave you"*
(Eph. 4:32, *AMP*).

Paul also wrote:

> *Clothe yourselves therefore, as God's own chosen ones (His
> own picked representatives), [who are] purified and holy and
> well-beloved [by God Himself, by putting on behavior
> marked by] tenderhearted pity and mercy, kind feeling, a
> lowly opinion of yourselves, gentle ways, [and] patience
> [which is tireless and long-suffering, and has the power to
> endure whatever comes, with good temper.] Be gentle and
> forbearing with one another and, if one has a difference (a
> grievance or complaint) against another, readily pardoning
> each other; even as the Lord has [freely] forgiven you, so must
> you also [forgive]* (Col. 3:12,13, *AMP*).

Shared Interests

It's important to share interest in your partner as a person, to discover what he/she has experienced during the day, to uncover any
upset feelings. This can involve listening and looking at each
other—without glancing at the TV or the paper on your lap. It can

mean listening without attempting to fix a problem unless asked to do so. If you're a man, it can mean giving more verbal responses and feedback when you listen, because women like to hear this so they will know you are listening. James 1:19 says to be "a *ready listener*" (*AMP*).

Showing Affection

Being consistently affectionate—and not just at those times when one is interested in sex—is a highly valued positive response. Sometimes nothing is shared verbally. It can be sitting side by side and touching gently or moving close enough that you barely touch while you watch the sun dipping over a mountain with reddish clouds capturing your attention. It could be reaching out and holding hands in public. It can be doing something thoughtful, unrequested and noticed only by your partner.

Or when your spouse has had a rough day, you may choose just to stroke her head, or rub his shoulders, instead of talking about it. Being so understood by your partner and having him or her meet your needs gives you the assurance that you have indeed married the right person.

Affection is demonstrated in many ways and displays. Years ago I heard the story of a couple who had been invited to a potluck dinner. The wife was not known for her cooking ability, but she decided to make a custard pie. As they drove to the dinner, they knew they were in trouble for they smelled the scorched crust. Then when they turned a corner, the contents of the pie shifted dramatically from one side of the pie shell to the other. He could see her anxiety rising by the moment.

When they arrived, they placed the pie on the dessert table. The guests were serving themselves salad and then went back for the main course. Just before they could move on to the desserts, the husband marched up to the table, looked over the number of homemade desserts and snatched up his wife's pie. As others looked at him, he announced, "There are so many desserts here and my wife so rarely makes my favorite dessert, I'm claiming this for myself. I ate light on all the other courses so now I can be a glutton."

And a glutton he was. Later his wife said, "He sat by the door eating what he could, mushing up the rest so no one else would bug him for a piece, and slipping chunks to the hosts' Rottweiler when no one was looking. He saw me looking at him and gave me a big wink. What he did made my evening. My husband, who doesn't al-

ways say much, communicated more love with what he did than
with what any words could ever say."

Acts of Caring

Of course there are many other ways to take positive action, showing that you care. I raise flowers all year long, and I know Joyce enjoys seeing them inside the house. Often, after I've made the coffee,
I cut her a rose and put it in a vase by her coffee cup. It's almost
become automatic now, but the motivation is the same. And often,
when I travel, Joyce slips a love note into my pants pocket.

Perhaps you're in the store and you see a favorite food your spouse
enjoys and you buy it for him or her even if you hate it. Or you
decide to stop at the store for an item and you call your spouse at
home or at work to see if there's anything he or she wants or needs.
You are "other" thinking rather than "self" thinking. You follow
through with the scriptural teaching in Ephesians 4:32 (*NIV*), *"Be
kind and compassionate to one another."*

An act of caring can be a phone call to ask if your partner has a
prayer request. Acts of caring can mean remembering special dates
and anniversaries without being reminded. I am amazed at the number of wives who have been deeply hurt by their husbands over the
years because they did not remember anniversaries or even birth-
days.

And their excuses are so lame. I've heard, "I just didn't remember"
and "I need to be reminded" and "We just didn't do that in our family." That's all such responses are—excuses! If the husband is sitting
in my counseling office, I simply ask him if he forgets to go to work
or to get involved in his hobby. Reluctantly he says no, and I go on
to let him know that I believe he is capable of learning something
new that will benefit both his life and his wife's. We then talk about
how he will do it. We don't accept excuses when it is obvious that
change can occur.

Showing Appreciation and Empathy

Another positive is being appreciative. This means going out of
your way to notice all the little positive things your partner does and
letting him or her know you appreciate them. It also means focusing on the positive experiences and dwelling upon those rather than
the negative (more will be said about this later). Working toward
agreement and appreciating the other's perspective is important.
Compliments convey appreciation, but they need to be balanced be-

tween what persons do and who they are. Affirmations based on personal qualities are rare, but highly appreciated.

Showing genuine concern for your spouse when you notice he or she is upset builds unity and intimacy in a relationship. You may not be able to do anything, but sharing your desire to do so may be all that is necessary. When your partner shares a problem with you, don't relate a similar problem you once had, tell him what to do, crack jokes to cheer him up, or ask how he got into that problem in the first place. Instead, listen, put your arm around him, show that you understand, and let him know it's all right for him to feel and act the way he does.

I'm sure you've heard the word *empathy* time and time again. This is the feeling of being with another person both emotionally and intellectually. It's viewing life through your spouse's eyes, feeling as he or she feels, and hearing his or her story through your mate's perceptions.

In marriage you have a choice to respond with empathy, sympathy, or apathy. Sympathy is being overinvolved in the emotions of your spouse. It can actually undermine your emotional strength. Apathy means you couldn't care less. There are no in-betweens.

Empathy includes rapport—knowing how your spouse would feel in most situations without him or her having to explain. You'll experience something together at the same time through the eyes of your partner.

Accepting each other for who you are and what you say is a positive. Acceptance means letting your spouse know that even though you don't agree with what he or she is saying, you are willing to hear him or her out. It means freeing your partner from being molded into the fantasy that you want him or her to be. It's more than tolerance. It's saying, "You and I are different in many ways. It's all right for you to be you and for me to be me. We are stronger together than we are separately, as we learn to complement one another." This doesn't mean spouses won't help to change each other—that's inevitable. But the purpose for which it's done, and the method, makes a world of difference.

The Lighter Side

Having a sense of humor and being able to laugh, joke, and have fun gives balance to the serious side of marriage. Some of what you laugh at will be private, and some will be shared with others. Having a sense of humor means you are able to laugh at yourself (even if it sometimes takes awhile!), and the two of you can laugh together. Sometimes the best memories are some of those hilarious incidents that happen even though your partner didn't think it was so funny at the time.

Several years ago while speaking at a family camp at Forest Home, California, such an event happened to Joyce and me. We were staying in a nice cabin, and since I'm an early riser I went down to the dining hall for an early breakfast. Joyce arose a little later and didn't eat a large breakfast, knowing that I would bring her back some fruit and a muffin. I entered the cabin and was just about ready to go into the bedroom with her food, when the door of the bathroom was flung open. Joyce, fresh out of the shower, said, "Don't go in there! It's still there! Don't take my food in there!"

I was shocked and said, "What!? What's in there?!"

"In there!" she said again, almost in tears by now. "It's still in the bedroom. It was terrible. And don't you dare laugh. It wasn't funny!" I still didn't know what she was talking about, but saying to a husband, "Don't you dare laugh!" is like a subtle invitation that may get played out later.

Finally, she calmed down and told me what happened. She had been resting in bed drinking her coffee when she decided to reach down and pick up her slippers. She found one, lifted it up, and then thrust her hand under the bed to find the other one. Now, Forest Home was using new humane mouse-traps that consisted of a six-by-six-inch piece of cardboard with an extremely sticky substance on it. When a mouse stuck in it, it was stuck permanently and would eventually die. Well . . . you can guess what happened. Not only did Joyce put her hand directly on the goo substance, but it also contained a bloated dead mouse! It was gross! (I have a picture of it.) As she said, she went ballistic with screams, trying to dislodge this disgusting creature from her hand.

As Joyce was telling me all this, she was shaking her hand and demonstrating how she had tried to dislodge the mouse from her hand. And the more she did this the funnier it got. I was biting the inside of my mouth to keep from smiling and all the time remembering those fateful words "Don't you dare laugh. It's not funny." I think she saw my struggle, because with an exaggerated pout she looked at me and said again, slowly, *"It's not funny."*

That's all it took. I was a dead man and I knew it. I laughed until the tears rolled down my face. I did take the mouse out and get rid of it. I also told Joyce that I would have gone into hysterics as well if that had happened to me, and that she had every right to be upset. After several hugs, she said, "I guess it was pretty funny at that." Now it's one of our favorite stories.

We also have many funny memories in which I was the source of the amusement. Just ask Joyce sometime and you'll hear a whole list of them.

A related positive in marriage is the sense of shared joy.[4] You share your partner's excitement and delight and you want your partner to be aware of what you're experiencing as well. Joy is a sense of gladness, not necessarily happiness. It's also a command from Scripture: We are to *"rejoice with those who rejoice"* (Rom. 12:15, *NIV*).

Avoiding the "Takens"

Another positive is never becoming complacent or taking one another for granted. A friend of mine described it in this way:

People in long-term marriages tend to take each other for granted. The most common of the "takens" include:

You will always be here for me.

You will always love me.

You will always be able to provide for me.

You will always be the same.

We will always be together.

Making these assumptions in a marriage is living more in fantasyland than on reality ridge. People who take things for granted are seldom appreciative of the everyday blessings in their lives. After a time, they come to believe life owes them these little gifts. They seldom say thank you for anything.

When you take someone for granted you demean him or her. You send the unspoken message. You are not worth much to me. You also rob this person of the gift of human appreciation. And to be loved and appreciated gives all of us a reason to live each day. When that gift is withdrawn or denied over the years, our spirits wither and die. People may endure this hardship and stay married forever, but they are only serving a sentence. In long-term marriages where one or both spouses are continually taken for granted, a wall of indifference arises between husband and wife. The longer the marriage, the higher the wall and the greater the human isolation. The way out of this woodpile is simple but crucial:

Start saying thank you and showing appreciation for anything and everything.

Be more consciously tuned in to what is going on around you.

Become more giving and affirming.

Specialize in the many little things that mean a lot: Bring each other flowers, take long walks in the country, lie on the floor in front of the fireplace, prepare breakfast in bed for each other, hold hands in public and walk in the rain, send caring and funny cards to each other in the mail, buy each other small gifts for no apparent reason.

Remember: A thirty-five year marriage does not guarantee year number thirty-six. Take nothing for granted just because you have it today.[5]

Keep in mind that in a healthy marriage . . .

You look out for "number 2" rather than number 1.

You energize your spouse rather than drain energy from him or her.

You eliminate blaming and shaming from the marriage.

You are willing to learn from your partner.

You end your disagreements with a feeling of resolve.

You feel better after a disagreement.[6]

These are just some of the positives that keep a marriage alive. Much more will be shared about this throughout the book. But what about you? On a scale of zero to ten, how would you rate the presence of these positives in your own marriage (zero being nonexistent and ten being super abundance)? How would your spouse rate these? (In the appendix you will find a marriage assessment form that will enable you to take a fresh look at your marriage.)

Destructive Forces in Marriage

At the same time that we measure positives, it is helpful to be just as knowledgeable about the factors that could destroy a relationship. Revelation 6 portrays the four horses of the Apocalypse: a white, red, pale, and black horse. This description has been used to describe destructive forces in marriage. They fit many unhappy marriages, even with their unique variations, because they follow basically the same downward spiral before they come to a state of disintegration and the marriage is overcome by negativity. When we see these behaviors in a couple's relationship, it's possible to predict with a safe amount of accuracy which marriages will most likely end in divorce. That's a bit frightening, isn't it? Especially if your own marriage fits the profile. The good news is that if a couple identifies this downward spiral, corrective action can be taken to stop it. I've seen this occur time after time over the years.

The four horsemen of the Apocalypse correspond with four of the most disastrous ways a couple could interact in order to destroy the marriage. These are *criticism, contempt, defensiveness,* and *stonewalling.*

As each of these behaviors becomes more a part of the marriage it seems that a couple's attention is then diverted from the positive to the negative. And soon they're consumed by the negative. As each of these attitudes or behaviors gains a foothold in the relationship, it opens the door for the next horseman to step through and enhance the destruction. Actually these four are contaminates. They infect the relationship with a toxic substance that gradually erodes the feelings of love.

Riding the Critical Horse

All couples will voice complaints from time to time. That's normal, and complaints can be voiced in a way that a spouse will hear them and not be defensive. For example, instead of focusing upon what annoys you, talk more about what you would *appreciate* your spouse doing. Your partner is much more likely to hear you and consider your request if you ride the horse of appreciation instead of the steed of criticism. Talking about what you don't like just reinforces the possibility of its continuing with an even greater intensity. The principle of pointing toward what you would like also conveys to your partner your belief that he/she is capable of doing what you have requested. Doing this consistently, along with giving praise and appreciation when your spouse complies, will bring about a change.

I've seen this in children as well as adults. The power of praise cannot be underestimated. I've also seen this principle work in raising our golden retriever, Sheffield—not that I'm comparing people to dogs. Sheffield was trained in the basics by the time he was four months old, and now he brings in the paper, takes items back and forth to Joyce and me, "answers" the phone and brings it to me, and picks up items off the floor and puts them in the trash. All it took was ignoring the times when he didn't do it right, and giving praise and hugs when he came through.

I don't think people are much different in this respect. Affirming and encouraging responses can literally change a person's life, because we do want and need others to believe in us. An unusual example of this is found in the Babemba tribe in southern Africa. When one of the tribal members has acted irresponsibly, he or she is taken to the center of the village. Everyone in the village stops work and gathers in a large circle around the person. In turn, each person, regardless of age, speaks to the person and recounts the good things he has done in his lifetime. All the positive incidents in the person's life, plus his good attributes, strengths, and kindnesses, are recalled with accuracy and detail. Not one word about his problem behaviors is even mentioned.

This ceremony, which sometimes lasts several days, isn't complete until every positive expression has been given by those assembled. The person is literally flooded by positives. When the people are finished, the person is welcomed back into the tribe. Can you imagine how all this makes persons feel about themselves? Can you imagine their desire to continue to reflect those positive qualities? Perhaps a variation of this is needed in marriages and families today.

Criticism is the initial negative response that opens the door for the other destructive responses to follow. Criticism is different from complaining in that it attacks the other person's personality and character, usually with blame. Most criticisms are overgeneralized ("You always . . . ") and personally accusing (the word "you" is central). A great deal of criticism comes in the form of blame, with the word "should" being included.

Criticism can be hidden under the camouflage of joking and humor. And when confronted about it, a person will avoid responsibility by saying, "Hey, I was just joking." It reminds me of the passage in Proverbs that says, *"Like a madman who casts firebrands, arrows, and death, so is the man who deceives his neighbor and then says, Was I not joking?"* (Prov. 26:18,19, *AMP*).

Faultfinding is a common form of criticism. It's a favorite response of the perfectionistic spouse. (For assistance in handling this problem in a marriage, see chapter 11 of *How to Change Your Spouse*, by Gary Oliver and this author.)

Criticism is usually destructive, but it's interesting to hear critics say they're just trying to remold their partners into better persons by offering some "constructive" criticism. But too often criticism does not construct; it demolishes. It doesn't nourish a relationship; it poisons. And often the presentation is like this description:

"There is one who speaks rashly like the thrusts of a sword" (Prov. 12:18, *NASB*).

Criticism that is destructive accuses, tries to make the other feel guilty, intimidates, and is often an outgrowth of personal resentment.

Criticism comes in many shapes and sizes. You've heard of "zingers," those lethal, verbal guided missiles. A zinger comes at you with a sharp point and a dull barb that catches the flesh as it goes in. The power of these sharp, caustic statements is seen when you realize that one zinger can undo twenty acts of kindness. That's right, *twenty.*

A zinger has the power to render many positive acts meaningless. Once a zinger has landed, the effect is similar to a radioactive cloud that settles on an area of what used to be prime farm land. The land is so contaminated by the radioactivity that, even though seeds are scattered and plants are planted, they fail to take root. Subsequently they die out or are washed away by the elements. It takes decades for the contamination to dissipate. The kind acts of loving words following the placement of a zinger find a similar hostile soil. It may take hours before there is a receptivity or positive response to your positive overtures.[7]

Another form of criticism is called *invalidation* and is often the cause of marital distress. When invalidation is present in a marriage, it destroys the effect of *validation,* as well as the friendship relationship of marriage. Sometimes couples get along and maintain their relationships without sufficient validation, but they cannot handle continual invalidation. This is yet another example of one negative comment destroying twenty acts of kindness.[8]

Invalidation is like a slow, fatal disease that, once established in a relationship, spreads and destroys the positive feelings. As one wife said, "The so-called friend I married became my enemy with his unexpected attacks. I felt demeaned, put-down, and my self-esteem slowly crumbled. I guess that's why our fights escalated so much. I had to fight to survive." To keep love and your marriage alive, keep the criticism out of it.

Instead of just being critical when a problem occurs, perhaps you could respond like the pilot in this story:

Bob Hoover, a famous test pilot and frequent performer at air shows, was returning to his home in Los Angeles from an air show in San Diego. As described in the magazine *Flight Operations,* at 300 feet in the air, both engines suddenly stopped. By deft maneuvering he managed to land the plane, but it was badly damaged although nobody was hurt.

Hoover's first act after the emergency landing was to inspect the airplane's fuel. Just as he suspected, the World War II propeller plane he had been flying had been fueled with jet fuel rather than gasoline.

Upon returning to the airport, he asked to see the mechanic who had serviced his plane. The young man was sick with the agony of his mistake. Tears streamed down his face as Hoover approached. He had just caused the loss of a very expensive plane and could have caused the loss of three lives as well.

You can imagine Hoover's anger. One could anticipate the tongue-lashing that this proud and precise pilot would unleash for the carelessness. But Hoover didn't scold the mechanic; he didn't even criticize him. Instead, he put his big arm around the man's shoulder and said, "To show you I'm sure that you'll never do this again, I want you to service my F51 tomorrow."[9]

Lobbing Shells of Contempt

The next step down the path of destruction is contempt—the intent to insult or psychologically abuse your spouse. That sounds harsh, doesn't it? But that is what happens. It's like using a mortar in a battle to lob shells into the enemy lines. But in a marriage you're lobbing insults into the person you promised to love. Negative thoughts and negative statements abound, and nothing is sacred. Name-calling, nonverbal actions, and mocking are all part of the pattern.

The Danger of Defensiveness

Contempt brings to the forefront the third and fourth elements of destruction in a marriage—*defensiveness* and *stonewalling*. These are natural protective responses intended to diffuse the attacks coming from the outside. Defensive statements are usually viewed as excuses, and often they are. Frequently they're accompanied by a counterattack. The greater the degree of defensiveness between a couple, the less the amount of emotional intimacy. Even though your partner's attack may be grossly exaggerated, unreasonable, and unfair, defensiveness and stonewalling are not your only options. Let's consider what you might be able to do instead.

Redeeming Destructive Forces

Realize that not all criticism is bad. Consider what God's Word has to say about criticism. *"It is a badge of honor to accept valid criticism"* (Prov. 25:12, *TLB*). *"What a shame—yes, how stupid!— to decide before knowing the facts!"* (18:13, *TLB*). *"Don't refuse to accept criticism; get all the help you can"* (23:12, *TLB*). *"A man who refuses to admit his mistakes can never be successful. But if he confesses and forsakes them, he gets another chance"* (28:13, *TLB*). Don't automatically assume that all negative criticism is invalid.

Evaluate the criticism for validity. I realize that this step may be easier said than done. Looking for value in destructive criticism may be like searching for a needle in a haystack. But you must ask yourself "What can I learn from this experience? Is there a grain of truth in what I am hearing to which I need to respond?" Asking questions like these will shift you from the position of the defendant in a relationship to that of an investigator. However unfair your spouse's attack, disregard the negative statements. Give your partner permission to exaggerate. Eventually the exaggerated statements will blow away like chaff and only the truth will remain. Keep searching for the grain of truth. Try to identify the real cause for his or her critical attack.

Clarify the root problem. Try to determine precisely what your spouse thinks you have done, or not done, that is bothering him or her. It's important that you understand the criticism from the other person's point of view. Ask specific questions such as "Will you please elaborate on the main point?" or "Can you give me a specific example?" Suppose your wife says, "You're the most inconsiderate person in the world!" That's a very general statement. Challenge her to identify specific ways you have acted inconsiderately. Ask for examples from your relationship. Keep digging until the root is exposed.

Think about the charge. At times, the process of investigating accusations and criticisms may overwhelm you with anger, confusion, or frustration. In the rush of these emotions, your mind may pull a disappearing act—it may go blank! You need time to think before you respond. How can you do this?

First I need to warn you against how *not* to do it. Don't ask "Can I take a minute to think about this?" Don't ask anyone's permission to take time to think. Also, don't say "Are you sure you are seeing this situation accurately?" This question gives your spouse the opportunity to make another value judgment on the issue. You are vesting him or her with unneeded power.

It is better to say "I'm going to take a few minutes to think this over" or "That's an interesting perspective. I need to think about it." Then ask yourself "What is the main point he is trying to make? What does he want to happen as a result of our discussion?" Sometimes it is helpful to clarify that point with your mate by asking "What would you like to be different about me as a result of our discussion? I'm really interested in knowing."

Respond positively and confidently. Once the central issue has been exposed, confidently explain your actions rather than withering defensively under the attack. I think people who criticize others expect their victims to be defensive, even though these critics sometimes say, "I wish they wouldn't be so defensive when I make a suggestion [their word for a critical demand!]." Critical people say they want their spouses to be nondefensive, but they are often shaken to the core when someone stands up to their criticism.

One man told me that he wished his wife wouldn't be defensive. I asked him, "How would you respond if you criticized her and she *wasn't* defensive?"

He looked at me, laughed a little, and said, "I guess I'd faint dead away."

I said, "You mean you expect her to be defensive, yet you wish she weren't?"

"Yes," he answered after a thoughtful pause. "I guess that sounds a bit strange. The very thing I want her not to do is what I expect her to do. I wonder if my attitude toward her is helping create her defensiveness."

Let's listen in on one husband's attempt to respond to his wife's criticism positively and confidently instead of defensively. The couple is talking in my counseling office. Sandra is bothered because Jim isn't as sociable as she is. He keeps putting her off when she tries to get him involved with other people. Sandra has a legitimate concern, but Jim also has a legitimate reason for not wanting to be involved, which he has never shared with her. Notice the communication process:

Sandra (quite angry): I'm really fed up. I've asked you time and time again about getting together with other people and you continue to refuse. I'm beginning to believe you don't like people. You're like a hermit. You just sit home and read.

Jim (good-naturedly): Am I really that bad? A hermit?

Sandra (with a slight laugh): You're much worse than that. I was giving you the benefit of the doubt.

Jim: Well, can you be more specific?

Sandra: You know when you're being antisocial. It happens at church and it happens when we're with my relatives.

Jim: I'm not sure about that. Can you give me an example?

Sandra: I can give you several. Last week when we were going out for dinner, I suggested that we invite John and Heather to go with us. You were upset because we hadn't planned it out beforehand. You have this thing about planning social activities weeks ahead. I wish you could be more flexible.

Jim: Are you saying that you'd like me to be more flexible? You want me to loosen up and be willing to do things without all that planning?

Sandra: That would sure help. I'd like to see you stop being so rigid. We would both be happier.

Jim: And you thought I was being antisocial the other night because I didn't want to invite John and Heather to join us on the spur of the moment.

Sandra: Yes, but that's just one example. It happens a lot.

Jim: Well, I guess that's something I can work on. I would also enjoy more of a social life, but I need more time to adjust to getting together with others.

Sandra: You've never told me that before. I
didn't realize our social activities
with others were such a difficulty
for you.

Even though Sandra, in her frustration, led off the dialogue with
an attacking, accusatory statement, Jim didn't let it throw him. And
that's the point. You can respond in a healthy, positive way regardless of the other person's style of criticism. Jim responded in such a
way that Sandra felt he was hearing her. And Sandra gained a deeper
understanding of their personality differences.

Agree with the criticism. No matter how hostile or destructive
the criticism may be, agree with it to a certain extent. By doing so
you will communicate to your spouse that he or she has been heard
and that you are not defensive.

For years I have used a book with my counselees called *When I
Say "NO," I Feel Guilty.* One of the two chapters I use is on a technique designed to handle another person's criticism without becoming defensive. This is called "fogging."

If a husband criticizes his wife as not being adventuresome or
wanting to go out much, she could respond with, "You know, you're
probably right. I'm not that adventuresome." When a response like
this is given without defensiveness or counterattack, where else
does the potential argument have to go except . . . nowhere! There
is nothing to fight against because there is no resistance.

Manuel Smith describes this response as similar to a fog bank.
Fog in our area of the country can be so thick at times that you can't
see anything ten feet away. Sometimes it seems heavy and sloppy.
But if you were to throw a rock at the fog bank, it would just keep
on going. It wouldn't bounce off or bounce back at you. There's no resistance.

And when a spouse criticizes you, his or her criticism has no effect when you don't participate with either defense or counterattack.

When you fog you will discover that you listen in a new way. You
hear what was said and respond to it at face value. It keeps you from
being defensive because you have quit thinking in terms of absolutes. You are now thinking in terms of probabilities, such as "There
is even a small probability they could be correct."

There are actually three methods of dealing with put-downs:
agreeing with truth, agreeing in principle, and agreeing with the
odds.

When you agree with truth it means you listen carefully for any seed of truth in the criticism and only the truth. If there is a put-down or some implied derogatory remark, ignore that. You can agree with the possibility that something is true.

> *Wife:* You're late again. I can never depend on you to be home on time.
>
> *Husband:* Wow—It's past seven. Time got away from me. You're right. I'm late.

An example of agreeing with a principle is seen in this discussion:

> *Wife:* It's going to be expensive to hire someone else to do all the tree trimming this year if you're not going to do it.
>
> *Husband:* That's true. It will cost more to have someone else do this for us.

Some spouses don't come out clear and straight with their criticisms. They try to be subtle and sneak in with their remarks. They use what I call sideswipe comments. An example would be the husband who says, "Most wives I know take time and fix up for their husbands before they come home at night." Instead of responding with "Are you saying I don't?" or "I fix up when I'm able to do so" or "*Now*, what are you criticizing me about?" there is an alternate response. One wife replies to such a comment, "Well, that's good that they do and it's nice that you notice that." This puts the responsibility back in the other person's lap to state a direct request. Your response will disarm your attacker and you will no longer have a real opponent.

There is a skill and process called *penetrating listening.* It's like some of our sophisticated weaponry used in war in which the bomb or missile penetrates deep within the defensive structure before it explodes. It works because it is not put off by the initial defense, but penetrates to where it will have the greatest effect. Listening that can penetrate by going beyond the anger or contempt in a partner's voice may pick up the core concern that is often disguised in the heat of a quarrel. If your listening is nondefensive, you will be less likely to respond defensively, and when you don't contribute any fuel to the fire, it soon dies out.

The Stonewalling Stage
When criticism, contempt, and defensiveness become permanent residents in a marriage, they strangle the flow of communication.

And communication is to a marriage what blood is to the body. Without it, you die. *Stonewalling* is one of the many descriptions of this last and worst stage.

At this state, both partners may feel like they're talking to a brick wall. There is little or no response. The loudest sound is silence, and the message it imparts is distance and disapproval. It's a method used more by husbands than by wives. The silent retreat irritates a wife and sends her the message that he doesn't love her. Men avoid conflict in marriage more than wives, and it upsets them more physiologically. When this condition becomes chronic it usually sounds the death cry for a marriage even when just one partner employs this tactic.[10]

It's difficult to maintain the five-to-one ratio of positive to negative when the four horsemen are racing through your marriage. The minute any of them begin to invade your marriage, it should be viewed as an unwelcome guest and exited. (Again I would urge you to read *How to Change Your Spouse* by Oliver and Wright for detailed assistance on what you can do. I will recommend this many times as a practical companion volume to this text. Another excellent resource is *What Your Mother Never Told You & What Your Father Didn't Know* by John Gray [HarperCollins].)

If these negatives have become a part of your marriage routine, are you ready to do (not try, but *do*) something new? Throughout this book, as well as others recommended, you will find better ways of responding. After all, if what you're doing now isn't working, why keep on doing it? There *is* a better way.

4
A Vision for Your Marriage

"I HAD A DREAM," my client said. "It seemed like a realistic dream at the time. I could almost see what was going to happen in the future. I was sure it was within reach. June and I both had so much to offer. We were in love but highly realistic. We were convinced that our marriage was made in heaven, and for awhile it seemed to be. But then that dream we had when we married began to fade and get a bit fuzzy. It wasn't at the forefront of our thoughts anymore. It was there, but so were a lot of other things in our lives. All too soon we were into routines and ruts. Our marriage wasn't fresh anymore. And here we are, fifteen years later, wondering what happened. Are we just like everyone else with a lackluster marriage? It feels like we're just drifting and too often on the edge of a whirlpool."

I've heard it many times in my counseling office—a marriage ending up where the couple never wanted it to be. So many marry with the belief, "We're getting married and because we're Christians and we love each other, we have what it takes for our marriage to work and to be what we want it to be."

But if I press them and ask "What do you really want your marriage to be?" the reply is often generalized and vague. When a couple responds "Marriage isn't what we thought it would be," only general disappointment is being voiced. What they really wanted from the marriage is vague, and that's a big part of the problem.

Drifting or Dreaming?

In one of his books originally titled *The Drifting Marriage*, a fellow counselor describes so well what happens to marriages. Listen to this description and ask yourself if it describes anyone you know.

Drifting is one of the most common forms of marital failure. In fact, I would venture to say that the majority of those couples found in our churches from Sunday to Sunday have marriages which are "adrift." Just think about that for a moment. Look across the pews. Would you guess that a majority of your friends have marriages that are in trouble? Probably not. Neither would they.

Drifting. Not only is it the most common form of marital failure, it is also the most dangerous. It is subtle. It is quiet. It is non-offensive. It sounds no alarms. It just gradually creeps into our lives. And then it destroys.

Step by step, the emotional deadness sneaks up on us as we move further and further away from our mates. The appearance of "all is well" is our placard. We fail to see the absence of real caring. Why should we see it? We have our preoccupations to keep us busy. The absence of emotional pain is accepted as a sign that everything is "fine." We have grown accustomed to the way things are.[1]

Drifting occurs because of a lack of purpose, the absence of personal and marital goals, and a vacuum where a sense of vision ought to be.

Do you have a vision for your marriage? Have you established specific goals for your marriage that you would like to achieve? Have you and your spouse discussed and evaluated where your marriage is and where you want it to be three to six months from now? I asked this of a couple in counseling and I received an interesting reply. "Norm, we don't even know what you're talking about. What do you mean a 'vision' for your marriage? And how can we think of what we want three to six months from now when we're just trying to survive on a day-to-day basis?"

Although many people feel that way, lasting marriages not only have the characteristics we have already described; they have senses of vision for their marriages as well.

Vision for the Journey

Here is my premise for this chapter: Unless you have a clear and precise understanding of where you are heading in your marriage, the probability of a successful journey is limited.

In the *King James Version* of Proverbs 29:18 there is a statement that is a foundation for a successful marriage. It reads, "*Where there is no vision, the people perish."* A paraphrase of this is "Where there is no vision, a marriage relationship stops growing and begins to crumble." Unless you as a couple have a clear understanding of where you are heading, the probability of a successful marriage is limited, and drifting could lead you to the driveway of a divorce court.

Having a vision for anything is like having a dream. But you know, sometimes dreamers are scoffed at. Joseph was a dreamer and was subject to ridicule from his brothers (see Genesis 37). Sometimes dreams fade if we receive too much negative reaction. Sometimes we start to disbelieve our own dreams and become content to remain right where we are.

But dreams can also be contagious. Do you remember the dream of the man that day in 1963 who stood in front of thousands of people and cried out again and again. "I have a dream"? His dream was for justice and equality for black people. He never gave up on his dream, and the dream of Martin Luther King Jr. is now part of mainstream American consciousness. Dr. David Seamands, who heard Dr. King cry out his dream that day, says simply. "That day I learned the awesome power of an awe-inspiring dream, and I returned home lifted and encouraged."

The diminutive Albanian woman we today know as Mother Teresa was nothing more than average early in her life. Her colleagues in the convent have remarked that she was nothing special as a student, as a leader or as a woman seeking to please God. However, after years of prayer and a spirit broken by Him, she emerged as a figure to be reckoned with, moved beyond complacency to a deep compassion for the poorest of the poor. Summoning courage unfamiliar to her, she requested that her religious order permit her to initiate a ministry in India to care for those who were so sick that no other people or organizations bothered to care for them.

Why risk her life and the few human comforts she knew to begin a life of even greater sacrifice and ignominy? Because she felt a special calling from God to reach out to "love the unlovable." She could very easily have continued her ministry as a nun, teaching in schools, leading young women to consider a relationship with Christ, even directing some special students toward a vocational ministry. Nobody would have questioned her love for God, her commitment to His Kingdom, her selflessness as a nun.

Yet, she knew that God had reached out to her with a special vision for what she could do to impact people's lives for His glory. And what an impact she has had, one that exceeds her innate intellect, courage and physical strength. She has felt compelled to change the lives of people because God has given her a special vision for outreach.[2]

The prophet said it for us: "*Your old men will dream dreams, your young men will see visions*" (Joel 2:28, *NASB*). When you have vision, you may find yourself battling upstream, but you'll experience God's blessing and His presence as you cooperate with His work in your life. When you see things as they could be, especially in your marriage, you won't let the odds overwhelm you. When you see things as they could be, you'll recognize obstacles, but you won't dwell on them.

Describing the Vision

In seminars I've had people ask me: What do you mean by a vision, especially having a vision for your marriage? I tell them that there are many ways to think about vision. Vision could be described as *foresight*, with the significance of possessing a keen awareness of current circumstances and possibilities, and of the value of learning from the past.

Vision can also be described as *seeing the invisible and making it visible*. It's having a picture held in your mind of the way things could or should be in the days ahead.

Vision is also *a portrait of conditions that don't yet exist*. It's being able to focus more on the future than getting bogged down with the past or present. Vision is the process of creating a better future with God's empowerment and direction.[3]

Here are some other thoughts describing what vision means:

Vision is the dominant force that controls your life and it impacts the choices you make as a person and a couple. It's what your thoughts lean toward when you are not focused on something else.

It can direct the type of relationships and friendships that you form. It's also what you pray about as you seek God's will.[4]

Vision as a Magnet

A vision should be like a magnet that draws us out of the past and into the blessings of the future. I thought of this recently while watching the popular film *Dances with Wolves*. I was greatly intrigued with the animal scenes. During the stampede scene there are hundreds of buffalo thundering across the plain. At one point a buffalo appears to be charging directly at an Indian boy. As I watched, I wondered, *How did the filmmakers get that buffalo to do what they wanted?*

I later discovered in a magazine article that a great deal of time had been invested in the scene with that one buffalo. In order to get the buffalo to cooperate, they conditioned it by feeding it Oreo cookies. It wasn't long before the animal would practically jump through a hoop to get to those round, chocolate, cream-filled cookies. So for the stampede scene they placed a pile of Oreos next to the Indian boy (and out of sight of the camera), and the cookies drew the buffalo in the right direction just like a powerful magnet.

Vision as Visualizing

One of the current figures in the field of effective management and character development is Stephen Covey. He encourages leaders to begin each day with a mental picture of the end of their lives as the criteria for everything they choose to do each day.

If you've ever followed golf you'll recognize the name of Jack Nicklaus as one of the legends of this sport. In order to accomplish what he wants in his sport he envisions what he wants to happen as well as how he will make it happen. Nicklaus writes:

> I never hit a shot, even in practice, without having a very sharp, in-focus picture of it in my head. First I "see" the ball where I want it to finish, nice and white and sitting up high on the bright green grass. Then the scene quickly changes and I "see" the ball going there: its path, trajectory, and shape, even its behavior on the landing. Then there's a sort of fade-out, and the next scene shows me making the kind of swing that will turn the previous image into reality.[5]

Here's what Chuck Swindoll says about vision:

> Vision is the ability to see God's presence, to perceive God's power, to focus on God's plan in spite of the obstacles. . . . Vision is the ability to see above and beyond the majority. Vision is perception—reading the presence and power of God

into one's circumstances. I sometimes think of vision as looking at life through the lens of God's eyes, seeing situations as
He sees them. Too often we see things not as they are, but as
we are. Think about that. Vision has to do with looking at
life with a divine perspective, reading the scene with God in
clear focus.

Whoever wants to live differently in "the system" must
correct his or her vision.[6]

Vision's Uniqueness

Vision is specific, detailed, customized, distinctive, sometimes
time-related, and measurable. In marriage, vision is a way of describing its activity and development.[7] The vision you have for your marriage may be uniquely different from another person's. Having a vision for your marriage is having a realistic dream for what you, your
spouse, and your marriage can become under God's direction. And
we need to seek what God wants for us and our marriages, because
without His wisdom what we achieve may be out of His will. We
need His wisdom, because *"The Lord knows the thoughts of man;
he knows that they are futile"* (Ps. 94:11, *NIV*).

Dr. Charles Stanley talks about vision for the Christian life:

The Lord often shows us a general picture of what we are to
do—and that broad overview tends to intimidate us and scare
us. We need to realize that the Lord doesn't leave us with a
giant goal or a great plan—He provides direction for all of the
small steps that are necessary for getting to the big goal.

Ask the Lord to show you the first step that you need toward the goal. Recognize that it will be only a step. Be patient
with yourself and with God's working in you. Do what He
shows you to do with all your strength, might, and talent.
And then look for the second step that He leads you to take.

The Lord doesn't catapult us into greatness; He grows us
into spiritual maturity.

He stretches us slowly so that we don't break.

He expands our vision slowly so that we can take in all of
the details of what He desires to accomplish.

He causes us to grow slowly so that we stay balanced.

The unfolding of God's plan for our lives is a process. Expect
to be engaged in that process for the rest of your life.[8]

And this is true for a marriage as well.

From Dream to Reality

What we need is vision that employs action.

This power of vision to fulfill needs and turn dreams into reality is what I call action-vision. Action-vision is an image of desired results that inspires us to action. It's more than just a snapshot from our hope chest. It's a visualization of the possibilities, the probabilities, and the process of making things happen.

Action-vision doesn't mean developing a tunnel vision of what we think our life should be like and then feeling we've missed the mark when it doesn't happen. Instead, it's recognizing the desires of our heart and being actively involved in the process of seeing them become reality or being willing to revamp the blueprints. In this mode of living, God's will is not some elusive dream, but a daily reality. It's a method of setting direction for the future that allows us to live fully today.[9]

How does all this apply to your marriage? What do you do? How do you do it? Where do you begin? A goal makes a dream become a reality, especially when you break down your long-range goals into short-range. For some it is easier to talk about having goals for their marriages rather than creating visions for them. The purpose of a vision or a goal is to bring change to your marriage.

Change as Positive

The word *change* means to make different, to give a different course or direction, to replace one thing with another, to make a shift from one to another, to undergo transformation or transition. Some see change as negative or threatening. I've even had some couples say, "Why fool around with something that's already working well? I don't think it could be any better." If that's true, wonderful. Personally, I think all marriages can improve in some way. Warren Wheebe has written:

We can benefit from change. Anyone who has really lived knows that there is no life without growth. When we stop growing we stop living and start existing. But there is no growth without change. There is no challenge without change. Life is a series of changes that create challenges, and if we are going to make it, we have to grow.[10]

Unfortunately, I see a number of couples who believe that their marriages can't be improved. This hopeless perspective makes a marriage become even more impoverished. But often this is an attitude rather than a fact of reality.

One wife who came for counseling basically wanted her husband to spend ten uninterrupted minutes a day talking with her. There was nothing wrong with this request. In fact, this is a necessity for any marriage if growth is going to occur. Two weeks later she returned for another counseling appointment, but she was quite upset. She complained because in the past two weeks they had sat down and talked only four times.

I think I shocked her with my reply. "That's outstanding," I said. "Remember during our first session you said you were hesitant to try because you didn't think it would work?"

"Yes," she said.

"Look at it this way," I continued. "There was improvement. You're on your way to reaching your goal. If you have a 15 to 20 percent improvement this soon, you're doing well. Of course you want to have this discussion every day, but that will take time. You must have done something positive and encouraging for this to happen so quickly. What did you do?"

And all of a sudden this woman was looking at what did happen, rather than what didn't happen. It makes a big difference.

Chuck Swindoll has written:

Change—real change—takes place slowly. In first gear, not overdrive. Far too many Christians get discouraged and give up. Like ice-skating or mastering a musical instrument or learning to water-ski, certain techniques have to be discovered and developed in the daily discipline of living. Breaking habit patterns you established during the passing of years cannot occur in a few brief days.[11]

Looking Forward

When you begin thinking about your goals or vision for your marriage, there are two basics to follow: (1) Be specific and (2) look forward rather than backward. I have a phrase for this second principle—be a tomorrow person rather than a yesterday person. Usually couples want to talk more about what they don't want rather than what they do want. When you focus on what you don't want, you tend to reinforce its existence by paying attention to it. It becomes more of a complaint, and it doesn't give you any help to achieve what it is that you want. If you tell your spouse what you don't want, he or she will hear it as a complaint and will probably become defensive.

So in creating your vision for your marriage, describe what you want rather than what you don't want. Don't describe what you want "less" of, but rather "more" of, because it's easier to notice a positive response rather than a decrease in a negative.

How would you respond if your spouse said, "Have you noticed that I'm less irritable than usual?" Compare that with "I think we are getting along better and we're kinder in our responses." Begin creating your vision by stating it in terms of what will be happening. This will make reaching your goals easier than if you focus on negatives that are happening less often.[12]

Being Specific

Now back to the first basic: Your vision statements or goals need to be specific, rather than vague. Look at the following goals:

- To be more respectful;
- To improve our sex life;
- To be more loving;
- To be more flexible;
- To be less self-centered.

The first four goals are much too general. And do you see the problem with the last goal? It's backward-looking rather than forward-facing. Don't focus on reducing the negative, but on increasing the positive! And when you increase positives, the benefits are such that they begin to crowd out the negative or problem behaviors. Keep in mind that the more specific your goals, the more attainable they are. And this means they must be reasonable.

Let's look again at the goals above, and this time make them specific.

We will show more respect for each other. Each of us can show interest in one another when we first meet at the end of the day. We will give each other at least one compliment a day. We will listen to one another without interruption even when we don't agree with what the other is saying.

We will improve our sexual relationship. We will read a book on sex aloud to each other and work toward making our sexual experience creative, satisfying, and exciting most of the time. We will both communicate clearly before 8 P.M. if we are interested in sex or not. We will also be more verbal before and during lovemaking.

We will be more loving verbally and nonverbally. We will both ask how we can help the other each day. We will say "I love you" to each other at least once a day. We will make love at least once a week. We will ask what the other wants to do on Friday and Saturday nights.

We will learn to be more flexible. We will learn to handle being a spontaneous guest for dinner, and spontaneously having guests for dinner.

We will see things from the other's perspective, giving ourselves two years to accomplish this. We will do a task the way our partner does it at least once before we encourage them to do it our way. We will work toward admitting it when we're wrong and be less defensive.

These are all goals that I've heard from couples. Do you see the difference? Keep them specific, futuristic, and attainable.

Planning the Process

Goal setting and priority evaluation are not all of the process, however. Developing your plan to attain the goal is the heart of the process. Planning moves you from the present to the future.

You must be flexible and adaptable because plans do change. Locking yourself into a dead-end approach would be as detrimental to your marriage as no goal setting at all. This fact is stated in the book of Proverbs: *"It is pleasant to see plans develop. That is why fools refuse to give them up even when they are wrong"* (13:19, TLB). Planning is a tool, a means to an end. It saves time and energy, and decreases frustration.

One husband described to me how he and his wife learned to plan their goals:

Before we were married, Evie's and my goals were just to get married. In the beginning years of our marriage, our major goals centered around my finishing seminary and getting into ministry. There were no goals for our life together as a couple except to be happy. Our first real mutual goal was to have a baby. It took us quite some time to realize that goal. Then it wasn't until we were in a seminar—a Christian Marriage Enrichment Seminar—about six years into our marriage that we thought about making mutual goals. This involved deciding upon them together and making them priorities in our lives.

The experience in the seminar of setting mutual goals and then within the next few months working to reach some of those goals was so beneficial to our marriage that we decided to keep setting and reviewing goals periodically. So we began to set aside a couple of days between two and four times a year to do this. They became what we like to call "honeymoon weekends." They may not be on a weekend. We sometimes go away on a Tuesday and Wednesday or Thursday and Friday. The principle is that we get away from our regular routine and demands on our time and we go someplace where we can spend sufficient time together.

We start on the first afternoon and evening by discussing goals that we previously set and evaluating the progress we've made. We also discuss setbacks and what adjustments we might need to make to reach the goals. We review the goals. About some goals we have made previously we say, "Well, that is not realistic," or "That is not practical," or "That is not so much a priority now as it was when we talked about it at the time."

Then we spend some time on the second day of our honeymoon weekend talking about goals that involve others. We talk about where we would like to be in five years as a couple, as parents, as ministers, as people in our neighborhood—trying to take into account all aspects of life, including our relationship with God. Then we talk about what we would like to be doing a year from the present time in order to be on our way toward these five-year goals. We then talk about what needs to be done now to get started.

Setting Your Own Goals

What can you do now to discover and set your goals? Ed Dayton and Ted Engstrom, in their book *Strategy for Living*, suggest six steps to setting goals. Respond to each of the following steps in the space provided.

Step 1: Understand Your Purpose
What would you like to do for your marriage, or what would you like your marriage to become? What is the general direction toward

which you would like your marriage to move? Make a statement about that.

_____

_____

_____

_____

_____

Step 2: Picture the Situation

Imagine your marriage relationship not as it is now, but as you would like it to be. What does it look like? Who are you with? What are you doing? What are the circumstances? Visualize and use your mental imagery.

_____

_____

_____

_____

_____

Step 3: State Your Immediate Goals

What things do you have to accomplish now if you are going to move toward your ultimate purpose in your marriage?

_____

_____

_____

_____

Step 4: Act

Pick out one of the goals for your marriage and start moving toward it. Remember that every long journey begins with the first step! And before you act, pray.

_____

_____

_____

_____

Step 5: Act as If . . .

Act as if you have already reached your goal. If you are going to start working toward that first goal, you are going to have to start acting as if you had really reached it. How would this impact all the other parts of your life? What would it say about your plans for the church, your family, and others? This may help you uncover some other goals that you need to consider.

Step 6: Keep Praying

If you are going to live life with a purpose, then you need to keep seeking God's leading in all this. Yes, you prayed before you acted, but pray also through the whole planning process. If you are expecting to live a life with God's purpose in mind, you had better be communicating with Him.[13]

How It Worked for One Couple

Over the years I have asked couples to develop such goals or vision statements for their marriages in the counseling office as well as in marriage seminars.

One of the best ways to capture the vision of how to develop your own goals is to see what others have done. The following is a vision statement a couple in their thirties developed and are now using to guide the direction of their marriage. They said their overall goal for their life and marriage was as follows: *"Love the Lord our God with all our hearts, our souls, and our minds"* (see Matt. 22:36–40). Specifically, our goals are to demonstrate this love to each other and others by:

Our Spiritual Well-Being

Walk together with Jesus and enjoy the journey (see Ps. 16:11).

Commit to spiritual growth through prayer, study, praise, and meditation—as individuals, as a couple, and together with other Christians (see Jer. 15:16).

Serve God wherever He leads us.

Our Marital Well-Being

Be encouragers by (see 1 Thess. 5:11):

Giving the other person the benefit of the doubt.

Believing in each other's dreams.

Affirming and protecting one another.

Being active listeners.

Cherishing and respecting each other.

Our Familial Well-Being
> Model Christlike love (see Eph. 5:22,33).
> Be accountable to God first for our family (see Gen. 18:19;
> 1 Sam. 3:12–14; 2 Tim. 1:5).
> Uphold our home as a haven.

Our Physical Well-Being
> Maintain our bodies through regular physical activity.

Our Mental Well-Being
> Share interesting topics that stimulate dialogue.
> Cultivate our love of books and reading.
> Take advantage of continuing educational opportunities.

Our Emotional Well-Being
> Recognize and acknowledge crises.
> Anticipate stresses and plan accordingly.
> Take advantage of available resources.
> Make lifestyle changes as needed to enhance our relationship.

Our Financial Well-Being
> Remember that our finances and material possessions have
> been entrusted to us by God (see Matt. 24:45,46).
> Support our church through tithes and offerings.
> Maintain a spirit of giving (see 1 Tim. 6:17–19).

Our Social Well-Being
> Because we as individuals gain energy through reflection,
> introspection, and solitude, we must accept responsibility for
> our social lives by:
> Developing and maintaining close and meaningful
> relationships.
> Seeking and creating social atmospheres that are
> comfortable for us.
> Having adequate preparation and renewal times surrounding social interactions.
> *Our relationship is a precious gift from God. We honor it
> as such, and will protect it from attack or neglect.*

Together for Others

Part of the calling of marriage is to do something together, to minister together, and to serve God together. We are called as believers to a mission to minister to others, and this means as married couples having a mission together.

One counselor stated:

> To try to keep love just for us . . . is to kill it slowly. . . . We are not made just for each other; we are called to a ministry of love to everyone we meet and in all we do. In marriage, too, Jesus' words hold true: in saving our lives we lose them, and in losing our lives in love to others, we drink of life more deeply.[14]

A family therapist said:

> When families reach out beyond their own worlds to serve others, they have a stronger spiritual bond. The call to Christ is the call to serve. . . . Every family we know that serves together regularly has a strong foundation and closeness that other families are missing.[15]

A wife said:

> Over 10 years of marriage, I have found that when my husband and I focus on our own needs, and whether they're being met, our marriage begins to self-destruct. But when we are ministering together, we experience, to the greatest extent we've known, that "the two shall become one."[16]

What is needed is *balance*. I've seen couples who focus exclusively on themselves to the exclusion of others, and those who focus exclusively on others to the exclusion of themselves.

I think one of the best mission purposes and a model for young couples today is to have a healthy marriage based upon the presence of Jesus Christ within the marriage. For years I have been dismayed by the responses of so many young couples who, when I ask if they have any models of healthy marriages, respond with, "No, we don't."

Sometimes you discover your mission as you move along in your marriage. It could be based on your experiences, or even on difficult times. In our own marriage, part of our mission to others is a ministry to couples who have disabled children, and to those who have experienced the death of a child. This focus developed because we've experienced both the raising of a disabled child as well as his death at the age of twenty-two. (See *I'll Love You Forever*, published by Focus on the Family.) From the pain we experienced and lessons we learned, we've been able to minister to others. God can do the same with the experiences of your life as well.

Well, where is your marriage going? Where do you want it to go? It's exciting to have a vision and a mission. It can make your marriage come alive in a new way, and it gives you a love that lasts!

5
Where It All Started

PEOPLE OFTEN ASK ME, "What's the cause of all the marital problems? Why can't people get along and love one another? What's the main issue?"

I have a simple answer: "The garden."

Usually that elicits a strange look, so I elaborate with five more words: "The fall of man—sin."

The world is still reaping the results of or damage from original sin—in the way we behave, the way we feel, and the way we think. And our *thoughts* are where it all begins. God pointed this out early on in Genesis: *"Then the Lord saw that the wickedness of man was great on the earth, and that every intent of the thoughts of his heart was only evil continually"* (6:5, *NASB*). In other versions "thoughts" is translated *imagination*. This is where it all begins—in our minds.

Storms of the Mind

I've never been in a hurricane and I never want to. The tremendous force of the violent, swirling winds devastates everything in its path and leaves behind a trail of destruction. Within a hurricane there is a place called the eye of the storm. It's a place of such calm that you wouldn't even know about the fury going on elsewhere. But it's directly related to the intense violent winds as they stem outward from this core.

It's not unlike what we see in many marriages. There is an eye of the storm in every person that can make or break any marriage. It's called our thought life, and it is marred. It has a bent toward negative thinking as a carryover from the fall of mankind.

Consider these examples. A husband comes home from work early and greets his wife with a hug and kiss. But in return she becomes angry and glares at him. Why?

A wife returns her husband's overdue books to the library and he becomes annoyed at her for doing so. Why?

A husband brags about his wife's cooking to a number of friends and she becomes furious at him for doing so. Why?

In each case the spouse's positive action brought an unexpected reaction from his or her partner. The anticipated reaction would have been appreciation, not anger. What happened? Why the negative reactions? Let's go back and look at the thoughts each spouse had in response to the positive overture.

In the case of the wife whose husband came home early, she thought, *Why did he come home at this time? Is he checking up on me? If there is anything undone, he'll criticize me. I don't need that.*

The husband who has the overdue library books thought, *I was going to take those back. I'm capable of doing that. She's trying to point out that I'm not responsible. She doesn't trust me to follow through so she's going to jump in and do it herself!*

The wife who was praised for her cooking thought, *He never praises me that much at home. He's just using me to get attention for himself from his friends. He probably wants me to compliment him on something now. I wonder what they think about me now.*

In each case these reactive thoughts just popped into their minds. Has something like this ever happened to you? Probably. It could be that your thought was based on some past experience so there is a reason for it. But in each case, regardless of the intent and purpose of the partner who did something positive, the reaction was such that it might limit a positive overture the next time.

Choosing How We Respond

We can all choose to react to what our partners do with a negative interpretation, a negative assumption, suspicion over their intent, or in a guarded and defensive way. On the other hand, we could also respond at face value to what was said or done, give the benefit of the doubt, seeing it as a positive step, and showing appreciation. In the *Amplified* version, 1 Corinthians 13:7 states "Love . . . is ever ready to believe the best of every person."

Your negative thoughts will generate anger, but if you correct them the anger will subside.

One of the ways to keep love alive in a relationship and to keep going in a positive direction is to be fully aware of your thoughts and beliefs about your relationship.[1] If the communication in your marriage could be better, look first at your thought life. If the way you behave toward each other needs improvement, look at your thought life.

The other day I went to the dictionary and looked up the word "slander." Do you know what it means? It's the utterance in the presence of another person of a false statement or statements, damaging to a third person's character or reputation.[2] It dawned on me that many of our thoughts about one another fall into that category. God knows all of our thoughts as well as everything else. Many spouses commit slander in their minds. I've heard many such comments in my counseling office. Actually some of the thoughts we have about our partners unfortunately fall into the category of character assassination rather than character adoration. And this character assassination style of thinking generates both conflict and distance in our marriage relationships.

Couples who have growing, fulfilling marriages have thought lives that are positive and healthy. What happens within the couples is a reflection of the inner workings of each person's mind and heart.

Many, however, struggle with defeatist beliefs. I've heard many of these beliefs over the years. But as people have worked at challenging these beliefs and becoming positive, I've also seen not only people themselves change, but their spouses and marriages as well.

Perhaps it would be helpful at this point for you to take a few minutes and write out your thoughts about your marriage and your partner, so you can become more aware of whether they are thoughts that promote or hinder growth in your marriage.

1. My positive thoughts about my spouse are

_____
_____
_____
_____

2. My negative thoughts about my spouse are

_____
_____
_____
_____

3. Beliefs I have that help my marriage grow are

_____
_____
_____
_____

4. Beliefs I have that keep my marriage from growing are

_____

_____

_____

_____

_____

Roadblocks to Belief

There are numerous patterns of thought that deaden and block a marriage relationship. Let me take you back to the counseling office so you can hear some of the common beliefs that impede progress.

One roadblock is *assuming.* Assumptions are usually negative. They portray the worst about another person. You make unfavorable judgments about your partner. You hear him singing in another room and you think, *He's just doing that to irritate me. He knows that bothers me.* But you don't really know that. You can't determine another person's motive.

One of the most bothersome thoughts, and a pattern of thinking that is difficult to change, is *overgeneralizing*—statements such as "He never listens to me" or "She's always late" or "You never consider what I want." What is said may be plausible to you if you're upset over a few incidents, but these words are like insecticide that drifts across a field and kills all the crops rather than just the weeds. A spouse hearing these statements usually gives up. When, in our eyes, our partners are *always* or *never,* we have condemned them and probably won't give them credit even when they please us. And overgeneralizing, again, begins in our thought lives.

There are times when for one reason or another we may *magnify.* This is the tendency to enlarge the qualities of another person, usually in a negative way. When a situation seems out of control we may tend to think this way. One husband I knew wasn't the best when it came to spending and saving money. Once, when some checks bounced, his wife shared some of her thoughts with me. "He is such a spendthrift." "He does this constantly." "We won't have enough money for the bills this month." "If we're late on the house payment again, they'll foreclose." And finally, "We're going to lose our house and it's all because of him." I think you could imagine the ensuing conversation.

Hopelessness as Blocking Belief

I've heard husbands and wives say, "Nothing can change or improve our relationship." Now that is a defeatist belief. It will not only keep you from attempting anything, but it will cause you to look at your spouse and the relationship through a negative filter. It becomes a self-fulfilling prophecy. It will keep you stuck.

Do you know what the results of this belief are? Let me give you several. And even if they don't fit you and your situation, they may fit someone you know.

With a belief such as this, you end up with a sense of resignation: "I'll just have to learn to live with this." You feel powerless and the downward spiral has started. You may begin to think less of yourself and that usually leads to thinking less of your partner. And when that happens your love and giving to your spouse begins to dry up.

I remember hearing one husband say. "I'm afraid my learning to live with it was the first step in learning to live without her." That's sad, especially since in the majority of situations change and growth are possible.

I've also talked with spouses who end up feeling like martyrs. Unfortunately, martyrs usually let their partners know what they have to live with. And in time, that hideous destroyer of marriages begins to put in an appearance—revenge. It may be hidden or blatant. All it does is cause the negatives to be set in cement.[3] (For more assistance see *How to Change Your Spouse* by Gary Oliver and H. Norman Wright, Servant Publications.)

If you or anyone else believes that nothing can improve your marriage, test this belief. Challenge it. Look at, define, and clarify some of the problems, then select one that appears to be the easiest to change. One husband wanted just to be able to have discussions with his wife without the usual defensive arguments that seemed to erupt constantly. He and I actually had an enjoyable time brainstorming different ways he could stay out of the argument and eliminate his defensiveness. We did the following:

1. He chose to believe that his wife wasn't out to get him or simply to argue with him out of spite. She might have some good ideas.

2. He committed himself not to interrupt her, not to argue or debate, and not to walk out on her.

3. He would respond to what she said by making such statements as: "Really," "That's interesting," "I hadn't considered that," "Tell me more," and "I'd like to think about that."

4. He also chose to think the following: *Even if this doesn't work the first time, I'll try it at least five times.*

5. He determined to thank her for each discussion, and when her response was even 5 percent less defensive, to compliment her for the way she responded.

Five weeks later, he called and said, "The fourth discussion was totally different. It's starting to work, Norm. You destroyed my belief that nothing can improve our relationship. There's a bit of hope now."

Perhaps it would help in countering our negative and hopeless beliefs to focus more upon passages from God's Word that are future oriented and filled with hope. For example, in Jeremiah we read, *"'For I know the plans that I have for you,' declares the Lord, 'plans for welfare and not for calamity to give you a future and a hope'"* (29:11, *NASB*).

Individual Action and Differences

Another defeatist belief is "My spouse won't cooperate and nothing can be done without her cooperation." Again, it's not true. We can't wait around for our partners' responses or cooperation before we take positive steps. I've had people say, "But if I do something, he may resent it or it could discourage him and make him feel bad about himself." He could, but even if he did you haven't forced him to respond in that way. And if you wait around for him to cooperate, you're just allowing his inactivity to control you. Is that what you want?

If you take the initiative, several positives are apt to occur. You won't feel so much like a victim. You'll be doing something positive, and if you initiate change or respond in a new way, your spouse may respond differently if he or she sees the possibility of something new happening. What have you got to lose? Nothing. But you do have everything to gain.

Another similar defeatist attitude is "My partner is the most entrenched, stubborn person I know. He/She is just not capable of changing." If you believe that, you will act accordingly, and he/she *won't* change, because you're not working to bring about change.

I believe everyone is capable of some change regardless of their upbringing, personality, nationality, and even age. I've heard wives say, "He's German, you know, and those men don't change." These are myths and false beliefs that we buy into and perpetuate. The reason most spouses don't change is because we believe they can't.

If we respond to them in ways that don't promote change, we often cripple their attempts to change by our own unbelief!

I've also talked to couples who felt that if they tried to improve their marriages and make them better, they may become worse. But if you don't put forth the effort, you'll never know. One wife told me, "It's tolerable now. It's not what I thought marriage would be but it's better than nothing. And it's better than being alone." Unfortunately, a year later, she was alone.

If you work at discovering new information and new approaches, there's as much possibility of the relationship improving as getting worse. And frequently a relationship may get worse for awhile on the path to getting better. But it's better to be a risk taker than to be paralyzed.

Some of the other defeatist thoughts I've encountered involve personal resistance to improving the relationship. Some have said, "Why should I have to be the one to put forth all the work and effort to change?" My response is, "Why *not* you?" It would show maturity on your part and a desire for something positive. This step is a reflection of your inner character. Whether or not it has any impact on the relationship, wouldn't there be a sense of satisfaction on your part if you took this step? Not too many people think about that.

Think of it this way. Your partner may not have the same perception that you do of what is occurring in the relationship. I'm amazed at how often levels of satisfaction in a marriage can vary. One couple graphically expressed this verbally when I asked each the question, "On a scale of zero to ten, how satisfied are you with the marriage relationship?" The husband replied with a resounding, "Eight!" whereas she said, "Three." That caused some discussion.

Many times I have seen this disparity in the responses to a Marital Assessment Inventory that I have couples complete prior to coming for counseling. I ask them to complete the question "How committed are you to remaining in your relationship?" and then, "How committed do you think your spouse is to remaining in your relationship?" They respond to this on a scale of zero to ten. I don't know how many times I've seen one respond by giving an eight or nine to his perception of his partner's commitment, while in reality his partner's commitment as evidenced by her own response was only a two!

Another reason it's beneficial for you to take the initiative is because the two of you may differ in your motivation as well as in your ability to change. The person who is more optimistic or can become more optimistic, or the one experiencing the most pain, could be more motivated to take action. And both people do not have to work at the relationship with the same degree of intensity.

Libelous Labels

Watch out for "crazy spouse labels." I've heard people say, "My spouse is crazy, has a character disorder, is enmeshed with mother, an alcoholic, a pervert, sick, impossible, a stubborn _____, etc."

My response to statements like that is not usually expected. I may say, "So if your partner truly is crazy or has a character disorder, why should that stop you from working on the relationship? If the other really is that way, and we don't know that for a fact, it might even be easier to get your partner to change." They'd never thought of it like that before. It's something to consider. Throw out undocumented, undiagnosed, and unreliable labels.[4]

Victim Phrases

Not only do your thoughts about your partner affect your marriage; your thoughts about yourself will also affect your marriage because of how you limit yourself. When I work with individuals or couples I look for what I call "victim phrases."

One of these phrases is "I can't." Do you say this to yourself about yourself or your marriage? Words like these are prompted by some kind of unbelief, fear, or lack of hope Any time you say "I can't," you're saying you have no control over your life or your marriage. It takes no more effort to say "It's worth a try" or "I'll try something new," and this approach certainly has more potential. It shows you've become more of an encouragement to yourself than a defeatist.

Victim phrases that can be a real problem are "That's a problem" and "That's going to be hard." These are self-fulfilling prophecies. Also, too often we amplify them to say "My spouse is a problem" or "It's hard to work on my marriage." Whenever you see what is occurring in life as a problem or a burden, you tend to become enmeshed in fear or even helplessness. Every obstacle brings with it an opportunity to learn, grow, and become a different person if you have the right attitude. Phrases such as "That's a challenge" or "It's an opportunity to learn something new" or "Living with my spouse provides an opportunity for me to learn something new" means you're on the right track.

Another victim phrase is "I'll never be able to do anything about my life, my situation, my marriage, my spouse, etc." If you say this, it's an indication of unconditional surrender to whatever is occurring in your life. You're saying in essence, "I'm stuck in cement and won't ever be able to move." It doesn't give you or God an opportunity to work in your life. You could say, "I've never considered that before" or "I haven't tried that, but I'm willing to."

The question "Why is life . . . my marriage . . . my spouse this way?" is a fairly normal reaction to the disappointments of life, and it's certainly all right to feel this way and verbalize it. But to choose to remain at this place and stick with this attitude is crippling. I've seen some stuck there for life!

Another phrase usually follows in its wake: "Life isn't fair." That's true. It's unfair and unpredictable and it won't always be the way we want. But we can choose to grow during these difficult times and learn to ask, "What can I learn at this time and what can I do differently?"

Such victim phrases keep us prisoners in our own minds. By using them we limit growth. We limit change. We act out the rehearsal script of our minds for ourselves and others.

Sometimes thoughts like these are called "crippling thoughts" or even "hot thoughts." They lead to feelings of hopelessness, anger, resentment, bitterness, futility, and depression. What you *feel*, you will *say*—directly or indirectly—and your partner will probably respond in such a way as to confirm your worst thoughts about him or her.

Many years ago a new jail was constructed in a small town in England. The builders said it was escape proof. Harry Houdini, the great escape artist known all over the world, was invited to come and test it to see if it really was escape proof. He had once boasted that he could escape from any jail, so naturally he accepted the invitation.

He entered the cell and the jailer closed the door behind him. Houdini listened to the sound of the key being slipped into the lock. The jailer then withdrew the key and left. Houdini took out his tools and started the process of working on that cell door. But nothing happened. It wasn't working out the way he expected. In fact, nothing that he did to unlock the door seemed to work. The hours passed. He was puzzled, because he had never failed to unlock any locked door. Finally, he admitted defeat. But when, in his exhaustion, he leaned against the door, it swung open. The jailer had put the key in, but never locked it. The only place the door was locked was in his mind. Too often we're not much different.

The point I'm trying to make is this: Thoughts like these create problems. They don't solve them. Whenever you have such a thought or any negative thought for that matter, confront it. Challenge it. Debate with it. Change it. Ask yourself, "If I didn't have this thought, what's a better one I could have?" "If I could change this negative thought into something positive, what would it be?" "If someone else were to describe my partner, what would his or her description be?"

Negatives Versus Forgiveness

Negative thoughts and labeling never provide a full picture of your spouse. They are limited, biased, and slanted in one direction. More importantly, they interfere with one of the ingredients most essential for a marriage to change, progress, and move forward. It's called forgiveness. Negative labels and thoughts block forgiveness. You have to see your spouse in a new light in order for forgiveness to occur. Can you forgive a person you label as callous, selfish, controlling, insensitive, manipulative, unbending, crazy, etc.?

Labels are false absolutes. They are developed to describe those who are different. They're used to make it easier to justify ourselves and to keep us from thinking. If we used our minds constructively, we would be able to see both sides of a person. Labels limit our understanding of what is occurring in a marriage, for we see the label as the cause of the problem. Why look elsewhere!?

Labels also keep us from looking at our part in the problem. We use labels to avoid looking in the mirror for fear of what it will reflect. When you treat your spouse *as if* he or she is a certain way and possesses a particular quality, he or she may begin to act that way. Our negative expectations often become self-fulfilling prophecies and we end up cultivating what we don't want to grow.

Do you and your spouse label each other? Are the labels positive and motivating, or negative and debilitating? Are these generalizations attached to descriptions such as *always* or *never?* If you do label your spouse, perhaps you could learn to correct the label and in your heart and mind give him or her an opportunity to be different.[5]

Sometimes I wonder whether we really know what forgiveness is. Forgiveness costs. It hurts. It doesn't always come easily. Forgiveness cannot be given out of fear, but only out of love and compassion. Forgiveness is an action that lets the other person know he or she is loved "in spite of." Forgiveness is no longer allowing what has happened to poison you. Sometimes you feel as though forgiveness isn't deserved. But it never is. That's what makes it forgiveness. It unfolds first as a decision to accept what you never thought would be acceptable. And negative thoughts and labels block that decision.

Consider these thoughts about forgiveness:

> In forgiveness, you decide to give love to someone who has betrayed your love. You call forth your compassion, your wisdom, and your desire to be accepting of that person for who he or she is. You call forth your humanness and seek reunion in love and growth above all else.
>
> Forgiveness is the changing of seasons. It provides a new context within which to nurture the relationship. The changing of the seasons allows you to let go of all that has been difficult to bear and begin again. When you forgive, you do not forget the season of cold completely, but neither do you shiver in its memory. The chill has subsided and has no more effect on the present than to remind you of how far you've come, how much you've grown, how truly you love and are loved.
>
> When forgiveness becomes a part of your life, little resentment is left. Anger may not vanish immediately, but it will wither in time. The hot core of bitterness that was embedded firmly in your being burns no more.
>
> Forgiveness comes first as a decision to act lovingly, even though you may feel justified to withhold your love.[6]

Forgiveness is a decision to wish another person well, to call upon God to bless him or her, and to show His grace to the person in a special way.

Challenging the Negative Slide

Here is an example of how thoughts can put a damper on an otherwise enjoyable occasion, and how to interrupt the downhill slide and move it back to the enjoyable level.

June and her husband, Frank, went to a movie and afterward Frank suggested they walk down to a restaurant and have a piece of pie. Let's look inside the mind of each as the conversation continued.

June's first thought was *Oh boy. He knows I've been trying to diet and lose weight. He's just thinking of himself as usual. You'd think he'd remember something as important as that.*

June responded with an exasperated, "No, I'd rather just go home." Frank thought, *Now what's wrong with her? We had a great time and now she's getting all bent out of shape. She sure goes up and down on her emotions.*

Frank said a bit irritably, "Fine. Just forget it."

They each walked to the car in silence, but this time something new was beginning to take place. They were both learning to recognize how their thoughts had been feeding the way they responded to each other, and so each one during their silence was working on challenging their statements or destructive thoughts.

June began to think, *Well, maybe he just didn't think about it. After all, he's not the one on a diet. I am. And he's probably hungry. I could have a cup of decaf.*

She also thought, *I guess I would prefer to go home and get some sleep. I've been overworked this month. I guess I must have snapped at him and I didn't need to. His request was innocent enough.*

At the same time Frank was thinking, *June has been pushing it at work recently. And it is 10:30. Maybe she's just tired and wants to go home.*

He also thought, *We've worked out other disagreements. I think we can work this one out.*

June, who had calmed down by this time, said, "I didn't need to snap at you. I guess I was thinking about myself a bit too much. I guess I was looking forward to some rest. And I realize, too, that you could be hungry."

Frank responded, "I appreciate your clarifying that. I know you've been working a lot. And I just remembered you're on a diet, and that eating pie in front of you might make you drool." And with that comment they both laughed and were relieved because they were learning to turn things around.

Prayer and Your Inner Dialogue

I've had counselees ask, "Is it really possible to change my thought life?" Yes! An emphatic yes, especially if you know Jesus Christ as your Lord and Savior. You won't change your inner talk or thought life by talking with your partner, but you will *by talking with God about it.* God has already communicated with us in various ways—through the gift of His Son as He speaks to us through His Word, and as we respond to Him when we pray.

When you pray, what is it like? Is it a natural experience for you? Do you use your own language and style of talking, or do you feel you must talk in a certain manner or phrasing in order to get through?

What we pray about is personal, but I would like to recommend one specific prayer: Ask God to refashion your thinking. This begins first by consecrating your imagination and thought life to God. Then ask Him to cleanse your thought life of anything that would hinder your growth and relationship with your spouse. This suggestion is in keeping with a passage of Scripture found in 1 Peter 1:13 (*KJV*), "*Gird up . . . your mind.*"

The word *gird* means mental exertion. We are called upon to put out of our minds anything that would hinder the growth and development of our Christian lives—and in this case, anything that would cripple our marriages. But this growth is accomplished by the working of God in our minds. As believers, the Holy Spirit can give us greater awareness of the thoughts that control our lives and greater access to the specific thoughts that need to be changed.

With God's assistance, we can develop a much greater sensitivity to our inner dialogues. On occasion we may feel hesitant to do this because we feel guilty about an old pattern of thinking. Here again our negative inner dialogues have kept us from honest expression— with God. He will not be surprised or amazed or shocked by anything we say to Him, since He is already aware of our thoughts anyway.

As I have asked people in counseling to commit their inner dialogues to God each day, I have also asked, "How do you envision God responding to your admission of your thoughts and pattern of thinking?" This usually provokes not only an interesting response but an indication of the person's image of God.

How do we pray then? First we admit that our thought lives need renewal and changing. Next, if we lack that desire, we envision Jesus Christ as willing to help us develop the desire to change our thoughts. Sometimes you may feel justified about your thoughts about your spouse. Often people find it helpful to start the day by asking God to help them identify and dissect their thoughts and then to reassemble them. Although we may or may not be alert to these, we *can* become aware of these inner conversations. We need to develop the ability to accurately observe them. Scripture tells us to *"bring into captivity every thought to the obedience of Christ"* (see 2 Cor. 10:5).

I remember a counselee once who asked me, "Norm, is it all right if I use my imagination in my prayers?" He went on to say, "I find that if I at times actually imagine myself in the presence of Christ, talking to Him, it has a greater impact on my life." I told him it was fine to do so.

Some people derive more benefit out of praying with their eyes open, others by being in a room by themselves and talking out loud. Some individuals, once they have identified their negative thinking patterns, take each distorted or negative thought, repeat it, and give it over to God. Still others almost act out their prayers by seeing themselves holding each thought in their hands and literally giving it over to Jesus Christ, who accepts it with His hands and takes it away. They conclude this process of prayer by dedicating their imaginations to God in a realistic manner, especially as it pertains to their partners. Actually they have relinquished ownership of their thought lives and imaginations to God. However you do it, whatever method works for you, give your thought life to God's control.

Some people resist this approach because it is so effective! I have found it so in my own life. Some people resist giving God control because they feel comfortable with their negative patterns of thinking. They know that any effort to change would take time, energy, and patience. In fact, some gain satisfaction from their thinking patterns, even though they do not follow the direction God desires! Here is a sincere and balanced prayer I once heard:

> Lord, I am at the place of asking You to take over my thought life and my imagination. I am asking that You not only clean them up, but give me the power to control my thoughts. I am learning which thoughts cause me the most grief and which ones help me. I am learning which thoughts help or hinder my marriage. I have to admit to You that I am a creature of habit. I know I have spent years developing this type of negative thinking. I do want to communicate better with others and with myself, and I need Your help. I ask You to cause me to be very aware of what I am thinking and its effect. Please remind me, and I will respond to Your prodding. If I revert back to my old way of thinking from time to time, help me not to fall back into being negative about myself because of this lapse. Help me to be patient with myself and with You. Thank You for hearing me and accepting me.

Thank You for what You will do for my thought life and inner dialogues in the future.

Some people find it helpful to conduct their own prayer sessions for the changing of their thoughts. Begin praying by affirming that the Lord is present, that you are loved by Him, and that you belong to Him. Take a pen and paper. Ask the Lord to guide your mind to thoughts you have regularly that hinder your relationships with others and with yourself. This is a private time between you and the Lord. You do not need to rush. If no thoughts come for a while, be patient. As thoughts enter your mind, write them down, but do not evaluate them. After a time, go back over the list and thank God for allowing you to remember these. Ask Him for His wisdom and guidance in changing your thoughts and in becoming aware of them at all times.

I have encouraged a number of individuals and couples to keep a daily log of their thoughts. A log or journal simply records personal insights concerning your thoughts, what you have learned about them, and how you have prayed for them. It also indicates progress in identifying, dissecting, and reconstructing your thoughts. When you write such a journal, respond to questions such as "What were the significant thoughts and feelings of this day?" and "How did I respond to them?" Write down the answers. The act of writing something down tells you that it is important.

Another variation of using a log or journal is expressing yourself in prayer. By writing out a prayer or putting it in the form of a letter to God, you give it greater thought and deliberation, and the experience can take on tremendous meaning. You may want to commit yourself to this approach for one week and at the end of that time evaluate what took place.[7]

Some couples have even done this together as a joint venture. When you are not threatened by the struggle your partner is having with his or her thoughts, you are able to offer support and encouragement. This does wonders for both your and your partner's thought life. And it gives you a love that lasts!

6
Transitions—Friends or Foes?

"MARRIAGE? Sure I can tell you what it's like," said my counselee, Ellen. "It's like driving on a bumpy road in a car with no springs. Other times, it's like riding on a four-lane highway, with everyone picking up speed. And you can't be sure what lies ahead.

"It's a journey on a road that varies from being straight and smooth to winding, steep, and rough—with a few unexpected detours thrown in for good measure. And even though you thought you had packed for every possible circumstance, you soon discover you still left something out."

Ellen was a wife who had hit one of those bumpy stretches in her marriage, with no end in sight. "Over the past few years," she said, "I've experienced stress and loss in some ways I never expected. And that's thrown me. I'm a careful, organized person; I look at life realistically. And I don't just consider what is happening now, but I plan for the future. When I was eighteen, I studied and reflected on the different transitions that I would experience. But when some of them arrived, they still surprised me. Why? I wasn't able to handle them as well as I thought I would. Why not? Instead of feeling challenged by them, I felt threatened. Why?"

Bends in the Road

Even though our day-to-day experiences can sometimes feel like drudgery, marriage is always full of twists and turns, bends in the road, U-turns, even temporary roadblocks and seeming dead ends. The journey uniquely blends acquiring and losing, receiving and giving away, holding and letting go. A loving, committed relationship helps us weather all of these moves.

From birth until death, life is a series of transitions. A transition is a bridge between two different stages of life. It is a period of moving from one state of certainty to another. But in between there is a time of uncertainty. One stage is terminated and a new one begun. As you know, any new change carries an element of risk, insecurity, and vulnerability—even change that is predictable and expected.

Following childhood and adolescence, for most people there is the transition from being single to being married, from the twenties to the thirties, the thirties to the forties, from being a couple to being parents, from being parents to the empty nest, from the empty nest to becoming grandparents, from being employed to retirement, and so on. These transitions are all fairly predictable and can be planned for to reduce the adjustment.

Every transition carries with it seeds for growth, new insights, refinement, and understanding. But in the midst of turmoil, sometimes the positive aspects seem too far in the future to be very real. There is also a sense of loss that may or may not be recognized.

One of the natural transitions of life begins in our first year. Our baby teeth come through after bouts of pain and crying. We have gained a valuable tool for continued growth. But one day, these hard-earned baby teeth begin to loosen and wiggle. Soon they either fall out or have to be gently pulled out. We must suffer this necessary loss to make room for our permanent teeth. Sometimes we end up losing these as well, and have to be fitted with false teeth. None of these transitions is easy or painless.

Dealing with Transitions

Some people wish life was like a video player. Then whenever they find a particular stage especially satisfying, they can just hit the pause button and remain there awhile. But life is not a series of fixed points. Stable times are actually the exceptions; transitions are the norm. Dr. Charles Sell uses an apt analogy to describe these normal transitions in life:

Transitions are mysterious, like an underground passageway I once saw in a tour through a castle. The castle's rooms were gigantic, the woodwork extravagant, and the huge beams in the inner part of the towers projected massive strength. But what captivated me the most was that underground tunnel. A half-mile long, the escape route led from the castle to the stables. It was strikingly different from the rest of the castle.

The vast ballroom offered its visitors the feeling of dignity. A sense of comfort overtook us in the luxurious bedroom suites. Serenity filled the garden room. But the secret tunnel was mysterious and unnerving. It held no comfortable chairs because it was not a place to rest. No artwork adorned its moist, dark stone walls. It was not a place to browse. The tunnel was not made for stopping. It was for those en route with a sense of urgency. It turned your mind to either the past or the future: either you would concentrate on the extravagant castle you were leaving behind or on the stables ahead.

Life's transitions are like that, going *from* somewhere *to* somewhere. The present circumstances may seem like a void. It would be pleasant to turn around and go back to the security left behind. But because that is impossible, it is necessary to keep groping for what is ahead; then there will surely be a resting place. Uncertainty cries out "How long?" And anxiety questions, "Will I ever get through this?"

Drawn to the past by warm memories and yearnings, the future simultaneously beckons with a mixture of hope and fear. Sometimes depression opens its dark pit. Above, the grass is green, the sun shining on gleeful men, women, and children. But those in transition feel distant from them, pressured by the urgency to get on, to get through and out. Each transition carries with it the death of the previous state and the birth of a new one.[1]

We are always moving from, into, through, and out of something or other. Resisting this process puts us at the mercy of what is happening. Which of the transitions in your life have given you the greatest sense of joy? Why? The greatest sense of loss? Why? What about your partner?

But most people do not plan adequately for transitions, and the new stages of life creep up on them unaware. Suddenly they feel carried away by a flood, totally out of control. That in itself can threaten a marriage. And to make matters a bit more tense, there can be those unexpected events that occur in the midst of predictable changes—miscarriage, marital separation and divorce, illness, disability, death of a loved one, loss of a job, relocation of the household, parents coming to live with you, an adolescent running away or using drugs, an automobile accident, fire in the home, changes in socioeconomic status, and tornadoes. The list never ends.

Sometimes we take on additional, unexpected new roles such as becoming part-time students while continuing as homemakers or full-time employees, or becoming foster parents while still parenting our own children. We may even exchange one significant role for another. You graduate from school and instead of being a full-time student, you are a full-time employee. You experience a death and must give up a loved one. What transition might you experience in the next five years? How do you think it will affect you and your marriage? What could you do to prepare for it now?

Some people seem to cope well with unexpected crises. They stay in control by taking on each situation one at a time, while delaying their response to others. Others are thrown into stressful upheaval when too many unanticipated events happen all at once. "Oh, no! Not something else!" we cry. "This is the last straw." We can begin to crumble when our resources seem to have been exhausted.

Stepping Through Transitions

What can we do when we're in the midst of a transitional struggle? First we need to identify what is making the adjustment particularly difficult. This can affect the health of our marriages.

Identifying the Problem

The problem may be a normal change of life, or one of the unexpected events mentioned above. But most problems encountered during such a transition center on one of the following:

1. We could be having difficulty separating from the past stage. We might be uncomfortable with our new role at this time of life.

2. We could be having difficulty making a decision concerning what new path to take or what plan of action to follow in order to negotiate this new transition.

3. We could be having difficulty carrying out this new decision because of a lack of understanding of what is involved in making the change. Perhaps we lack enough information concerning expectations for ourselves and others. We could also be struggling with our own lack of preparation for this transition.

4. We may already be in the midst of this transition, but we may be having difficulty weathering the period of adjustment until the new changes have stabilized. Again, we could be lacking information or resources that are needed to make the change secure.

To move effectively through a time of transition in marriage, I would recommend an orderly progression of steps. First of all we need to *identify the target problem* in terms of the specific difficulty that we feel at this time and what we are willing to work on. Second, we need to *identify the target goal,* that is, the situation in which we feel we could move ahead. This goal includes specifying what it would take to feel competent in moving forward in our lives again. The third step is to *identify the tasks* that need to be accomplished in order for a smooth transition to occur. And it helps if you *work together as a couple* going through this stage of growth. If you are presently facing a transition, you may want to stop and discuss this now.

Some transitions are quite normal, but nonetheless involve major changes. People marry, have children, the children go to school and then move into adolescence and adulthood. Other events can be more wrenching, affecting us in ways we never expected. We've identified some of these.

Positive events can have the same effect, such as a move, a promotion, the birth of twins, or finally having a baby after seventeen years of being without. Some adults bypass many of these natural transitions, especially if they never marry or if they die in their forties.

A sudden change can become a threat to whatever marital balance has been achieved. It tends to reawaken personal insecurities that the marriage has successfully overcome or held in check. You've noticed how sick people tend to fall back into childish ways—they become terribly dependent, demanding, and unreasonable. Similarly, some people regress in other kinds of emotional crises. Long-conquered patterns of behavior reassert themselves, at least until the first impact of the shock has been absorbed.[2]

During any major transition, people must restructure how they view their roles in life and plan how to incorporate the changes. They need to put forth a tremendous effort to give up old patterns of thinking and activity to develop new ones. Whether or not this transition becomes disastrous depends upon the person's ability to handle this process of change in a healthy way.

One of the greatest determinants of whether a transition involves excessive stress and crisis potential is the timing of such an event. Serious difficulties can occur when the accomplishment of tasks associated with a particular stage of development is disrupted or made extremely difficult. For example, an athletic husband suddenly becomes a paraplegic because of a diving accident, and must rethink his whole life.

Ordinary Passages

Predictable transitions do not have to become major storms in our lives. We don't need a satellite weather picture to tell us they are coming. Just consider your age and what stage you and your spouse are in. What is the next event looming close on your horizon? You can prepare for it and even rehearse mentally what you will do when those events occur. And you can gather new information to assist in the transition process.

A teacher who realized he would have to retire in ten years determined to expand his interests. He began to take courses at the local college in subjects he thought he might have an interest in. He took up photography and began reading in areas he had never considered before. He also began developing a list of projects he would like to tackle, health and finances permitting, upon retirement. Since there would be a significant loss in his life—his job and his livelihood—he planned in advance for a variety of replacements and worked through some of those feelings of loss.

He also had the foresight to develop hobbies that could be enjoyed whether his health was good or poor. By anticipating what was to come, he eliminated the possibility of the transition becoming a crisis. That is very important because studies indicate that many men have a serious and often unsuccessful adjustment when they retire. Depression hits many, and the suicide rate more than triples for men over the age of sixty-five!

More and more retirees seek out the so-called comfort and support of a retirement community. Jim Smoke puts a different perspective on this option:

> Retirement communities are filled with once-important people who are living out their lives in personal obscurity. While most probably enjoy their new life of leisure, many others turn to drugs and alcohol, the silent killers in scores of retirement enclaves across America, to deaden the pain caused by loss of identity and self-worth. Prescription drugs follow close behind as the killer of past dreams and present realities. As a result, in many instances retirement kills people quicker than most diseases. It happens because it takes something from them that many are not ready to give up: their identity. Mundane card games and craft classes after a daily round of golf cannot give meaning and purpose to life after one has impacted others' lives for 40 years.

In most cases, retired men lose their identities quicker and more often than retired women, perhaps because many women consider themselves still "employed" as homemakers, wives, and mothers. There are abundant tales of retired husbands following their wives around all day long, looking for some form of meaning and fulfillment.[3]

Patrick Morley, in his excellent book *Two-Part Harmony*, shares this about older age:

Once I was invited to preach the Father's Day sermon at a particular church. When I arrived I was taken aback by how few men appeared to be of fathering age.

I asked the youth pastor, "What percentage of the congregation would you estimate to be elderly (over sixty-five)?"

"Seventy percent," he immediately responded.

"And of those, what percentage would you say are lonely?" I further inquired.

"All of them."

Recently a retired man told me, "The notion that when you retire your financial needs will go down is a myth. The trouble is that you build yourself into a certain lifestyle. It's not that easy to just up and change everything."

"How much money is enough, then, to retire?" I asked.

"You can never have too much retirement income," came his reply.

There are two great problems in retirement: *loneliness* and *money.*

As a general rule, the quality of our relationships in retirement will mirror the quality of our relationships today. Loneliness is a choice, one that we make years before we retire— a decision we are making right now. True, some people won't be lonely even if they retire to the North Pole and talk to penguins all day. For most of us, though, the decisions we make right now determine whether we will be lonely in retirement.

We can avoid loneliness in retirement by sound planning and making some investments in other people's lives. The Bible proclaims that we reap what we sow.

There are two ways to be lonely: One is to be alone; the other is to have nothing in common with your mate. No married person ought ever to be lonely.[4]

These words of wisdom need to be considered decades before we get to this stage.

If moving through the various stages of life went smoothly and everything were predictable, life would be fairly easy for most mature individuals. But two factors must be considered. First, many of us are not yet mature enough nor able to take responsibility because we are stuck in our own development at an earlier stage. We may be age thirty or thirty-five chronologically, but only twenty emotionally. And second, as I mentioned earlier, some changes either come in like sudden invaders or do not occur in the time sequence that we have anticipated.

Some roles in life are not replaced by other duties, leaving a void, such as retiring from work without finding a fulfilling task in retirement, or losing a spouse without remarrying.

There are also physical changes such as the loss of one's hearing, being confined to a wheelchair for years and then regaining the ability to work, or moving from being thin to becoming obese.

Changes: "On Time" and Otherwise

Transitions can be swift or gradual and may have either a positive or a devastating impact upon our lives.

Most people have heard of the phrase "male midlife crisis." But did you know that only a minority of men experience a full-blown midlife crisis—and that this crisis is not inevitable? All men do go through midlife transition, which is a normal change. But we can fairly accurately predict the man who is a candidate for a full-blown crisis. He is the person who:

- Builds his sense of identity upon his work or occupation, which becomes the source of meaning in his life;
- Is out of touch with his emotions or feelings and has not learned to accept and express them;
- Has not learned to establish close intimate friendships with other men.

Now this is a simplified evaluation, but it does hold true for most men. A man does not have to go through this crisis that in most cases creates a crisis for his family and fellow workers as well. He does have a choice.

Even if we don't stop to think about it, we all have timetables for our lives. In premarital counseling, I ask couples when they plan to become parents, graduate from school, move to a higher level of responsibility in their careers, and so on. Some of them have developed very precise timetables. Most people have their own expectations for when certain events will occur—a sort of "mental clock" that tells them whether they are "on time" or not in terms of the family life cycle.

When an event does not take place "on time" according to someone's individual expectations, a crisis may result. Many mothers face an adjustment when the youngest child leaves home. But this predictable stage can be planned for in advance. When the child does not leave home at the expected time for some reason, a crisis can often occur for both parents and child.

Having an event happen too early or too late in our plans can deprive us of the support of our peer groups. June, for example, wanted a child early in life but didn't have one until three days after her thirty-seventh birthday. Consequently, she lacked the support of many other women her age. Surrounded by women who were having their first child in their early twenties, June felt unable to develop any close friendships at this stressful time of her life. Most of her contemporaries had gone off to work.

By being off schedule, we may also feel deprived of the sense of pride and satisfaction that often accompanies such an event. Some people have worked out mental timetables for advancement in their work. But what happens if that sought-after promotion occurs two years prior to retirement rather than fifteen years earlier? We can begin to wonder: Is it really recognition for accomplishment or merely a token gesture? When an event occurs later than expected, its meaning is often lessened.

On the other hand, having an event occur too early can also limit us from preparing adequately. A young mother who is widowed early has to support her family during a time when most of her friends are married. An oldest son may suddenly have to quit college and take over the family business because of some unexpected event, even though he feels ill equipped for this new role.

My wife and I entered the "empty nest" stage approximately seven years ahead of schedule. When our daughter, Sheryl, moved out to be on her own, we should have been left with a thirteen-year-old son at home. But he was a profoundly mentally retarded child, much like an infant, and he had left home at the age of eleven to live at Salem Christian Home in Ontario, California.

We had planned for his leaving for two years by praying, talking, and making specific plans and steps to follow. Therefore, his departure and that of our daughter were fairly easy transitions. But when Sheryl told us a year and a half later that she wanted to come back home and live for a while, we faced a more difficult adjustment. We had very much enjoyed being just a couple again and hadn't expected her to return.

Transitions Connected with Aging

When we are young, some of our losses are celebrated as much as they are mourned. Most of the early ones are developmental and necessary. We can accept these natural transitions fairly easily. But often we focus on the gain without remembering that it usually carries some loss along with it. When we face the developmental changes connected with aging, the losses affect us much more heavily because the attached gains are often lacking.

Those over forty usually experience more of the releasing and losing part of the family journey that goes hand in hand with the gathering and accumulating. R. Scott Sullender describes this later stage of life:

> The middle years of adult life are spent building. We build a family, a career, a home and place in the community. It is a time for planting roots deep into the soil of our psyches. We build memories that last a lifetime. We form deep emotional attachments with one another. The latter half of life, however, is a time when what has been built up gradually dissolves. One by one (or, sometimes, all at once) we must let go of family, career and home.[5]

Many transitions in life are related to aging. As we grow older, our childhood dreams and beliefs often begin to crumble or change. Then come the physical losses attending the usual aging process. Ironically, one change typical of middle age involves gain . . . those unwanted pounds and inches! We gradually lose our youth, our beauty, our smooth skin, our muscle tone, our shape, our hair, our vision and hearing, our sexual ability or interest, and so on.

In the later years, losses take on a different flavor. They seem to be more frequent, permanent, and in many cases, negative. Who rejoices over losing hair and teeth, or graduating to bifocals or even trifocals? We don't usually call these "growth experiences." Our losses seem to build on other losses.[6]

In our younger years, we may have one or two physical problems, which are often correctable. But later on, bodily ailments accumulate faster than our abilities to resolve them. Muscles don't work as well or recover as quickly. Our response time slows down. Our eyeglasses prescriptions need to be changed more often. One day we suddenly notice that people seem to be talking in softer tones. We soon have to turn up the television volume along with the thermostat!

Marriage After Midlife

Some definite changes impact marriages at this time.

Harold Myra was publisher of *Christianity Today* and was middle-aged at the time he wrote "An Ode to Marriage," a poem about marriage in the middle years. His poem illustrates the problems and potentials of midlife marriage.

"You know, it could happen to us," you said to me,
sitting in your favorite chair as we sipped coffee,
digesting the news of the latest couples splitting up.
"No matter how great we think we have it,
      if all those people can break up
      it could happen to us.
We're humans like them.
It is possible."

I didn't answer for awhile.
We were both incredulous at the news.
Men and women of maturity
         decades-long marriages
         so many have exploded, one after another.
Almost every week, another set of names.
Not him! Not her!
They're too sensible, too solid.

"You're right," I finally admit.
We've never joked about divorce,
         never brought it up as an option.
We declared total commitment to each other
         and must reaffirm that always.

But maybe realizing it could happen to us
   helps us make sure it won't.

How terrible to think of an argument
   someday when one of us feels
   the need for the ultimate weapon,
"Well, obviously there's no sense staying together.
We're just hurting each other,
   just keeping each other trapped."
Those are words mouthed in kitchens
   and bedrooms of "mature" Christian homes.

Remember how our love began?
Years ago, I offered you my arm
   that September night we first went out.
You reached for it
   as we leaped a puddle together.
Then you walked just close enough
   to show you liked it.
I glimpsed your face under the streetlight,
   excitement splashing gently on it. . . .
No commitment—just beginnings.

My arm pulled you that January eve
   tight beside me in that car.
Midnight. Time to leave.
"Good night" wasn't quite enough,
   and our lips touched gently
   in a kiss as light as angel cake.
"I like you," it said.
   but nothing more.

November air had rough-scrubbed our faces.
As we wrestled playfully
   in your parent's farmhouse.
That moment I knew
   and breathed into your hair,
"I LOVE YOU."
The words exploded around us.
They meant far more than "you're nice."

They meant commitment.
Your words came back to me
          in firm, sure sounds:
"I love you, too."
And our kiss of celebration
          was the beginning of a new creation.
Yes, I chose you.
Out of all the lovely girls I knew.
I chose you.
How marvelous are the women of planet Earth,
          hair flaring in the wind
          rich browns and golds
          a thousand delicious shapes
          girls who laugh saucily
          girls who read Browning
          girls who play sitars
          girls who fix carburetors.
Of all those fascinating possibilities,
I chose you.
Decisively. Permanently.
Is that self-entrapment?
Was a commitment made in youth
          to bind me a lifetime?
Ah, but it was as strong as birth,
          a fresh creation,
          soon to be a new flesh,
          you and I as one.
We chose each other.
We created something new under the sun.
You to shape me
          and I you,
          like a Luther Burbank original.
We, our own new creation,
          to produce fruit wholly unique,
UNIQUE IN THE UNIVERSE!
Then the wedding
          flying rice and honeymoon
          days and nights together.
Two persons
          as unalike as birch and cypress
          had chosen each other.

The heavens laughed
        and the sands of earth
        lay ready for the tender feet
        of our newborn self.
Does time change all that?
Were we naive? Now, after we have
        loved, argued, laughed, given birth,
        what does it mean
        when I hold you and say,
        "I love you"?
Without the young-love ecstasy,
        is it required rote
        or reaffirmation of our new creation?

"I love you."
My temples don't pulse as I say it.
My body does not ache for coupling,
        not as it did.
Yet the words carry more fact
        than ever they did in courtship.
They embrace a million moments shared. . . .

Standing together
        atop Cadillac Mountain
        and aching to absorb the blue-white-green
beauty. . . .
Or angrily expounding to each other in the kitchen
        about our particular stupidities,
        then sharing a kiss ten hours later. . . .
Bonding moments, holding us together.
How easily those bonds could be tyrannical.
"You always forget. . . . " "You never think. . . . "
And bitter moments bite into their flesh
        with binding ropes that tie them to the
        time and place instead of to each other.
Yet bonds can be a
        thousand multicolored strands
        of sorrow, joy, embarrassment,
        of anger, laughter shared
        as we watch God maturing us,
        as we gently tell each other

of our joys, our fears,
even of our fantasies.
Rope is rope.
Experiences are much the same:
crabby days
laughing days,
boring days.
We'll go through them "in love,"
by commitment to each other.
sharing, forgiving,
not blaming, not hurting.
Yet when we do hurt,
we ask forgiveness,
so the ropes will bind us together.

For if they don't
they'll wrap around our throats,
so that each struggle will tighten the noose,
and we'll have to reach for the knife to cut the
bonds.
"I love you."
It sounds trite—
but not if it's remembering
the thousands of strands
of loving each other when we don't feel lovely.
of holding each other,
of winking across a room,
of eating peanut butter sandwiches beside the
surf. and of getting up in the morning thousands of
times, together,
and remembering what we created
the day we first said "I love you,"
Something permanent
and growing
and alive.[7]

Frequency and Finality

The nature of losses as we age is compounded by their growing frequency. We don't usually lose many of our friends through death early in life. But in our later years, such loss becomes much more frequent. The longer we live, the more friends and relatives we usually lose. Visits to the funeral parlor become almost second nature.

We seem to handle loss best when it is infrequent. But after midlife, we typically move into a time zone of accumulated losses. It can be difficult to handle the next one when we are still recovering from the present one. Our coping skills soon become overtaxed. If they were never highly developed to begin with, serious and frequent losses can hit us like a freight train.

Losses in later life often loom with growing finality. Losing a job at age twenty-seven simply means we have to look around for a new one. But losing a job of many years' duration at age fifty-seven can mean big trouble. Now what—especially if demand for our skills has significantly decreased over the years?[8]

Family Transitions
These later years carry such numerous changes—many of which are out of our control—that we need to face how we feel about what is happening to our family lives.

One of the biggest transitions your marriage faces is the time when your children leave home. Sometimes both generations look forward to this day with joyful anticipation. Greater freedom looms on the horizon for the parents as well as the child.

But once more the gain carries inherent losses. Parents must face a significant change in the amount of control they have over their kids. If the kids choose a lifestyle contrary to the way they were raised, many parents battle feelings of failure. Children may have been the mutual bond that held the husband and wife together. What might happen when that glue is no longer there? I've heard some couples say, "Yes, it's true our children are leaving and we're losing them from the home, but our gain will be our grandchildren." But what if the grandchildren are delayed for ten more years, or never arrive at all?

Having our children leave home doesn't mean just empty rooms, but emptiness in other ways as well. When our children marry, it is their choice of when and if they will have little ones of their own. Sometimes parents seriously violate boundaries by their persistent insistence that their children "get with it" and have children. We must always ask if our concern is primarily for the child, for ourselves, or for our own marriage.

Any major transition has the potential of becoming contaminated by side effects and personal feelings.[9] Having completed the major

task of parenting may stimulate emotions ranging from relief to sad-
ness over the loss. Some still attempt to live out their own lives
through the lives of their children—with predictable consequences
for both. For many the most painful feeling of all is no longer being
needed—often a symptom of having based one's self-esteem and
identity solely in the life of the offspring.

I have counseled with a number of parents who were extremely
bitter when their children left. As one parent said, "I really feel left
out now. They didn't turn out the way I wanted and now that they've
moved 2,000 miles away, what chance do I have to influence their
lives?"

Other parents become bitter because their overly indulged children ended up becoming takers, adults who didn't learn to give and
respond in the same manner as their parents. Perhaps they were
trained too well.[10]

Here are many of the typical thoughts parents have expressed
when the time comes for their children to leave home. The range of
feelings runs the gamut.

"I miss the early years with my children. I was so tied up in work
at that time."

"The nest doesn't seem to empty as fast as I want. They're sure
slow in moving out."

"I looked at that small chair and started to cry. It seemed like
yesterday my son was sitting in it."

"I'm sure I'll be glad when they leave. But won't I feel useless?"

"That room seemed so empty when he left."

"I'm looking forward to a new job! This time for pay!"

"Now that they're gone, we sit, we don't talk, don't look at each
other. Nothing!"

"Parenting is hard work and I want to get out of this job."

"We married at twenty and had the first one at twenty-two. The
last one came at thirty-four. He left when he turned twenty-one.
Why didn't someone tell us it would take twenty-nine years until
we were alone again as a couple!"

"We're adjusted to their being gone. I hope none of them divorce
or lose a job and have to move back. I like this setup!"

"I don't want to build my happiness on when they call, write, or
visit. I need my own life now."

"They left too soon, married too young, and had kids too soon. I
hope they realize I'm not their baby-sitter. I raised one family, but
I'm not going to raise another!"

"I've done what I could. They're in the Lord's hands now. And I guess they always have been, come to think of it."[11]

When people are learning to fly a plane, an instructor is constantly by their sides in the cockpit until their first solo flight. That day is a huge event for most novice pilots, the time to launch out on their own and put into practice what they have learned. Both instructors and students can be scared. If a novice pilot is pushed to solo too soon, he or she could either crash or develop a pattern of mistakes that is difficult to change.

As parents, most of us pour ourselves into our children. They're one of our greatest investments. But unfortunately, I've seen many people build their lives around their children and end up feeling absolutely empty when they are no longer around. Life goes on, however. The normal life span of today means that we could spend two-thirds as much time in the period after child rearing as we do while going through it.[12]

Making Positive Transitions

Where do we go from here? What can we learn from those who seem to cope better with the predictable changes of life as well as some of the sudden ones?

People who make positive transitions are people who face life and prepare in advance. They are also able to adjust and sort out which crisis needs to be handled first. For example, one man was facing the crisis of his wife being seriously ill in the hospital. Then the next day a major crisis threatened his business. Instead of attempting to juggle both and deal with them as problems of equal weight, he decided that his wife's recovery was most important and nothing else was going to deter him from helping her. Thus in his own mind the business crisis receded in importance. The second crisis did not add as much to his level of stress as you might expect. By making the decision he did, he was able to stay in control. That is important. When we feel as though we are in control, we handle life better.

If you find that you are facing or are in the midst of a transition, here are some suggestions:

1. Look at the stage of life you are leaving. Are you fighting leaving it in any way? What is there that you do not want to give up or change? What makes you uncomfortable with the new role? What

would make you more comfortable? Find someone with whom you can discuss your answers to these questions.

2. If you are having difficulty making a decision regarding a new change or determining what plan to follow, seek the advice of someone you respect whose insights will help you.

3. Make a specific list of what is involved in making this change in your life. Look for the information through reading and asking others about their own experiences.

4. Spend time reading the Psalms. Many of them reflect the struggles of humanity, but give the comfort and assurance that are from God's mercies.

5. Identify specifically what you need to do at this time that will help you feel as though you have some control of the situation. And remember that being in control does not mean that you have all of the answers, or that you know the outcome or when the situation will be resolved. Being in control means that you have given yourself permission not to have all of these questions answered. You have told yourself that you can handle the uncertainty. Being in control means that you have allowed Jesus Christ to come and stand with you in this time of uncertainty. His presence gives you the stability and control you need.

Christ's strength is what you need. *"My grace is sufficient for thee: for my strength is made perfect in weakness"* (2 Cor. 12:9, KJV).

Transitions are opportunities to apply our faith. And we as believers have a greater opportunity to handle crisis than others. Hear what David Morley says about this.

> The change that is so threatening to the nonbeliever is an opportunity for the Christian to exercise his faith and to experience the process of true Christian maturity. The mature Christian is a person who can deal with change. He can accept all of the vicissitudes of life and not deny nor complain about them. He sees them all as the manifestation of God's love. If God loves me, then He is going to provide an experience that makes life richer and more in line with His will. To the Christian, "All things work together for good to them that love God . . . " (Romans 8:28). How often we hear that Scripture quoted. How little we see it applied to real-life experiences. What God is really saying is that we should comfort ourselves with the thought that what happens in our lives, victory or defeat, wealth or poverty, sickness or death, all are

indication of God's love and His interest in the design of our lives. If He brings sickness to us, we should be joyful for the opportunity to turn to Him more completely. So often in the bloom of health, we forget to remember the God who has provided that health. When we are in a position of weakness, we are more likely to acknowledge His strength, we are more likely to ask His guidance every step of the way.[13]

Transitions and a Love that Lasts

I've had some people come right out and tell me that having a strong marriage is impossible to attain, especially in view of life's inevitable changes. Having seen many quality marriages over the years, I can't agree. Each couple will be at different levels in how well they deal with transitions, but as long as they have in mind the goal of preparing for transitions, are working toward it, and are able to perceive progress, I would call their marriage healthy.

Not every element of the marriage relationship will always be operating to the fullest degree. We all work toward ideals for which we aim rather than targets on which we can score a bull's-eye. Perfection will never exist in this life, but that doesn't keep us from working toward the goal. Perhaps these ideas offered by David Morley can give you a new sense of vision. Remember, without a vision, a person or a marriage can perish.

In the latter part of the 1980s, a series of movies called "Back to the Future" proved to be popular. Unfortunately, many couples live the same way today. They create for themselves a limited future for their marriages by projecting the past and the present upon them.

By becoming stuck in the dilemmas that seem so endless, married couples can fail to remember that there is a future. Especially for Christians, that future is filled with hope. Too many overwhelmed men and women mentally condemn the future to be an unhappy continuation of the past. Norman Cousins once said, "We fear the worst, we expect the worst, we invite the worst."[14]

Scripture holds out a sure promise for our marriages as well as our individual lives: "'For I know the plans I have for you,' declares the Lord, 'plans to prosper you and not to harm you, plans to give you hope and a future'" (Jer. 29:11, NIV). When you capture the truth of these words, your marriage has a limitless future.[15]

7
I Married an Alien . . . but from What Planet?

IT WAS TEN O'CLOCK on a Wednesday morning. My first appointment was scheduled to arrive in just a minute and I looked at the names. It was a new couple whom I had never seen before. They were referred by a pastor from one of the large evangelical churches in the area. The call had come in the day before, and since I had a last minute opening, I was able to schedule them. But there had been no opportunity for them to complete the customary preliminary forms that would have given me a great deal of information. We would just have to find out the difficulties during their first session.

Herb and Sue came in and sat down, a well-dressed middle-aged couple. After a few minutes of casual conversation, I asked, "What brought you to the place of wanting to see a counselor? What are your concerns?"

Herb looked at me, leaned forward and said in a quiet, tense voice, "I want to know just one thing. I've been married to this woman for seventeen years and I can't understand why we've had seventeen years of fighting. Hassle, hassle, hassle. That's all our marriage is— *one big hassle!* We can't agree on anything. We are so different, I'm not sure we should even be married! I don't have this problem with people at work—we get along great. Now *you're* the so-called expert. You tell me why there's so much conflict in our marriage. Do other people have this many problems?"

Sue looked up and interrupted at that point to share her opinion. The next fifteen minutes seemed to escalate into a small-scale border war, and I felt I was right in the middle of it. They interrupted, raised their voices, made accusations, and threw critical barbs back and forth. Finally I raised my voice, interrupted and said, "Thank you!"

They stopped and looked at me, and then back at one another. "Thank you?" Herb said. "For what?"

"For answering your own question of a few minutes ago. You asked why you have so many conflicts. That last fifteen minutes just exposed the answers. Would you like to know what I heard?"

They both looked at me and Sue said, "Yes, I would like to hear. We've been trying to figure it out for years. What did you discover?"

I looked at both of them and said, "You asked for it, and here it is. I heard some of the most common issues that create problems for the majority of couples. I heard unresolved issues from your past, Sue, and you both have unfulfilled needs and expectations. You haven't accepted your personality differences and you are still trying to make the other person into a revised edition of yourself. You engage in some classic power struggles and you keep the conflicts alive by the intense, vicious circles you've built up. Finally, you've never learned to speak the other person's language. Now that's just for openers.

"I don't mean to be overly simplistic, but the bottom-line cause for our conflicts is our sinful natures, which leads me to another question. Where is Jesus Christ in the midst of your relationship? Have you invited Him to bring healing to the issues that are creating your conflicts? Many of these are symptoms of deeper issues."

They looked at each other silently and then back at me, nodding their heads in agreement with what I had just said. I continued:

"You're looking for a marriage of peace and harmony and one that is fulfilling. You've spent seventeen years building negative patterns. That's the bad news. The good news is *you can change.* I don't mean change your personality. The couples who make it in marriage are not carbon copies of each other. They are people who have learned to take their differences through the process of acceptance, understanding, and eventually complementation. Differing from another person is very natural and normal and can add an edge of excitement to a relationship."

A Spouse from Star Trek?

Differences. How do you learn to adjust to the differences in your partner without losing who you are? How do you learn to appreciate another person's uniqueness? How can you learn to live with this person who is so, so different from you? As one wife said, "It's not just that I married someone who's a foreigner! At times I feel like I married an alien from another planet! Did I join the cast of *Star Trek* or marry someone left over from the film series *Star Wars?* Help!"

I've heard them all—questions, complaints, pleas for help. For years people have asked me the question "When you marry, do you end up marrying someone who is your opposite or someone who is similar?

My answer is, "Yes." I'm not copping out by saying that, because the answer is yes. It's both. There will be some similarities as well as opposites, and you have to learn to adjust to both. Think of it like this:

We marry for our similarities.

We stay together for our differences.

Similarities satiate, differences attract.

Differences are rarely the cause of conflict in marriage.

The problems arise from our similarities. Differences are the occasion, similarities are the cause.

The differences may serve as the triggering event, as the issue for debate or the beef for our hassle, but it's the similarities that create the conflict between us.

The very same differences that initially drew us together, later press us apart and still later may draw us near again. Differences first attract, then irritate, then frustrate, then illuminate and finally may unite us. Those traits that intrigue in courtship, amuse in early marriage, begin to chafe in time and infuriate in the conflicts of middle marriage; but maturation begins to change their meaning and the uniqueness of the other person becomes prized, even in the very differences that were primary irritants.[1]

Differences abound in any marriage. Generally, they can be divided into two types. The first includes those that can't be helped, such as age, race, looks, home, and cultural background. Your personal body metabolism will affect where you want the temperature in the home, whether you wake up bright and eager, ready to face the day, or whether you need an hour to get both eyes focusing. These differences cannot be changed.

But the other type of difference involves those that can be changed. These can include personal habits in the bathroom or at the dinner table, whether you like to get up early and your spouse enjoys sleeping late, or whether one likes going out three nights a week and the other prefers watching television at home. I'm amazed at how small learned behaviors, such as having the bed covers tucked in rather than having them loose or eating a TV dinner rather than a four-course dinner on a tablecloth, become such major issues in marriage.

Staying Flexible in Our Strengths

We are all different. We're mixtures of various tendencies and preferences. And these are neither right nor wrong. The problem arises when one of these tendencies becomes so strong and dominant that our strengths become weaknesses. This condition fails to allow for alternate ways of responding to life. As a result, we become entrenched in our own styles and threatened by differences. Remember this: The person who has the greatest flexibility and who can respond to situations in a variety of ways will derive the most out of life and impact the greatest number of people!

What are some of these tendencies that draw us to each other but can end up being a pain in the neck? Well, some of us are thinkers and some are feelers. Some of us are savers and some are spenders. Some of us are amblers and some are scurriers. Some of us are inner people and some are outer people. Some of us are bottom-line and some are ramblers.

The factor of timing becomes an issue for many couples as they attempt to deal with marital adjustments. We all have different internal clocks within us. Some of us use a calendar to tell time, others a stopwatch. Often these two people marry each other. The wife needs ten minutes to get ready; her spouse needs an hour. The husband wolfs his food; his spouse chews each bite five times. One spouse tells a story in three minutes and the other takes ten to tell the same story.

Problem-Solving Styles

The way people approach problems and attempt to solve them can also become an issue in a marriage. Some individuals are leapers; others are lookers. Leapers do look, but it's usually back over their shoulders after a decision is made. This has often been called the intuitive approach, whereby a solution just "leaps into a person's mind." Rarely are the answers totally correct, but neither are they totally wrong. Leapers tend to rely upon past experiences to make their quick formulation of an answer to a problem.

Then we have the lookers. They are the calculators, the people who tend to do things "by the book." They look at a problem, identify the elements in it and then come up with a solution. And they often tell you that both their approach and their solution is right. And guess what. They are right most of the time! This really frustrates the leapers. But the lookers need all the available data for their decisions to be correct.

Both approaches have strengths and advantages. If you need a quick decision in an area that is not all that important, the leaper is the best one to decide. But when you have a problem that is quite important and you need all the facts, the looker is the best approach.

No couple is compatible when they marry. The challenge of marriage is to learn to become compatible. Some accomplish this within the first few years, some within ten to fifteen years, some . . . , well, unfortunately some never do. I know. I've seen them in my counseling office, some at seminars, some informally. But the sad part about this is that it doesn't have to be that way.

I don't care how different a husband and wife are, it's possible to learn to adjust, to adapt, to live in peace and harmony, to be compatible. I've seen it happen. One of the delights of counseling is to see couples both in premarital counseling and those who have been married for thirty years discover how to understand, accept, adjust to, and honor their partners' uniqueness.

Messages from the Trenches

I've worked with this issue for years. I've taught about it and written about it in several books. And yes, I'm going to write about it here, although in a different way. I'm going to let married individuals tell about their spouses and themselves and what they have learned. I won't give any guarantees, but I suspect that you are going to identify in some way with one or several of these people. Hopefully, you can learn from what they have learned.

These accounts are from those who have been married for awhile. Some of them struggled through this process before the pieces came together. These are people who have learned to apply and experience God's Word in their lives including these important passages:

Let the peace of Christ rule in your hearts, to which indeed you were called in one body (Col. 3:15, NASB).

Be of the same [agreeable] mind one with another; live in peace (2 Cor. 13:11, AMP).

Tom's Tale

"My name is Tom. I'd like to tell you about my outgoing, social wife. That's what I call her now, and that's what I called her before we married. But after about two years of marriage I started calling her 'Mouth'! She talked and talked. She even talked to herself. Now me, I'm just the opposite. I don't talk much at all. At first I was attracted to her mouth. Then I was repulsed by it. My ears get exhausted.

"I couldn't understand why Jean had to think out loud so much. It's like she wanted the whole world to know about her wild ideas. And it's not just because she's a woman. I've seen men who are the same way. But it seemed like she would start talking before she engaged her brain. At times I felt like my space was invaded by her giving a running commentary on everything or saying the same things over and over or wanting an immediate response from me on a question I'd never had a chance to think about. Man, all that stuff wore me out.

"There were even times when I'd go to the garage to putter around (and find some peace and quiet) and Jean would come out there, bring up a subject, ask my opinion, arrive at her own conclusion before I could think about it, thank me, and walk out. I'd just stand there shaking my head and wonder *Why even ask me?*

"When we go to an activity, it's like she knows everyone there and wants to stay forever. It seemed like she would never run down or get enough socializing. I've seen men like that, too. I always wondered how they did it. It drains me, but seems to give her a shot of adrenaline!

"Oh, and wait until you hear this: I think I'm a caring guy. I do give compliments. Maybe not as many as I could, but I don't think I could ever give enough to Jean. She is so capable and gifted. But it seems like she doesn't believe it unless I or someone else tell her. I used to wonder why she would come and ask me how she did or how she looked when the answer was obvious. Fantastic!

And something else that bugged me—Jean is better about this now—she would interrupt me when we talked. It takes me longer to get things out and reach a conclusion. So, if I talked or thought too slow I either got interrupted or she finished my statement for me. We had a good discussion (argument) over that one. But she's much better now, and I don't avoid discussions with her. Sometimes I remind her that our speed of thinking and speaking is different and that helps.

"When we have a conflict I think (or used to think) there was just too much talking about the problem. Jean had the belief that if we just talked it through a bit more everything could get resolved. Resolved! A few more words would be the last straw. We eventually learned to put some time limits on each segment of the conversation so I could have time to think. Then I was ready to continue. I also worked on sharing my first reaction without having to do so much thinking and editing.

"Now and then I've said to Jean, 'Honey, I want you to resolve this, but for me to continue since I'm getting worn down, why don't you write out what you're thinking or put your thoughts on the computer. Then I can read them over and be able to respond. OK?' That's worked well for us. That way Jean doesn't get as loud either, since I really tend to withdraw when that happens. I used to tell her, 'You're not going to get me to respond by shouting at me. It won't work.' Now I say, 'I want to hear you. I would appreciate it if you would say it softly and give me a chance to respond.'

"Sometimes I would ask her, 'Why are you bringing that up again? We've already talked about it.' Jean would say, 'No, we haven't.' And then we'd argue over whether we had or not. This went on for years until one day I heard her say, 'Could it be that you rehearse conversations in your mind and then think that we've already talked about it?' Bingo!—that's exactly what I do, and when she said it, I realized it. Fortunately, we've learned to laugh about it. Sometimes I catch myself and say, 'Yeah, I did talk to you about it . . . in my head.'

"Sometimes I worry about what Jean says to others about us and our intimacy. You know, our lovemaking. She likes to talk about it when we're not even doing it, and sometimes during a romantic time she wants to talk. That's not me. I don't say much, but I've learned that this is what Jean enjoys. And it's getting more comfortable.

"What has really helped me (and us) is to realize that there's nothing wrong with Jean the way she is. That's just her. It's the way she's wired. I guess it's the way God created her. She's OK. I'm OK. We're just different and we can learn to adjust.

"I've learned to appreciate the fact that she's helped me be more social and involved with other people. It's become apparent that Jean needs more interaction and time with people than I do. Now I'm glad to provide it. It's all right for her to go places and gab, and I can stay home or get together with one of my male friends.

"It's really helped me to understand that Jean needs to talk out loud to figure things out. And it doesn't mean that she's going to do what she's thinking out loud. She's just thinking. I've learned not to assume.

"We're not perfect, but we are much more accepting. We've learned to be creative in the ways we approach each other. And it is a lot more peaceful."

Jean's Journey

Jean shared the story of her own journey.

"Well, I'll try to be brief (that's a joke!). I'm an outgoing, talkative person who for some strange reason was drawn to a quiet, reserved, thoughtful man. I knew we were different when we were dating, but never realized just how much until we were married. When it really hit me was the evening I figured out that Tom seemed to be avoiding me. Even when I was talking to him it seemed like he couldn't wait until I quit talking. And his responses were shorter and shorter. It was as though he thought if he said less I wouldn't have so much to respond to. I guess it was true, because eventually I'd get fed up and socialize on the phone. I actually felt rejected and hurt because I wasn't getting enough talk out of Tom. I couldn't figure out why he was like that. At first I thought, *That's just the way men are.* But others I dated weren't always like that. In fact, I've known women who are like Tom. So I figured it's just the way he's wired and put together.

"I just love getting together with others. I get energized by them. But it doesn't take long (at least it seems to me) for Tom to get worn out at a party and want to leave early. I've even seen him just sit off to one side by himself or go into another room for awhile just to be alone. I used to think, *What is wrong with that man?* Then, I began to discover that Tom needs some quiet time and space to get energy back. That's draining for me, but it perks him up.

"He is friendly and communicates well, but he doesn't go out of his way to connect with people. I've got scads of friends. He's satisfied with just two. See, there's the difference—just two! That wouldn't be enough for me. I need more people to talk with. And I love interruptions. They're just great, but they really bother Tom. It's like he needs to know ahead of time that he's going to be interrupted.

"One of our biggest conflicts is, or was, in the area of communication. I like to get things resolved, and that means talking through every part of an issue. But when we talked, or when I talked, the more he seemed to retreat. So I figured I'd just keep after him and he's bound to open up. No such luck! He'd retreat, clam up, or say, 'I don't know.' I admit, I want answers right now. I used to say, 'Tom, tell me right now. You don't need time. For Pete's sake, tell me!' And then nothing. Silence. It's like I just short-circuited his thinking ability. And later on I discovered I did!

"Tom is more of what they call an inner person. Through some reading I discovered he's the kind of person who likes to think things through in the quiet privacy of his mind without pressure—and then he's got a lot to say! Little did I know this at first. Now when I need his feedback or a discussion, I just go to him and say, 'Tom, here's something I'd like you to think about. Put it on the back burner where it can simmer for awhile and when it's done, let's discuss it.' He appreciates it, and we talk more. And lest you think he always uses a Crockpot to cook, he doesn't. Sometimes it's a microwave! After I did this for awhile, he said to me, 'Thanks for recognizing and respecting my need to think things through in the privacy of my mind.' That felt good, because I like compliments.

"I've had to learn he isn't comfortable thinking and talking fast out loud. That's my world, not his. A few times we got into a conflict and I pressured him so much he just let fly with an outburst that seemed extreme. I learned not to push. It's better to let him think first.

"I've also learned to not interrupt Tom with every thought that pops into my head. I'm finally learning to edit and pick times when I can have his attention. I know my thinking out loud used to bother him, because he thought I meant every word of it. I just like to sort things out, and I don't care who knows it. So now I just warn him, 'Tom, I'm just thinking out loud again. You can relax, because I'm not going to rearrange all the furniture in the house today.'

"You know, I used to think that Tom's quietness and withdrawal at times was a passive-aggressive way of getting back at me. But it wasn't. God made me unique and made Tom the way he is. I just didn't understand it. Twice this last month he actually did some thinking out loud with me, which was wonderful. I know it was difficult for Tom, but it was great to see him put forth that effort. I hate to admit it, I really do, but now I see some value in being alone and quiet, too . . . sometimes . . . just a bit.

"I've also learned that when I encourage him to be who he is, I receive more of what I need, too. The other day I knew he was frazzled, but I wanted to talk. Usually, I would have forced the discussion or tried to, but I remembered a couple of passages from Proverbs, *"Don't talk so much. You keep putting your foot in your mouth. Be sensible and turn off the flow!"* (10:19, *TLB*). And, *"Self-control means controlling the tongue! A quick retort can ruin everything"* (13:3, *TLB*).

"So I said, 'You look like you need some recouping time. Why don't you go read or do whatever and maybe we could talk a bit later.' And we did talk—quite a bit. And I am learning to write him notes, too.

"Tom understands things that used to really get me. He's better at it, but I've learned that a few of his words mean a hundred of mind. When he gets a big smile on his face and doesn't say much, I say, 'It looks like that smile is about 500 of my words.' And he says, 'You've got that right. I just love good translators!'

"So I've learned to give him time and space, and not to interrupt when he talks. And I don't assume anymore that he doesn't have opinions or want to talk. He's selective and more methodical. I use a scatter-gun approach."

Sheri's Story

Let's consider another couple—Sheri and Fred, who have been married for twenty-two years. Sheri says:

"After I married Fred, the relationship was just okay. At times I felt pinned down or restricted by him. It's like he was so mechanical and precise he'd take the fun out of everything. It's as though we'd both look at the world and even though we stood in the same place, we saw something different.

"Fred seemed to have a clipboard, and was making a list of the facts. It's one thing to be literal, but at least from where I was coming from he was extreme. I know I'm not always the most practical, but Fred is overly so . . . and realistic . . . at least that's the way he sees himself. I love possibilities and speculation, but he didn't seem to see the value of it.

"We had so many arguments over (he says) my answers. I mean, he'd ask, 'What time will you be getting home?' and I'd say, 'Around five o'clock.' That wouldn't do it for him. He needed to know the exact time. If I bought something, it wasn't enough that I'd tell him it was around forty dollars. He wanted to know it to the penny.

"For several years he wouldn't ask me for directions anywhere. I mean anywhere. Even inside a building. Fred wants a detailed, step-by-step map. I can find where I'm going with instructions like, 'It's a couple of blocks or signals down seventeenth and you'll pass some kind of a school on the left, then in a little while you'll turn right and the store is, uh, let's see, two or three blocks on the right. Oh, you can't miss it.' That's not good enough for Fred. He says it's not precise enough.

"The future intrigues me much more than what's going on at the present time. There are all sorts of surprises waiting to be discovered. Fred looks at things and wants to know if it will work or won't work. I'd rather think of the possibilities.

"Whenever we buy something that needs to be put together, Fred can't wait to get into the box and find the instructions. He loves to follow them exactly. A friend of mine asked me to think of a word that would describe Fred. The first word that came to mind was predictable. I could set the clock by him. I can tell you what time he gets up, leaves the house, and what he has for lunch. He'll drive the same streets to work or church, even though we've got several options.

"You can imagine what our communication was like. I don't have the same problem with some of my other friends. But at least I always know the subject we're talking about when Fred brings it up—he identifies it very precisely.

"Actually our relationship is much better. One day we had this big argument—I mean BIG. We both got upset and said the same thing. It's funny now that I think about it, but we each said, 'There's nothing wrong with the way I see things. It makes sense to me. If you'd just try my way for a change then you'd see. And you'd understand me better. We're not wrong, just different.'

"Then I said, 'Our statement has some real possibilities. Let's look at it.' And Fred started laughing at what I said. So did I. But then he went on. 'What if, using your idea of a possibility, just what if each of us became a little bit more like the other when we're talking and working together.' When he used the word possibility, I knew it could work.

"So we're both responding differently. You know what I'm doing? First of all, I'm saying to myself it's all right for Fred to be practical, pragmatic, and literal, following instructions to the letter of the law, liking routines, and never seeing the big picture. He's got me to help him experience another way to live life. When we interact, talk, play, work, or whatever, I ask myself, 'How would Fred see this? How would he describe it? How would he respond?' For me, it's become an adventure to package my responses in a way that fits him. It's fun and I can speculate about it at the same time.

"So when I talk to Fred, I've learned (as much as possible for me) to give him some specifics or the bottom line first. Then he seems to be better able to listen to me. It's like I have to give him one point and then I can lead him to the next and the next and the next. Personally, I'd rather throw out the whole bale of hay any which way and then sift through it! But, you know, when I present something in his format, I'm able to see the pros and cons of it clearer, too. So I guess there is a benefit.

"It also helps when I ask him to listen to my wild dreams and ideas even though (and this is the important part) we may never ever do this. Once I even said, 'And before you tell me the reasons this wouldn't be practical, let me share them with you.' Boy, Fred never said a word, but he sure looked at me with all kinds of respect. Then he's willing to listen to my suggestions of why it might work.

"I used to think Fred's lack of enthusiasm for my dreams was, well, something personal, like he didn't care for me. But I discovered he's just more cautious and factual. I wished he would dream with me more, and he's doing better. He's helped me enjoy what is going on at the present. And there really is a lot happening right now. This helps him, because often he felt I didn't appreciate what he was doing right then—it seemed like I always wanted more. When I listen to his routine stuff, then he listens to me. I guess I need his practicality."

Practical Fred

"I'm Fred. Someone asked me what attracted me to Sheri. Excitement. My life was fairly routine. She brought a lot of fun and excitement into my life. But after we married, it seemed to get old in a hurry. She seemed scattered and going in several directions at once. She was always looking for some new possibility.

"When we plan a vacation, it really doesn't start for me until we get there. But for Sheri, it seems to start as soon as we mention it! She goes wild with all sorts of ideas and there it is again—possibilities of this and that. She loves the unknown. And even after it's over it seems like she's doing the same thing! I mean, when she describes what we did and where we went her perceptions are so different from mine that I wonder if we were on the same vacation. The word *exactness* isn't in her vocabulary. I ask her for something and I hear 'It's over there somewhere.'

"When I ask a simple question, all I ask for is a simple, clear, concise answer, not a hundred speculative possibilities. But she is doing better. And I've also learned that even if she gives me four or five sentences of background details, when she does give me the exact answers then I've got a very complete picture. She just takes longer and puts it in a different order. That used to drive me up a wall. Now I relax and realize it will just take a little longer, but she'll get to the point. And sometimes by hearing all that other stuff first, I listen to it better and learn about some things that are helpful. I've even said, 'Honey, here's an idea. Speculate on it for a while and then give me some alternatives.' She loves it.

"She says I nitpick, but I think she takes an incident and blows it way out of proportion. It's amazed me for years how she and the women friends who are just like her can carry on a conversation. They start a sentence and never finish it, but jump to another one and don't finish that before jumping to the next and the next. And yet, they seem to understand each other. I've tried. I mean I've tried, but it's beyond me. I've learned to say, 'Sheri, I want to hear what you have to say, and it helps me if you could condense it and finish a sentence before going on. I'll stick with you better.' And it's worked.

"I've learned that Sheri's mind and body might be two different places. We could be watching a movie together and I'm really into it, but I'll ask her a question and she's thinking about something else. I've just accepted that as part of our differences.

"I have learned that we approach projects differently. Years ago her lack of looking at the directions and following her hunches instead drove me up the wall. Now I do one of two things, because figuring things out on her own is like a game to her. I either just wait and eventually she'll ask for some help, or I say, 'Do you want me to read the directions first and go over it step by step, or do you want to wing it?' This seems to help.

"We have different definitions for words such as *No, Later, Sometime,* and *I'll get it done.* I usually ask, 'Can we clarify that?' or 'Whose definition are we using?' That's cleared up a lot of misunderstanding.

"After years of frustration, we've both learned to adjust some. Sheri has broadened my horizons. Because of her, I've followed her lead sometimes and had some great experiences. I've learned that her (what I call) restlessness is just her, and I haven't caused it. She's just a person of vision more than I am. And we've been able to discuss that it's important to me to have her notice my present efforts and contributions. I used to think she was just unappreciative, but that's not the case. She's just looking forward, that's all.

"It's best, too, when I bring something up to give her an overall general view rather than a bunch of little details. She likes it when I ask her questions, and listen. What used to be a problem for us isn't now We are learning to accept that we're different and . . . we need each other's differentness to make us complete. I wish we had started out our marriage on that note."[2]

Growing Through Differences

These two couples as well as so many others have gone through the typical stages of adjusting to conflict. You're vaguely aware of them when you marry. You certainly wouldn't say at that time that your partner is different—more likely "unique." But after a while it is . . . different. At first you may try to *accommodate*. You tolerate, overlook, or deny differences to avoid conflict.

Then you *eliminate,* or try to purge the differences in one another by demanding, pressuring, or manipulating.

But then you *appreciate,* because you discover the differences are necessary and indispensable. They're essential.

And because of this you are able to *celebrate* them. You delight in them. You welcome them. You encourage their growth.[3]

Couples discover through this process that they didn't marry the wrong person. Think about this:

In reality, we marry the right person—far more right than we can know. In a mysterious, intuitive, perhaps instinctive fashion we are drawn by both similarities and differences, by needs and anxieties, by dreams and fears to choose our complement, our reflection in another.

We always marry the right person, and the discovery of that rightness moves us into the third marriage within a marriage. We at last begin to appreciate what we had sought to eliminate.

As we discover that we knew more than we knew when we chose whom we chose, appreciation begins to break into a gentle flame. In appreciation, we discover that people who marry each other reflect each other. There is a similar level of maturity, a parallel set of self-understandings and self-acceptance in most couples choosing each other. The two express their self-image and self-valuation in the person selected.

People who marry each other complete each other in a puz-

zling yet pronounced way. The missing is supplied, the imbal-
anced is brought into equilibrium, the dormant is enriched
by what is dominant in the other.[4]

Well, what do you do now? Study your partner. Study yourself.
Decide how you could respond differently. Expand your knowledge
of gender differences, personality differences, and how to speak in
a language that your partner understands. We've just scratched the
surface here. If you want to learn more, read chapters 4–9 of *How to
Change Your Spouse* (Servant Publications) and *What Your Mother
Couldn't Tell You and Your Father Didn't Know* by John Gray (HarperCollins).

You may be surprised and amazed by what you discover. And you
know what? It will be worth the minimal amount of time it will
take to bring a new and better level of harmony and adjustment to
your marriage. It's an ingredient for a lasting marriage. It will help
you celebrate your differences.

The adventure of marriage is discovering who your partner really
is. The excitement is in finding out who your partner will become.

8

You Can Choose What Works
in Your Marriage

Y EARS AGO a couple came to see me with a particular problem. As we talked about what was occurring that brought them in, I discovered that this issue seemed to occur about every three to four years. I assumed that each time it happened they sought out a counselor, but that wasn't the case. This was the first time they had sought professional help.

I asked them, "Is this a continual issue in your marriage, or did you resolve it each time it happened?"

They said, "Oh, we were able to resolve it all the other times. But this time we thought we'd get some outside help."

I replied with, "Well, I'm not sure you need me. If you were able to resolve it before, why don't you just do what you did before? It sounds to me like it worked. If it was effective, why not do it again?"

They looked at me with an expression of, "Now, why didn't we think of that and save the money we're spending today?" Often this is the case. Look to see how you worked through issues before and do it again. If it worked once, it can work again. It can even be refined so it will work better the next time.

But you have to make up your mind to choose to find what worked.

Choosing the Sweet Life

Life is full of choices. Some are difficult; others are easy. But everything goes back to a choice. We can choose to love or not love. We can choose to be committed or not to be committed. We can choose to look for the best or for the worst.

If you have ever read about or observed various animals, you may have discerned the difference between the habits of buzzards and bees. Buzzards search for food by flying overhead and looking for dead animals. When they find the decaying animal, they move in to gorge. And the riper the better. This is what they want. They have made their choice.

Honeybees, however, have different habits. They search for nectar that is sweet. They are very discriminating as they fly through the various flowers in a garden. Some flowers just don't contain what the bees want, so they move on. They make a choice about where they settle in and feast. Both the bees and the buzzards find what they are seeking. They make choices.

Couples make choices, too. And I've seen couples who remind me of both the buzzards and the bees.

What Is Working in Your Marriage?

The suggestions I'm going to give you in this chapter may already have been said in one way or another in earlier chapters. But they need to be expressed again in this fashion. Why? It's simple. Because they work. I have seen them work in the lives of couples. These ideas are not original. I draw from anywhere I can to discover what works, so it can be passed along to help others.

If I were to meet you and talk with you about your marriage, I would ask you one question: "What's working?" A simple question, yet significant. I would want to know what works in your marriage. If I held a marriage seminar with 100 couples and asked everyone the question "What are the problems and difficulties in your marriage?" What do you think would be the outcome after everyone shared? There would be a dark cloud of doom and despair. Everyone would probably leave discouraged and with a lack of hope. I doubt if many would have benefited from their time together. I'm not suggesting that we overlook or ignore the problems. But there are better ways to solve them.

If I were to ask every couple to share "What is working for you?" what a different atmosphere and outcome we would have following the meeting. Couples would have been encouraged and challenged by what they heard. They would have discovered new ways of revitalizing their own marriages.

Let me turn to sports for a minute. I enjoy baseball. Sometimes even the best of the hitters face a drought. They fall into what we call a hitting slump. And they try and try to break out of it. They consult with their hitting coach and analyze what they're doing wrong so they can get back on track. Many will get videos of themselves while batting to see what they can learn. The videos they select will make the difference. Some will look at videos when they're in a slump and watch their worst performances. They think if they focus on this they can learn what they're doing wrong and correct it. Unfortunately, this doesn't work very well.

Others select older videos that show them in a hitting streak and doing fantastic. They watch and observe what they were doing that worked. Soon they're able to get back to that level. They concentrated on what was working.

Marriage isn't all that different. The best step any couple can take is to focus on what is working. This is the best way to solve problems. I'm sure there are many times when you and your spouse get along. Can you describe specifically what you and your spouse do differently when you do get along? Think about it. Identify it.

Exceptional Times

I've heard many couples in counseling say, "We don't communicate." Often I ask about the times when they do communicate. I'm asking for the exceptions. Sometimes I have to be persistent and keep asking, especially when couples are full of pain and despair. At times the progress is slow, but soon I hear an exception to "We don't communicate."

One husband said, "Last Sunday after church we went out to lunch, just the two of us and we talked all right. It wasn't bad." They were able to come up not only with this exception but several others. And what happened is that these exceptions began to counter the absolute belief that "We can't communicate." This is the beginning step to building a sense of hope and optimism. The exceptions begin to diminish the problems.

Too often the longer a couple is married the more they see their partner as incapable of changing. This can be in the realm of habits, behavior, or even attitudes. But as you talk about exceptions you discover that under certain conditions and circumstances your partner is different. As one wife shared, "I used to believe that Jim wasn't interested in sharing his feelings with me. But when we go away on a trip for a few days, and especially when we get away from that darn phone, he seems to relax and get his mind off of work. Those are the times when he does open up. I wish that somehow we could create those conditions more frequently." And in time they did. She discovered that some changes were possible given the right setting.

Road Maps and Windows

Another benefit of bringing out exceptions is that they might provide a road map showing the direction to take to increase the positives in their marriage. Discovering an exception might be the window a person or couple needs to try a new path that will improve their relationship. It may help them develop a plan. So much of what happens in counseling is plan making. This was drilled into me by a man I studied under in the late '60s—Dr. William Glasser. And I've never forgotten that principle. But the plan must be your own and individualized for your relationship.

Jim and Renee were a middle-aged couple with a marriage that had stagnated. Fortunately, they realized this and one day they each stayed home from work. They went to a small restaurant that was out of the way and quiet. They told the waitress they needed a booth for several hours and would be eating both breakfast and lunch. They also promised a healthy tip. When asked why they did this, Jim said, "We wanted to get out of the house into a neutral area and the restaurant was cheaper than a hotel room. And being in public might keep us from getting overly upset."

They both talked about how they wanted their marriage to be different twelve months from then. After they agreed on what they wanted, they identified three to five steps that both would take in order to reach their goal. They agreed to take one evening each month (on the fifteenth) to go out to dinner to measure progress and refine their plan. It worked, and it was much more economical than going to seek assistance from a marriage counselor.

A final benefit of looking at an exception is that it might enable you to discover a strength. In turn, this will strengthen the relationship. It's a step of encouragement because it lets a couple know they've been doing something right after all. Perhaps this is an example of what Paul was talking about when he said:

> *Whatever is true, whatever is worthy of reverence and is honorable and seemly, whatever is just, whatever is pure, whatever is lovely and lovable, whatever is kind and winsome and gracious, if there is any virtue and excellence, if there is anything worthy of praise, think on and weigh and take account of these things [fix your minds on them]* (Phil. 4:8, AMP).

Choosing Hope over Futility

We as Christians are called to be people of hope rather than despair. We are called to be people who confront obstacles and find a way to overcome them rather than to resign ourselves to a sense of futility.

It's strange, but I've found that some people don't really want to discover the exceptions to the problem. Perhaps they don't want to hope, for fear they'll be disappointed. Some see the exceptions as just that—a rare exception that just happened. But we also struggle with selective remembering, and the painful experiences tend to lock in and persist. We emphasize failures instead of successes.

But it doesn't have to be this way. We can choose another direction. Let's consider the suggestions that numerous marriage counselors have offered to assist couples in having fulfilling relationships.

What Worked Back Then?

I've never worked with any couple that doesn't get along some of the time. We all get along well part of the time, and I realize for some it might be just 20 percent of the time. That's all right. It's enough. In order to have a lasting marriage, the first step to take is to discover what each of you are doing during the times you do get along. You can do this by yourself or with your partner. Brainstorm and figure out what each was doing before and during that time. Be sure to concentrate more on what *you* were doing than on what your partner was doing. This is the beginning point for any change. What were you thinking and feeling when you were getting along? Then plan to do more of it . . . regardless of what your partner does.

Sometimes people have mental blocks against identifying current expectations. If this is your problem, think back to a time when your marriage had some satisfying times in it. Often I will have couples plot out charts of the history of the satisfaction level of their marriages. They're asked to identify the best experiences they've had since their marriages. "Best experiences" may have been times of just getting along. For some that's positive! And as we discuss these in detail, we talk about how we could create some of the same experiences right now in their marriages. Here is an example of the chart, and one husband's evaluation. The * indicates his level of satisfaction.

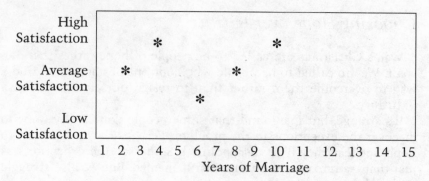

Here is the husband's analysis of his chart:

Best Experiences

Two years—I felt loved and accepted by you. You had an interest in me and my work.

Three years—I think you needed me to help with Jimmy, and that was a good experience.

Six years—Seemed to communicate real well without fighting for a few weeks.

Eight years—Started praying together twice a week.

Nine years—Had a week's vacation with no kids or in-laws; talked a lot and made love every day.

This is a good way to discover what worked in the past, to recall what we learned from it, and to put it into practice now.

Perhaps all of us couples need to ask ourselves the question "During the positive times in our marriage, what did we enjoy doing that we haven't been doing?" Then do it. Positive behaviors and responses create positive feelings. Biblically we are called upon to behave in specific ways—and nowhere does it ever say to wait until you feel like doing it.

Communicating Caring Behaviors

Over the years I have used a pattern for increasing positive behaviors for couples in both counseling and in seminars. I've talked about it and written about it before. It goes by various names such as "caring behaviors" or "cherishing behaviors." Let me present it in a way that you can do it yourself.

Ask each other the question "What would you like me to do for you to show how much I care for you?" The answer must be positive, specific, and something that can be performed daily. The purpose of each action must be to increase positive behavior, not to decrease negative behavior.

"Please greet me with a hug and a kiss" is positive.

"Don't ignore me so much" is negative.

"Please line the children's bikes along the back wall of the garage when you come home" is more specific and thus better than "Please train the children to keep their bikes in the proper place."

Ted would like Sue "to sit next to him on the sofa when they listen to the news after dinner." This is positive and specific. It's better than asking her to "stop being too preoccupied and distant" (a negative and overly general request).

Sue would like Ted "to kiss her good-bye when they part in the morning." This is positive and specific, which is different from "stop being so distant and cold" (a negative and overly general request).

Avoid making vague comments by writing down beforehand your answers to the question "What would you like me to do for you to show how much I care for you?"

The small, cherishing behaviors *must not concern past conflicts.* Your requests must not be old demands. That is, the requests must not concern any subject over which you have quarreled.

The behaviors must be those that can be done on an everyday basis.

The behaviors must be minor ones—those that can be done easily.

These requests should, as much as possible, be something only your partner can fulfill. If they are things that a hired hand could perform, they may create problems. For example, if they are mostly task-oriented like "wash the car," "take out the trash," "clean out the camper," "have the dishes and house all cleaned up by the time I get home," etc., they do not reflect intimacy and the cultivation of a personal relationship. Some better responses would be, "Ask me what excites me about my new job," or "Turn out the lights and let's sit holding hands without talking," or "Rub my back for five minutes."

Each list should include fifteen to eighteen items. Listing as many as eighteen creates more interest and makes it easier to follow through with requests. When you give your list to each other, the only discussion you may carry on about the list is to ask for clarification if it is needed.

Now it will be your commitment to do at least two items each day on your spouse's caring list, whether or not he or she is doing any positive behaviors on your list.

Here are some suggestions for your "caring" list:

1. Say "hello" to me and kiss me in the morning when we wake up.
2. Say "good-night" to me.
3. Sometimes bring me home a pretty flower or leaf.
4. Call me during the day and ask "How's it going?"
5. Put a candle on the dinner table and turn off the light.
6. Hold me when we're watching TV.
7. Leave me a surprise note.
8. Take a shower or bath with me when the kids are gone.
9. Kiss or touch me when you leave for work.
10. Tell me about your best experience during the day.
11. Hold my hand in public.
12. Tell me I'm nice to be around.
13. Praise me in front of the kids.
14. Ask me how you can pray for me.

Many of the cherishing behaviors you request of your spouse may seem unimportant or even trivial. Some may be a bit embarrassing because they may seem artificial at first. That's all right. These small behaviors set the tone of the relationship. They are the primary building blocks for a fulfilling marriage. They establish an environment of positive expectations and change negative mind-sets.

When the lists are completed, exchange them with each other.

Discuss the cherishing behaviors you have requested of each other. Don't be hesitant about telling your spouse how you would like to have the cherishing behaviors done for you.

For example: "Ted, remember the way you used to bring me a flower when we were first married? You presented it to me when you met me at the door—after you had kissed me. It made me feel really loved."

During the discussion it is likely that both of you will think of a few more cherishing behaviors that you would enjoy receiving. Add them to the lists. The more the better, providing the lists are approximately equal in length.

The basic principle behind this approach is this: If couples will increase their positive actions toward each other, they will eventually crowd out and eliminate the negative. The consequences of behaving in a positive way override the negative. In addition, behaving in a loving, caring way will generate the habit of responding more positively, and can build feelings of love.

How Much Is in the Bank?

Perhaps the following concept will illustrate the process in a different way. One of the metaphors used to describe a couple's interaction is that of a bank account. There are variations of this, but one is called a Relationship Bank Account.

As is true of any bank account, the balance in the Relational Bank is in flux because of deposits and withdrawals. Relationship deposits vary in size just like our monetary deposits. They could be a kind word or action or a very large gift of love. Withdrawals also vary. A minor disagreement could be small, but a major offense could drain the account. Zingers are definitely a withdrawal, and so is defensiveness.

When you begin thinking of your relationship in this way, you can be more aware of deposits and attempted deposits as well as what constitutes a withdrawal. Naturally the larger the balance, the healthier the relationship. And just like a monetary account, it's best to have sufficient reserves in your Relational Bank Account. Unfortunately, many couples live with their balances at a debit level.

There are two types of currencies in relational accounts—his and hers. Each may have a different valuation and could fluctuate from day to day. There is a difference in this type of bank—it's the "teller" or receiving person who sets the value of a deposit or withdrawal.

If there is a large balance in the account, a few small withdrawals don't impact the account that much. But if the balance is relatively small or hovers around zero, a small withdrawal is definitely felt. The ideal is to keep the deposits high and the withdrawals low. And each partner needs to be enlightened by the other as to what he or she perceives as a deposit or a withdrawal. What is a deposit for you? For your spouse? What is a withdrawal for you? For your spouse? It may help you to discuss this concept for clarification.[1]

Sometimes I find couples might want changes that are reasonable but unattainable at first. But over the long haul they can be accomplished. Trying for the unattainable breeds discouragement. It's better to work on very small attainable goals in order to eventually achieve the possible. Achieving a number of these small steps may in time resolve the major problem. It's better to spend time working on something you can achieve than something you can't.

Breaking Vicious Cycles

A different example of this is found in an approach that some marriage counselors use to help couples break free of the vicious cycle of reinforcing undesirable behaviors on the parts of their partners. There is a way to break a pattern on your own. It's not a matter of ignoring the behaviors, but making sure you're not helping to promote it anymore. It involves doing basically what a marriage counselor would have you do if you were in his or her office. But it does take cooperation from both the husband and the wife.

The first step is to agree not to become defensive at whatever is written or said. The second is for each one to write out three problem behaviors each would like changed in their spouse. They should be listed one to three to indicate the level of importance.

The third step is to list your own reactions to each behavior to identify how you might be reinforcing this behavior. This is a very important part of the solution. The final step is to list desirable or positive behaviors you would like from your partner. Here is one wife's list:

I. Problem Behaviors of Spouse I'd Like Changed
   A. I dislike his constant complaining. He complains about everything.
   B. I dislike the way he forces his ideas, wants, and desires on me. He tries to mold me and shape me to conform to his expectations.
   C. I dislike the way he never compliments me without qualifications.

II. My Reaction to These Behaviors
   A. I tell him that that's the way it is and he can't do anything about it. Often, I say nothing and just keep it inside.
   B. I am usually hurt by this and get angry and try to say something that will hurt him in return. I also tell him that I'm sorry that I'm not what he wants me to be.
   C. I respond by usually saying nothing—just keeping it inside. Just some kind of recognition would really help.

III. Desirable or Positive Behaviors of Spouse
   A. It's nice when he gets excited about something we can both do.
   B. I like it when he compliments me in front of other people.
   C. I appreciate his doing the dishes.

This is a list from her husband:
I. Problem Behaviors of Spouse I'd Like Changed
    A. She has no desire for sex. She laughs when kissed—shows no sexual interest at all.
    B. She walks away from me when I am talking to her. She usually tells me to shut up.
    C. She spends the little time we have together picking up things, taking showers, doing odd jobs, etc.
II. My Reaction to These Undesirable Behaviors
    A. My first reaction was to kiss her. When I found out that this turned her off I stopped, trying not to push what obviously annoyed her.
    B. I usually get mad and say things again to make sure she understands.
    C. I usually sit there although sometimes I say something to her. It makes me feel as though her housework is more important than me.
III. Desirable or Positive Behaviors of Spouse
    A. She is a good cook.
    B. She works uncomplainingly.
    C. Keeps house clean.
    D. Very good mother to baby.
    E. Very organized.
    F. Dependable.
    G. Thoughtful about many things.

The next step is quite different from what some would expect. This entails keeping a weeklong record of the number of times problem behavior number three—the least threatening behavior—occurs. This is not done to blame or react to your spouse, but to help each one become aware of his or her own reinforcing response to the behavior.

We begin with the least threatening behavior because it is easier to work out a mutual agreement with an easier problem. This should help any couple to proceed to the other more serious behaviors that need to be eliminated.

The way to eliminate a problem is to replace your reinforcing behaviors and increase the desired behaviors that your partner appreciates. Some partners verbally commit to each other that they will no longer respond the way they have, but let the problem behavior slide by. This takes patience, commitment, and prayer, but . . . it works.[2]

Foolish Questions

Remember when you were a child and your parents came into the room to break up a fight between you and a sibling or another child? What do you remember saying? What do kids say today when this happens? "He (or she) started it." And it continues throughout our lives. We get into a disagreement with our spouses and we either think or say, "You started it!" And if we verbalize it we usually frame it in the worst possible way by saying, "Why do you always have to start an argument?"

Fighting words. Ever said them? Ever heard them? "Why" is one of the worst ways to phrase a question. It puts the person on the defensive. Even if a person knew the answer to "why"—and often he or she doesn't—would he give the reason? And "always" is a gunpowder word. It's inflammatory. It incites a defensive posture, attitude, and response. And "have to" implies intent in a blaming way. You probably get the picture—bad phrasing of a question.

I don't think anyone is going to admit to starting the argument or fight anyway. Besides, regardless of who initiated it, would it continue if the other party didn't join in and participate? Not likely.

Instead of looking to see "who started it," what might happen if you concentrated more on "How did it end?" When you look at how disagreements end, you may find some solutions to use the next time and even shorten the disagreement. Learn from your solutions, achievements, and successes. For some it's when they say things like:

> "I see your point of view."
> "I guess I've never considered that."
> "I've never thought about it that way before."
> "I think I understand."
> "You're right."
> "I'm willing to give it a try."[3]

One of the principles I've learned about crises and losses in life is that eventually as people recover, they are able to discover something positive or beneficial from the experience amidst the pain and anguish. Sometimes it takes several months for the discovery to be made.

In marriage situations such as disagreements or hassles I think the discovery can be made earlier. The reason it often isn't is because we don't look for it. When a problem arises, instead of constantly looking for the negative outcome, look to see what is constructive about it. It may be there but either hidden or overlooked.

Some couples have discovered the following as expressed in their own words:

"We are more patient with one another after we confront a problem or have a disagreement."

"It takes me a while to see her point of view, but the only way I consider it is when we argue."

"I don't like getting angry, but I do feel better when I don't keep it bottled up."

"It's upsetting at the time but we sure become more intimate afterward."

The Power of the Unpredictable

Another way to bring out positive changes in a relationship is to do the unexpected. That is, doing something different when you know that what you're doing just isn't working. I learned about this in the early 1960s in a book I was reading in graduate school. The writer talked about it in relation to raising and disciplining children. Since I was a youth pastor at the time I wondered if it would work with teenagers and especially in large meetings.

Since most of us are predictable, and continue to respond in the same way (including me), I began to think, *When some kid begins to cut up and create a disturbance, how do I usually react? How do they expect me to respond?* Once I figured that out, I purposefully did something different. Because they weren't expecting it, they couldn't defend against it. I found that it worked. Then as I moved into counseling couples I wondered if it would work in their relationships. I experimented. It did.

Unexpected Tactics

Some of the unpredictable things I have seen couples do are as follows:

1. Instead of telling her husband not to get angry but to calm down (which never worked), a wife suggested that he needed to be angry and raise his voice. She pulled two chairs together and said, "Let's sit down and make it easier on ourselves." Interesting! He calmed down and sat down.

2. When a husband came in late occasionally because of traffic, instead of snapping at his wife when she complained that he should have called, he simply said, "Sorry," and gave her a tape that he had recorded in the car—complete with traffic noise—giving a report

every five minutes of where he was and how fast the traffic was moving. There was no argument, and the next time he was late there was a different response from his wife.

3. Instead of telling her husband that he was yelling again (which he would always deny), a wife turned on a tape recorder in plain view of her husband. This did the trick and the yelling stopped. Not only then but the next time when he started to yell, as he saw the tape recorder he stopped yelling.

4. On a humorous note, a husband shared with me that he hated being predictable when he came into the house at night, so he thought up different ways of greeting each person when he arrived home. Some days he said he would crawl in the doggy door and surprise everyone. He might surprise them, but he could get shot in the process!

A therapist who is one of the leaders of this approach shared one of her own family experiences:

> Knowing that a particular approach is entirely ineffective has no impact whatsoever on my choice of actions during subsequent crises. I find this to be a truly curious phenomenon. Consider what happened one evening at my house during dinnertime.
>
> Since I rarely prepare a homemade meal for dinner (my husband is the gourmet cook), I expect punctuality (and appreciation) when I do. Although my husband is generally considerate about informing me of his schedule, he occasionally "forgets," returning home later than usual without a phone call to advise me of his plans. There seems to be an uncanny correlation between the extremely infrequent occasions I decide to prepare a meal and his "forgetting" to come home on time.
>
> The sequence of events, when this occurs, is always the same. By the time he walks in, I have already tried calling several locations hoping to track him down. Dinner is ready and I mumble about the food getting cold. I suggest to my daughter that we begin without dad so that our food will still be hot. She senses my growing impatience. Later (what seems like years later) the door opens and I carefully plan my revenge—I will silently pout until he asks me, "What's wrong?" and then I will let him have it!
>
> As he enters the room he greets us and seats himself, commenting about how good dinner smells. Then he cordially obliges by asking, "What's wrong?" and I jump at the opportu-

nity to tell him. He defends himself and accuses me of being unreasonable. Things generally deteriorate from there. This particular plan of attack never works. I know this but my behavior belies this awareness.

However, something unusual happened one particular evening. The dinner scene was unfolding as usual when he walked through the door thirty minutes late. I was rehearsing to myself what I would say when he asked the million-dollar question. He predictably entered the room, said hello to us, sat down and began to eat. A couple of minutes passed and he did not inquire, "What's wrong?" "He's probably starving," I thought, reassuring myself that my attack was imminent. He then turned to my daughter and asked her how her day went in school. She launched into a ten-minute monologue consisting of the longest sentence I have ever heard. I thought she would never stop talking. After all, I was still waiting for my invitation to explode.

When she finally finished, instead of addressing me, my husband began to tell her some details of his day at work. She listened politely as I felt rage building inside: "What nerve, he didn't ask me why I am pouting!" I waited a while longer though I couldn't help but become mildly interested in the conversation. Without realizing it I found myself joining the discussion. The remainder of the meal was very pleasant.

When I realized what had happened I asked my husband why he decided to talk to our daughter instead of asking about my silence. He replied, "You always tell your clients to do something different when they get stuck, but you never follow your own advice. I thought I would give it a shot." It's just awful to have your own weapons used against you![4]

Surprise Attacks

One of the most common conflicts I've heard is when a wife wants to share about her day with her husband, and the response is often not what she is looking for. Frequently, after about thirty seconds, when a husband realizes that this is going to take awhile, he tunes back into the TV or begins rereading his newspaper.

Why does this happen so much? Simply because most men need to have a goal or a focal point. While a wife is sharing her feelings, and especially if she isn't talking in a linear fashion, a man is looking for the main point or bottom line. When he realizes it's going to take awhile, he relaxes mentally and focuses on his viewing or reading. And many a man thinks he is still listening. Part of his mind is still with her. It's sort of scanning her words to see when she makes a point that calls for some response from him.

The typical—and worst—way a wife can respond is to confront her husband and say, "You're not listening!" This doesn't work for two good reasons. Many men heard this from their mothers, and now they feel they're being talked down to like a child again. They feel blamed. Second, they *do* hear their wives with a part of their minds. What they aren't doing is giving their full and individual attention—which is what wives really want. They want their husbands to reflect James 1:19 when it says to be "a ready listener" (*AMP*).

Wives usually do one of two things, or both. They attack with the "You're not listening" statement and/or walk away hurt and upset. Neither works.

Why not do the unpredictable? How? One way is to say what you really want and, if a husband is bottom line, put it in his language style. As one wife said, "Tom, when you begin looking at the newspaper again, I don't feel I have your full attention. That's what I really want from you. When you do I can share what I have to say much faster and more concisely. Then you can get back to your own reading or TV much quicker. And I'll feel good about it, too." I think most men will not only hear this, but understand.

Another wife did something totally different. When her husband turned away to read or look at the TV, she stopped too and just sat and waited. After awhile he realized she had stopped talking and he stopped and looked up. She said, "Thank you. I only need three to five minutes more and it helps me to have your full attention. Will that be all right with you?" This kind of approach usually gets the desired response. And whenever you get what you want, always thank the person.[5]

The Forgetfulness Fight

Another common issue in marriage is "remembering and forgetting"—one partner asks the other to do something and the partner forgets. The opportunity to attack presents itself and the partner who forgot responds in a defensive and protective way.

You've probably asked questions like "Did you pick up the dry cleaning?" (or books at the library, photos, my prescription, bread, milk, etc.). That's a good question. It's positive. Much better than "I hope you didn't forget to . . . " or "I didn't see what I asked you to get and I was clear about how important it was. Did you forget again?"

Once you've asked in a positive way, respond in the same way if your spouse hasn't done it, with statements like "That's OK." "It's no problem." "Maybe we can get it tomorrow." If there is a time pressure ask a question that solves a problem and can lead to a solution:

"Honey, we need it tonight. Do you have any suggestions?"

"Honey, we need it tonight. Do you want to run back for it? Or I could if you can take over this project."

"Since we need it for this evening, I wonder if you could call one of the other couples to bring it?"

Whatever you do, do something different if your usual response doesn't work.

Accentuate the Positive

If you want your marriage to grow, focus on solutions, not just the problems. That's the message of this chapter. Switch the use of your imagination to a positive direction rather than a negative focus. I think most people create complete full-length mental pictures of themselves engaging in marital combat with their spouses, and thus they are prone to make that a reality. When you use the same energy and time to focus your imagination and concentration on what's working as well as the solution, you begin to expect that to happen. Act as if it is going to happen and talk as if it is going to be a reality.

This is nothing new. This procedure has been refined in the field of sports, especially tennis, racquetball, bobsledding, and skiing. In skiing, for example, the athletes will stand at the top of the ski run, close their eyes, and make the downhill run step by step in their minds. They see themselves making the precise moves at the right time as fast as possible. You actually see their bodies bob and weave as they go through the run in their minds.

I've used this rehearsal technique when playing racquetball, especially if I'm making bad shots and losing. When I concentrate on what I'm doing wrong, I continue to lose. But when I remember to concentrate on what works and what I will be doing in the next shot, I play better. It's as simple as that.

This is an important principle in your marriage, too. Concentrate on what you will be doing either differently or positively. Then commit it to prayer—don't attempt to do it without the Lord's guidance and power. When you visualize your intent to be different or loving or accepting, you move toward that reality.

Perhaps it would be helpful to look at your marriage now, and consider what you like about your relationship that you would like to see continue. Talk together about what you can do to ensure that it does continue.

As you can see, everything suggested in this chapter is simple. Not at all profound. But over the years I've wondered why more couples don't follow these principles. As one husband put it, "Norm, I just never thought about it like that before. Now that I do, it makes sense."

I think the potential for what can happen is summarized in this poem:

I will be with you
no matter what happens
to us and between us.
If you should become blind tomorrow,
I will be there.
If you achieve no success
and attain no status in our society,
I will be there.

When we argue and are angry,
as we inevitably will,
I will work to bring us together.
When we seem totally at odds
and neither of us is having needs fulfilled,
I will persist in trying to understand
and in trying to restore our relationship.

When our marriage seems utterly sterile
and going nowhere at all,
I will believe that it can work,
and I will want it to work,
and I will do my part to make it work.

And when all is wonderful
and we are happy,
I will rejoice over our life together,
and continue to strive
to keep our relationship growing and strong.[6]

9
Spiritual Intimacy in Marriages That Last

THE YOUNG WOMAN in my office was animated, though not so upset. "I never dreamed what has happened in our marriage during the past year was possible," she said. "We've gone along for years just sort of ho-hum. Nothing bad, nothing spectacular—just steady. I guess we were in a rut. It was comfortable, and I guess we felt, or I did, that this was the way it would always be. But Jim came home from that men's conference and made all kinds of changes. Even though they were mostly positive, it took me awhile to adjust.

"The first thing he did was come up to me and apologize for not telling me that he prayed for me every day, and had for years. How would I have ever known?! In fact, that's what I started to say, but I caught myself and thanked him for telling me. A week later he 'casually' asked me how I would feel about praying together and reading from the Bible occasionally. I have to laugh now because it's like he wanted me to but wasn't sure how I would respond. So we did.

"I can't explain why or what happened, but there is this incredible sense of bonding or closeness now that we never had before. We pray, we read, we share. Sometimes I call him and pray a sentence prayer for him over the phone. He does the same. And our sex life is a whole different story. Others have seen our relationship change. And when they ask, we tell them. I guess we're finally experiencing what the Bible says about cleaving in the full sense of the word."

Spiritual bonding. Spiritual intimacy. Spiritual closeness. Desired, yet avoided. Available, yet illusive for so many.

Difficult, but Desired

When partners are asked the question "How close are you spiritually as a couple?" there are usually two responses. Many say, "We're not spiritually close," or "We're not as close as we could be." The second response is, "I think we would like to be." Many couples, when they finally talk about it, discover they would like to be closer spiritually, but they were uncomfortable dealing with it. It was difficult, so it was never discussed.

I hear couples say, "We need to. We want to. We don't." What keeps us from developing this area that can bring an even greater depth to the other dimensions of intimacy?

Some couples say, "We really don't know any couples who do, and we're not exactly sure how to go about it." Perhaps there is a lack of role models for us to follow because we don't ask others what they do. We would be embarrassed if asked, so we feel others would be as well. And we avoid putting them on the spot.

Still other couples say, "We just don't have time. With our schedules we hardly have enough time to say 'hello' to each other, let alone have devotions together."

To relate together spiritually means creatively meshing two people's schedules. And yet, we have the greatest time-saving gadgets. When either an individual or a couple states they don't have time to develop the spiritual intimacy in their marriage, I say, "I don't agree. I've never met anyone who couldn't work out the time. It may take some creative juggling, but it's a choice—like so much of the rest of life. You have to be flexible, committed, and have realistic expectations for what you want to have happen in the relationship."

Others have said, "We're not at the same place spiritually in order to share this together." Perhaps praying or reading the Bible together would be the very process that would enable them to become more unified spiritually.

Some people have simply asked, "Why? Why develop this? Why do this? I'm not sure of the benefits." If a couple says this to me I won't even debate the issue with them or try to convince them. But I can say this to them: "I don't know if anyone could really explain why or convince you. Perhaps the best way to discover the benefits is just to try it for a week. Then evaluate the process to see if it does anything for you. Anyone can give one week of his or her life for an experiment such as this."

The Risk of Isolation

People can have strong, individual, personal relationships with the Lord, but never invite their partners into their lives to experience the spiritual journey together. When one partner wants this and the other resists overtly or just drags his or her feet, it can have a damaging effect upon the relationship.

A friend of mine shared his experience before he and his wife decided to develop this dimension of their relationship:

> When it came to the day to day sharing of our own spiritual journeys (the real test of spiritual intimacy), it wasn't there. Privacy was the rule.
>
> Jan would want us to read something together, and I would be too busy. She would want us to pray, and I would be too tired. She would share something deeply personal, but I would not respond. I would listen intently, but my sympathetic stares were followed with deafening silence. On the rare occasions when I did respond, it was only with a summarization of what she had said, an acknowledgment, but never a personal reflection.
>
> To Jan, my avoidant behavior communicated that I was not interested in spiritual matters and, to some extent, that I did not care about her needs. Gradually my excuses and my silence took their toll and she tired of her efforts. The requests for my involvement, the statements of her need, the times of her own personal sharing—all of these tapered off. Jan seemed to resign herself to the fact that it just was not going to happen. For whatever reason, we were not going to be spiritually intimate. Our sharing would be limited to crises.
>
> With Jan's resignation came some resentment. This was not a seething-caldron type of problem, but on occasion it would become clear that "resignation" had not brought "resolution." Jan still desired the closeness that was missing, and the disappointment was frustrating.[1]

Many marriage partners today feel close to their spouses in every way except spiritually. In that area they feel isolated. Often this isolation cannot be kept in check, and it may creep into other areas of a couple's life and impact those areas, too. And the more one person wants to be close spiritually and the other resists, the more resentment will build.

Many couples find themselves in this bind, but it can be over-come.

Sharing Your "Inmost"

What is spiritual intimacy? For that matter, what is intimacy? There is a great deal of confusion about this word because so many people think it simply refers to a sexual relationship. The word actually comes from a Latin word, *intimus,* meaning "inmost."

Intimacy suggests a very strong personal relationship, a special emotional closeness that includes understanding and being understood by someone who is very special. Intimacy has also been defined as an affectionate bond, the strands of which are composed of mutual caring, responsibility, trust, open communication of feelings and sensations, and the nondefended interchange of information about significant emotional events. Intimacy means taking the risk to be close to someone and allowing that someone to step inside your personal boundaries.

Sometimes intimacy can hurt. As you lower your defenses to let each other close, you reveal the real, intimate, secret *you* to each other, including your weaknesses and faults. With the real you exposed, you become vulnerable to possible ridicule from your partner. The risk of pain is there, but the rewards of intimacy greatly overshadow the risk.

Although intimacy means vulnerability, it also means security. The openness can be scary, but the acceptance each partner offers in the midst of vulnerability provides a wonderful sense of security. Intimate couples can feel safe and accepted—fully exposed perhaps, yet fully accepted.

Intimacy can occur outside of marriage commitment and without the element of physical love. Women can be intimate with women and men with men. The closeness of intimacy involves private and personal interaction, commitment, and caring. We can speak of intimacy between friends as well as intimacy between spouses.

Intimacy can exist without marriage, but it is impossible for a meaningful marriage to exist without intimacy. For two hearts to touch each other, intimacy is a must. If you don't know how your partner thinks and feels about various issues or concerns, he or she is somewhat of a stranger to you. And for two hearts to be bonded together, they cannot be strangers.

It is often assumed that intimacy automatically occurs between married partners. But I've seen far too many "married strangers." I've talked to too many husbands and wives who feel isolated from their spouses and lonely even after many years of marriage. I've heard statements like:

"We share the same house, the same table, and the same bed, but we might as well be strangers."

"We've lived together for twenty-three years, and yet I don't know my spouse any better now than when we married."

"What really hurts is that we can spend a weekend together and I still feel lonely. I think I married someone who would have preferred being a hermit in some ways."

No, intimacy is not automatic.

Dimensions of Intimacy

Actually there are several dimensions of intimacy. It's not limited to one quality such as sex. Several elements are involved in creating an intimate relationship. Many relationships have gaps in them for one reason or another. You may be close in two or three areas but distant in others. If you feel you have a close, intimate relationship, but you're distant in a couple of them or even one, there is work to be done. Let's consider the various dimensions before looking at the spiritual aspect, because they all relate.

Emotional intimacy is the foundation for relating in a couple's relationship. There is a "feeling" of closeness when this exists, a mutual feeling of care and support coming from each person. You share everything in the emotional arena, including your hurts and your joys. You understand each other, and you're attentive to your spouse's feelings.

Social intimacy involves having friends in common rather than always socializing separately. Having mutual friends to play with, talk with, pray with, and give reciprocal support to is reflective of this important dimension.

Sexual intimacy is taken for granted in marriage. Many couples have sex but no sexual intimacy. Performing a physical act is one thing, but communicating about it is another. Sexual intimacy involves satisfaction with what occurs. But it also means you talk about it, endeavor to meet your partner's needs, and keep it from being routine. There is an understanding of each other's unique gender needs, and flexibility in meeting them.

There is even the dimension of *intellectual* intimacy—the sharing of ideas and the stimulation of each other's level of knowledge and understanding. You are each different, and you have grown because of what your partner has shared with you.

Joyce and I have become much more involved this way in the last ten years of our marriage. We share or point out some idea or save something we learned in an article, book, newscast, or TV program. We value each other's opinion. For this dimension to exist, you need mutual respect. You cannot be threatened by the sharing, but must value what's given.

Recreational intimacy means you share and enjoy the same interests and activities. You just like to play together, and it doesn't have to be competitive. You have fun together, and it draws you closer together.

Sharing Your Spiritual Selves

Then we come to *spiritual* intimacy. Just to keep everything in balance, even though this dimension may be more significant than others, you need the others in order to be complete, too. I've seen some couples who have spiritual intimacy but lack social and recreational. That's out of balance.[2]

In his book *The Spiritually Intimate Marriage*, Don Harvey has the most complete definition that I've found. He says spiritual intimacy is:

> Being able to *share* your spiritual self, find this reciprocated, and have a sense of union with your mate.

> Based on this definition, spiritual intimacy is something that we do, something that we feel, and something that is *interactional*.

> *Sharing* is something that we do; it is a behavior. It is an act of self-disclosure, of opening yourself up to someone else and privileging them with a genuine glimpse of who you really are. The variety of what can be shared is enormous. At one time it may be more of a cognitive nature: You may share your beliefs and insights. Or, delving a little deeper, you may share your misbeliefs: your doubts and apprehensions. At times you will share your feelings. This will include both the good (joy and peace) and the bad (fear and pain). There will be times of victory and growth, and there will be times of dismay, when burdens, struggles, and seeming failure weigh you

down. All of this represents your spiritual self, and this is what is shared in an intimate relationship.

A sense of union is emotional. It is something that we feel. There is a sense of acceptance, of being known for who you really are and knowing that is okay. You know that you are cared for spiritually, that at least one person is praying for you. With this sense of union is the feeling that you are spiritually "in tune" as a couple—that this is truly a marriage.

Finally, to *find it reciprocated* implies an interactional element. You cannot stand alone and experience intimacy. That is isolation. Intimacy is not a one-person game; it requires two of you. Depthful sharing that is not reciprocated by a mate will not lead to closeness. There must be an effort by you and your mate if intimacy is to be approached. It takes two.[3]

I know couples who worship regularly together, but there is no spiritual intimacy. I know couples who read the Scripture regularly together, but have no spiritual intimacy. I know couples who pray and share together sporadically, but are lacking in spiritual intimacy. I know some couples who don't pray and share, yet have spiritual intimacy.

What's the difference? It seems to be in their attitudes. Spiritual intimacy is a heart's desire to be close to God and submit to His direction for your lives. It is the willingness to seek His guidance together, to allow the teaching of His Word in your everyday life. It's a willingness to allow God to help you overcome your sense of discomfort over sharing spiritually and learn to see your marriage together as a spiritual adventure. It's a willingness to enthrone Jesus Christ as Lord of your lives and to look to Him for direction in your decisions, such as which house to buy, where to go on vacations, or which school is best for the children. It means He will direct both of you, and change your hearts to be in agreement rather than speak just through one of you.

Lordship and Control

Spiritual intimacy in marriage requires both partners to submit to the leadership and lordship of Christ, instead of competing for control. One author wrote:

We can gather all the facts needed in making a decision. We can thresh out our differences as to the shape and direction our decision should take. We can put off the decision while we allow the relevant information to simmer in our minds. Even then, however, we may be uneasy: we still don't know what is best to do, and the right decision just won't come.

When we turn to the Lord Jesus Christ and open our consciences to His Spirit's leading, some new events, remembrances, and forgotten facts will come to us. A whole new pattern will emerge. We can then move with abandon in a whole new direction which we had not previously considered. Looking back, we may conclude that God's providence delivered us from what would have been the worst possible decision. Jesus as Lord made the difference between deliverance and destruction.[4]

When Jesus is Lord of your marriage, it relieves you of the problem of experiencing a power struggle. Jesus expressed something interesting to His disciples when He said, *"You know that those who are regarded as rulers of the Gentiles lord it over them, and their high officials exercise authority over them. Not so with you. Instead, whoever wants to become great among you must be your servant"* (Mark 10:42,43, *NIV*).

Earlier we talked about the dominant-submissive relationship, and how intimacy cannot develop in this style of marriage. It's true for spiritual intimacy as well.

I've seen marriages in which one member dictates the spiritual dimension by selecting the church they attend, the meetings attended, what magazines and books are allowed, as well as which Bible version is the accepted one! It's difficult to see how this reflects Paul's words: *"Outdo one another in showing honor"* (Rom. 12:10, *RSV*) to each other.

Even in a spiritually intimate marriage, faith differences may surface occasionally, but that's normal. With tolerance for diversity couples can have a shared faith relationship that includes his faith, her faith, and their faith.

Requirements for Spiritual Intimacy

Some couples seem to be able to develop spiritual intimacy and others never do. What makes the difference? Spiritual intimacy has the opportunity to grow in a relationship that has a degree of stability. When the two of you experience trust, honesty, open communication, and dependability, you are more willing to risk being vulnerable spiritually. Creating this dimension will increase the stability factor as well.

For a couple to have spiritual intimacy they need shared beliefs as to who Jesus is and the basic tenets of the Christian faith. You may have different beliefs about the second coming of Christ, or whether all the spiritual gifts are for today or not. One of you may enjoy an informal church service while the other likes a high church formal service, or one of you may be charismatic and the other not. It's important that your beliefs are important to you. You've made them something personal and significant for your life. There can still be spiritual intimacy within this diversity.

We hear about mismatched couples when one is a Christian and one isn't. You can also have a mismatch when both are believers but one wants to grow, and is growing, and the other doesn't and isn't![5]

A wonderful way to encourage spiritual intimacy is to share the history of your spiritual life. Many couples know where their spouses are currently, but very little of how they came to that place.

Use the following questions to discover more about your partner's faith:

1. What did your parents believe about God, Jesus, church, prayer, the Bible?
2. What was your definition of being spiritually alive?
3. Which parent did you see as being spiritually alive?
4. What specifically did each teach you directly and indirectly about spiritual matters?
5. Where did you first learn about God? About Jesus? About the Holy Spirit? What age?
6. What was your best experience in church as a child? As a teen?
7. What was your worst experience in church as a child? As a teen?
8. Describe your conversion experience. When? Who was involved? Where?
9. If possible, describe your baptism. What did it mean to you?
10. Which Sunday School teacher influenced you the most? In what way?
11. Which minister influenced you the most? In what way?
12. What questions did you have as a child/teen about your faith? Who gave you any answers?
13. Was there any camp or special meetings that affected you spiritually?

14. Did you read the Bible as a teen?
15. Did you memorize any Scripture as a child or teen? Do you remember any now?
16. As a child, if you could have asked God any questions, what would they have been?
17. As a teen, if you could have asked God any questions, what would they have been?
18. If you could ask God any questions now, what would they be?
19. What would have helped you more spiritually when you were growing up?
20. Did anyone disappoint you spiritually as a child? If so, how has that impacted you as an adult?
21. When you went through difficult times as a child or teen, how did that affect your faith?
22. What has been the greatest spiritual experience of your life?

The Gift of Praying Together

How important is prayer together as a couple? Vital. No other way to put it. It's vital. Think of praying together as a couple not as a duty, a drudgery, or a negative mandate. It is a gift from Him. Over the years I've collected statements or quotes from others whose words have encouraged and challenged me in my own marriage. Reflect on the following statements about prayer. Consider their truth. Explore how they can infuse your life with a new depth of togetherness and closeness.

Prayer is an awareness of the presence of a holy and loving God in one's life, and an awareness of God's relations to one's husband or wife. Prayer is listening to God, a valuable lesson in learning to listen to one another. In prayer one searches the interior life for blocks to personal surrender to God, evaluating one's conduct in the quiet of prayerful mediation. At times prayer may be rich with confession and self-humbling, or with renunciation and higher resolve to fulfill God's best. Praying together shuts out the petty elements of daily conflict and anxiety, permitting a couple to gain a higher perspective upon their lives, allowing their spirits to be elevated to a consideration of eternal values and enduring relationships. Prayer helps a couple sort out unworthy objects of concern and helps them to concentrate on the nobler goals of life. All the threatening things that trouble a pair can find relief in the presence of God; humbling themselves before Him, they humble themselves before one another—an invaluable therapy. In this way the couple comes to honest estimates of themselves and one another. Unbecoming self-assurance and stubborn independence give way before the recognition of their inadequacy to meet divine standards of life; thus, two people are led to seek God's help and the support of each other.[6]

It is only when a husband and wife pray together before God that they find the secret of true harmony, that the difference in their temperaments, their ideas, and their tastes enriches their home instead of endangering it. There will be no further question of one imposing his will on the other, or of the other giving in for the sake of peace. Instead, they will together seek God's will, which alone will ensure that each will be fully able to develop his personality. . . . When each of the marriage partners seeks quietly before God to see his own faults, recognizes his sin, and asks the forgiveness of the other, marital problems are no more. Each learns to speak the other's language, and to meet him halfway, so to speak. Each holds back those harsh little words which one is apt to utter when one is right, but which are said in order to injure. Most of all, a couple rediscovers complete mutual confidence, because, in mediating in prayer together, they learn to become absolutely honest with each other. . . . This is the price to be paid if partners very different from each other are to combine their gifts instead of setting them against each other.[7]

Lines open to God are invariably open to one another for a person cannot be genuinely open to God and closed to his mate. Praying together especially reduces the sense of competitiveness in marriage, at the same time enhancing the sense of complementarity and completeness. The Holy Spirit seeks only the opportunity to minister to whatever needs are present in a marriage, and in their moments of prayer together a couple gives Him entrance into opened hearts and minds. God fulfills His design for Christian marriage when lines of communication are first opened to Him.[8]

There is a sense in which marriage is a three-story affair. There is a third floor of the spiritual where we worship to-

gether, where we appreciate God together, where we pray together. If we disagree here, a certain disunity will seep down
into the second floor, which is our emotional and mental
state. This will lead us to disputes, mental and intellectual
debating and haggling; and this division on the second floor
naturally seeps down into the physical relations of the first
floor and takes the deepest desire from them. Everything that
is crowned is crowned from above! Unless in the marriage
relationship there is an "above", some spiritual rapport, it is
difficult for the physical relationship to be at its best.[9]

Scripture also tells us to pray:
*"As for me, far be it from me that I should sin against the
Lord by ending my prayers for you; and I will continue to
teach you those things which are good and right" (1 Sam.
12:23, TLB).*

*"You haven't tried this before, [but begin now]. Ask, using
my name, and you will receive, and your cup of joy will overflow" (John 16:24, TLB).*

*Don't worry about anything; instead, pray about every-
thing; tell God your needs and don't forget to thank him for
his answers (Phil. 4:6, TLB).*

Always keep on praying (1 Thess. 5:17, TLB).

*Admit your faults to one another and pray for each other
so that you may be healed. The earnest prayer of a righteous
man has great power and wonderful results (James 5:16,
TLB).*

How to Start

How do you start praying together as a couple? Why not begin by
praying by yourself for your partner? Do it daily, earnestly, hopefully,
specifically. Ask God to bless and to lead your spouse. I know couples who call one another during the day to tell them they're praying
for each other. Other couples ask each other before they part for the
day, "How can I pray for you today?" At the conclusion of the day,
it gives you something to discuss. When I'm on a trip, I've found
notes in my clothes from Joyce stating that she is praying for me.

The easiest way to begin praying together is to take the time and set a time to do it. I've heard so many say that with their schedules it's almost impossible. I disagree. Creativity and flexibility can make it happen. You can put your arms around each other for thirty seconds and pray before you leave for the day or after dinner. Couples can pray together over the phone when they're apart. Creative couples write their prayers and send them to each other via the fax machine. With cellular phones couples can pray while driving (hopefully with their eyes open) and make contact in this way.

When you start praying silently together at home, perhaps it's best just to share some requests, then pray silently together. There is no threat to this.

Praying aloud is something you grow into. It may take a while to develop a comfort level. Communication doesn't always have to be vocal. We're bombarded with noise all the time. Sometimes couples struggle with audible prayer, because they don't communicate very much with each other on anything else. Or one spouse feels that the other is much more articulate and fluent. It could be true, but this is not a time for comparison or competitive endeavor. It's a time for learning to accept who you are. I've always felt my wife's prayers were much more detailed and in-depth than mine. But this has never hindered me from praying aloud.

I like the journey that Charles and Martha Shedd experienced in learning to pray together.

> We would sit on our rocking love seat. We would take turns telling each other things we'd like to pray about. Then holding hands we would pray each in our own way, silently.
>
> This was the beginning of prayer together that lasted. Naturally, through the years we've learned to pray in every possible way, including aloud. Anytime, anywhere, every position, every setting, in everyday language. Seldom with "thee" or "thou." Plain talk. Ordinary conversation. We interrupt, we laugh, we argue, we enjoy. We hurt together, cry together, wonder together. Together we tune our friendship to the Friend of friends.
>
> Do we still pray silently together? Often. Some groanings of the spirit go better in the silence.
>
> "I've been feeling anxious lately and I don't know why. Will you listen while I tell you what I can? Then let's pray about the known and unknown in silence."
>
> "This is one of my super days. So good. Yet somehow I can't

find words to tell you. Let's thank the Lord together in the quiet."

Negatives, positives, woes, celebrations, shadowy things—all these, all kinds of things we share in prayer. Aloud we share what we can. Without the vocals we share those things not ready yet for words.

Why would this approach have the feel of the real? Almost from the first we knew we'd discovered an authentic new dimension.

In becoming best friends with each other, we were becoming best friends with the Lord.

And the more we sought his friendship, the more we were becoming best friends with each other.[10]

What God Does Through Couples' Prayers

One of the other reasons for praying silently has to do with the unique way God has created us in both our gender and personality differences. Most men prefer to put things on the back burner and think about them for awhile. Thus, if a man has the opportunity to reflect on what he wants to pray about, he would eventually be more open to praying. Extroverts find it easier to pray aloud because they think out loud; whereas introverts need to think things through silently in their minds before sharing. Silent prayer is less threatening. Some prefer reflecting for awhile first and writing out their prayer. There is nothing wrong with this.

There are numerous benefits from praying together. When a man and woman marry they no longer think and act as a single person. It is no longer "I" but "we." All of life is then lived in connection with another person. Everything you do affects this significant person. You're a team of two, and when both of you participate, you function better. When you confront problems and crises in your life (and you will), it's a tremendous source of comfort and support to know that here is another person who will pray for you and with you. When you're struggling financially, or with problems at work, when you have tough decisions to make, or a medical crisis, to be able to share the burden with your spouse lightens the load.

Couples need to pray together for the health of their marriages. When you married, you entered into a high-risk adventure. The vows you took at your wedding will be attacked on all sides. Praying together will make your marriage stronger as well as help to protect you from reacting sinfully toward your spouse.

Scripture's promise about the effectiveness of prayer includes the prayers of married couples. Jesus said, *"Again, I tell you that if two of you on earth agree about anything you ask for, it will be done for you by my Father in heaven. For where two or three come together in my name, there am I with them"* (Matt. 18:19,20, NIV).

Couples who have prayer lists and see the results of answered prayer will be encouraged as they see how God works in their lives.

When couples pray together it has an impact on disagreements, conflicts, and anger expressed toward each other. When you see your spouse as a child of God, valuable and precious in His sight, someone He sent His Son to die for, wouldn't that have an effect on how you pray for him or her? In the book *If Two Shall Agree* by Carey Moore and Pamela Roswell Moore, Carey puts it plainly:

> To place Christ at the center of our homes means, of course, to tell Him, "You are our God," not just at prayer time but all day long. I cannot be careless or insensitive in what I say to Pam and then pray with her. Nor can either of us treat anyone else rudely or engage in gossip and criticism or allow conceit and pride to rule our relations with others, and expect God to hear our prayers at the end of the day.
>
> Praying together involves the family finances, how we spend our time, what we do for entertainment, the thoughts we dwell upon when we are apart. I cannot be dishonest or profligate or stingy in money matters and then pray with my wife for His blessing on our economic life. Nor can we be cavalier with the way we spend money on clothes or a vacation or a new car, and then pray for the poor. I cannot harbor jealousy or hatred or lust or self-conceit in my thoughts, nor can Pam, and then expect God to hear us as we pray. When we come into His presence God searches our hearts. *"Surely you desire truth in the inner parts"* (Psalm 51:6).[11]

Help from the Holy Spirit

Have you ever felt like this when it comes to prayer?—"I just don't know what to say when I pray. Sometimes I'm at a loss for words."

If you've ever felt this way, you're not alone. We've all felt like this at some point. Often it's when we attempt to pray that we become very conscious of a spiritual struggle in our lives. As we sit down to pray, our minds wander. Every few minutes we sneak a look at the clock to see if we've prayed enough. Has that happened to you when you pray alone? It has to me. But it's interesting that when couples pray together it happens less often.

The Holy Spirit is God's answer when we don't know how to pray.

You and I cannot pray as we ought to pray. We are often crippled in our prayer lives. That's where the work of the Holy Spirit really comes into play. He helps us in our prayer lives by showing us what we should pray for and how we ought to pray. That's quite a promise!

J. B. Phillips translates Romans 8:26,27 in this manner:

> The Spirit of God not only maintains this type within us, but helps us in our present limitations. For example, we do not know how to pray worthily as sons of God, but his Spirit within us is actually praying for us in those agonizing longings which never find words. And God who knows the heart's secrets understands, of course, the Spirit's intention as he prays for those who love God.

One of your callings in marriage is to assist your partner when he or she needs help. You are always to be listening for a call for assistance. Similarly, there is someone looking out for us when we need help in our prayer lives: the Holy Spirit. There are several specific ways that He helps us.

First, *the Spirit intercedes for you* when you are oppressed by problems in life or when you feel down on yourself. He brings you to the place where you can pray. Your ability to begin praying is prompted and produced by the working of the Holy Spirit within you. There may be times when all you can do is sigh or sob inwardly. Even this kind of prayer is the result of the Spirit's work.

Second, *the Spirit reveals to your mind what you should pray for.* He makes you conscious of such things as your needs, your lack of faith, your fears, your need to be obedient, etc. He helps you identify your spiritual needs and bring them into the presence of God. He helps you by diminishing your fears, increasing your faith, and strengthening your hope. If you're at a loss to know what you need to pray for about your partner or even what to pray for together, ask the Holy Spirit to intercede for you.

Third, *the Spirit guides you by directing your thoughts* to the promises of God's Word that are best suited to your needs. He helps you realize the truth of God's promises. The discernment that you lack on your own is supplied to you by the Spirit. Perhaps you're looking for a verse to apply to your marriage. Again, help is available through the Spirit.

Finally, *the Spirit helps you pray in the right way.* He helps you sift through your prayers and bring them into conformity with the purpose of prayer.

When you experience a crisis, it may be difficult for you to talk. But you and your spouse can hold each other in your arms and quietly allow the Holy Spirit to pray for you. This is called the silent prayer of the heart.

When you are having difficulty praying, remember that you have someone to draw on for strength in developing your prayer life.

Keeping Your Appointment with God

When is the best time for a couple to pray? You decide for yourself. It may vary or it may be set. There will be all kinds of interferences from the phone and TV, and child interruptions and exhaustion. But a commitment to be faithful in prayer can override excuses. Jim Dobson shares a situation he and his wife, Shirley, experienced:

> I'll never forget the time a few years ago when our daughter had just learned to drive. . . . It was during this era that Shirley and I covenanted between us to pray for our son and daughter at the close of every day. Not only were we concerned about the risk of an automobile accident, but we were also aware of so many other dangers that lurk out there in a city like Los Angeles. . . . That's one reason we found ourselves on our knees each evening, asking for divine protection for the teenagers whom we love so much.
>
> One night we were particularly tired and collapsed into bed without our benedictory prayer. We were almost asleep before Shirley's voice pierced the night. "Jim," she said. "We haven't prayed for our kids yet today."
>
> I admit it was very difficult for me to pull my 6'2" frame out of the warm bed that night. Nevertheless, we got on our knees and offered a prayer for our children's safety, placing them in the hands of the Father once more.
>
> Later we learned that [our daughter] Danae and a girl friend had gone to a fast-food establishment and bought hamburgers and Cokes. They drove up the road a few miles and were sitting in the car eating the meal when a policeman drove by, shining his spotlight in all directions, obviously looking for someone.
>
> In a few minutes, Danae and her friend heard a "clunk" from under the car. They looked at one another nervously and felt another sharp bump. Then a man crawled out from under the car. He was unshaven and looked like he had been on the street for weeks. He tugged at the door attempting to open it.

Thank God, it was locked. Danae quickly started the car and drove off . . . no doubt at record speed.

Later, when we checked the timing of this incident, we realized that Shirley and I had been on our knees at the precise moment of danger. Our prayers were answered. Our daughter and her friend were safe![12]

We keep appointments with others, and make sure we're always available for certain TV shows. Similarly, when you establish a specific time or pattern for prayer and keep to it consistently it becomes a regular part of your life. Some couples pray in their kitchens, family rooms, bedrooms, cars, or on walks. Work out what's best for you.

The Content of Your Prayers

Sometimes it helps to read prayers out loud that others have written. For years (even since college!) off and on I've used a book of daily prayers by John Baille called *A Diary of Private Prayer*. Reading the Psalms aloud can be a prayer. You can pray about everything and I mean everything.

Recently I found a fascinating resource that personalizes passages of Scripture into prayers for a husband and wife. It's called *Praying God's Will for My Marriage* by Lee Roberts. It simply takes passages of Scripture and rewords them. By reading these aloud for awhile, any couple could learn to do this for themselves. Here is a sampling:

I pray that my spouse and I will be swift to hear, slow to speak, slow to wrath: for the wrath of man does not produce the righteousness of God (James 1:19–20).

I pray that my spouse and I will always love the Lord our God with all our heart, with all our soul, with all our mind, and with all our strength and that we love our neighbor as ourselves (Mark 12:30–31).

I pray that when my spouse and I face an obstacle we always remember that God has said, "Not by might nor by power, but by my Spirit" (Zechariah 4:6).

I pray that if my spouse and I lack wisdom, we ask it of You, God, who gives to all liberally and without reproach and that it will be given to us (James 1:5).

I pray that because freely my spouse and I have received, freely we will give (Matthew 10:8).

I pray, O God, that You have comforted my spouse and me and will have mercy on our afflictions (Isaiah 49:13).

I pray that my spouse and I will bless You, the Lord, at all times; and that Your praise continually be in our mouths (Psalm 34:1).

I pray to You, God, that my spouse and I will present our bodies a living sacrifice, holy and acceptable to God, which is our reasonable service. I pray also that we will not be conformed to this world, but transformed by the renewing of our minds, that we may prove what is that good and acceptable and perfect will of God (Romans 12:1–2).[13]

Can you imagine the effect on your relationship when you literally bathe yourselves with God's Word as a prayer? Try this for a one-month experiment. Then note the difference in your marriage.

Prayer is one of the best ways to experience closeness. When your partner is discouraged, go up to him/her and hug him/her, and pray a one-line prayer of support. You can do this with your eyes open and looking him/her in the face. When he/she is upset or stressed, you could touch him/her on the arm and pray, "Lord, give strength and peace, lift the pressure, and show me how to support my loved one." This in itself can be supportive.

Before or after making love you could thank God for your spouse's love and physical attributes as well as for the gift of sex. Praying about sex? Why not? It's God's idea. It's His creation. It's His gift. How would you like to pray the following prayer?

Thank you, O Redeemer,
   for letting me express love through sex.
Thank you for making it possible
   for things to be right with sex—
   that there can be beauty and wonder
   between woman and man.
You have given us a model for love in Jesus.
He lived and laughed and accepted his humanity.
He resisted sexual temptations
Which were every bit as real as mine.

He taught about the relationship of husband and wife
  By showing love for his bride the church.
Thank you that he gives me
  the power to resist temptations also.
Thank you that real sexual freedom
  comes in being bound to the true man Jesus.
Everywhere there are signs that point to the sex god:
  Books declare that sex is our savior;
  Songs are sung as prayers to sex;
  Pictures show its airbrushed incantations;
  Advertisers hawk its perfume and after-shave
  libations.
Help me know that sex is not salvation.
Help me see instead that there is salvation for sex.
For the exciting sensations of erotic love,
  I offer you my thanks.
For the affirmation of self-giving love,
  I offer you my thanks.
Lord, you replace sexual boredom with joy;
  You point past sexual slavery to the hope of purity;
  You enable sexual lovers to be friends;
  You teach how to replace lust-making with
  lovemaking.
Would I have any hope for sexual responsibility
Without the power you give?
Would I ever be a covenant keeper
Without the fidelity you inspire?
Thank you, Lord, for a love that stays when the bed
  is made.
Help me to keep my marriage bed undefiled—
  To see it as an altar of grace and pleasure.
Keep sex good in my life,
  Through your redeeming love.
Teach me to say:
  "Thank God for sex!"[14]

Testimonies About Couples' Prayers

What has prayer done for couples? Listen to some of these testi-
monies:

"We both feel that communication with God deepens . . .
the spiritual and emotional intimacy we share with one an-

other," one couple wrote. "Prayer is the means by which we build upon the Lord's love for us as the foundation of our marriage, and the medium by which we achieve spiritual agreement (Amos 3:3). The goal of our prayer life is spiritual unity, emotional oneness and marital harmony."

"Sharing our spiritual lives," said Joel and Maria Shuler, "is one of the ways we work at being truly intimate. We believe that God wants us to be one, to be united in every way possible. Our total couple intimacy is enhanced by our couple prayer. When we listen in to each other's private conversation with God, we are at our most vulnerable. It is a gift we give to each other, a special time." This is from a couple who found praying together "awkward" at first.

Joel and Maria are Catholics and have been committed to prayer together since Joe's conversion from Judaism some ten years ago. "At first," they recall, "we had to pray mostly traditional prayers" from a book, but Maria knew them so well she would run ahead of Joel. At one point their inability to pray at the same pace struck them as very funny. "We laughed so hard we couldn't continue with the prayer; but the experience freed us up to be more comfortable and natural before the Lord," Maria says.

"We believe that God wants us to be united in mind, heart and body. We work toward unity in every area of our lives, and have much to glean when we share our faith and spirituality with each other. We see how we complement and learn from each other, and thank God for bringing us together. God, Joel and I are like a three-ply cord that is woven and intertwined."[15]

Resources for Spiritual Intimacy

If you're looking for a practical book to assist you in your prayer life, the best one I've found and used is *Conversation with God* by Lloyd Ogilvie (Harvest House).

There are numerous devotional books for individuals to use for their own personal time, and these can be used by couples as well.

The daily reading can be read aloud together, or each one can read it individually and then share what it means to him or her. When something you read doesn't connect with you, it's both honest and healthy to say, "Today's devotion just didn't speak to me. Perhaps another time it would." Sometimes my wife, Joyce, and I will comment on what we each read in our own devotional material. Or it could be a passage of Scripture.

Until recently there wasn't very much available in devotional materials for couples. In 1990 the book *Quiet Times for Couples* (Harvest House) was released, and the response to it showed the hunger of couples for something that would help them grow closer spiritually. By reading the daily information aloud to each other, hundreds of thousands of couples have discovered a structure that works for them as well as one that is not overly time-consuming. The material often includes one or two discussion questions to assist couples in applying the Scripture to their marriages.

Reading aloud together as a couple develops an interesting dynamic in the relationship. When you read aloud to each other, you are each aware of what the other has read or heard and you feel a greater sense of motivation to follow what was shared. Reading the Scripture aloud and letting it speak to and guide you in your life will also tend to draw you closer together.

A simple way to implant God's Word in your heart and mind is to take one chapter from a book of the Bible and read it out aloud every day for one month. Why? A speaker I heard in Westmont Chapel in 1958 challenged us by saying, "If you will read the same chapter from the Bible out loud for a month it will be yours for life." He was right. It works. It's one way of following the admonition in Psalm 119:9,11 (*AMP*): "*How shall a young man cleanse his way? By taking heed and keeping watch [on himself] according to Your word [conforming his life to it]. Your word have I laid up in my heart, that I might not sin against You.*"

Dwight Small summed it up well:

> The lordship of Christ becomes very real when it is known through the Scriptures. Marriage goals are then conformed to the pattern set forth in the believer's relation to Christ. Of all that two people might study and share, nothing can match the influence of God's Word upon their lives.[16]

One of my favorite authors is Max Lucado, particularly because of his penetrating, insightful writing style and his focus on the life and ministry of Jesus. Some of his books include *God Came Near* (Multnomah Books), *No Wonder They Call Him the Savior* (Multnomah Books), *When God Whispers Your Name* (Word Inc.), *The Applause of Heaven* (Word Inc.), and *And the Angels Were Silent* (Walker and Company).

The books *Intimate Moments With the Savior* (NavPress) and *Incredible Moments with the Savior* (NavPress) by Ken Gire are very informative and inspirational. *The Pleasures of God* by John Piper (Multnomah Books) will broaden your own understanding of God, as will *The Knowledge of the Holy* by A. W. Tozer (HarperSanFrancisco).

The following are daily devotional books that can be used by couples in their daily devotions: *100 Portraits of Christ* by Henry Gariepy (Victor Books), *My Daily Appointment With God* by Lucille Fern Sollenberger (Word Inc.), *Hymns for Personal Devotions* by Jerry B. Jenkins (Moody Press), *Quiet Times* by Max F. Anders (Wolgemuth & Hyatt), *God's Best For My Life* by Lloyd Ogilvie (Harvest House), *Two-Part Harmony—A Devotional for Couples* by Patrick M. Morley (Thomas Nelson), and *Quiet Times for Couples* by this author (Harvest House).

10
How'd They Do That?

We HEAR SO MUCH about couples whose marriages don't last. Often the question is asked, "What went wrong?" Perhaps we've been asking the wrong question. I'd rather know about couples who have *stayed* married, and ask another question: "What did you do right?"

For this reason I decided to look for couples who have been married for a lifetime, and try to discover what they did that made it work. And find them I did. They're all around us. You would be amazed at how many there are. At the church my wife and I attend, there is a Homebuilders class that was started fifty-six years ago. Out of that class alone, fifty-two couples have celebrated their Golden Wedding Anniversaries.

Voices of Experience

For the purpose of this study, I actually ended up interviewing a number of couples from another congregation in Orange County, California, who had been married from forty-seven to sixty-five years. They were asked the following questions:
1. What has been the most fulfilling or positive experience in your marriage? Describe in detail.
2. Describe how you developed your spiritual relationship together.
3. What three things have you done yourself that have helped your marriage?
4. What three things has your spouse done that have helped your marriage?
5. What were (or are) the three greatest adjustments you had to make in marriage and how did you do it?
6. If you could start your marriage over again, what would you do differently?

It was fascinating to hear their stories and see the diversity, yet discover the common themes in these marriages. Even though the couples interviewed began their marriages during much different times, they still have a message to share with the present generation. Most of them married during the Great Depression or during World War II years. They began their marriages during a survival time in our society. The pressures were different, yet similar in many respects.

Listen to some of the selections from their stories. Some were brief, whereas others went into detail. I have let their statements stand largely as they were originally written, feeling that they communicate more realistically than they would with a lot of polishing and editing.

What do you identify with? How is your experience similar or dissimilar? What can you learn from them? And by the way: What will you be able to pass on to the next generation?

Both Trust and Space

One couple married forty-seven years told about the most fulfilling or positive experience in their marriage. They said it was . . .

"The love we share. I don't think anything surpasses that. I think the biggest thing in our marriage is love and trust, and trust is of utmost importance.

"Our generation is so different from the present one, as in yours everything has to have an answer. I don't think that really falls in at all in our way of thinking and doing. I love her and trust her. You just need to go along and trust each other and love each other every day.

"I think the biggest thing is not to let little things bother you."

Another couple married fifty-four years shared what they did to help their marriage. They said,

"We've allowed each other space, feelings, and ideas that we would discuss and just give each other understanding, supporting one another in ideas and whatever we wanted to do apart. Freedom to be ourselves.

"And communication, I think, is one of the main things. We worked together. Whenever there was a problem, we'd discuss it.

"Having a commitment and the Lord in our lives got us through. We never entertained anything other than this was a lifelong togetherness. And that we would work together and share and support one another. So we didn't consider that an adjustment; it just came natural."

Through Tough Times

A couple married for sixty-five years shared their story.

"We married during the depression in 1929, and those were really tough times. We didn't have one nickel to rub against the other. There just was no money. We couldn't get a job. It was hard on both of us, but we managed.

"I was only out of work for eleven months. We picked up a little extra money on the side by going down to my uncle's farm and bringing chickens back, dressing 'em and selling 'em just to pay bills. That was the Great Depression.

"The Lord just kept us going day by day. Then we had to move in with my wife's mother. I don't know how she put up with us. There were three daughters in a five-room bungalow with an attic, a basement, and one bathroom. And each one had kids.

"But everybody was loving."

The husband shared about his spiritual journey:

"My mother and dad had just started life together on a small farm with one of my sisters who was just a year and a half old. My dad was killed in an accident. I was born two months later and Mother died right after that. I was raised by a great-aunt and great-uncle. But I was church-housed from day one, from what I can recall. I went through what they call catechism and examination, and automatically became a church member.

"When I was about twenty years old, I moved to the Chicago area and I met my wife there. The fellow I was working for, his brother was getting married. He married a girlfriend of hers. That's where we met. Then I started going over to her house, naturally. I went over there one Sunday and she said, 'Are you going to church with us tonight?'

"I said, 'Sure.' They were going to a Baptist church around the corner from her. That's the first time in all those years I heard I had to accept Christ as my Savior. Listening to that preaching all those years and never been told that I had to accept Christ. But from there on I met the Lord, learned to love the Lord, and I've tried to work with Him ever since. Maybe not doing the best that I should, but I've tried.

"I still don't recall us arguing all those years, my wife's mom and dad or any of us.

"Oh, sometimes you'd get angry, you know; it's only natural. But it cools off real fast. You want to kill each other sometimes, but it worked out just fine. We never had any overnight arguments that lasted very long. But we enjoyed each other."

His wife shared that what she did to help the marriage was to have their kids and help raise her husband's nieces and nephews.

"Living a Christian life was the most important part of it. That's what we had to do, because we had a real hard life after we moved to the country. His folks moved in with us. His sister had six months to live and had four children. She moved in with us, and we had the kids for two or three years, four children after she died. The father wouldn't support them. We also had his old aunt who raised him, and she was ninety when she died. And an uncle who was a drunk! Fortunately we didn't have all of these people at the same time.

"Life was hard for many years with all the children, but we still kept trusting the Lord. My old uncle came back to the Lord, too.

"Something else that helped our marriage was we were very good at working together. We always worked together. I always let him think he was the boss and it worked out real good.

"One thing he wouldn't let me do was let me buy anything on time. And I helped him that way. I knew what I would get if I bought anything on time. One thing I hated was for him to scold me.

"And regardless of what we made, when we came to the Lord we felt we should tithe. Even when we only had a dime, we tithed. And I think through that the Lord has helped us, too."

Divorce Wasn't an Option

Another couple explains:

"We've been married forty-seven years. Our most positive experience has been that we have had a mutual love, devotion, and commitment to each other, and to Jesus Christ, as well as for our four children and nine grandchildren.

"There has never been any doubt about our true love for each other and for God. We have each been confident of our faithfulness to one another, without concern or jealousy, and divorce has never been accepted as an option to escape our difficulties.

"Our spiritual progress during our marriage has been staggered. However, it did not present a problem until thirty years ago when one of us knew we had come into a much deeper relationship with Christ, leaving the other mate feeling seriously neglected for some time. When that mate realized through agony, and prayer, that self-control needed to be exercised, and that the other mate was not at the same spiritual high at that same time, and was in fact being neglected, we worked through it with God's help in revealing the truth to us.

"The three things we have done that have helped our marriage have been being completely devoted to my husband, eagerly and joyfully assuming the responsibilities of a homemaker, and I have always tried to keep myself attractive at all times so my husband would be proud of me."

"For me, [the husband] I have never given her cause to worry about my whereabouts, or my association with the opposite sex. I worked diligently to be a good provider, but not at the expense of neglecting time with my family. I've also continually expressed my devotion and loyalty to my wife, our children, and our parents, as being second only to my Lord and God. My career and church responsibilities followed after them, but I have [since my conversion two years after we were married] been a faithful spiritual leader in our home.

"Our greatest adjustments were [in the area of] financial responsibility. In the earlier years of our marriage we did not always agree upon major expenditures and investments. However, over the years confidence was established that the husband had the responsibility, and most of the time profit was realized.

"As a husband, my temper created considerable discord. However, with prayer and discussion, over the years, considerable improvement has been acquired. It has been very important for us to verbally discuss the hurt and embarrassment this problem has created."

"As a wife, my lack of showing affection through touching and caressing, and lack of sexual desire have generated many hurt feelings in the middle and later years of our marriage. Through many agonizing discussions and prayer we have struggled with this problem. God has helped us through prayer to be willing to understand each other, and be willing to die to self. Without our Lord's intervention and support, we may have not have been able to get through those times.

"If we were starting our marriage over again now, as a wife I would not attempt to keep our home in such immaculate condition as to neglect my family's wifely and motherly needs. I would put Christ first, and spend more time with my children and husband. I also would surrender my all to the Lord at the beginning of our marriage, and pay much more attention to my husband, trying more diligently to fulfill his cravings and desires."

"As a husband, I would exercise more self-control in openly expressing my temper, spend even more time with my children in helping them at school, and teaching them the essentials of leading a holy and God-fearing life. I would try to be more sensitive to my wife's fears of my spending too much money on cars and boats.

I failed to clarify to her satisfaction that such transactions had hobby benefits to me, as well as being secure and profitable investments."

Commitment Conquered Casualties

A couple married for fifty-eight years shared:

"I think the most fulfilling thing in my life [the husband's] is the fact that my wife has always been committed to me and to our marriage. We haven't really had a lot of bad experiences in our life. We've had a few casualties, but not anything personal or real sad things except loss of family or that kind of thing. But her commitment to our marriage has really been the most fulfilling thing in my life.

"Our spiritual relationship developed by devotions and attending church and being active in church. We always read in the morning from a devotion book, *Bread of Life*, and we have our prayer.

"We have always been involved in church over the years, as a matter of fact, over our whole life, even before we were married. We pray together and if we ever have a problem, we are right there together. I think that's the key to it, to look to each other. When we got married, you got married and were committed to that. That's the way it was going to be.

"The three things that have helped our marriage were our devotion to each other, we always tried to live within our means, and we tried to be a good mom and dad and not cause too much friction.

"When we were married, people didn't have much. If we came from good families, then we had good families. But we didn't have anything, really. And we didn't expect a lot. The Lord has always been good to us. We have had a real successful life, I think. We were committed to each other to start with and we served the Lord at a church doing different things with young people. But the commitment to serving other people, not just ourselves, was important.

"The greatest adjustment we had to make was first living on our income. You wouldn't believe this today, but I was making $2.50 a week when we first got married. We didn't have any debt, and we saved money on that. It's hard to believe, but that's true. We didn't finish up that way, but we started that way.

"[Second,] we had to adjust, basically, to being committed to the other person. We both did the same thing. That was the first adjustment. You're not free anymore. You're committed to a marriage and to loving each other. So it's a different style within our culture. We don't have that today.

"I had to make the adjustment to being responsible for somebody else, too.

"We never really had a serious problem. I know that sounds unbelievable, but it's true. I'm satisfied. I don't think I would do anything differently if we were able to go back. That's not to say that we're perfect, 'cause we're not. But we're human beings that God deals with, and He's brought us along all these years. We've been married for a long, long time. And I hope we have many more years.

"If we had any advice to give to couples, it would be just be true to each other. Love each other. I remember one thing I told my wife, 'If I did anything wrong, and you want to correct me, don't tell anybody else. Tell me first.' And I think she's always done that. Again, we're not perfect. I'm not trying to play it up.

"I think I would tell young couples today that the first thing to do is to make sure you love each other and that the Lord has brought you together to be one. It's easy to make a commitment today and then break it. But if you make a commitment, it's a commitment."

Joint Commitment to Christ

A couple who had been married fifty-two years shared:

"The thing that's meant the most to us from the start is, we knew the Lord. We knew where we were in the Lord as far as who we were responsible to. And when we joined as one, our priority was to serve the Lord Jesus Christ. So regardless of what situation we find ourselves in or have found ourselves in, it's always been a priority in everything. Every decision is made on the basis of how we can best glorify the Lord Jesus Christ—whether it be moves, of which we made many, or whether it be decisions of a family nature.

"We've had joys and we've had sorrows along the way. Our background was such that I felt like we were conditioned for marriage. We were conditioned for those problems that do come up in our lives: the joys, the sorrows, and the changes that have to take place. And I would say the entire span of our marriage has been something that we are very thankful for. We couldn't ask, I don't think, for anything better.

"The thing about it, is the fact that we had not known each other for too long [when we married]. And it was all during the early war years. There were a lot of decisions that had to be made. Whether you get married before you leave, or you wait. And so I'm confident that we made the right decision. We felt that the Lord led us in that. I was gone for the first four years of our marriage, primarily. Before

I went overseas, she was able to be with me two or three different times, and so I feel like the Lord led in all of this."

Christ Conquers Physical Problems

A couple married fifty-five years shared:

"I think as we look back over our marriage, one of the most fulfilling things has been the enjoyment of each other. And the fact that God led us together and the fact that even to this day we still enjoy being together.

"Then, our trust in each other. I knew he was faithful—just as much as I knew that I was. And then one of the greatest things of course has been our family—our three boys, even through the trials and tribulations of adolescence.

"And we've just always had that pride in each other's accomplishments, whatever we did.

"Our spiritual relationship started before we were married. I was not a Christian and she was. I did find the Lord. And it's been [something] we've been able to hold onto all of our lives. As a matter of fact, I made that decision before we were married, and she agreed with it, that we would make our friends within the church rather than to cultivate my friends' friendship.

"One thing that hindered us was she had an auto accident five weeks after we were married. She was in a body cast for the first year of our marriage. Her spine had been crushed. We were afraid that had we been kids (we were older, I was twenty-six and she was twenty-three) we would not have stayed together, because that was a difficult time. We borrowed everything we could possibly borrow from the bank. We had no money, but we had each other.

"We always have been able to pray together out loud and really, really know what the other was placing before the Lord. I think our spiritual relationship was developed by putting Christ first. He has been the glue that has really held our marriage together through the physical difficulties."

When asked about what they had done to help their marriage, the wife shared:

"It took many years financially to come out of the accident. And I was willing to go back to teaching. Well, I loved it! But I was willing to go back to teach even though we had a family. I think that was a help in our marriage. And I know that I tried to live within our means. I know that I really tried to make a happy home and not [have] a long list of things when he came home to jump on him, whether it be what the kids had done or what happened. It was more of the positive things we shared. Of course we shared the negative, too. We have a plaque that says 'Happiness is homemade.' And that is so true. But unhappiness is also homemade."

The husband shared:

"Well, I guess my work habits had a lot to do with it. I worked long hours, but when I came home, as she said, she had a pleasant place for me to be. She had food ready at the table. And we took lots of trips. We had a happy family. We had some family troubles, maybe. But I think that would be my main thing. We have always kept Christ [at the] center in our family, too."

His wife added:

"The things that I felt that he put into our marriage were his great patience and his unselfishness of putting his family first to his best ability. You always knew what he was going to be like. He wasn't up in the clouds and then down. I could always depend on him being the same. When he came home from work, I didn't have to worry or bite my nails thinking. *What's going to happen today that's going to make him tired?* or anything like that.

"Then his patience with me was wonderful. I was in a brace for about six years off and on, and he had great patience with me and understanding. When I would have to lie down and take it easy for awhile, he never looked at me or came through the room saying, 'Are you down again?' or 'Here you go again' or anything like that.

"Then he had the first of a series of heart attacks before heart surgery when he was just in his early forties. I think our physical difficulties gave us both an understanding. We were both given enough physical limitations, handicaps you may say, even though we've never felt that the other one was handicapped even with his stroke."

They talked about their greatest adjustments. The husband said,

"I think my greatest adjustment for the first six weeks was going from the single life to the married life. I had always been in a home where I did what I wanted, when I wanted, how I wanted. My folks seemed to depend on me for that. And then, being married at twenty-six, I had made my own decisions. I never consulted anyone else. It was hard for me to consider anyone else after I got married, because I could do and come and go. I would always come home, but it was hard for me to let her in on what I was doing, financially or whatever.

"After the [accident], our first year was dictated for us. We had no money; she lost her job. I didn't have enough money. I had a good job, but it wasn't enough to pay the doctor bills. So that was a tough adjustment. It was kind of a forced adjustment. We just did it."

The wife shared,

"I think that was the hardest thing for me, too. If we had just been out of high school, just kids, our marriage probably wouldn't have lasted with my being down and having to be hospitalized for a long time. Then having to go back to living with my parents was an adjustment. When we look back, we are so thankful that it didn't happen when we had our children or later in life.

"And I think, of course, about his stroke, although we're so thankful it isn't worse, we're so thankful his mind wasn't affected. That has been an adjustment. The retirement hasn't been an adjustment for us, because he's never really retired. So this adjusting to his stroke at this time of life has been one of the hardest. But then it's just day by day. We have each other. We look at so many of our friends who have lost their mates. We've just been so thankful. It has been hard for him. Because you grieve with any loss. And acceptance comes after that grief."

Her husband shared,

"I have to fight pity parties. I don't have many, but I do fight having them. When you get an arm that won't work and a leg that won't work, and to begin with, my side wasn't working, and I couldn't talk, you go through quite a bit."

"I Would Have Made More Cornbread"

The husband continued:

"If I were starting my marriage over, I couldn't really think of anything I would do differently. I was in love with her when I married her and I have been every minute since then. But I think I would try communicating [better], sharing what I was doing better. That would be the one thing I would do.

"Also, rather than making a decision, I would talk it over with her before I make it. I think [those are] the only things I would change."

In concluding this interview, his wife said,

"And I think our earlier years and up 'til the recent years in our disagreements, I had the very ugly habit of bringing up past things. Not just disagreeing on what we were disagreeing about, but bringing up, 'Well, if you hadn't done that' or 'If I hadn't done that' or 'If we hadn't done that, such and such wouldn't have been' and all of that. But I did not hold grudges. I truly learned to overcome that. I think I would say sooner, 'I'm sorry.'

"I knew he loved little white navy beans and ham and cornbread.

So I knew that when we needed to make up, I needed to make navy beans and ham and cornbread. And I think I would just make more cornbread."

"We Will Make It Work"

These couples have probably seen and experienced more change in their lifetimes as couples than any previous generation. It wasn't easy for them. But something held them together. Perhaps the theme that runs through these few examples and the hundreds of other stories I've heard over the years is that concept emphasized earlier in the book—commitment. For these couples, divorce was not an option. Instead, there was an attitude of "We will make it work."

I've often wondered what it would be like if we lived in a society that did not have anything called divorce. What if it just didn't exist? You were totally and fully bound and committed for life, till death do you part. But then I realized, we do! As Christians, our perspective of the world is different from that of nonbelievers. Scripture tells us, *"Do not be conformed to this world"* (Rom. 12:2, *NKJV*). We are called to be different. And that difference means building a marriage that lasts, regardless.

Incompatible couples don't have to divorce, for all couples are incompatible to some degree.

An affair doesn't have to destroy a marriage. Yes, it may be painful and violate trust, but it also provides the opportunity for a couple to experience repentance, God's grace, forgiveness, and restoration. I have seen dozens of couples who have recovered from unfaithfulness, and today have strong marriages that reflect the presence of Jesus Christ.

Abusive marriages don't have to result in divorce when there is repentance.

Some couples look for reasons to justify the dissolution of their marriages. I've had couples tell me their marriages are painful because it's chaotic. My response? Let God do what He did in the creation of the world. "In the beginning, God created out of chaos. . . . " And He still does.

I've had couples tell me that dissolving their marriage was necessary to take away the pain and allow them to experience joy. Recently, though, I came across an illustration written by a friend. In all four Gospels there is the story of the rich young ruler who came to Jesus and asked Him what he must do to inherit eternal life. Jesus told him what he must do, but he was not willing to do what Jesus said. The Gospel writers saw what happened, for Mark 10:22 says, *"At this the man's face fell. He went away sad, because he had great wealth"* (NIV).

But in another portion of Scripture (see Luke 19), we read the account of another rich man, Zacchaeus. He accepted Jesus' invitation, repented, and did what Jesus asked.

Describing the differences in these two events, my friend wrote:

One man left in sorrow and the other embraced Jesus with joy. What do these two passages illustrate? Simply this: There is no joy in moving apart—*there is only joy in coming together.*

No one walks away—whether it be from spiritual light, a relationship with God, or a marriage—with happiness. Walking away is always accompanied by sorrow and oftentimes regret. There is no joy found in moving apart. Joy is only found in coming together—in accepting spiritual light, in embracing the arms of the Savior, and in restoring strained relationships. There is joy—true joy—in reconciliation.

Reconciliation is God's grand spiritual design. It is a focal point in Scripture throughout both Old and New Testaments. It is why Jesus came—to provide a way whereby man could be reconciled to God. It is God's plan and goal. It should be our way of life; we are to live reconciled lives. When there is reconciliation, whether it be between God and man or within a marriage, there is joy—true joy.[1]

What about you? What can you do to move closer to Jesus Christ? To your spouse?

Incidentally—what do you want to be able to say about your marriage when you've been married as long as the couples who shared in this chapter? Give it some thought. Now is the time to be doing what needs to be done so you can say, "It was very worthwhile." Perhaps the following poem sums up what the couples in this chapter have been saying and will give you an idea of what can be said after you've been married fifty years.

On the Eve of Their Golden Wedding Day
John C. Bonser

"Our Golden Wedding Day draws near,"
  the husband said.
The elderly woman, smiling, raised her head,
"Will you write me a poem as you used to do?
That's the gift I'd like most from you!"

The old man, agreeing, limped from the room,
Went out on the porch in the twilight's gloom,
Leaned on the railing and reminisced:
"Often we sat here, shared hopes, and kissed.

"Dear Lord, how the years have hurried by—
Those memories of youth make an old man sigh!
Now we grow weary and bent and gray,
What clever words can I possibly say

"To show that I love her just as much
As I did when her cheeks were soft to my touch,
When her eyes were bright and her lips were warm,
And we happily walked with her hand on my arm!"

So the husband stood while the evening breeze
Echoed his sigh through the nearby trees
Till the joys they had shared in days long past
Merged into thoughts he could voice at last,

And he went inside and got paper and pen;
Sat down at the kitchen table and then
Carefully wrote what his wife had desired:
A gift as "golden" as a love inspired.

"Sweetheart, dear wife, my closest friend,
With you my days begin and end.
Though time has stolen strength and youth,
It cannot change this shining truth:
Our love has lasted all these years
While hardships came and sorrow's tears.

We've met each test and gotten by,
And I will love you till I die!
We are not rich in worldly wealth
But we own nothing gained by stealth,
And you remain my greatest treasure,
My source of pride and quiet pleasure.
I wish you all the happiness
With which two loving hearts are blessed;
You were, and are, my choice for life,
My girl, my lady, my sweet wife!"

The poem finished, the husband arose,
Went into the room where his good wife dozed
And tenderly kissing her nodding head,
"Wake up, 'sleeping beauty,' and come to bed!"[2]

Appendix

Instructions

Answer each of these eleven questions. Then fill in the Satisfaction Scale that follows. After both of you have completed these two exercises, select a time when you can be together privately and share your responses. Covering each item may require two or three sessions. Be sure to focus on what you want and what you can do for the future.

1. Describe how much significant time you spend together as a couple, and when you spend it.
2. Describe five behaviors or tasks your partner does that you appreciate.
3. List five personal qualities of your spouse that you appreciate.
4. How frequently do you affirm or reinforce your spouse for the behaviors and qualities described in numbers two and three?
5. List four important requests you have for your spouse at this time. How frequently do you make these requests? What is your spouse's response?
6. List four important requests your spouse has for you at this time. How frequently does he/she make these requests? What is your response?
7. What do you appreciate most about your partner's communication?
8. What do you do to let your spouse know that you love him/her?
9. What does your spouse do to let you know he/she loves you?
10. What has been one of the most fulfilling experiences in your marriage?
11. What personal and marital behaviors would you like to change in yourself?

Satisfaction Scale

Instructions

Use an *X* to indicate your level of satisfaction in each element of your relationship listed below, with 0 = no satisfaction, 5 = average, and 10 = super, fantastic, the best.

Use a circle to indicate what you think your partner's level of satisfaction is at the present time.

1. Our daily personal involvement with each other.
      0   1   2   3   4   5   6   7   8   9   10

2. Our affectionate romantic interaction.
      0   1   2   3   4   5   6   7   8   9   10

3. Our sexual relationship.
      0   1   2   3   4   5   6   7   8   9   10

4. The frequency of our sexual contact.
      0   1   2   3   4   5   6   7   8   9   10

5. My trust in my spouse.
      0   1   2   3   4   5   6   7   8   9   10

6. My spouse's trust in me.
      0   1   2   3   4   5   6   7   8   9   10

7. The depth of our communication together.
      0   1   2   3   4   5   6   7   8   9   10

8. How well we speak one another's language.
      0   1   2   3   4   5   6   7   8   9   10

9. The way we divide chores.
      0   1   2   3   4   5   6   7   8   9   10

10. The way we make decisions.
       0   1   2   3   4   5   6   7   8   9   10

11. The way we manage conflict.
       0   1   2   3   4   5   6   7   8   9   10

12. Adjustment to one another's differences.
    0   1   2   3   4   5   6   7   8   9   10

13. Amount of free time together.
    0   1   2   3   4   5   6   7   8   9   10

14. Quality of free time together.
    0   1   2   3   4   5   6   7   8   9   10

15. Amount of free time apart.
    0   1   2   3   4   5   6   7   8   9   10

16. Our interaction with friends as a couple.
    0   1   2   3   4   5   6   7   8   9   10

17. The way we support each other in rough times.
    0   1   2   3   4   5   6   7   8   9   10

18. Our spiritual interaction.
    0   1   2   3   4   5   6   7   8   9   10

19. Our church involvement.
    0   1   2   3   4   5   6   7   8   9   10

20. The level of our financial security.
    0   1   2   3   4   5   6   7   8   9   10

21. How we manage money.
    0   1   2   3   4   5   6   7   8   9   10

22. My spouse's relationship with my relatives.
    0   1   2   3   4   5   6   7   8   9   10

23. My relationship with my spouse's relatives.
    0   1   2   3   4   5   6   7   8   9   10

Select any three responses that have a score of 3 or less, and indicate what needs to occur for you to have a higher level of satisfaction. Also discuss how you have tried to work on this issue.

Endnotes

THE SECRETS OF A LASTING MARRIAGE

Chapter 1

1. Original source unknown.

2. Thomas F. Jones, *Sex and Love When You're Single Again* (Nashville: Thomas Nelson Publishers, 1990), pp. 93–96.

3. From the book *Finding the Love of Your Life* by Dr. Neil Clark Warren and published by Focus on the Family. Copyright © 1992, Neil Clark Warren, pp. 81,82. All rights reserved. International copyright secured. Used by permission.

4. Jeanette C. Laves and Robert H. Laves, *'Til Death Do Us Part* (Harrington, N.Y.: Park Press, 1986), p. 179, adapted.

5. Bernard I. Morstein, *Paths to Marriage* (Newbury Park, Calif.: Sage Publications, 1986), p. 110. Original source unknown.

6. Warren, *Finding the Love of Your Life*, pp. 97–99, adapted.

7. From *How to Change Your Spouse (Without Ruining Your Marriage)*, © 1994 by H. Norman Wright and Gary Oliver, Ph.D. Published by Servant Publications, Box 8617, Ann Arbor, Michigan 48107. Used with permission, pp. 24–25.

8. Paul Tournier. Original source unknown.

9. Taken from *Growing Strong in the Seasons of Life* by Charles R. Swindoll, Inc. Copyright © 1983 by Charles R. Swindoll, Inc. Used by permission of Zondervan Publishing House, pp. 66, 67.

10. David L. Leuche, *The Relationship Manual* (Columbia, Md.: The Relationship Institute, 1981), p. 3, adapted.

11. David Augsburger, *Sustaining Love* (Ventura, Calif.: Regal Books, 1988), p. 100, adapted.

12. Jones, *Sex and Love When You're Single Again*, pp. 86–87, adapted.

13. H. Norman Wright, *Finding Your Perfect Mate* (Eugene, Oreg.: Harvest House), 1955, material adapted.

14. H. Norman Wright, *Holding on to Romance* (Ventura, Calif.: Regal Books, 1992), p. 81. Used by permission.

15. Mike Mason, *The Mystery of Marriage: As Iron Sharpens Iron* (Portland, Oreg.: Multnomah Books, 1986), p. 65. Used by permission.

16. Rebecca Cutter, *When Opposites Attract* (New York: Dutton, 1994), p. 189, adapted.

17. Wright, *Finding Your Perfect Mate*, portions adapted.

18. Donald Harvey, *The Drifting Marriage* (Grand Rapids: Fleming H. Revell, 1988), p. 213.

19. Warren, *Finding the Love of Your Life*, p. 171.

20. Barbara Ascher, "Above All, Love," *Redbook* (February 1992).

21. *Marriage*, Second Edition by Robert O. Blood, Jr. Copyright © 1969 by The Free Press, a Division of Simon & Schuster, Inc., pp. 10–11. Reprinted with permission of the publisher.

Chapter 2

1. Karen Kayser, *When Love Dies* (New York: The Guilford Press, 1993).

2. Ibid., p. 6, adapted.

3. Ibid., pp. 20–24, adapted.

4. Charles Swindoll, *Come Before Winter* (Portland, Oreg.: Multnomah Books, 1985), p. 239.

5. Peter Krather with Bill Burns, *Affair Prevention* (New York: MacMillan Publishing Co., 1981), p. 68.

6. Kayser, *When Love Dies*, pp. 21–87, adapted.

7. From *How to Change Your Spouse (Without Ruining Your Marriage)*, © 1994 by H. Norman Wright and Gary Oliver, Ph.D. Published by Servant Publications, Box 8617, Ann Arbor, Michigan 48107. Used with permission, p. 209.

8. Adapted from Robert Paul Lieberman, Eugene Wheeler and Nancy Sanders, "Behavioral Therapy for Marital Disharmony: an Educational Approach," *Journal of Marriage and Family Counseling* (October 1976): 383–389.

9. Kayser, *When Love Dies*, p. 153, adapted.

10. Ibid., p. 152.

11. Lewis B. Smedes, *Forgive and Forget* (New York: HarperCollins, 1984), pp. 128–129.

Chapter 3

1. John Gottman, *Why Marriages Succeed or Fail* (New York: Simon & Schuster, 1994), pp. 41–47, adapted.

2. Ibid., p. 57, adapted.

3. Ibid., adapted.

4. Ibid., pp. 58–61, adapted.

5. Jim Smoke, *Facing 50* (Nashville: Thomas Nelson, 1994), pp. 40–41.

6. Paul Pearsall, *The Ten Laws of Lasting Love* (New York: Simon & Schuster, 1993), pp. 298–299, adapted.

7. Clifford Notarius and Howard Markman, *We Can Work It Out* (New York: G. P. Putnam's Sons, 1993), p. 28, adapted.

8. Ibid., pp. 123–124, adapted.

9. Dale Carnegie, *How to Win Friends and Influence People* (New York: Pocket Books, 1936), pp. 41–42.

10. Gottman, *Why Marriages Succeed or Fail,* pp. 70–102, adapted.

Chapter 4

1. Donald Harvey, *The Drifting Marriage* (Grand Rapids: Fleming H. Revell, 1988), p. 11.

2. George Barna, *The Power of Vision* (Ventura, Calif.: Regal Books, 1992), pp. 21–22. Used by permission.

3. Ibid., pp. 28–29, adapted.

4. Phil Grand, "The Task Before Us," *European Bookseller* (May/ June 1991): 48, adapted.

5. Reproduced by permission from GOLF MY WAY by Jack Nicklaus with Ken Bowden, published by Simon & Schuster, New York, NY, 1974, p. 79.

6. *Living Above the Level of Mediocrity,* Charles Swindoll, Copyright © 1987 Word, Inc., Dallas, Texas. All rights reserved, pp. 94–95.

7. Barna, *The Power of Vision,* pp. 96–98, adapted.

8. Charles Stanley, *The Source of My Stength* (Nashville: Thomas Nelson, 1994), p. 166.

9. Sheila West, *Beyond Chaos* (Colorado Springs: NavPress Publishing, 1991), p. 60.

10. Taken from a "Back to the Bible" radio broadcast.

11. Charles R. Swindoll, *Come Before Winter . . . and Share My Hope* (Portland, Oreg.: Multnomah Books, 1985), pp. 331–332.

12. Michelle Weiner-Davis, *Divorce Busting* (New York: Summit Books, 1992), pp. 109–110, adapted.

13. Edward R. Dayton and Ted Engstrom, *Strategy for Living* (Ventura, Calif.: Regal Books, 1976), pp. 55–56, adapted.

14. James H. Othuis, *Keeping Our Troth* (San Francisco: Harper San Francisco, 1986), pp. 133–139.

15. From the book *When Love Is Not Enough* by Steve Arterburn

and Jim Burns and published by Focus on the Family. Copyright © 1992, Stephen Arterburn and Jim Burns, p. 6. All rights reserved. International copyright secured. Used by permission.

16. Julie Hatsell Wales, "Letters," *Marriage Partnership* (Winter 1991): 8.

Chapter 5

1. Aaron T. Beck, *Love Is Never Enough* (New York: HarperCollins, 1988), pp. 108–110, adapted.

2. *Webster's New World Dictionary.* Third College Edition (New York: Simon & Schuster, 1994), p. 1,259.

3. Gary J. Oliver and H. Norman Wright, *How to Change Your Spouse (Without Ruining Your Marriage)* (Ann Arbor: Servant Publications, 1994), pp. 52–53, adapted.

4. Beck, *Love Is Never Enough*, pp. 155–160, adapted.

5. Paul W. Coleman, *The Forgiving Marriage* (Chicago: Contemporary Books, 1989), pp. 47–52, adapted.

6. Ibid., pp. 22–23.

7. H. Norman Wright, *How to Speak Your Spouse's Language* (Grand Rapids: Fleming H. Revell, 1986), pp. 148–151, adapted.

Chapter 6

1. Taken from *Transitions* by Charles M. Sell. Copyright © 1985. Moody Bible Institute of Chicago. Moody Press. Used by permission, p. xi.

2. Clark Blackburn and Norman Lobsenz, *How to Stay Married* (New York: Cowles Books, 1968), p. 196.

3. Jim Smoke, *Facing 50* (Nashville: Thomas Nelson, 1994), pp. 148–149.

4. Patrick Morley, *Two-Part Harmony* (Nashville: Thomas Nelson, 1994), pp. 234–235.

5. Reprinted from *Losses in Later Life* by R. Scott Sullender, © 1989 by R. Scott Sullender. Used by permission of Paulist Press, p. 54.

6. Ibid., p. 3, adapted.

7. Harold Myra, "An Ode to Marriage," *Moody* magazine (May 1979): 60–62.

8. H. Norman Wright, *Recovering from the Losses of Life* (Grand Rapids: Fleming H. Revell, 1991), pp. 15–17.

9. Sullender, *Losses in Later Life*, pp. 54–55, adapted.

10. Ibid., p. 61, adapted.

11. Mel Roman and Patricia E. Raley, *The Indelible Family* (New York: Rawson, Wade Publishers, Inc., 1980), pp. 205–206, adapted.

12. Thomas Bradley Robb, *The Bonus Years,* Foundation for Ministry with Older Persons (Valley Forge, Penn.: The Judson Press, 1968), p. 64, adapted.

13. David C. Morley, *Halfway up the Mountain* (Grand Rapids: Fleming H. Revell, 1979), p. 26.

14. Michelle Weiner-Davis, *Divorce Busting* (New York: Summit Books, 1992), p. 45.

15. Some material in this chapter has been adapted from H. Norman Wright, *Seasons of a Marriage* (Ventura, Calif.: Regal Books, 1982); and *Family Is Still a Great Idea* (Ann Arbor: Servant Publications, 1992).

Chapter 7

1. David Augsburger, *Sustaining Love* (Ventura, Calif.: Regal Books, 1988), p. 40.

2. Concepts adapted from Otto Kroeger and Janet M. Thuesen, *Type Talk* (New York: Delacorte Press, 1988) and *Sixteen Ways to Love Your Lover* (New York: Delacorte Press, 1994); and David L. Luecks, *Prescription for Marriage* (Columbia, Md.: The Relationship Institute, 1989).

3. Augsburger, *Sustaining Love,* p. 38, adapted.

4. Ibid., pp. 54, 56.

Chapter 8

1. Clifford Notarious and Howard Markman, *We Can Work It Out* (New York: G. P. Putnam's Sons, 1993), pp. 70–73, adapted.

2. Alan S. Gurman and David G. Rice, *Couples in Conflict* (New York: Jason Aronson, Inc., 1975), pp. 268–269, adapted from "A Behavioral Exchange Model for Marital Counseling" by Alan F. Rappaport and Janet E. Harrel.

3. Michelle Weiner-Davis, *Divorce Busting* (New York: Simon & Schuster, 1992), pp. 130–133, 126–128, adapted.

4. Ibid., pp. 148–149.

5. John Gray, *What Your Mother Couldn't Tell You and Your Father Didn't Know* (New York: HarperCollins, 1994), pp. 176–179, adapted.

6. Elizabeth Achtemeier, *The Committed Marriage* (Philadelphia: Westminster Press, 1976), p. 41.

Chapter 9

1. Donald R. Harvey, *The Spiritually Intimate Marriage* (Grand Rapids: Fleming H. Revell, 1991), p. 24.

2. Ibid., pp. 42–45, adapted.

3. Ibid., pp. 45–46.

4. Howard and Jeanne Hendricks, general editors, with LaVonne Neff, *Husbands and Wives*, (Wheaton, Ill.: Victor Books, 1988), p. 158.

5. Harvey, *The Spiritually Intimate Marriage*, pp. 54–56, adapted.

6. Dwight Small, *After You've Said I Do* (Grand Rapids: Fleming H. Revell, 1968), pp. 243–244.

7. Paul Tournier, *The Healing of Persons* (New York: HarperCollins, 1965), pp. 88–89.

8. Small, *After You've Said I Do*, p. 244.

9. Louis H. Evans, *Your Marriage—Duel or Duet?* (Grand Rapids: Fleming H. Revell, 1972), pp. 98–99.

10. From "How to Start and Keep It Going," by Charlie and Martha Shedd, cited by Fritz Ridenour in "Praying Together," *The Marriage Collection* (Grand Rapids: Zondervan Publishers, 1989), pp. 442–443.

11. Carey Moore and Pamela Roswell Moore, *If Two Shall Agree* (Grand Rapids: Chosen Books, Baker Book House, 1992), p. 111.

12. James C. Dobson, *Love for a Lifetime* (Portland, Oreg.: Multnomah Books, 1987), pp. 51–52.

13. Lee Roberts, *Praying God's Will for My Marriage* (Nashville: Thomas Nelson Publishers, 1994), pp. 1, 9, 19, 28, 115, 162, 227, 267.

14. Harry Hollis Jr., *Thank God for Sex* (Nashville: Broadman Press, 1975), pp. 109–111.

15. Moore and Roswell Moore, *If Two Shall Agree*, pp. 194–195.

16. Small, *After You've Said I Do*, p. 243.

Chapter 10

1. Donald Harvey, Surviving Betrayal (Grand Rapids: Baker Books, 1995), pp. 36–37.

2. Used by permission of the author, John C. Bonser, of Florissant, Missouri.

Can You Hear Me Now?

Harnessing the Power of Your Vocal Impact in 31 Days

By Kate Peters

A comprehensive book that will help you understand how your voice impacts your ability to get what you want, with exercises and suggestions that you can use TODAY.

Narrative Development
1077 Pacific Coast Hwy. #341
Seal Beach, CA 90740

Library of Congress Pre-assigned Control Number pending
Peters, Kate.
   Can You Hear me Now? / by Kate Peters.
     p. cm.
     ISBN 0-9776407-0-1

Printed in the United States of America

www.VocalImpact.net

Cover Design by Gail Richards
Layout by Chad Huebner

Attention: Corporations and Schools
This book is available at quantity discounts when purchased in bulk for educational use, business, and training. For information, please contact Narrative Development Corp.

Narrative Development

This book is dedicated to the late Roger Ardrey, whose expert guidance and friendship helped me understand how to use my voice and inspired me to help others do the same.

Table of Contents

Acknowledgements

My father was a man of few words; my mother was a woman of many. They had been married for nearly 50 years at the time of my father's death. The miracle of their marriage was that they were in love to that day. When asked the secret of their successful relationship, both would answer, "Great communication." My parents inspired this book.

During my college years, I studied voice, diction, acting, and psycholinguistics. I began teaching voice in graduate school and have had many talented and receptive students over the years. In addition, my experience as a performer has been vast and varied. A three-year job in corporate America was an education in communication all by itself! My teachers, students, audiences, co-workers, and the experience of Life itself informed this book. I am grateful to my employees at Narratus and all the members of Team Cabaret—past, present, and future—for what they have taught me. I would especially like to thank the late Roger Ardrey, Seth Riggs, and Dr. Ronald McCauley.

I became acutely aware of the problems that poor communication can create in relationships when I went through a divorce. The experience created an urgency within me to discover the principles of effective conversation and conflict resolution. My children will say that I became obsessed with the search. In fact, I knew I might have gone too far when, in the midst of a disagreement, my daughter turned to me and said, "And don't use any of your communication tricks on me!" However, I see plenty of evidence that our family has benefited from my obsession, and I think they will finally agree with me. My family—especially Katy, Katherine, Joey, and Ali who have had to live it—actively supported the research of this book.

Acknowledgements

Producing a book is a process that takes many talented people. I wish to acknowledge the work of the following professionals who made this book a reality: Tim Sweeney for helping me begin the transformation from files to chapters, Adrienne Cooksey for her help with permissions clearance, Christine Frank for the index and the enthusiastic response to my book, and Gail Richards for the cover art and her sense of humor. I am extremely appreciative of Rick Schank for his thoughtful consideration of the design of the book, and to Kris Elftmann for seeing the possibilities. Thanks go to George Kyle who gave me advice as well as moral support. I am extremely grateful to Gary Hernandez, whose editing was thoughtful, educational, and very affirming. I also want to thank his daughter who helped ensure the exercises made sense by trying them out. Jan King of E-women Publishing Network gave me expert guidance maneuvering the book publishing waters. Above all, I owe a huge debt of gratitude to Chad Huebner who worked intelligently and artistically on this project with me for many months, enduring last minute changes, complete "about-faces," and the drudgery of picky details, not to mention late night trips to Kinko's.

Finally, there is one special person whose presence in my life keeps me happy as well as honest. His ever-present love and encouragement are the reasons that I wrote the book. His curiosity and passionate pursuit of Life inspire me everyday. He gives me emotional and financial support, and he always "has my back." I am grateful to Doug for sharing his life with me and encouraging me to share what I know. Without him, this book would still be an idea scattered across separate folders on my desktop. Thank you, Doug.

All my life I have played with the sounds that I create with my voice. I am a singer, an actor, and a public speaker. I'm also a mom, a business woman, and a teacher. I have noticed that I change the way I use my voice according to the role I am in. This doesn't mean that I am pretending—it means that the sound of my voice is affected by my perceptions and emotions. And so is yours.

Try listening to people speaking on the phone while you are in the room. You can't see to whom they are speaking, but you can hear their voice change as they converse with different people. And that's what this book is about. It's about understanding how your voice represents you and works for you; it's about gaining control of those sounds and deliberately changing them to help you create the life you want; it's about taking charge of your voice, one of your most valuable possessions, and making it an asset in your relationships with others.

"Open the door, dear children; your mother is here, and has brought something back with her for each of you." But the little kids knew that it was the wolf, by the rough voice. "We will not open the door," cried they, "you are not our mother. She has a soft, pleasant voice, but your voice is rough; you are the wolf!"'

Grimm Brothers,"The Wolf and the Seven Little Kids"

Introduction ·

Can You Hear Me Now? is about you. It celebrates the opportunity you have to be heard in a world where there is a lot of noise. It is my sincere belief that everyone has a voice that needs to be heard; it is my special pleasure to help you use your voice so that it can be heard. Ultimately, this book is about learning to use your voice to get what you want.

"...words mean more than what is set down on paper. It takes the human voice to infuse them with the shades of deeper meaning."

–Maya Angelou, *I Know Why the Caged Bird Sings*

"*The impact of your voice on your listeners is equally important to your success, if not more, than the clothes you are wearing and the words you are speaking.*"

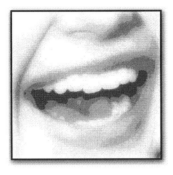

Your Voice,
Your Impact,
Your Choice

Your Voice, Your Impact, Your Choice

Like many others, you have dreams, goals, and aspirations. You want to be successful, you want to motivate others, you want to have an impact on the world around you. But what does your voice have to do with that? In recent years, more and more people have given a great deal of attention to personal power and how it relates to an individual's success. If you are like other success-minded people, you've already focused on improving your image/brand by dressing for success, increasing your self-confidence through risk-taking exercises, appreciating yourself more through affirmation, and boosting your personal power through motivational reading. Yet you can do all of these things and still fail to convince others of your personal power if you don't take your voice into account.

You know that communication is important. You know that there are communication styles that work and those that don't. You may have gone to seminars, read books, and even studied professional presenters, and yet you still are not getting the results you want. You're still not reaching your potential in sales, you're still not getting the audience to respond, and you're still not communicating effectively with your partner. What you may not realize is that your voice may be hindering your success. Worse, you may be running out of time to fix the problem.

Your Voice, Your Impact, Your Choice

For the first 30 seconds that you speak, people are assessing your voice rather than really hearing what you say. They are trying to see how your voice aligns with how you look and how you present yourself. If they don't know you, they're trying to figure out who you are. If they do know you, they're trying to figure out what's going on with you. The impact of your voice on your listeners is equally important to your success, if not more, than the clothes you are wearing and the words you are speaking.

The good news is that there are plenty of things you can do to improve your voice and, consequently, improve your chances for success in all you do. By improving your vocal skills, you will have more tools to deliver your message. By improving your vocal skills, you will be able to speak more clearly, more convincingly, and more often for longer periods of time. By improving your vocal skills, you will improve your chances of success by minimizing vocal distractions. People will be more likely to hear what you want them to hear, because you will be able to create a sound that will immediately make it easier for others to want to listen to you.

Your Voice, Your Impact, Your Choice

If your sound doesn't match how you represent yourself, people may question your integrity. If you want to close a million dollar sale, you may want to sound friendly, but you can't sound like you are joking around. A big burly man with a high-pitched, nasal voice may be amusing to many people, but he may also be irritating to others. A woman with a percussive speech pattern may seem pushy, while a man with the same kind of speech pattern may seem strong.

Many people fail in their communication simply because the inflections, pitch, or speed of their words don't align with their message. If you need to negotiate in your work, you need to have a speech pattern that supports negotiations. If you want others to trust you, you have to sound trustworthy. Your pitch, speed of delivery, and intensity of sound can imply such things as friendliness or hostility, tolerance or prejudice, and weakness or strength.

Your voice, your impact, your choice

You are not stuck with the voice you have. What we call "voice" is actually a set of integrated muscles, cavities, and cartilage within the body. And even though voices are as varied and unique as hair color and eye color, they are as moldable and flexible as the rest of us. You go to the gym to get the rest of your body in shape--you can work out to get your voice in shape, too. Exercising your body makes you stronger and more confident; exercising your voice makes it stronger and more appealing. A strong, vibrant voice makes you sound more confident.

Our voices are created through imitation. We imitate sounds we hear. Many successful people have imitated the actions, sounds, and styles of their mentors. Perhaps you have, too. Imitation has probably helped you, but it's not the only answer. Let's face it, you are unique. There is not another person on the planet like you. You may look like your father, but you are not him. Likewise, there is not another voice exactly like yours. You may sound a little like your sister, but you'll never sound exactly like her. Similarly, your thoughts offer a different perspective on life. The world wants to hear what you have to offer, and the world wants to hear your unique voice.

Summary:

Perhaps you are reading this because the title has piqued your curiosity. Many CEO's, public statesmen, and great conversationalists have learned the value of training their voices.

Your Voice, Your Impact, Your Choice

They have learned that aligning their vocal image with their sense of purpose and intention often results in impact beyond their expectation. The same can be true for you.

The fact is, you are already projecting a vocal image. You are already making an impact on others with your voice, but the impact you are making with your voice may not be the one you want to make. So, change it. If you want to change your voice, you have to be aware of how you sound and what you like and don't like about your voice. To accomplish this, you have to listen to yourself and others. You have to become aware of the sound you are creating and the effect it has on others. Most importantly, you have to be willing to change the sound. And finally, you have to know how to make that change in such a way that you don't create problems with your voice.

The good news is you have the power to align your voice with your image. You can choose to have your voice more fully support your sense of who you are and what you want to do with your life, and you can have a healthy, vibrant sound. This book is full of ideas, tools, techniques, and exercises that can help you. Let's get started.

"People have to talk about
something just to keep their
voice boxes in working order
so they'll have good voice boxes
in case there's ever anything
really meaningful to say."

—Kurt Vonnegut, Jr., *Cat's Cradle*

"In spite of the proliferation of e-mails and junk mail, most of our communication still requires the use of the human voice."

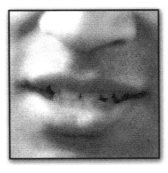

Communicating Well

Communicating Well

Conversation vs. personal expression

Before we explore the actual sound of your voice, let's discuss the basics of good communication. The truth is, much of our verbal communication is meaningless noise. We speak without thinking, we add verbal filler to our thoughts, and we pontificate our personal ideas rather than exchange them with others. We then wonder why our relationships are a mess and why we can't get others to listen to us. Well, there is a difference between personal expression and conversation.

Conversation is an exchange and requires a response from others.

Personal expression represents a point of view, but does not require a response from others.

When it comes to your voice, conversation and personal expression are both important, but most people get the two confused. For example, in conflict we want cooperation, but we often orate and thus close off any chance of exchange. Other times we may want to state our case but leave ourselves open for unintended conversation, thus undermining our position.

Communicating Well

To communicate well you need to be clear about how to use conversation and personal expression.

Good conversation requires being appreciative of another point of view. It involves an exchange of ideas or points of view and is used in dialog with others

- To work effectively as a team
- To understand another's needs and desires
- To minimize conflict
- To negotiate
- To invite learning

Good personal expression requires confidence in speaking. It presents the point of view of the speaker and is used in solo situations

- To lecture to or educate another
- To express a point of view where dialog is not required
- To perform as an actor
- To orate
- To describe the value of a process, system, product or even a person

Good conversation and personal expression have three things in common: They require you to listen, to be clear, and to have vocal skills that support your words.

Communicating Well

Listening

To be a good communicator, you need to be a good listener. To be a good listener, you need to be objective and to want to hear what others have to say. Listening is essential to all communication -- it supports the sharing of ideas and the expression of points of view. It is obvious to most that good conversation involves listening to others, but few realize that listening is essential even in personal expression. Although many question the wisdom of talking to yourself, it is always important to listen to yourself.

> "*Don't use meaningless exclamations, such as 'Oh, my!' 'Oh, crackey!', etc.*"
>
> —Oliver Bell Bunce, *Don't, A Manual of Mistakes and Improprieties More or Less Prevalent in Conduct and Speech*

Developing good listening skills for conversation

All listening is basically biased. We bring our own story or history to whatever we do. Often, we listen to others so that we can find a space to jump in with our comments. We forget what the other person is saying because we are so focused on our personal expression.

Yet there are many benefits to actually hearing what another person is saying. Some of them are as follows:

- You create an environment in which people can express themselves more clearly. By confirming what you have heard the other person say before you comment on their remarks, and by insisting that they do the same, you minimize confusion and misunderstandings in conversation.
- You create a more relaxed environment for exploration and learning. When people feel heard, they are more likely to put aside their own defenses and be open to productive discussion.
- You ensure better understanding. If you can wait to prepare a response until you are sure that you have heard the other person clearly, your response is more likely to be appropriate.
- You become more present in the conversation. You have to pay attention in order to listen. You will learn more and be able to add more to the conversation.
- You develop better relationships with those to whom you are listening. By listening carefully to others and taking the time to validate that what you have heard is what they said, you create an atmosphere of trust in which others feel they are important to you.

Start using at least one of these ideas for an entire day, in every conversation you have. If you already do these things, teach someone else how to improve their communication skills by using what you know.

Communicating Well

For most of us, good listening in conversations is something that needs to be learned. It is more than just being quiet while someone else speaks. It is listening with intent to hear, not just reply. Here are some ideas that can help you become a better listener.

- Ask open questions without judgment or criticism so that others stay open to conversation.
- Refrain from telling others your experiences until asked or until it's your turn.
- Rephrase what the other person has said to reflect your understanding and to be sure you have heard what they said.
- Honor the speaker; don't interrupt. Let the person complete all they have to say and allow a pause before you respond.
- Hear what the other speakers are saying from their perspective rather than your own. Try to remove your own filters.
- Ask open questions, e.g., How...? What...? And I wonder if...? Whenever possible, try to end what you've said with an open question that encourages others to add their thoughts or ideas.
- Honor time commitments. Be on time. If you have agreed to meet for an hour and need more time, schedule another meeting.
- Tell the truth without malice. If you are angry, cool down before talking so that you don't say something you may later regret.
- Avoid judgmental remarks. Such remarks infer that you think you are more important, smarter, or more powerful than others. Judgmental remarks create a situation where others are less open to honest conversation.
- Use "I" words when stating your perspective. For example: Say "When you speak to me that way, I have a hard time believing that you have heard what I told you," instead of "You never listen

to me." Or you might say, "I like the way you stated that," instead of "That's the way you should say that." Speak about what you feel or think. You cannot really know what another person is feeling, even though you may think you can.

Developing good listening skills for personal expression

You depend on your voice to help you communicate, so you need to understand that your voice can either be attractive to others or it can be unattractive, that is, stressed or strained. Just as your physical appearance, your voice can represent you either effectively or ineffectively. The question is, how do you make the switch from creating your voice through reaction and imitation to creating your voice through thoughtful application of knowledge? The answer is, you start by listening objectively.

The original purpose of your voice was not speech. The muscles and cavities you use for speech were intended for chewing, swallowing, and breathing—in short, for survival. Humans were driven to develop verbal skills as a need to communicate more effectively. Speech was, and still is, a secondary function. Thus the only "natural" way to speak is what you learn through imitation. However, in the process of studying language development, singing techniques, and speech pathology, humans have discovered that some sounds work for them and some don't, and some work well under one circumstance but not under another. Research has shown that a person cannot re-create a vocal sound that they cannot hear.

Communicating Well

Ear-voice coordination is as important to a speaker or singer as eye-hand coordination is to a tennis player. To learn more about the way the ear and voice work together, please refer to the books in the bibliography by Alfred Tomatis and Don Campbell.

Here are some ways to apply listening skills to develop better personal expression:

- Sing often, even if you don't feel that you have a good voice. The act of singing will strengthen your vocal muscles.
- Give talks. Join a public speaking class or club. Volunteer to be an advocate for your business or church.
- Respond to what you hear. Express your thoughts when there is an opportunity. Jump in when you have the opportunity to share your perspective.
- Practice saying hello to people in different ways. Try "Good morning," "Hi, there," "Hello. How are you today?" Pay attention to the different responses you get from others.
- Practice a talk you are preparing using many different inflections and pitch variations in your delivery. Listen to yourself as you do this and then try something else.
- Listen to yourself as you speak and analyze what you are doing. Record yourself talking to someone else or while speaking extemporaneously on a topic. Then listen to the recording and analyze how it sounds and what impression the delivery gives you. You may want to use some of the questions in the vocal image journal provided in this book.
- Listen to the voices of others to compare your voice with theirs. Do you speak higher or lower? What expressions do others use that you don't?

- Work with a voice professional. If you want to improve or heal your voice, it's always helpful to work with a vocal professional. Be sure that you feel comfortable with them and that they have solid credentials as a technician. Degrees in speech therapy or applied voice are such credentials.
- Imitate your favorite actor, singer, politician, teacher, etc. Try to determine if your voice feels different from your normal vocal delivery.

Clarifying Intention

Good communication requires clarity; clarity requires clear intention. Too often we go into a presentation or a discussion without a clear intention for our communication. We are then surprised that our message comes across confusing and ineffective. Unclear intentions result in unclear communication.

Intention guides communication just as it guides action. For example, you might go into a discussion with the intention of solving a problem, sharing ideas about a favorite subject, or just to become acquainted with others. You may develop a talk with the intention of educating, entertaining, or soliciting. You may sing a song to move people, make them laugh, or just help them to relax. The reason you do what you do is your intention.

There are exercises later in this book that will help you develop good listening skills for personal expression. Spend some time every day doing just that.

Communicating Well

Discovering intention in conversation

Discovering your intention in communication is sometimes more difficult than it would seem. It requires you to be clear about what you want and how you want others to perceive you. As you uncover your intentions, you may begin to see how you unwittingly sabotage your own communication. For example, if you believe you have the intention of closing a sale, but your real intention is to get the other person to like you, you may not have as much success closing the sale. In addition, you may not get the other person to like you. On the other hand, if you set your intention on closing the sale, you will probably be more open to creative ways to accomplish your goal, and you may also gain a friend.

Think of a recent conversation where you felt that you did not get the response for which you were hoping. What was your original intention for having the conversation? Did you align your remarks and responses with your intention? Did your intention somehow change during the conversation? What did you actually accomplish? Is what you accomplished different than what you originally intended? What do you think your real intention was?

Write your thoughts here: _____

_____

_____

Now think of a recent conversation that was successful for you. What was your intention going into it? Did that change? What did you hope to accomplish? In retrospect, was your intention the same as what was accomplished? If it wasn't, then what do you think your real intention was?

Write your thoughts here: _____

_____

_____

_____

_____

_____

_____

"Speak when you are angry and you will make the best speech you will ever regret."

–Ambrose Bierce

Communicating Well

When you are planning to have a discussion, especially if it is an important one, be sure to think through your intention.

Begin by asking yourself what you hope to accomplish. Be as clear as possible about what you want the end result to be. It can be helpful to imagine the discussion is already finished, and envision the most desirable conclusion. You may wish to reach a decision. You may hope to enlist others in a project or raise some money. You may want them to buy your product or agree to help you with a task. You may want people to leave with a certain feeling. Perhaps you want them to leave knowing what action to take. You may want them to leave feeling satisfied and happy. Whatever the desired conclusion, be as clear about it as possible so you can plan the discussion with the results in mind.

Be sure to state your intention clearly to yourself and to the others involved. For example, if you are interested in coming to an agreement with a group, state what the desired goal is, such as, "We are going to take a couple of hours today to create a plan for the meeting next Friday." You will be surprised what a powerful tool this simple act can be.

Take time to invite your partners in conversation to state their own intentions or to agree on an intention that works for all of you. Write it down for everyone to see. For example, if you are planning a meeting, you might ask everyone to state what they hope to accomplish in that meeting. List all of the intentions people bring to the table and prioritize them. You may discover you have an overall intention and several lesser intentions. Everyone will feel included, and it will be more possible to have the kind of conversation you want to have.

As the conversation progresses, remind yourself of your intention and check to see if you are staying focused on it. Don't let the conversation get stuck on details that can be handled by a different discussion or by a sub-committee.

If you find that your intention changes during the conversation, identify the new intention in order to clarify your communication. Be open with the change. For example, if my intention is to plan a course of action with your help, but you don't want to help, my intention probably needs to change. I might say, "Now, I want to understand why you don't want to help."

It is possible to get to a solution instead of staying "stuck" in a difference of opinion by setting this as one of your intentions: We agree that we can disagree and still find an answer.

Communicating Well

Discovering intention in personal expression

Personal expression, as described earlier, is a solo act. From that standpoint, your intention in personal expression will usually involve the representation of your personal perspective. You will seek to persuade, to inform, or to entertain others. However, if you truly need or want to communicate something, you need to consider others in your intention. Although their intention may not be the same as yours, it may intersect with yours. This can be important for communication. For example, just because you have a solution to sell, doesn't mean they intend to buy from you, even if they need a solution.

Be careful not to make the mistake of thinking you have something to say that others need or want to hear. If you make this assumption, you will miss out on the opportunity to consider how to frame your message for your particular audience. For instance, a political comedian may be hysterically funny to one party and offensive to another. No matter how persuasive, a pharmaceutical rep may have a hard time convincing a convention of naturopaths that his product is viable. The most eloquent teacher in the world will not necessarily persuade a group of restless middle school teenagers to sit and listen to him for hours.

Communication always involves an audience. You can think of intention in communication of personal expression as something akin to good marketing. You need to know who you are, what you do, and why anyone should care. When you consider these points, you can usually get quickly to the heart of what it will take to make an impact on your listeners.

As a performer on stage, I expect that the audience is usually there out of a desire to see the performance. However, on one occasion my show became the destination for a large group of high school students who were the target audience of an educational outreach program. Although my intention was to perform the show and get a good response from the audience, I mistakenly thought that their intention was to sit and watch the show. In truth, their intention was to take advantage of a day away from the normal grind of school. The hoops and hollers and cat calls were totally different from the usual audience response. I quickly changed my intention from performing well to merely surviving that afternoon!

But what about communicators who have persuaded their audience to listen when the audience didn't want to listen? A client of mine was a speaker at a large convention. He was to give his presentation on the last day of the three-day conference. His intention was to motivate the attendees to use the information they had been given during the convention. When he walked onto the stage, he knew right away that he had a difficult task in front of him because everyone else was just as tired and overloaded as he was. Nevertheless, he began his speech with a joke, as usual,

Communicating Well

and moved on to his next point, illustrated by his elaborate PowerPoint presentation. The audience was restless, on their phones, and some were even talking. He sensed that their intention was just to get through this final session and go home. He believed that he had a job to do and that it was an important one. So instead of proceeding as planned, he stopped, turned off the projector, put down his notes and walked out in front of his podium.

Looking out at his audience, he said, "I think I am forgetting why I am here, and so are you." He paused, and everyone became silent. "We are here to celebrate the accomplishments of this great company and figure out how to move it to the next level. Now, I know that we are all tired so I'm going to do this a little differently than I had planned." He then proceeded to break the crowd down into small groups, and give them topics to discuss amongst themselves on which they would report to the larger group. People began responding. When the session was finished, some of the groups even decided to finish their discussions in the restaurant. He had succeeded in aligning their intentions with his and instead of losing the audience, his session was remembered as amongst the best in the conference.

His achievement is a testament to the power of aligned intention. It is the direct result of the speaker's ability to use his voice to communicate and then secure an audience alignment with a clear and focused intention.

Communicating Well

When you speak in front of others, you will have more impact if you consider your intention when planning your presentation. Build it in to your talk and your actions. State it out loud. Let it guide your choices in physical expression as well. Granted, such preparation will be difficult when you are asked to speak on the spur of the moment. In those situations, you can still find an intention to help you communicate effectively.

Consider who your audience is and why they are there. Your intention can be seen as the intersection of why you are there and what you have been asked to do. Ask yourself the following question, "Why should my audience care about what I am saying?" Here you are considering the value of the content of your message. Then consider the intention of your audience by asking, "Why are they listening to me?" Here you are considering what convinced your audience to take a seat at your presentation in the first place. Again, your intention should reside in the place where these two answers intersect.

Communicating Well

Summary: To realize your potential vocal impact, you must communicate well. The key to effective communication is clearly understanding your intention and how that intention aligns with your listener. Below are some tools that can help you identify and remain aware of your intention. Try at least one of these now.

1. Create a life purpose statement and a work purpose statement. A purpose statement is a brief description of what you do and why you do it. For example, my work purpose statement is "to find the strengths of each person's voice and to help them express themselves in ways that are supportive of their lives and their work, thus enabling people to bring more of themselves and their talents to the richness of the human experience."

2. Once you have created these statements, keep them in your notebook, date book, laptop, and on your desk— places where you will be able to read them throughout the day as you prepare talks, sales pitches, or discussions.

3. Create a personal statement of intention for each project or product you represent. Keep in mind, a personal statement of intention is different from a purpose statement. A personal statement of intention is specific to the project or conversation at hand, but is also related to your purpose statement. For example, my purpose as an artist is "to show how our voices are at once unique and the same." However, my intention in talking to a an online distributor may be to persuade them that they want to market my music. On the other hand, I will have a different intention when I am in conversation with a fan: I may intend for them to like me, download my music, or attend a concert. In all these instances, my personal statement shapes my communication

with others. Discovering and remembering your intention will help you stay on track and accomplish more.

4. At the next event you attend, when people ask what you do, instead of answering with your job title, answer them with a personal statement of intention, a personal mission statement, or your intention for attending the event.

5. If you are an artist, create an artist profile statement that describes who you are and what message is in your art. Use that to shape your intention in every personal communication about your art. For more information on the concept of an artist profile, refer to the work of Tim Sweeney in the bibliography.

6. Research the purpose of the organizations and businesses with whom you communicate. Find ways in which their purpose and your intention intersect. Use that as a filter in your communication with them.

Communicating Well

Use the space here to create a life or work statement of purpose. Use the statement to guide your personal expression:

Now create another version of your statement of purpose. Limit the statement to 20 words or less. You are creating an "elevator pitch," an answer that describes your purpose quickly and clearly in answer to the question, "Who are you and what do you do?"

_____

_____

_____

Now create a statement of intention for a conversation or presentation you are planning in the near future. Let your statement of purpose guide your statement of intention.

_____

_____

_____

_____

_____

_____

_____

_____

Communicating Well

The sound of your voice is important to good communication

In spite of the proliferation of e-mails and social media posts, most of our communication still requires the use of the human voice. The rest of this book focuses on the sound of your voice and how it impacts your ability to get what you want. In the three scenarios below, I will give you a taste of the next chapters. In addition, I'll also offer some suggestions that you can use today to start having more impact with your voice.

Scenario #1: You've done your research. Your product will solve their problem. Your intention is clear. You have decision makers listening and you know that their intention is to buy this week. They like your product. You make your presentation, but they don't buy. You think it's because you didn't have the right words to say or the right price.

Explanation: They had a hard time hearing you and you sounded like you weren't sure of yourself.

Suggestions: Check your posture. You will appear more confident if you stand or sit up straight. If you are not cutting off your air by slouching or standing back on your heels, you will have more energy in your voice.

Beware of moving too much. You will appear more confident if you don't pace or wander around the room. If you must move, do so and then stay still for a few minutes. Then move again.

Scenario #2: You are from New York and your spouse is from California. You disagree about an important issue. You practice listening to her. You make sure she knows that you have heard everything she has said and that even though you may disagree, you still love her. Nevertheless, at the end of the exchange you still feel misunderstood, and so does she. She thinks you sound like you end every sentence with a demand.

Explanation: There are differences in cultural speech patterns that can impede understanding. A typical New York accent has a masculine cadence and often sounds demanding to non-New Yorkers. A Californian accent has a feminine cadence and is open-ended. Comments made in a California accent may sound unsure or unfinished to a New Yorker.

Suggestions: If you are trying to communicate with someone of a different gender or geographic location, be aware of speech patterns that are different and make allowance for them. In addition, if you interact with people from a different background, a different industry, or from a different nationality, spend some time familiarizing yourself with their home turf and what is important to them. Learn some of the words and phrases that characterize the speech of their area. I recommend reading Deborah Tannen to learn more about how your background affects your speech.

Communicating Well

Scenario #3: You have created a wonderful presentation for a seminar you are conducting on a popular topic. The room is full. You notice that people start checking their phones as you speak. On the attendee surveys the participants indicate, they love the topic, but they rate you with low marks. You decide that next time you'll add more special effects to the PowerPoint slides.

Explanation: Perhaps you spoke too fast or your voice was monotone. In such a case, using technology to spice up your presentation may not always help.

Suggestions: Many people think that technology will help them to be more interesting. The truth is that people will always be more interesting to other people than slide shows. Do not expect technology, no matter how innovative, to do anything more than simply enhance your presentation. Spend some time on your delivery: vary the pitch, vary the volume. Get up close and personal with the audience. Get them involved where you can. Invite interaction if you are not comfortable doing all of the talking all of the time. Tell some jokes. Laugh. And finally, make an impact with your voice by putting into action the information and exercises learned in the rest of this book.

"The devil hath not, in all his quiver's choice, an arrow for the heart like a sweet voice."

–Lord Byron, "Don Juan"

" Your vocal power contributes to or detracts from the impact you have on others."

Vocal Power

Vocal Power

This book is dedicated to helping you discover the difference between a voice that helps you and a voice that hinders you. We are going to study two important aspects of your voice. One is your vocal image, the other your vocal power. They are the two key components of your voice as it relates to others. Remember, your voice is both a sound and a representation of your ideas and beliefs. You can change it or keep it the way it is. It's your voice and your choice.

Creating the powerful effect you want with your voice is a matter of understanding how vocal power is physically created, knowing what acoustic properties have the most effect on others, and learning what you can do to influence those things. It's about the resonance of your voice and how to use your vocal muscles.

Let's start with vocal production, or how you actually produce your vocal sound. Here is a simplified description of what happens when you speak or sing: First, sound travels on air, so you have to breathe out. As the air moves from your lungs through your trachea or windpipe, it passes between your vocal folds (also called arytenoids and vocal cords), and brings those muscles together. They vibrate and sound happens. You then use your throat, tongue, lips, and jaw to shape the sound into words.

There are properties of sound that are determined by the shape and size of your vocal folds and some that are determined by the shape and size of your body. People with higher voices generally have smaller vocal folds than people with lower voices. Sound resonates through your bones as well as the cavities in your head and in your chest. In this way, bigger people may have more resonant voices than smaller people. Whatever the voice, it can be expressive and powerful if leveraged properly.

Vocal power is all about the impact your sound has on others. Over the years important characteristics of sound have been discovered regarding its impact on the ear, and even on the brain, of both the speaker and the listener.

Research has shown that certain sounds have the power to energize the cortex of the brain, and that this charging is a major function of the ear. Specifically, sounds that are rich in overtones, or harmonics, have been shown to slow down brain waves and reduce heart rate and respiration in much the same way as meditation.

"In a booming voice, declare to yourself 'I am the barbeque king.' Say it again. And again. Believe it."

–Bergren, Cox, and Detmar, *Improvise This*

Obviously, you don't want to put your audience into a trance-- or worse, put them to sleep! Fortunately, it also happens to be true that a voice rich in overtones is louder, stronger, and even healthier than other voices.

Vocal Power

What are harmonics and overtones, and why are they important to you? Harmonics are inherent in all sound. Sound is vibration, and pitch is the subjective experience of the frequency or rate of that vibration. Each pitch is made up of tones called partials. The lowest partial in each pitch is the one we hear the strongest, and that pitch is called the fundamental. All of the partials that are higher than the fundamental are called overtones, or harmonics. These overtones are mathematically related to each other. However, sound can be produced with different degrees or intensity of overtone activity, and, vocally, this is determined by the size of the vocal apparatus, the shape of the resonating chamber, as well as where the sound is allowed to resonate. In other words, you have to consider your own physical makeup, as well as where the sound vibrates in your body. In short, overtones are a good thing and you want to make sure your voice has them.

If you have a piano, you can perform an experiment that will let you hear overtones first hand. First, depress the c above middle c without actually sounding the note. Keep it depressed and play middle c. You will hear the c above middle c ring. This is because it is in the overtone series for middle c.

Singers may have an advantage over non-singers with respect to vocal power, because increasing the overtone activity in vocal sound has been the focus of singers for centuries. In fact, if you want to increase your vocal power, studying singing can significantly help. Indeed, Tomatis and Campbell state that singing may be essential to good health and vitality! However, without ever studying singing, you can use some of the tricks that good singers use and start to make more powerful sounds right now.

In order to create overtones, singers are taught to create their sound so it resonates in "the mask," which is the area in the front of the skull, behind the upper front teeth and the nose and up into the eyes. The traditional Italian school of singing called Bel Canto has been teaching mask resonance since the 17th century. The reason has primarily been the appeal of the voices trained in this method. Another reason is that mask resonance creates a minimum amount of stress on the vocal folds and affords a great deal of vocal flexibility.

Try it now. Say "Mmmmm." See if you can feel the buzzy sensation in the front of your face. That's mask resonance. I have included exercises to help you identify and develop mask resonance. They involve starting with simple humming.

By the way, some people think that mask resonance is the same as nasality. It is not. Many people are afraid of any nasality in their sound, so they work to create a sound that is low-pitched and that resonates in the throat. Potentially, there are several problems with this approach. Overtones are eliminated and, to have sufficient carrying power, you have to push and strain your voice. Don't make that mistake. Mask resonance is a combination of nasal and mouth resonance. If a voice sounds too nasal, it is as incorrect as one that has no mask resonance. The sound you are looking for will produce a pronounced vibration in the nasal area and on the upper palate just behind the front teeth. It's not stuck in your nose.

Research on the effect of sound on the brain combined with best practices in singing shows that what is good for the singer or speaker is also good for the listener. This is true vocal power: a sound with great flexibility that is healthy, dynamic, and easy to produce will make others take notice and listen.

By using the exercises presented in this book, you can begin to make some changes yourself. If you have questions, don't hesitate to contact me at www.VocalImpact.net.

"We learn by practice. Whether it means
to learn to dance by practicing dancing
or to learn to live by practicing living,
the principles are the same. One becomes
in some area an athlete of God."

−Martha Graham, "I am a Dancer"

" Exercising your body makes you stronger and more confident; exercising your voice makes it stronger and more appealing."

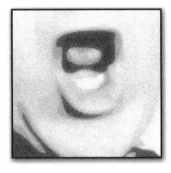

Vocal Power Exercises

Vocal Power Exercises

Exercise

A powerful vocal sound is the result of good vocal technique that uses mask resonance, an environment that supports the speaker, good vocal habits, and an awareness of how you sound to others. You have control over some of these things all of the time, including how you produce sound and where it resonates. You also have control of how well you are prepared as a speaker and how much knowledge you have of each speaking situation. The exercises here will help you create the sound you want.

You should do these exercises once a day for at least five minutes, gradually increasing that time to about thirty minutes a day. Practice in a room where there are minimal amounts of curtains and carpeting that will absorb the sound. If you must practice in your car, try to do some practicing in a more "live" environment as well. The room ambience will help you hear yourself better. It will also make the sound easier to produce.

One of the best live environments for practicing is (surprise!) your shower. Not only do you get lots of resonance, but the moisture in the air is good for your vocal folds and lungs.

Vocal Power Exercises

Basic Posture Awareness

Before doing the rest of the exercises, you need to make sure that you are physically supporting your voice. So let's address basic posture awareness. Think about how you stand and sit during the day. Are you supporting your voice with your posture? You'll get a better sound if you feel energetic. Do you hold yourself erect, or do you slump over at a desk? When you talk on the phone, do you constrict your breathing by hunching over your chair? Do you speak low and soft as if to make sure nobody hears you except the person you are speaking with on the phone? While using your mobile phone, do you catch yourself almost yelling into the phone to make sure you are heard on the other end?

If any of these descriptions fit your behaviors, make adjustments now: Sit forward in your chair when you are on the phone or speaking with others. And stop talking on your mobile phone while you drive. Besides being dangerous, road noise and the sound absorption quality of automobile interiors make most cars bad acoustical environments for speaking. When you cannot hear yourself, you are motivated to increase your volume but are unaware that you are doing so. This is not good because it results in vocal fatigue. (You can learn more about this in the chapter called "Vocal Problems.") If you are not sitting when you speak, stand tall and keep your energy forward like an athlete ready to move.

Vocal Power Exercises

Spend some time each day practicing posture awareness:

Stand up straight, with your feet about 12 inches apart and one foot slightly in front of the other. Put your weight evenly on both feet, or forward on your feet rather than back on your heels. Your knees should not be locked. Imagine that you are a marionette and that there is a string coming out of the crown of your head, pulling you up just a little so that you feel buoyant and energetic. This is the preferred posture for optimal support of your voice, whether singing or speaking. Practice reading or speaking out loud as you stand in this position. Then walk forward a few steps, keeping your body erect and in the same basic position. Finally, walk around the room as you speak, projecting your voice. Imagine that there are people seated in a classroom listening to you. Don't shout, but speak up.

 **The old posture exercise of walking around with a book on your head is not as silly as it sounds. Try it.**

Vocal Power Exercises

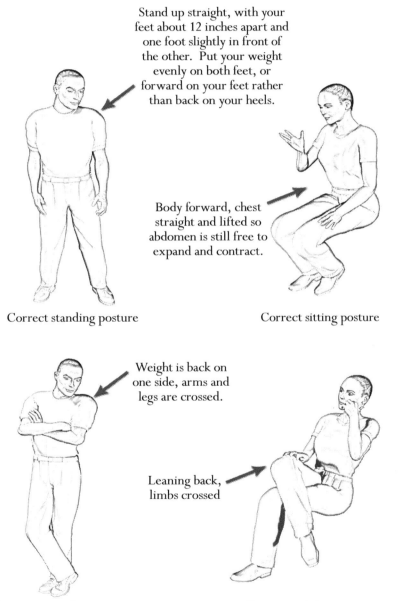

Stand up straight, with your feet about 12 inches apart and one foot slightly in front of the other. Put your weight evenly on both feet, or forward on your feet rather than back on your heels.

Body forward, chest straight and lifted so abdomen is still free to expand and contract.

Correct standing posture

Correct sitting posture

Weight is back on one side, arms and legs are crossed.

Leaning back, limbs crossed

Incorrect standing posture

Incorrect sitting posture

Vocal Power Exercises

Breathing Exercise #1:

Stand in the basic posture described above. Count slowly to ten as you breathe in deeply, letting the air first drop into the abdomen, and then expanding the lower rib cage.

At the count of ten, your lungs should be fully expanded. Now hold the air for another ten counts.

Slowly exhale on ten counts, keeping your ribs expanded, and paying special attention to the front of the rib cage around the solar plexus. (This area should stay open. If your rib cage drops in that area, practice squeezing your back together at the base of the rib cage on the next exhalation.)

Let your abdomen contract as you exhale.

When you have expelled all of your air, quickly let the abdomen relax and inhale again. This time inhale more quickly, for only five counts.

Hold the air again for ten counts

Exhale slowly on a hissing sound, emphasizing the "ss." Increase the exhalation to 12 counts.

Continue with three more breaths, with the inhalation taking three counts, holding for ten counts, and the exhalation taking 15 counts. Your first goal is three counts on inhalation, ten counts while holding your breath, and 15 on exhalation. If this is too difficult, do whatever you can do, but practice daily and work toward this goal.

Sometimes people get stuck here. If you're one of those people, contact me at Kate.Peters@VocalImpact.net.

Vocal Power Exercises

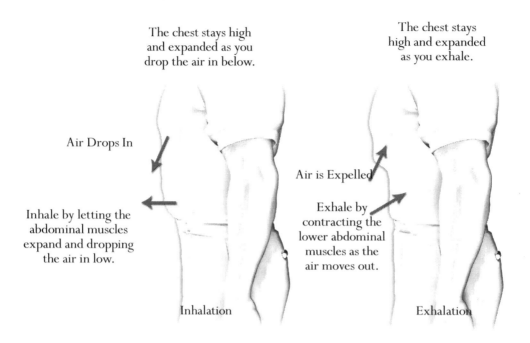

The chest stays high and expanded as you drop the air in below.

The chest stays high and expanded as you exhale.

Air Drops In

Air is Expelled

Inhale by letting the abdominal muscles expand and dropping the air in low.

Exhale by contracting the lower abdominal muscles as the air moves out.

Inhalation

Exhalation

Breathing Exercise #2

You will need something to read that you know well.

Do the following:

Stand in the basic posture described above, drop the air in low, quickly filling your lungs and expanding your lower rib cage.

Exhale on 20 counts, keeping your rib cage from falling in the front at the solar plexus.

Inhale and exhale again in the same manner.

Now breathe using the same process, but instead, on the exhalation, read several sentences out loud, keeping your awareness on your breathing.

You will probably not be exerting yourself as much as you were when you were doing the breathing exercise, but the posture and muscle involvement will be the same. Always practice breathing before doing the other vocal exercises, and before doing any public speaking.

Breathing with a friend
Exercise #3

Try practice breathing with a friend. You will both need to be comfortable with a hands-on practice session. Practice these three ways to check each other's breathing.

First, on the inhalation, put one hand on your friend's lower abs and have her push out against your hand. This will help to isolate the muscles needed for inhalation.

Vocal Power Exercises

Secondly, on the exhalation, make sure she doesn't let the lower ribs fall. Do this by putting your hands at the base of her ribs in front. This works best if you "hug" her from behind, placing your hands just under the lower ribs in front.

Finally, have her exhale slowly, trying to exhale every bit of air. While doing so, put a little pressure on her lower ribs on her back to remind her to squeeze her ribs together as she exhales the last bit of air. Be careful—a little bit of pressure is all that is needed.

Other Things to Remember About Breathing

I had been teaching voice for quite sometime when I had an important realization: I have learned a lot about living by learning a lot about breathing. Frankly, breathing is essential for living. It is natural and reflexive. It should be easy, but when the physical demands of singing are added to this natural process, problems may arise. Now, isn't that just like life itself? One day things are going along smoothly, and then next day some demands are made upon us that suddenly engage us in the complexities of balancing, controlling, and analyzing what once seemed so simple and natural. After my realization, I decided that if I wrote down some rules for better breathing, I might have some tools for better living.

Breathing Lessons

• Remember to breathe.

• Take good care of your body. It is your instrument.

• Practice conscious breathing.

• Gradually increase your capacity to breathe by gently, but consistently, challenging your "limits."

• Work to make your breathing appear effortless. You will feel more confident if your breathing looks effortless.

• Plan to breathe.

• Breathe into each phrase and keep the breath flowing with energy.

• Breathe into your entrance. The entrance is often the hardest part.

• Keep the air flowing even after the final word. The cut-off, or final word, also takes breath.

• Give yourself time to breathe, even when there's not much time to breathe.

• Use your breath well, especially if you don't have much time to breathe.

• Master your breathing. Breathing isn't everything—talent, practice, and skill are also important—but if breathing is a problem, it's a lot harder to demonstrate talent and skill.

Vocal Power Exercises

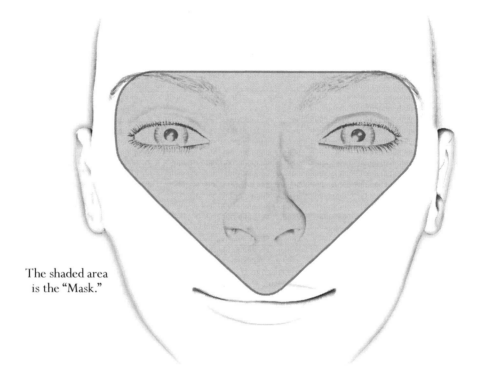

The shaded area is the "Mask."

Using Mask Resonance
Exercise #1: Learning to identify mask resonance

Even in an untrained voice, there is a simple way to find mask resonance.

Say, "MMMMMMMMMM." Can you feel that buzzy sensation in the front of your face?

Put your fingers on your face, next to your nose and across your cheekbones.

Now, say it again, "MMMMMMMMMMMM." You can probably feel a vibration in your fingers as well as your face.

Now say, "AAAWWW." You may not feel much vibration in your face, but you might feel it in your throat. The "aw" sound resonates more in your throat and less in your nasal pharynx.

Now say, "memory."

Repeat it slowly, "m-e-m-o-r-y." This word vibrates in the nasal pharynx.

Now alternate two words until you feel the difference. Say "fought," "memory," "fought," "memory."

Vocal Power Exercises

Now try saying "factor," "father," "fought." If you say it in this order, you will feel the vibrations dropping lower with each vowel.

Repeat: "factor," "father," "fought," paying close attention to the sensations in your head. Can you feel the sound created in your nasal pharynx, mouth, and throat in accordance with each vowel?

Now say, "Mimi," "mine," "Mop." The same sensations occur, but because of the "m" there is a little more mask resonance in each word than with the previous set of words.

True mask resonance is a combination of mouth and nasal pharynx resonance. You can learn to say all of your words using some mask resonance.

Exercise #2: Learning to use mask resonance

Take a few sentences from a presentation, a magazine article, or a book. Write the sentences below, one sentence for each of the lined sections. Highlight all of the m's, n's and v's.

Physical preparation: Make sure you are using the basic posture described above. Take three breaths, checking your breathing to make sure it is low and that your chest doesn't fall as you exhale. As you do the following, check your posture and breathing from time to time:

Read out loud, preceding each sentence with "MMMMMMMM." Exaggerate each one of the highlighted letters. Overdue the mask resonance, as if you were using a cartoon voice.

MMMMMMM _____

_____

MMMMMMM _____

_____

MMMMMMM _____

_____

Vocal Power Exercises

Exercise #3: Using mask resonance

Now write the same sentences below in paragraph form. Again, highlight the m's, n's, and v's.

Make sure you are using the basic posture described above. Take three expansive and conscious breaths, checking your breathing to make sure it is low and that your chest doesn't fall as you exhale. Then do the following, checking your posture and your breathing from time to time:

Read the paragraph out loud, first with your cartoon voice, over-emphasizing the mask resonance, and then in a more relaxed, normal speaking voice. You should still be aware of that buzzy mask resonance in the front of your face, even as you relax its intensity.

Pick another paragraph and write it here. Read it out loud several times. Can you feel the mask resonance in your speech? If not, go back and repeat Exercises #1 and #2 and then return to this paragraph.

_____

_____

_____

_____

_____

Practice this approach daily, especially if you have a presentation to give. Use different ads or articles in magazines to read out loud to keep your practice interesting and to challenge yourself with a variety of moods and styles of delivery. Choose something funny, something serious, something informative, something lively, something dry. Make sure you are using the correct basic posture. In addition, always precede your vocal exercises by checking your breathing to make sure it is low and that your chest doesn't fall as you exhale.

Humming before a presentation or meeting will do more than just help you remember to use mask resonance. It will also help relax you. In fact, five minutes a day of humming is an excellent way to de-stress your body.

"*Your vocal image sends a message separate from your words. It can contribute to or detract from your credibility.*"

Vocal Image

Vocal Image

Let's define vocal image as "The impression that people get of you from the sound of your voice." Vocal image is the synthesis of rhythm, pitch, tone, volume, and the inflection of a voice. Your vocal image sends a message separate from your words. It can contribute to or detract from your credibility. It makes wordless statements about your character, emotional state, economic status, education, age, gender, and lots more.

"A man's style is his mind's voice. Wooden minds, wooden voices"

–Ralph Waldo Emerson

Whether you're aware of it or not, you already have a vocal image. You've created your vocal image by imitating vocal patterns you heard as a child while you were developing language. These were probably speech patterns of your family, teachers, and perhaps even public figures whom you admired. During adolescence you were likely influenced by your peers and by characters in pop culture. In your adulthood you might have changed your vocal image again to create a sound that you felt would be more effective in your job. The point is that vocal patterns are learned. You are not stuck with the one you have, especially if it is not healthy or helpful. You've created what you have now. If you want to, you can create something else that works better for you.

Vocal Image

Creating the vocal image you want

Let's explore what you have already created. Again, your "vocal image" is the impression that people get of you from the sound of your voice. You need to become aware of that impression. By taking an inventory of the vocal patterns you hear in your own voice, and by studying those of speakers whose voices you find interesting or even annoying, you can begin to discern productive and unproductive patterns of speech. At this point, you can then eliminate your unproductive patterns and begin to create new, more useful patterns of sound. You can also determine where and when to best leverage them. For now, I'd like you to consider and observe the vocal patterns you hear while engaging in and listening to conversations today.

The best way to become aware of your vocal image is to record yourself in a variety of situations and then listen to yourself. Over the next several pages you will have the chance to further explore your vocal image and make notes about your voice in a guided learning experience. The written work will enhance your awareness of your voice even more.

Vocal Image

Preparation for Vocal Image Awareness Exercises

Over the next ten days try to become more aware of your vocal image so that you can create the one you want. Each day consider a different aspect of your vocal image and write down your observations. Take time to also consider the same aspect of vocal image in others that you hear. Through this awareness, you will have a chance to hear yourself clearly and to change what you want to change. Remember, you cannot change what you cannot hear.

 Besides listening to your recordings, it can be useful to get someone else's opinion of your vocal image. However, be careful about relying too much on any one person. If you want to know how others perceive you from the sound of your voice, ask several and take all comments into account before deciding what, if anything, to do to change that image.

"There is no index of character
so sure as the voice."

–Benjamin Disraeli

"By taking an inventory of the vocal patterns you hear in your own voice, and by studying those of speakers whose voices you find interesting or even annoying, you can begin to discern productive and unproductive patterns of speech."

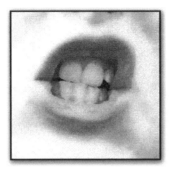

Vocal Image
Awareness Exercises

Vocal Image Awareness Exercises

Getting Ready

Make a recording of yourself speaking. If you have recordings of yourself already, you can use those. You will use these recordings to refer to as you consider various characteristics of your voice. Here is what you need to record:

Record yourself talking out loud in normal conversation for two to three minutes.

Record yourself reading two pieces of contrasting material for two to three minutes.

Record yourself giving instructions without using a script for two to three minutes.

You may work on one of these a day or several each day. The pace is up to you; however, you will be more successful at changing unwanted patterns if you pay attention to one vocal characteristic at a time. You can even spend an entire week paying attention to one aspect of your speech before moving on to the next. Make sure you also continue practicing mask resonance and breathing using the exercises previously covered.

Vocal Image Awareness Exercises

Day 1

Listen to your recordings. Consider the rhythm of your speech. Is there a consistent rhythmic pattern? Rhythm is a pattern of sound that is created by contrasts and alterations of different recurring sounds. Speech can have patterns that are formal, as in a poetic rhythm like "iambic pentameter." You may have a rhythm to your speech that you are not aware of at most times. You may also use a phrase that has a rhythm to it. Listen for those kinds of patterns of sound. Also consider whether or not your words and ideas flow easily. Are there spaces between them that don't make sense? On the other hand, do you give enough space in between ideas and phrases?

Silence can be a wonderful tool for a speaker. Do you use it? Teachers sometimes use silence to get their students' attention. Composers use silence to create dramatic effect. It is far better to use silence than verbal fillers such as "um." Don't be afraid to build silence into your presentations when you want to accentuate a point. Silence is a great tool to get someone's attention , especially when they are expecting you to say something.

What effect does the rhythm of your speech have on your vocal image?

Vocal Image Awareness Exercises

Now write down your observations.

_____

_____

_____

_____

_____

_____

_____

_____

_____

_____

_____

Not everyone understands this right away.

If you have any questions, be sure to contact me

at Kate.Peters@VocalImpact.net

Vocal Image Awareness Exercises

_____

_____

_____

_____

_____

_____

_____

_____

_____

_____

_____

_____

_____

The best way to break a habit of speech is to first exaggerate it and then change it drastically several times in several different ways when you are practicing.

Vocal Image Awareness Exercises

Day 2

Listen to your recordings. Consider the pitch of your speech. Pitch is a property of sound that describes the actual frequency of the sound waves that produce a particular sound. A faster sound wave produces a higher sound, while slower sound waves produce lower sounds. Pitch is not determined by the loudness or volume of sound, but rather by the notes we use when we speak. Yes, we use notes when speaking just as we do when singing. Speaking notes, however, are random, informally ordered, and usually of less duration. Some people actually sound like they are singing when they speak, whereas others use so little variety we call them "monotones." Some people think that a low voice is sexier than a high voice. Some people think a high voice sounds younger. The most interesting voices use a variety of pitch in their sounds. What about your voice? Is it pitched high, low, or somewhere in between? Is there variety in your pitch, or is it more of a monotone? What effect does the pitch of your voice have on your vocal image? What do you observe in others?

Write your thoughts here. _____

_____

_____

_____

_____

_____

_____

_____

_____

_____

_____

_____

_____

_____

_____

_____

_____

If you have trouble understanding the concept of pitch, or trouble discerning high and low tones, contact me. You may have a hearing problem, or you may be part of the 1% of our population who is actually tone deaf. Either is possible, but neither is likely.

Vocal Image Awareness Exercises

Vocal Image Awareness Exercises

Day 3

Listen to your recordings. Consider the tone of your voice. Is it rich or thin? Is it scratchy or smooth? Is your voice breathy or clear? Does it sound husky? Does it sound mellow? Does it sound whiny? Does it sound compressed or constrained, or does it sound free and open? Is it pleasant to listen to? Is it strong or weak? Listen to other voices, too. How would you describe the tone of other voices? Sometimes a voice needs more air in it, sometimes it needs less. Sometimes it needs more energy. More energy can be created by using better posture, better breathing, and better resonance. Notice how your voice changes as you do the exercises. How does the tone of your voice or others' voices affect vocal image?

Write your thoughts and observations here. _____

_____

_____

_____

_____

_____

_____

Vocal Image Awareness Exercises

Vocal Image Awareness Exercises

Be sure to practice the exercises using mask resonance. Also remember to practice breathing consciously several times during each day. You'll feel better and sound better too!

Vocal Image Awareness Exercises

Day 4

Listen to your recordings. Consider the volume of your vocal sound. Can you hear yourself when listening to the recording? Are you whispering? Are you shouting? Do you mumble or under articulate when you speak? Do you over articulate? If you speak too softly, you can project a weak image; if you speak too loudly, you may sound forceful, anxious, or even angry. You can use volume to emphasize your words or ideas. Contrast is an important part of communication, and it is a good idea to change your volume from time to time in order to keep people's attention. You can also use volume to add drama to what you say. Try emphasizing your words by speaking more quietly at times, without diminishing the energy. Note: Speaking softly does not necessarily mean speaking with less intensity. Sometimes there can be more intensity in a quiet sound, which can also be engaging. Listen to other speakers. What do they do with volume? How does the volume of your voice affect your vocal image?

Write your thoughts and ideas here. _____

_____

_____

_____

_____

_____

_____

_____

_____

_____

_____

_____

_____

_____

_____

_____

_____

_____

As people increase their volume, they often increase their speed of delivery as well. If you find that you speak too fast, try speaking a little more softly, being careful not to lose energy as well.

Vocal Image Awareness Exercises

Vocal Image Awareness Exercises

Listen to your recording. How do you sound emotionally? Do you like what you hear? You can get help from watching films or TV shows. You can fairly easily identify the emotions that characters are portraying in a film. Since you can be more objective with them, listen to their voices to hear what they are doing to create the sound of that particular emotion. You can listen again and again to the same part of the show and carefully analyze it. Here is an example of what you are listening for: When someone feels sad, their voice may get soft and sound weak. When they are angry, it may get louder and sound forceful. If you have a loud voice that sounds stern, you may have a vocal image that makes you seem angry. When you are aware of how you sound emotionally, you can change it. What are the emotions that the film characters are portraying and what makes them sound like they are feeling? Try on emotions and listen to their "sounds" in your voice.

Then ask yourself, in general, if your voice sounds like you are feeling any particular emotion. Does this serve you by creating the vocal image you want to create, or would you like to change it?

Write your thoughts and observations here. _____

_____

_____

Vocal Image Awareness Exercises

Vocal Image Awareness Exercises

Vocal Image Awareness Exercises

Day 6

Listen to your recording. Consider the clarity of your vocal production. Could someone else understand what you are saying? Clarity of sound is created by using mask resonance and by effectively using articulation mechanisms—your tongue and lips. Your tongue and lips need to work independently of each other. If you find that your articulation seems a bit "lazy," try isolating your lips and tongue in some tongue twisters. Try them slowly, repeating them several times and speeding up gradually as you get better at them. Here are some to try:

1. Unique New York
2. Red lorry, yellow lorry, red lorry, yellow lorry
3. Three free throws
4. The myth of Miss Muffet
5. Tim, the thin twin tinsmith
6. Peggy Babcock
7. If Stu chews shoes, should Stu choose the shoes he chews?
8. Brad's big black bath brush broke.
9. Give papa a cup of proper coffee in a copper coffee cup.
10. She sifted thistles through her thistle-sifter.

Also, when listening to your recording, consider the speed of your vocal production. Do you speak too quickly or just fast enough? Do you like what you hear? How does the clarity of your sound affect your vocal image?

Write your thoughts and observations here. _____

_____

_____

_____

_____

_____

_____

_____

_____

_____

_____

_____

_____

_____

_____

If you stumble over a word during a presentation, take the time to clarify yourself. If you go on thinking no one noticed, you are wrong. Chances are they all noticed. Admitting that you made a mistake and correcting it will make you appear more human and approachable.

Vocal Image Awareness Exercises

Vocal Image Awareness Exercises

Day 7

Listen to your recording. Consider the ease of vocal production.
Does your voice sound natural or made up? Does it sound forced
or contrived? Sometimes, a voice sounds constrained due to the
lack of air in the sound. Be sure that your breathing is low and
expansive and that you use your air when you speak. If you find
yourself holding air back, then practice speaking with a breathier
sound until the air flows more freely in your voice. Often a lack
of air in the sound also means that your voice will get tired easily
or feel strained more often than others. Consider how the ease of
your vocal production affects your vocal image? Do you like what
you hear, or would you like to change it?

Write your thoughts and observations here. ⎯⎯⎯⎯⎯⎯

Vocal Image Awareness Exercises

Vocal Image Awareness Exercises

_____

_____

_____

_____

_____

_____

_____

_____

_____

_____

_____

_____

_____

_____

_____

_____

_____

A good way to get air moving in your voice is to practice walking while talking. If you want to try this, be sure that you move with purpose and direction rather than just meandering around the room.

Vocal Image Awareness Exercises

Day 8

Listen to your recording. Consider any repetitive vocal habits. Consider the vocal patterns of your family, teachers, and friends. What patterns in your own voice do you recognize as those that sound like someone else in your family, on TV, or in your workplace? Do you use an accent that is not natural to your background? Does it work for you? Do you like what you hear? Habits are difficult to break, but if you don't like a particular pattern that you use, the first step in breaking it is to recognize it. Once you recognize it, you can then begin making a different choice in pronunciation, wording, or rhythm. If it's a pattern of sound, you can choose to create a different one. Another habit that people often have is to use fillers when they are thinking or to use pop phrases as habitual conversation fillers. Do you do that? Listen for "um," "uh," "you know," and "like." You may also ask someone else to listen to you speaking and remind you to pay attention to your fillers. How do your habitual vocal patterns affect your vocal image?

Write your thoughts and comments here. ⸻

⸻

⸻

⸻

_____

_____

_____

_____

_____

_____

_____

_____

_____

_____

_____

_____

_____

It is better to say nothing than to say "um." When you notice that you are about to use a filler, don't say anything. This may be uncomfortable at first. However, you will gradually become used to speaking without fillers.

Vocal Image Awareness Exercises

Vocal Image Awareness Exercises

Listen to your recordings. Consider the cadence of your sentences. Cadence is the general inflection or movement of your voice at the end of your sentences. Do your sentences end mostly "up" or mostly "down" in inflection? Do you often sound like you are asking a question, even when you are not? Do you often sound like you are demanding something or giving orders even when you are not? Sentences have feminine cadences and masculine cadences. These are not gender specific, but rather just descriptions of the sound. A feminine cadence is open, inquisitive, and can seem friendly and inviting. In a feminine cadence, the voice is raised at the end of a sentence. It invites conversation from the listener. We typically hear the feminine inflection in a question, but it also can be present in statements, though less pronounced. A masculine cadence is more closed and can sound authoritative and strong. In a masculine cadence, the voice falls at the end of the sentence. This cadence sounds definitive and may not invite comments from others.

To hear the difference, say the sentence, "I want you to take a look at this." First, use a final cadence that sounds almost like a question, with your voice rising. Then say it while lowering your pitch at the end of the sentence. The first is a feminine cadence; the second is masculine. A good speaker uses both types of cadences, but uses them when they are needed. You can learn

Vocal Image Awareness Exercises

more about cadence and other cultural speech patterns by studying the work of linguist, Deborah Tannen. One piece is listed in the bibliography at the end of this book. After studying cadence, consider your voice. How does the general cadence of your sound affect your vocal image?

Write your thoughts and comments here.

You can learn a lot about cadence by listening to audio books and podcasts. Without visual stimuli, you are more likely to hear vocal inflections. Listen for cadence to determine how it is used by different readers.

Vocal Image Awareness Exercises

Day 10

Consider the content of your speech. Your vocal image can be affected by your choice of words. It can be affected by the way in which you express your ideas. Your choice of words reflects your perspective on the world and your intentions. Some people are always selling something. Others are always asking for something. Some people are generally optimistic and some negative. Some people have difficulty expressing themselves because they think that they need to impress others with sophisticated vocabulary when it is not natural. Others feel they need to "dumb down" their words for an audience. The result may be an audience that feels patronized. Do you use words appropriate to your audience? Do you use words appropriate to your level of education? Are your expressed thoughts reflective of your economic status and expectations of life? Is your content instructive, engaging, conversational, persuasive? What do you want it to be? Do you express your thoughts clearly? Do you like what you hear? Consider how the content of your speech affects or reflects your vocal image.

Write your thoughts and comments here. _____

_____

_____

_____

Vocal Image Awareness Exercises

Vocal Image Awareness Exercises

_____

_____

_____

_____

_____

_____

_____

_____

_____

_____

_____

_____

This is a good place to ask yourself if you clearly state your intention in the content of your speech. Being clear about intention helps us to be clear about content.

"*A healthy sound gives you more control and is more likely to impact others in the way you want.*"

Vocal Problems

Vocal Problems

Some people use their voices in ways that are damaging to their vocal health. Most of us have experienced such damage at least once. For instance:

- Do you ever feel like your throat is sore after a day of meetings?
- Do you ever come home feeling like you just can't say another word?
- After a long day of talking, do you ever get hoarse or have laryngitis?
- After you give presentations, do feel like your voice is rough or swollen?
- Do you find that you have to clear your throat a lot during the day, even during a day of normal conversation?
- Does your voice often feel dry, irritated, or raspy?
- In the worst case, have you ever had to cancel a presentation because your voice was shot?

Well, this is not normal. The good news is that in most cases it is not necessary either.

Your voice is a part of your body and, as such, needs physical care. There are ways to stand, to breathe, and to physically produce the sound that are more likely to produce a healthy voice. A healthy sound gives you more vocal control and is more likely to impact others in the way you want. Vocal control is what I call vocal power. Your vocal power contributes to or detracts from the impact you have on others.

Vocal Problems

Your voice is made up of a set of muscles that needs proper care and training to function at its best. If you don't take care of your voice, you may hurt it and start to experience problems with it. Sometimes problems like the ones I listed above are the symptoms of serious damage that only a doctor can help you cure. For instance, the damage can manifest in vocal nodules or polyps. It is always a good idea to see an otolaryngologist if the problems persist for longer than a couple of days, or if they happen often. In most instances, however, the problems can be cleared up before they become serious. In that case, we call them signs of "vocal fatigue."

Some signs of vocal fatigue are frequent hoarseness, chronic throat clearing, a limited pitch range, and a lack of vocal endurance. If you have some or all of these signs of vocal fatigue, it's a good idea to figure out what may be causing the fatigue. There are also some simple things you can do to make vocal fatigue less possible. Let's explore some scenarios that will illustrate possible problems as well as solutions.

Vocal Problems

If you have signs of vocal fatigue, you may have used your voice for too long.

As a speaker, it is possible for you to talk for a couple of hours without harm. However, anything more than a couple of hours with no break and no vocal rest is usually too much for most people.

Suggestions: Plan breaks in your presentations to rest your voice. As you rest your voice, your audience can reflect on your messages thus far.

If you have signs of vocal fatigue, you may have pushed the limits of your endurance.

As mentioned earlier, the harmonics in sound are the carrying power for the speaker or singer. However, many people try to get vocal power through "muscling" the sound, that is, lowering the pitch and pushing the voice. Muscling is a common cause of vocal fatigue.

Suggestions: If you need to use your voice in public speaking for more than a couple of hours at a time, you can build up its endurance. You will need to build endurance gradually, and you need to have good vocal technique. Try the following:

- Practice speaking at home as if you were giving a presentation. Start by practicing for an hour at a time. If your voice still gets tired, practice for less than an hour. Gradually increase your practice sessions until you can work in two-hour periods without any signs of vocal fatigue.

- Practice your talks using mask resonance.

- Practice singing. Use practice scales on syllables such as mum, ney, no, ma, and yang.

Vocal Problems

If you have signs of vocal fatigue, you may have tried to overcompensate for a bad acoustic environment.

Keep in mind that when the environment changes, you will probably change the way you use your voice. Every time you go into a new environment, your experience of your voice will change. In addition, your environment can be either "friendly" or "unfriendly" to your voice. A friendly speaking environment is one in which there is some echo in the room that bounces your sound back to you. In a friendly room, you will automatically feel a freedom and ease of sound production. Your car is NOT such an environment. Your shower is!

Suggestions:

You need to be able to hear yourself. If you cannot hear yourself, you will over produce sound without even knowing that you are doing so. This is one of the most common causes of vocal fatigue. Use a sound system with a monitor whenever possible. Create some acoustic feedback in the room by using a tiny bit of reverb. Be careful you don't get so much feedback that the sound becomes muddy or barn-like. You can also use the acoustic properties of the room to help ease your vocal production. To use the acoustic properties of the room, you will need to test different areas in the room until you find the spot from which your voice carries the best and also comes back to you. Have someone listen while you speak. Most likely, you will get more feedback from an elevated spot such as a stage. You can also increase feedback by speaking across the room into a corner. Don't be afraid to use people to help you determine how you sound in a room. If you cannot hear yourself very well anywhere that you stand, assign someone the task of listening throughout your presentation and signaling to you when you are too loud or too soft. Don't hesitate to ask your audience if they can hear you from time to time.

Make sure everyone can see you and you can see them. You are less likely to yell if you feel people can see you and if you can see how they react to your talk.

Be close to the audience whenever possible. Move among them when you speak. Bring them into your talk. Let them do some of the talking for you whenever possible.

If you are going to speak in a new setting, take time to try it out before the actual event so there won't be any surprises. Remember the acoustics will change a bit when the room is full of people,-- human bodies absorb a lot of sound!

Also, practice speaking in many different environments so you can start building a large experience base. The more environments you speak in, the less surprises you'll have. The less surprises you have, the more confident you'll become.

Vocal Problems

If you have signs of vocal fatigue, you may have used your voice when it was already fatigued or tired.

Sometimes you have to speak at a conference. Sometimes you have to give a lot of presentations, classes, or workshops and you may not be accustomed to doing so. Many teachers get hoarse during the first week of school because they haven't been speaking for extended periods or for large groups during the summer months.

Suggestions:

Be sensitive to how your voice feels. If it starts to feel tired, rest it as much as possible, even if that means being quiet during your breaks.

Drink warm liquids or ones that are at room temperature. Avoid iced drinks.

Avoid eating foods that create phlegm, such as dairy products, sugar, and spicy foods. There may be some that are not on this list that you find irritating to you. Avoid those as well.

Get plenty of rest when you need to use your voice a lot. Many people fail to follow this bit of old wisdom. Remember, your voice is part of your body and needs proper rest before a vocal workout.

Drink plenty of fluids. The vocal apparatus is a low priority organ, which means when you are exerting yourself, the high priority organs, such as the heart, receive fluids first. Yet the vocal folds need fluid for lubrication. You may need extra fluids when you are doing a lot of public speaking.

If you have signs of vocal fatigue, you may be imitating bad vocal patterns.

Many of us have grown up with bad vocal habits that we learned from our family, a favorite teacher, or any other speaker we may admire. We may have created vocal sounds that are too high, too low, too loud, too light, too forced.

Suggestions:

The most important step in re-training a voice for vocal health and power is listening. Listen to singers who have a natural, easy production. Listen to voices that are resonant and have carrying power without sounding forced. Once you have found the sensation of the sound in the mask, listen to see if you hear that in other voices. Remember, we tend to duplicate whatever we hear. Make sure that what you focus on when you listen is what you want to reproduce when you speak.

Most vocal problems can be remedied with exercise; however, some are more serious. If you find that your voice is always sore or husky no matter what you do, see an otolaryngologist.

"The question is, how do you make the switch from creating your voice through reaction and imitation to creating your voice through thoughtful application of knowledge?"

Practical
Application
Journal

Practical Application Journal

A practical application journal will help you continue to develop awareness. Awareness, in turn, will help you make changes that can last a lifetime. Without awareness, you will probably continue to make the same choices that you do today. I'm reminded of a story. A man was speaking to people passing a street corner in a small town in California. He was standing by a car with two small children, pointing to the car animatedly and passionately but speaking in a language that people passing by did not understand. Finally, a concerned woman stopped to help. With obvious relief in his voice, he spoke to her. She struggled to understand and shook her head as if to say, "No, I don't understand." In response, he spoke louder. Again she shook her head. He spoke louder and louder until the woman threw her arms up in frustration and walked away.

At times, all of us are like that man and woman. Sometimes we resemble the man in the story. When we feel misunderstood, we get louder and louder in a language that no one understands. when we should be taking the time to try to communicate more clearly. Sometimes we resemble the woman in the story: when we misunderstand others or feel misunderstood ourselves, we give up and walk away when we should try to slow things down to clarify the situation or try to see things from another perspective. In most cases, it does not have to be this way. Clear communication is a skill that can be developed with awareness and practice.

Practical Application Journal

As humans, we are passionately driven to communicate. We want to be heard. We want to be understood. The sound of another voice and the touch of another hand are among life's most precious offerings. In the end, connection with others is at the core of our desires. To the extent that you create clear communication, you open the door to connection. Creating clear communication takes consistent, focused attention and work, but it is work that will bring the greatest rewards that life has to offer. When your intention, your message, and your voice are all clear, others cannot help but listen and feel more confident about who you are and what you stand for. There is no doubt that this will help you get more of what you want out of life. More importantly, when you communicate clearly, your ideas have more impact, your point of view carries more weight, and the unique talents and gifts that you have to share are more accessible to others. In other words, when your voice is strong and clear, you not only get more from life—you can give more to life.

Practical Application Journal

Use the following pages to keep a journal of your observations on how you are using your voice.

Use this portion of the book every day for 31 days.

Keep the journal on your desk or carry it with you so you can write down your vocal observations after you have finished a conversation. You don't need to write more than a couple of sentences or phrases. The act of doing this is all that is required to continue developing your awareness of your voice. After awareness comes conscious control. Soon, you will not only understand the dynamics of your voice, but you will be able to use them to your advantage.

Try to write your observations three times during the day. It is sometimes best to plan to write in your journal at the same time everyday. For example, write in it when you first arrive at your desk so you can capture your thoughts on how you used your voice at home and on the way to work. Write in it after lunch, so you can think back on how you used your voice while having lunch with others. And finally, write in it before going home, so you can observe the state of your voice over a period of a day.

Also, be sure to review your journal weekly.

Practical Application Journal

After reviewing what you have written in the preceding pages, write down five things that you like about your voice.

1. _____

2. _____

3. _____

4. _____

5. _____

Now write down five things that you would like to change about your voice.

1. _____

2. _____

3. _____

4. _____

5. _____

Day 1

Start by looking at your list of changes. Write one of these on the top of the page for the next five days. Study that aspect of your voice for one full day. Consider what you can do to make that change.

The first thing I want to change about my voice is ————————————————

——

AM: ——

——

——

——

——

——

——

Noon: ——————————————————————————————————————

——

——

——

 { **Consistent and frequent practice makes it easier to change habits. Consider how much time you are willing to give to developing your voice. Even five minutes a day is better than one hour once a week.**

120

PM:

Day 2

Study an aspect of your voice that you want to change today. Consider what you can do to make that change. Listen to others and compare your sound with theirs. If you still don't know what to do, you can contact me through my web site at www.vocalimpact.net.

The second thing I want to change about my voice is _____

_____

AM: _____

_____

_____

_____

_____

_____

_____

Noon: _____

_____

_____

_____

PM:

Day 3

Study an aspect of your voice that you want to change today. Consider what you can do to make that change. If you still don't know what to do, you can contact me through my web site at www.vocalimpact.net.

The third thing I want to change about my voice is _____

_____

AM: _____

_____

_____

_____

_____

_____

_____

Noon: _____

_____

_____

_____

PM:

Day 4

Study an aspect of your voice that you want to change today. Consider what you can do to make that change. If you still don't know what to do, you can contact me through my web site at www.vocalimpact.net.

The fourth thing I want to change about my voice is _____

_____

AM: _____

_____

_____

_____

_____

_____

_____

_____

Noon: _____

_____

_____

_____

PM:

Day 5

Study an aspect of your voice that you want to change today. Consider what you can do to make that change. Try a new approach. If you still don't know what to do, you can contact me through my web site at www.vocalimpact.net.

The fifth thing I want to change about my voice is _____

_____

AM: _____

_____

_____

_____

_____

_____

_____

_____

Noon: _____

_____

_____

_____

PM:

Day 6

Look at your list of things you like about your voice. Write one of these on the top of each page for the next five pages. Study that aspect of your voice for one full day. Consider how that strength affects others. What does it say about you separate from your words? How can you use that strength more effectively to present the vocal image you want?

The thing I like best about my voice is _____

_____

AM: _____

_____

_____

_____

_____

_____

_____

Noon: _____

_____

_____

_____

PM:

Day 7

Study one aspect of what you like about your voice all day today. Consider how that strength affects others. What does it say about you separate from your words? How can you use that strength more effectively to present the vocal image you want?

The second vocal strength I have is _____

_____

AM: _____

_____

_____

_____

_____

_____

_____

Noon: _____

_____

_____

_____

PM:

Day 8

Study one aspect of what you like about your voice all day today. Consider how that strength affects others. What does it say about you separate from your words? How can you use that strength more effectively to present the vocal image you want?

The third vocal strength I have is _____

_____

AM: _____

_____

_____

_____

_____

_____

_____

Noon: _____

_____

_____

_____

PM:

Day 9

Study one aspect of what you like about your voice all day today. Consider how that strength affects others. What does it say about you separate from your words? How can you use that strength more effectively to present the vocal image you want?

The fourth vocal strength I have is _____

_____

AM: _____

_____

_____

_____

_____

_____

_____

_____

Noon: _____

_____

_____

_____

PM: ——————————————————————————————————————

Day 10

Study one aspect of what you like about your voice all day today. Consider how that strength affects others. What does it say about you separate from your words? How can you use that strength more effectively to present the vocal image you want?

The fifth vocal strength I have is _____

_____

AM: _____

_____

_____

_____

_____

_____

_____

Noon: _____

_____

_____

_____

_____

PM: _____

By focusing on your strengths, you also build self-confidence.
People will hear that in your voice!

139

Day 11

How are you using your voice today in telephone conversations? Is it different from how you use it in person with others? Check your posture as you speak on the phone. Sit tall and forward in your chair. Make sure you can breathe properly. Observe this throughout the next two days and write down your observations.

AM: _____

_____

_____

_____

_____

_____

_____

_____

Noon: _____

_____

_____

_____

PM:

Day 12

How are you using your voice today in phone conversations? Is it different from how you use it in person with others? Check your posture as you speak on the phone. Sit tall and forward in your chair. Make sure you can breathe properly. Observe this throughout the day and write down your observations.

AM: _____

_____

_____

_____

_____

_____

_____

_____

Noon: _____

_____

_____

_____

_____

PM: _____

It can be useful to have a friend or business associate agree to be your
voice buddy. In this role, you call them daily to get encouragement
to make the changes you want to make. Their job is to be supportive,
especially on days when you are less inspired to do the work. Your job
is to be open to their feedback.

Day 13

How are you using your voice today in one-on-one conversation? Is it different from how you use it on the phone or in large groups? Check your posture as you speak. Make sure you can breathe properly. Observe this throughout the next three days and write down your observations.

AM: _____

_____

_____

_____

_____

_____

_____

_____

_____

_____

_____

Noon: _____

_____

_____

_____

Questions or comments?
Visit my website at
www.VocalImpact.net.

PM:

Day 14

How are you using your voice today in one-on-one conversation? Is it different from how you use it on the phone or in large groups? Check your posture as you speak. Make sure you can breathe properly. Observe this throughout the day and write down your observations.

AM: _____

_____

_____

_____

_____

_____

_____

_____

_____

Noon: _____

_____

_____

_____

_____

PM: _____

Today, practice listening in all of your conversations. Practice some of the techniques described in the chapter on communicating well.
Write your personal statement of intention at the top of the page in your journal every day.

My personal statement of Intention:

Day 15

How are you using your voice today in one-on-one conversations? Is it different from how you use it on the phone or in large groups? Check your posture as you speak. Make sure you can breathe properly. Observe this throughout the day and write down your observations.

AM: _____

_____

_____

_____

_____

_____

_____

_____

_____

_____

_____

Noon: _____

_____

_____

_____

PM:

My personal statement of Intention:

Day 16

Does your voice ever get tired during the day? Does it feel dry or croaky? Make sure you drink enough water to keep your voice lubricated. For the next five days, keep a bottle of water close by and become aware of the effect that water, or the lack of it, has on your voice. Also, pay attention to how long conversation affects your voice. Re-read the chapter in this book on vocal problems and try some of my suggestions. See which ones you can begin to implement right away to keep your voice healthy.

AM:

Noon:

PM: _____

Set a 32 oz. bottle of water on your desk or counter and drink all of it during the course of the day to ensure you get enough fluids.

151

My personal statement of Intention:

Day 17

Does your voice ever get tired during the day? Does it feel dry or croaky? Make sure that you drink enough water to keep your voice lubricated. For the next five days, keep a bottle of water close by and become aware of the effect that water or the lack of it has on your voice. Also, pay attention to how long conversation affects your voice.

AM:

Noon:

PM:

My personal statement of Intention:

Day 18

Does your voice ever get tired during the day? Does it feel dry or croaky? Make sure that you drink enough water to keep your voice lubricated. Keep a glass of water close by and become aware of the effect that water or the lack of it has on your voice. Also, pay attention to how long conversation affects your voice.

AM: _____

_____

_____

_____

_____

_____

_____

_____

Noon: _____

_____

_____

_____

Visit my website for more exercises and information that can
help. Or e-mail me at Kate.Peters@VocalImpact.net.

PM:

My personal statement of Intention:

Day 19

Does your voice ever get tired during the day? Does it feel dry or croaky? Make sure that you drink enough water to keep your voice lubricated. Keep a glass of water close by and become aware of the effect that water or the lack of it has on your voice. Also, pay attention to how long conversation affects your voice.

AM: _____

_____

_____

_____

_____

_____

_____

_____

Noon: _____

_____

_____

_____

PM:

My personal statement of Intention:

Day 20 _____

Does your voice ever get tired during the day? Does it feel dry or croaky? Make sure that you drink enough water to keep your voice lubricated. Keep a glass of water close by and become aware of the effect that water or the lack of it has on your voice. Also, pay attention to how long conversation affects your voice.

AM: _____

_____

_____

_____

_____

_____

_____

_____

Noon: _____

_____

_____

_____

PM:

My personal statement of Intention:

Day 21

Continue to observe how you use your voice and how it feels during the day. Make brief notes on your observations.

AM: _____

_____

_____

_____

_____

_____

_____

_____

_____

_____

Noon: _____

_____

_____

_____

{ **Keep a little notebook with you when you give presentations or lectures. Make notes in it afterwards regarding the use of your voice. Take special note of any comments people make about the sound of your voice. Evaluate whether or not your intention was clear and aligned with your audience.**

PM:

My personal statement of Intention:

Day 22

Continue to observe how you use your voice and how it feels during the day. Make brief notes on your observations.

AM: _____

_____

_____

_____

_____

_____

_____

_____

_____

Noon: _____

_____

_____

_____

_____

PM:

My personal statement of Intention:

Day 23

Continue to observe how you use your voice and how it feels during the day. Make brief notes on your observations.

AM: _____

_____

_____

_____

_____

_____

_____

_____

_____

Noon: _____

_____

_____

_____

_____

PM:

My personal statement of Intention:

Day 24

Continue to observe how you use your voice and how it feels during the day. Make brief notes on your observations. Evaluate your vocal impact and your vocal power. Is it changing? Where do you need to concentrate your awareness to increase impact and power?

AM: _____

_____

_____

_____

_____

_____

_____

_____

_____

_____

Noon: _____

_____

_____

_____

PM: ⎯⎯⎯⎯⎯⎯⎯⎯⎯⎯⎯⎯⎯⎯⎯⎯⎯⎯⎯⎯⎯⎯⎯⎯⎯⎯⎯⎯⎯

My personal statement of Intention:

Day 25

Continue to observe how you use your voice and how it feels during the day. Make brief notes on your observations.

AM: _____

_____

_____

_____

_____

_____

_____

_____

_____

Noon: _____

_____

_____

_____

_____

PM:

My personal statement of Intention:

Day 26 _____

Review the notes you have taken over the last 25 days. What has changed? What do you still need to work on? Make plans for your vocal health. Make plans to choose the vocal image you want.

Write your new goals below: _____

_____

_____

Practice now so that you create new, healthy vocal habits. Practice your new approach three times a day for the next five days.

AM: _____

_____

_____

_____

_____

_____

_____

_____

Noon: _____

Visit my website for more exercises and information that can help.

170   Or e-mail me at Kate.Peters@VocalImpact.net.

PM:

My personal statement of Intention:

Day 27

Continue to practice daily and write your observations regarding how you use your voice in ordinary conversation and special situations such as presentations.

AM: _____

_____

_____

_____

_____

_____

_____

_____

_____

_____

Noon: _____

_____

_____

_____

_____

PM:

My personal statement of Intention:

Day 28

Continue to practice daily and write your observations regarding how you use your voice in ordinary conversation and special situations such as presentations.

AM: _____

_____

_____

_____

_____

_____

_____

_____

_____

_____

Noon: _____

_____

_____

_____

_____

PM:

My personal statement of Intention:

Day 29

Continue to practice daily and write your observations regarding how you use your voice in ordinary conversation and special situations such as presentations.

AM: _____

_____

_____

_____

_____

_____

_____

_____

_____

_____

Noon: _____

_____

_____

_____

_____

PM:

My personal statement of Intention:

Day 30

How are you doing? Observe how far you have come. Take a moment to reflect on your successes.

AM: _____

_____

_____

_____

_____

_____

_____

_____

_____

Noon: _____

_____

_____

_____

_____

PM:

My personal statement of Intention:

Day 31

You've done it! Congratulations for staying with the program all the way to the last day. Today is a day to celebrate!

Share a coffee with a friend and notice that nice buzzy feeling of mask resonance as you talk about what you've accomplished.

AM: _____

_____

_____

_____

_____

_____

Have lunch with your team. State your intention, which is to celebrate and have a good time. Make sure they are on board with you and that their intentions are aligned with your own. Have a good time. OR go make a speech in the park. You know how to do it so others will listen! _____

Noon: _____

_____

_____

_____

_____

_____

_____

_____

_____

Tonight, plan to spend some quiet time with a close friend or significant other. Listen to them. Practice letting them know that you hear them. OR if you have plans to go out to a business event, get ready with your voice as well as your clothes. You know how to sound great!

PM: _____

_____

_____

_____

_____

_____

_____

In the days and years ahead, you will continue to benefit from the work you have done over the last six to eight weeks. Continue to practice daily. Remember, you are an evolving being. You are not stuck with the voice you have! If you ever need help, please visit my web site at www. vocalimpact.net or e-mail me at Kate.Peters@vocalimpact.net.

Have fun! Speak well!

Glossary

Arytenoids: Commonly called the vocal cords. A small set of muscles at the top of the trachea used to create vocal sounds. Also referred to as vocal folds.

Cadence: The general inflection or movement of the voice at the end of a sentence.

Chest voice: Usually the lower notes in a voice, the lowest register, so called because the lower notes often cause a pronounced vibration in the chest cavity.

Conversation: Communication between at least two people. A verbal exchange requiring a response.

Diaphragm: The bowl-shaped reflexive muscle at the base of the lungs that is used for inhalation.

Elevator pitch: A very short description of what you do or who you are that is complete enough to pique a listener's interest. It is given this name because it should be short enough to tell someone with whom you are riding on an elevator.

Head voice: Usually the high notes in a voice, the upper register, so called because the upper notes in a vocal range typically have a pronounced resonance in the head.

Glossary

Mask resonance: A reverberation of the sound in the front of the face and into the nasal pharynx and nasal cavities.

Nasal pharynx: The passageway behind the mouth and nose.

Nasal cavities: The sinus cavities and nasal pharynx.

Nasality: A pronounced vocal resonance in the nasal cavities, without much resonance in the mouth.

Otolaryngologist: A physician who specializes in the health and diseases of the ear, nose, and throat.

Personal expression: Communication that expresses a perspective or opinion and does not require a response.

Pitch: A property of sound that describes the frequency of the sound waves that produce a particular sound. Faster sound waves produce a higher pitch; slower sound waves produce a lower pitch.

Resonance: The reverberation or repetition of sound in the environment in which it was created. There is resonance in the body as well as resonance in the surrounding area when someone speaks. Resonance also refers to "richness" or "thinness" in sound.

Glossary

Rhythm: A pattern of sound that is created by contrasts and alterations of different recurring sounds.

Room ambience: The feedback or resonance of sound in a room.

Solar plexus: Popularly refers to the soft, vulnerable area at the center front of the upper torso just below the diaphragm and at the base of the stomach. The true solar plexus is the largest nerve mass in the abdominal cavity and is behind the stomach.

Statement of intention: A statement that describes what you hope to accomplish in a given situation.

Statement of purpose: A description of the motivation behind your life choices. It usually describes the values that drive you.

Vocal apparatus: The physical structure within the body that creates the voice. Includes the muscles used to create sound and change pitch as well as the resonating chambers and the muscles used for breathing, support, and articulation.

Glossary

Vocal coach: A person who specializes in the interpretation of vocal music, but not necessarily a specialist in vocal technique.

Vocal fatigue: Muscle fatigue of the arytenoids when they are strained or overused. The results of vocal fatigue are problems such as hoarseness, laryngitis, a tired or achy feeling in the voice, and a wobbly jaw.

Vocal folds: see arytenoids

Vocal image: The impression of someone from the sound of her voice.

Vocal nodules: Calluses on the arytenoids caused by chronic or excessive irritation while speaking or singing.

Vocal polyps: Blisters or cysts on the arytenoids.

Vocal power: How vocal sound impacts a listener.

Bibliography

Angelou, Maya. *I Know Why the Caged Bird Sings.* New York: Random House, Inc., 1997

Bergren, Cox, and Detmar. *Improvise This.* New York: Hyperion, 2002

Bunce, Oliver Bell. *Don't: A Manual of Mistakes and Improprieties More or Less Prevalent in Conduct and Speech.* 1880, reprint Pryor 1982

Campbell, Don. *The Mozart Effect: Tapping the Power of Music to Heal the Body, Strengthen the Mind and Unlock the Creative Spirit.* Dresden, TN: Avon Books, 1997.

Cooper, Morton. *Winning with Your Voice.* Hollywood: Frederick Fell Publishers, Incorporated, 1990.

Graham, Martha. *Blood Memory.* New York: Doubleday, 1991.

Herbert-Caesare, Edgar F. *The Voice of the Mind.* Boston: Crescendo Pub. Co, 1963.

Leeds, Joshua. *The Power of Sound: How to Manage Your Personal Soundscape for a Vital, Productive & Healthy Life. Rochester: Inner Traditions* International, Limited, 2001.

Riggs, Seth. *Singing for the Stars: A Complete Program for Training Your Voice.* Van Nuys: Alfred Publishing, 1998.

Rivers, Dennis. *The Seven Challenges: A Workbook and Reader about Communicating More Cooperatively.* Santa Barabra: Dennis Rivers publisher, 2001.

Bibliography

Sweeney, Tim. *Tim Sweeney's Guide to Releasing Independent Records.* Audio CD. TSA Books, 2003.

Tannen, Deborah. *That's Not What I Meant! How Conversational Style Makes or Breaks Relationships.* Westminster: Ballantine Books, 1991

Tomatis, Alfred A. *The Ear and the Voice.* Trans. Roberta Prada and Pierre Sollier. Lanham: The Scarecrow Press, 2005.

Vonnegut, Kurt, Jr. *Cat's Cradle.* New York: Holt, Rinehart & Winston, 1963

Index

Index

Contact Info

Web Site . . . . .www.vocalimpact.net

Email . . . . .Kate.Peters@vocalimpact.net